The African Past Speaks

The
African Past Speaks

Essays on Oral Tradition and History

Edited by

JOSEPH C MILLER

DAWSON · ARCHON

First Published 1980

© Wm Dawson & Sons Ltd 1980

Wm Dawson & Sons Ltd, Cannon House
Folkestone, Kent, England

Archon Books, The Shoe String Press, Inc
995 Sherman Avenue, Hamden, Connecticut 06514
USA

British Library Cataloguing in Publication Data

_____

The African past speaks.
  1. Bantus–History
  2. Oral tradition–Case studies
  3. Oral history–Case studies
  I . Miller, Joseph Calder
  967'.007'2   GN656   79–67841

ISBN 0–7129–0951–6

Archon ISBN 0–208–01784–4

Filmset in 10/12 point Times
Printed and bound in Great Britain
by W & J Mackay Limited

Contents

List of Illustrations

Maps

Figures

Preface

Unconventional sources, particularly oral narratives, were the methodological anchors around which the nascent discipline of African history swung during the 1960s. Archeology, botany, linguistics, ethnography, artistic creations, and numbers of other fields of study formed a disciplinary gauntlet through which professors put ardent student historians.[1] No specialty seemed too esoteric or too technical for mastery by enthusiastic researchers who, forewarned and forearmed, spread out across the African savannas and woodlands in search of hidden records from the past that would reveal a depth and continuity of history in Africa worthy of the respect of an initially doubting world.

Specialists in some of these other disciplines at first joined the historians in applying their skills to the recovery of the African past, with only the gentlest of urgings that fundamental methodological difficulties might lurk behind the apparent ease with which the historians claimed plants, carvings, artifacts, and words as solutions to the riddles of African history. But others remained outside the sphere of euphoria created by the historians and soon expressed reservations about the haste with which untrained novices were in some cases applying highly technical methodologies to issues they understood only in part. Among the first nonhistorians to flash the cautionary warning light were anthropologists, who had behind them several decades of thinking about oral narratives as ideological or cosmological constructs. Some of these anthropologists opposed the historians' claims to find descriptions of the past in oral traditions in tones no more restrained than those of the historians who asserted their faith in the straightforwardly accurate nature of oral sources. For the anthropologistical doubters, the same oral performances were no less straightforwardly functional charters or mythical constructs, devoid of discernible relationship to past conditions. This volume presents the responses of some historians to the countercharges made by structuralist and functionalist anthropologists. These historians, although generally working on traditions from Bantu-speaking peoples of central Africa, raise methodological issues present throughout the continent and else-where in the nonliterate world. The introduction phrases these questions of methodology in terms of the contrast between literate and nonliterate modes of communication in an effort to render more widely relevant the lessons discussed here in cases from the Bantu-speaking world. The exception of non-Bantu-speaking Madagascar, which conforms to the general principles outlined, would seem to support the point.

African historians who use oral sources in the late 1970s have learned from the doubts of others about the evidence that they study. They have also gained sophistication from criticisms originating within their own discipline, from colleagues who have reminded the profession that the burst of enthusiasm over less familiar sorts of source left seriously neglected during the 1960s and early 1970s the painstaking criticism of documentary sources essential to the discipline of history.[2] With respect to oral narratives from the more remote epochs of the past, the category of oral source discussed in the following essays, most historians still believe the narrative traditions allow glimpses into areas of the past not revealed by other sorts of data. They continue to accept Jan Vansina's seminal methodological treatise (*Oral Tradition*, Chicago, 1965, but first composed in 1959–60) as a fundamental justification of the value of oral tradition as historical source and an outline of methodological principles that can be developed and applied to specific fieldwork problems.

In *Oral Tradition* Vansina seemed to have his eye on doubting historians more than on potential sceptics in other disciplines. Few historical fieldworkers anticipated the doubts implanted by social and structural anthropologists who emerged as the primary critics of oral traditions as history. Those who continued to seek history in oral African societies in the late 1960s and early 1970s thus had to reconcile their received faith in the historicity of the traditions with their growing recognition that the anthropologists were saying something that they could not ignore. The essays collected represent an interim response by historians who accept much of what anthropological critics have written, particularly the structuralists. The historians here conclude that if they now believe less of what they hear in oral sources, they can justify more rigorously their acceptance of that bit of each narrative that they accept as historical.

Because the historians' response has arisen in reply to functionalist and structuralist anthropological criticism, it tends to follow the broad orientation of these fields in arguing the historicity of the narrative traditions in ideological and social structural terms. The introduction confines itself to these issues in presenting a synthetic statement of how intellectual history seems to work in a verbal environment, where reading and writing are not present. Yet this phrasing of the argument does not relinquish the relevance of these studies to political economy and neoMarxism, important influences in African studies today. Several of the contributors remark on the pervasive influence of the 'colonial situation' on how Africans now tell their history. It is my feeling, though one I have not here explored in detail, that the general tendencies outlined in the introduction would explain this specific case of recent African intellectual history, the imposition of colonial rule, as well as they do other cases more remote in time.

The presumption is therefore that there is little unique in the general pattern of how African oral narrators behaved in the twentieth century (in so far as their profession survived the arrival of literacy), but it would require another lengthy essay to document this hypothesis. Several recent studies of oral traditions have provided very useful examples of how traditions came to be first written down in the context of highly political battles with colonial authorities and with other Africans enmeshed in the same colonial net.[3] It would be a short step from this recognition to extend the discussion to comprehend the methodology and concepts of neoMarxism or political economy. Such an extension would add some new emphases to the discussions found here and would doubtless change some of the terminology of the debate, but I doubt that it would alter the basic conclusion that historians can study the past through African oral narratives. Indeed, reflection on the materials presented here may suggest to others what is apparent to me: that the clichés and sociological emphases of the traditions parallel in several suggestive ways the neoMarxist search for the interrelationships of economy, society, and ideology. African oral narrators, if this approach withstands critical scrutiny, may thus have anticipated the political economists' search for the identification of change at the level of basic structures in the 'social formation'.

The remoter periods of the African past languished in neglect during the early 1970s, half-submerged in the wake of disillusioning recognition of the problems of extracting history from oral narratives, combined with the turn toward colonial history and toward economic and social issues in Africa. However, several recent conferences, panels at professional association meetings, and special issues of scholarly journals indicate renewed interest in the earlier centuries that fascinated the first African historians in the field. The themes featured in this revival are often new, with demography, economics, political economy, agricultural history, and other similarly nonpolitical foci reflecting the shape of the field in the late 1970s. It may be assumed that the restudy of oral sources will play an important part in the coming search for answers to these questions. It is toward the methodological precision requisite in this endeavour that this book of essays is directed.

As editor, I am grateful to the contributors for drawing essays that focus on methodological issues of doing history in oral societies out of fieldwork often more immediately oriented toward other concerns. It was their work that converged on the issues discussed in the introduction. I had the good fortune to know Dr. Roy Willis at a time in the formulation of my present notions about history and oral traditions when his work, graciously shared, greatly stimulated my own. Several of the authors first wrote their essays for a panel held at the Twelfth Annual Meeting of the African Studies Association in 1976. Readers who know the numerous studies of Professor Vansina since the publication of *Oral Tradition* will recognize that his work has paced many of the advances in methodology applied here, as the notes to the introduction acknowledge.

Joseph C. Miller
Charlottesville, Virginia
May 1979

Notes

1 For example: Daniel F. McCall, *Africa in Time Perspective* (Boston, 1964), but see also the early issues of the *Journal of African History*. As Wyatt MacGaffey trenchantly remarked: 'African historiography became the decathlon of social science.' 'African History, Anthropology, and the Rationality of Natives', *History in Africa*, vol. 5 (1978), p. 103.
2 One of the primary concerns of *History in Africa* (1974–   ).
3 Thomas Q. Reefe, *The Rainbow and the Kings* (forthcoming), and Robert J. Papstein, 'The Upper Zambezi: A History of the Luvale People, 1000–1900' (PhD dissertation, University of California, Los Angeles, 1978), *inter alia*.

1. Introduction: Listening for the African Past*

JOSEPH C MILLER

The echoes of the past reverberate, sometimes faintly, in the oral narratives of societies without writing, but historians must listen very carefully if they hope to discern the significance of what is said for reconstructing former times according to literate historical standards. Their difficulties in understanding arise from the contrast between modes of communication in cultures based on the written word (in which history as most of us know it acquired its distinctive characteristics) and in cultures where reading and writing were absent, like most of those in Africa. The written document, which in literate cultures bridges the divide between the historian's present and the past that he or she studies, did not exist in most African cultures before the present century. No direct expressions of the remote African past survive in the way that documents do in literate cultures. Yet, other sorts of true evidence from the past do survive in oral form in African societies, though often indirect, muffled, and mixed in complex ways with information from the present. The essays in this volume illustrate how Africanist historians separate historical evidence from all other sorts of element in perhaps the most problematic sort of oral historical source—the narrative oral tradition.

The historian must approach the oral tradition as 'evidence', whatever scholars in other disciplines may choose to do with the same narratives. Evidence (the 'echoes' alluded to at the outset) the historian takes as something that bears witness to a vanished time because it has *survived unchanged* from then until the historian examines it. Historical method is essentially concerned with tracing the exact relationship between the evidential remnants in the present and their origins in the past. In no other category of spoken evidence—including personal reminiscences, songs, chants, formulae, and others—is this relationship of the words the historian hears now to times past more puzzling than in narrative oral tradition.

1

An oral tradition is a narrative describing, or purporting to describe, eras before the time of the person who relates it. This definition of oral tradition differs slightly from the conventional one, which terms 'traditions' any spoken report removed by even a single previous telling from a direct eyewitness account.[1] That definition stresses the fact of 'transmission' by word of mouth from one person to another. The intent here is rather to emphasize the narrative style. Increasing distance between the teller and the event forces a historian in an oral environment to develop techniques for remembering and recounting that have no equivalents among literate historians. Some 'transmitted' stories, to be termed extended personal recollections, do not exhibit these peculiarly oral hallmarks and so must be distinguished from the narrative oral traditions.

The conventional concentration on the 'transmission' implies that tellers of the tales—here termed narrators, or oral historians, to distinguish them from the literate historians (or 'historians') who may attempt to make sense of what they do in terms of western concepts of history—incorporate in their narratives at least some elements they have heard from someone else. These elements must have been transmitted only by word of mouth. The series of such transmissions establishes a 'chain of transmission' down through time that links elements of the testimony heard by the literate historian to the remote period to be reconstructed.[2] The 'chain of transmission' thus forms the essential tie between the historian's present and a past, permitting use of the transmitted elements as historical evidence.

As originally applied, this notion seemed to establish the words of the narrative as evidence analogous to the words of a documentary source in a literate culture. The implication was that the words, or detectable distortions of them, had survived, though spoken rather than written in the oral environment. Past times could thus be reconstructed more or less directly from the tales as told. The analogy appeared close enough that Africanist historians embraced the narrative level of the traditions as valid evidence from and about the past, taking care only to reconstruct the proper wording through analysis of the chains of transmission from a presumed original telling down through the various versions of it extant in the present. Recognition was slower to come that factors peculiar to the oral environment altered the correspondence of the words heard to the past sought as events receded in time relative to their telling. The narrator's words often did not themselves come from the past. The

documentary analogy thus broke down, and with it hopes of retriev-
ing the past by use of the earliest versions of this method.

Challenges to this simple view of the historicity of African oral
traditions came first from anthropologists, specialists in nonliterate
cultures, whose predecessors had long since dismissed the possible
historical meaning of oral literature. They did not pause to consider
the nature of narrative traditions as evidence, in the ways that
historians must raise the issue, but based their doubts instead on
how oral traditions seemed to convey meaning. They thus chose to
treat the historians' 'oral traditions' as 'myth'. For one school of
anthropology, including most British social anthropologists, the
truth about 'myth' had been transmitted down a chain anchored in
the sociology of Emile Durkheim and given a functionalist twist by
Bronislaw Malinowski.[3] Most oral traditions, in their view, fell into
a category labeled 'mythical charters', stories meaningful primarily
in the homology they exhibited between their narrative structure
and the social and political institutions of the people who told them.
Social anthropologists who could demonstrate a close correspondence between story and current social structure saw no need to
look further in the oral traditions. They concluded that the traditions merely confirmed the present and challenged historians to
prove them wrong. They in fact left historians the option of showing
that they were not wholly right.[4]

French structuralist anthropologists delivered a blow from a
slightly different angle to the historians' faith in the historicity of
their oral traditions, particularly as the structuralist case was argued
by some British proponents of the method.[5] Structuralists generally
examined 'myths' in terms of their logical structure, seeking
explanation for them in religious beliefs and cosmology rather than
in social institutions. Structuralist analysis placed the goddesses,
heroes, men and women, animals, and other elements of a narrative
oral tradition in relationship to one another in the same ways
that the tellers of the tales contrasted basic cosmological
categories—nature and culture, hot and cold, sun and moon, and
many others. The structuralists' convincing demonstrations of these
homologies, particularly prominent in traditions of origin that purported to account for the beginnings of society or culture, make
awkward the historians' assertions that magical hunters emerging
from primeval forests to found great kingdoms could in fact amount
to much more than ahistorical fabrications of recent myth-makers.
By generalizing these conclusions to all oral narratives in which
homologies could be detected, some structuralists tried to argue

3

that no tradition could illuminate the past. But they too left a loophole by failing to deal with the traditions as evidence.

Although some historians have been momentarily discouraged by the theoretical elegance of the anthropologists' assaults on oral tradition, others wedged open the logical cracks in these arguments.[6] They responded by agreeing that oral traditions function quite efficiently as 'mythical charters' and by conceding that many narratives exhibit prominently the cosmological categories of the people who tell them. But, these historians continue, none of that proves that oral traditions do not also convey useful information from the past. Nor, they point out, is literate history entirely free from similar functions and aspects. They conclude that oral traditions remain useful as history, though often not in quite the ways believed by the first scholars to employ the narratives for historical purposes.

The papers in this collection represent the maturation of these latter trends in the use of African oral traditions as sources for history. Each attempts to demonstrate exactly how one may extract knowledge about the past from oral narratives. They do so by shifting their focus from the words of the 'tradition' as the primary unit of analysis, thus abandoning the old documentary analogy in its simplest form. They instead examine how oral historians construct their narratives, what evidential materials they have at hand, and by what procedures they combine these into purported representations of the past. These authors have moved from examining the means by which an entire 'tradition' might have been transmitted through time to studying how its miscellaneous components have come to the oral narrators who combine them into finished stories. These historians thus perceive a composite of many diverse parts rather than a single integrated 'tradition'. Each of the parts bears its own individual relationship to the past, or sometimes only to the present. Each of those from former times has come in its own way, often transformed in the process, from the past to which it may relate into the present in which it exists.

This methodology thus concentrates as much on the oral historian who provides the narrative as on the completed artifact, the tale as told. The salient characteristics of oral tradition then emerge as products of the way people in oral cultures think and talk about the past. Their ways of thinking and talking in turn depend in significant part on the oral mode of communications they employ. Emphasis falls here on listening and understanding in addition to careful reconstruction of chains of transmission. These essays proceed to develop historical conclusions on the basis of the historian's essentially empirical logic, 'doing history' by confirming every piece of evidence through adducing a second independent source in agreement with the first. If more theoretical justifications are needed, anthropologists of the very schools from which have come the most prominent critics of using oral traditions for historical purposes turn out to have provided them.

Each of the contributors to this collection, with the exception of the concluding one, confronts a methodological issue, usually a theoretical objection raised by an anthropologist against the historical use of oral traditions. He or she then presents a case study that produces history from materials that seem at first glance to lie more in the province of the anthropologist than in that of the historian. Generally each contributor presents in summary form a corpus of oral tradition, educes from it a conclusion about the past, and then employs the historian's standard technique of testing its historical content against independent confirming evidence. Although the interpretations agree in rejecting the extreme presentistic implications of myth charters and cosmological speculations, their historical conclusions vary as widely as do their sources of confirming data, whether in linguistics, ethnography, ecology and economic constraints, other sorts of oral data, functional correspondences between the narratives and social or political institutions, or documented contemporary descriptions. Most essays tackle traditions of origin, the most myth-laden and difficult of all to interpret. One focuses on a large but sometimes neglected genre of private narratives rather different from such public traditions as the stories of origin. Two trace the permutations of historical materials in a literizing environment, where oral specialists availed themselves of the technology of writing. The final paper looks at the known psychological properties of the human memory and what they imply for unraveling the meanings of oral traditions. This chapter's emphasis on the individual human mind makes it an appropriate conclusion: the volume as a whole stresses the need to examine how oral historians work in nonliterate cultures and stresses knowledge of their techniques as the key for deriving information from the past from narrative traditions.

Some Terms and Concepts

African oral narrators are creative artists who consciously attempt to preserve an accurate record of the past as they perceive it.[7] Such professional historians may not be present in all oral cultures, but they clearly exist in the societies studied by the contributors to this volume and may be typical of many parts of Africa.[8] Their techniques and their professionalism go far toward enabling the present authors to reconstruct western-style history from the stories they have heard. The achievements of such individuals in preserving a record of the past in oral cultures are an underlying theme in the essays that follow. This humanistic and individualistic emphasis becomes most explicit in the concluding chapters where Cohen stresses the role of individuals in the unconscious preservation of the past and where Vansina analyses the individual human memory as it influences the conscious preservation and transmission of knowledge.[9] The focus on individual narrators and on how they compose their historical narratives allows the historian to analyze how oral historians perceive their world, in particular how they visualize the past, and what may be the materials—evidence, cultural standards of truth, art, and style, conceptions of change—with which they work. If the historian can understand how the oral narrator puts together a story, then he or she is in a better position to pull apart the construction and to decide where in it lie bits of evidence that illuminate the past.

These techniques allow literate historians to deal also with even deliberate fabrications. Conceptualization of oral traditions as complex ethnographic features plays down the conscious narrative as a direct or literal representation of the past. Numerous critics have shown this level to be structured, falsified, and twisted in many ways.[10] But if historians can split apart the complex product of the oral historian's evocation of the past, whether intended as true or false, they may infer conditions from it of which the oral narrator may be unaware or may try to conceal. This methodological position renders oral traditions 'evidence in spite of themselves': that is, evidence that reveals the past in ways of which its authors could not have been cognizant and could therefore not have fabricated. According to the standards of modern historiography, historical inferences of this sort are more valuable than mere acceptance of a straightforward narrative. This approach accepts the oral traditions as secondary authorities that may be criticized as primary sources.[11]

Recent studies on oral tradition have identified three principal types of element from which oral historians compose historical narratives: clichés (or stereotypes), episodes, and personal reminiscences.[12] On these elements work several forces inherent in the tellers' and listeners' mental processes. These forces are particular to the oral/aural environment of the nonliterate cultures where oral traditions are important means of preserving knowledge of the past. Such tendencies, often working in ways quite unperceived by the oral historians and their audiences, combine with the use of clichés, episodes, and personal reminiscences to produce distinctive features of oral tradition, to be treated here under the headings of structuring and selection, epochs, 'magical' causation, anachronisms, genealogies, and variation—all features commonly noted but too often summarized vaguely and unhelpfully as 'myth'. An oral tradition undifferentiated as cliché, episode, and reminiscence cannot divulge its historical content. Oral performances treated as 'myth' and thus not distinguishing structuring, anachronisms, epochs and the like, appear misleadingly to stand in some sort of contrast to 'history'. By taking the perspective of an oral historian, as artist, the narrative may be understood as influenced by the way he thinks, by the way his audience reacts, by his methods of preserving and transmitting information, and by the way that he and his audience interact in terms of the culture that they share. The fact that much of these processes is unperceived allows the oral narrator to leave rough edges ('seams' in the language of Sigwalt's chapter on the Shi) that become the historian's clues in analysis of them.[13]

The *cliché* is a highly compressed and deceptively simple statement of meaning that refers to a much more complex reality, sometimes in the past. It is also a stereotype in the sense that it reduces a great deal of variation to a single unified representation, but it is more than a stereotype because, while the term stereotype may connote unconscious and inherent inaccuracy, clichés are deliberate and purposeful simplifications and thereby accurate in some respects. Clichés may occur in several linguistic forms, but they are commonly proverbs, sometimes songs or chants, and typically in oral traditions elementary narrative themes like the arrival of a foreign hunter who settles as a king among local people.[14] Anyone who has read or heard oral traditions will immediately call to mind a variety of other equally widespread images—autochthonous people of small stature who once lived in caves, the 'drunken king', and magical crossings of rivers are some that occur in the case studies presented here. Specialists who have worked intensively with oral materials will easily add a much larger number of clichés characteristic of the culture they know best.[15] Nearly all contributors to this collection have identified clichés in the oral traditions they discuss, and such stereotypes are clearly present even where the authors do not point to them.

7

The features that unite all of these forms of cliché are that they are short, often dramatic or striking, sometimes phrased in structured language, and because of all this *easily remembered*. One may argue that oral historians have given these clichés their distinctive forms at least in part in order to render them memorable. This functionalist explanation of why clichés appear in narratives implies that oral historians employ them to tell history to preserve a reliable referent to a past that they can no longer tangibly perceive and with which they might otherwise lose touch. This introduction will argue not only that some clichés refer to the past, because at least in origin someone quite consciously intended them to do so, but also that they refer to the past in ways that historians working in the western literate style of history might understand.[16]

Episodes are the narrative stories that oral historians develop to explain historical clichés in the present.[17] Oral historians customarily phrase these stories in terms of interactions between a relatively small number of human individuals, thus giving the episodes an intimate and personal quality. Commonly, they construct narratives with an eye toward their aesthetic integrity and lend them a sense of immediacy and vividness by freely embroidering the cliché with an almost limitless variety of related images. Most of these elaborations are not historical evidence, in the sense that they have not come down unchanged from past times. Despite their purported reference to former times, they are invented by the oral historian from materials in the present. Since these elaborations may be anachronistic, often almost wholly presentistic, the historian cannot use them to infer anything about the past. It is rather the cliché at the center of the episode that attracts the attention of the historian, since the cliché is what serves the oral narrator as a mnemonic device recalling for him a single historical point or the rough outline of the episode he intends to develop. It is therefore the cliché that each generation hands down to members of the next, who may remember it and use it even after it has become archaic and has lost its original meaning for those who continue to pass it on. The cliché at the center of the episode, not the details of the narrative, is what may bear information from and about the past.

Once the structure of a narrative episode is understood as a historical narrator's idiosyncratic elaboration built around a core of possibly historical matter, one may draw several conclusions about the larger patterns created when people recite these stories. Even when narrators combine several episodes dealing with a single historical figure or theme into a larger story, as they commonly do, none bears any necessary historical relationship to another. The oral narrator's juxtaposition of episodes does not allow the historian to infer historical sequence from the order in which they happen to be told or to argue causation from events portrayed in a preceding episode to events mentioned in one that follows.[18] Nor does the degree to which narrative elaborations of a given cliché converge in detail from performer to performer, or from performance to performance by a single oral narrator, constitute proof of historicity. Unanimity may result from a variety of conditions in the present—the complexity of the points to be made (as Sigwalt argues in his chapter on the Shi), politically enforced concurrence, or fashions in style of historical performing—rather than from uninterrupted accurate transmission from a single source in the past.[19] Realization of episodes in the context of interaction between oral narrators and their audience lends them a public quality, expressing generally held agreement about the significance of what happened rather than private observations of concrete detail. Thus, the narrative episodes are complex and normally spontaneous creations subject to analysis in a variety of modes—as art, as structure, as ethnography, as politics—even as they also contain a cliché at their center that may be historical.

Personal reminiscences are not oral traditions, since they do not come from before the time of the people who tell them, but they are the sources from which narrators create oral traditions. They are simply what people remember of their own experience. They resemble oral traditions in that they are already highly complex products of the human memory interacting with a culture[20] but they differ in being relatively straightforward representations of events, relying less on clichés and episodes than do oral traditions. Personal reminiscences frequently describe occurrences in terms closer to those familiar to western historians in written sources than do traditions. They are private recollections rather than public evaluations of an event. The historian normally encounters multiple and selective reminiscences about any given event, as numerous and as various as were the people who originally witnessed it or have since formed an opinion about it. This multiplicity and variety also distinguish personal reminiscences from oral traditions, which tend toward a social consensus and are more stereotyped, less numerous and differ from one another over a narrower range. All these characteristics make historical analysis of personal reminiscences analogous to standard literate historical methods of compilation and comparison of the narrative level of variant accounts. Oral

9

traditions are not subject to similar analysis, since variation in the content of narrative episodes or in the content of the clichés employed may or may not come directly from the past the historian wishes to reconstruct.

The life-span of personal reminiscences is short, unlike that of traditions, but time transforms them into oral traditions that may survive indefinitely. Since a personal reminiscence in an oral culture cannot survive independently of the individual who holds it, these data reach back something less than a human lifetime, a period of time shorter than people live by the number of years required for the perceptual and remembering abilities of the human mind to form in childhood.[21] The first step in transforming a personal reminiscence into a tradition occurs when a few particularly memorable such reminiscences pass into the following generation as extended personal recollections, stories one remembers and repeats from one's grandparents or other older members of a community after they are dead. These memories generally reach their practical limit with the death of the grandchildren of the youngest people who originally witnessed an event. This range often amounts to 120 or 130 years, but memories of socially significant events like genealogies, marriages, and former places of residence in certain contexts may extend back much further in time.[22] Beyond the time horizon at which the private recollections fade out, professional oral historians then convert the few that become part of the public stock of oral traditions into cliché-based narrative episodes.[23]

Vansina's contribution to this volume surveys one of the factors that condition this transformation: the effects of the human memory on the remembering and reproduction of past events. He points out how the human mind tends to recall concrete images more clearly than abstractions, for example. This bias is entirely consistent with the typical phrasing of oral traditions in personalistic terms. Remembering, Vansina notes, is also a process of structuring in at least two ways. The mind fills in logically necessary steps in a sequence that may have been actually observed only in part, and it makes remembered specific events conform to pre-existing assumptions about reality in general. The influence of these aspects of memory in producing structured and narrative oral traditions appears obvious. Vansina's stress on the collective—or some would say cultural—aspect of memory is as important as is his outline of the processes of the individual mind. The mnemonic code by which perceptions are logged into the memory and then retrieved later is a collective system. Witnesses from sharply differing cultures therefore inevitably differ in their recollections of the same event, particularly if it is a complex, diffuse, and multifaceted event like most of those to which oral traditions allude. Divergent perceptions and recollections rooted in cultural differences, of course, lie at the very heart of the difficulties western historians and anthropologists experience in recognizing how oral traditions may illuminate the past in spite of their exotic phrasing.

The collective aspect of memory assumes particular importance in understanding oral traditions, owing to the intense effect of public performance on the form and content of tradition.[24] Once perceptions of a happening have been coded and stored in the memory, as Vansina points out, that recollection will always exist. In an oral culture, it exists in only a very limited sense since it is realized in conscious form principally as it is performed before others. There is no equivalent to a written diary or book of private remembrances in which the writer carries on a purely personal and internal dialogue about his or her recollections. Since the oral performance takes place only in a context of intense interaction between the person holding the memory and the audience who hears about it, recollections repeatedly recited before others, although individual in origin, soon absorb perceptions of and feelings about the event in question shared by all who are present. Thus the recollections assume a collective character. The perceptions of others become part of a person's own memory of what happened. Repetition of the memory gives the original perception a thick overlay of undifferentiated realizations of the sort Vansina illustrates with an example of someone going to the shop to purchase bread. The individual recollection becomes standardized, streamlined, and edges closer and closer to a shared cultural norm approximating 'what must have been'. The contribution of group performances to structuring and to the formation of clichés must be enormous. Memory in an oral culture is even more a shared phenomenon than it is in a literate culture where people create private mnemonic devices—notes, diaries, and the like—to retain accurately their early idiosyncratic impressions of an event. With writing, one streamlines one's recollections to a similar degree, but the interaction is with one's own recorded impression, made at a time not long after the event, rather than with the later beliefs of others.[25]

The consequences of oral modes of communication on how people manipulate and retain information are becoming increasingly well known, though not always specifically applied to the

11

historicity of oral traditions.[26] Anthropologists of religion, myth, and other forms of thought in nonliterate societies have sometimes doubted that history could exist there by questioning whether Africans and other participants in oral cultures are 'rational' in the same sense that westerners hold themselves to be 'rational'. Arguments against the 'rationality of natives'[27] tend to posit some sort of 'primitive mentality' and to seek analogs for it in mystical constructions of the anthropologists' own making or among children (the only nonliterates!) in western cultures.[28] The studies in this volume assume, sometimes implicitly, the position dominant among anthropologists today, that is, that nonliterate people think in very much the same ways as do persons in literate cultures, whether these ways be designated 'rational', 'nonrational', or varying mixes of the two.[29] The undeniable differences between the formulation of ideas by people reared on writing and by people in oral cultures are explained, according to this logic, by the technology of communications. Thinkers aided by techniques of reading and writing can store larger amounts of information, array vastly more of it simultaneously for analysis, consider the relationships between different elements of it in greater detail, and phrase more abstract judgments about it than can similar thinkers in an oral environment. The difficulty of remembering, conceptualizing, and transmitting and preserving information by oral methods encourages oral historians to render their traditions in precisely the form observed: a few memorable clichés surrounded by spontaneous elaboration. They also preserve for the future only a tiny selection of all the information available when the past was present. Nothing survives without someone's conscious decision that it should. Historians should expect to find evidence from the past preserved differently in oral cultures from the often accidental forms in which they are accustomed to finding historical data in their own literate environments.

Structuring, an aspect of traditions that has received widespread attention from anthropologists following Claude Lévi-Strauss,[30] results from the collective aspect of memory working on historical data in an oral environment. Most, though assuredly not all anthropological studies of structure have tended to treat it in an exclusively synchronic sense, making only slight efforts to account for its origins in time. Those that thus neglect history leave the false impression that the only logic present in oral narratives is one consisting of sets of congruent pairs of contrasting concepts. The classic examples, to which several of the authors of the following papers refer, stress such oppositions as 'nature/culture'. Packard prefaces his historical explication of the Bashu myth of Muhiyi with a structuralist-style analysis that shows how such an underlying contrast is congruent with numerous other levels of meaning: 'pastoralist/agriculturalist', 'civilized/savage', 'giver of food/receiver of food', and so on. Structuralist anthropologists would usually argue that such static and synchronous structured contrasts, although secondarily realized through telling as sequenced narratives, are the primary meaning or oral traditions. They thus see most narratives as cosmological speculations only incidentally phrased in pseudohistorical form and in fact bearing no relationship to events that occurred in the past. Structure, for them, expresses the speculations and conclusions of nonliterate people about the world in which they live rather than preserving an accurate memory—consciously or unconsciously—of specific past circumstances.

'Structuring', the gerund form used here, contrasts with the anthropologists' nominal term 'structure' in its implied emphasis on the process by which representations of real events might acquire phrasings that also express fundamental cosmological beliefs or perceptual categories of the people who tell them. The term takes for granted the result of this process, which anthropologists designate as 'structure', and goes on to ask how narrators might have added it to originally circumstantial descriptions of reality. The authors in this collection would agree that a large category of myth is primarily, perhaps purely, cosmological and speculative. However, most would add that for the societies in which they have worked they find other structured tales that are also historical. By looking at structuring, they separate structure from history by tracing their distinct origins, even as most would also accept the argument that in practice each element exists as an aspect of the other.[31] Following sections of this introduction show how structuring turns personal reminiscences into oral traditions over time, as the chronological distance increases between an event and its recollection and recitation.

Historians working with oral traditions have found particularly misleading a particular form of structuring that bears a deceptively similar appearance to the chronological units (usually years) in western history. Oral historians group the clichés in sets, here termed *'epochs'*[32] in order to provide an abstraction that may refer to whatever concrete forms narrators in particular cultures may choose to give them. In societies where states are an important feature of the remembered past, for example, the oral historians commonly represent these epochs as the reigns of kings. In general, they define the sets they recall according to whatever referents they can distinguish in their own experience, including age-grades and variations in rainfall as well as monarchs. Their epochs may be as crude as the logically minimal three-part sequence of 'time of origins/distant past/recent past', or they may be nearly as refined as the calendar years that are the equivalents of these epochs in the literate western chronology. The epochs may also resemble years if they fall in an invariable sequence of numerous small units of nearly equal duration,[33] but in other cases they may be fewer in number, uneven in length, and unstable in their order. The logical status of epochs in oral traditions, parallel to that of years in western history, has led some literate historians to attempt to infer chronology from remembered kings' reigns, but the irregularities present in many epochal sets of this type have prompted a strong critique of techniques of this sort.[34] A firm chronology can exist only when the evidence from the past bears marks (usually dates in the case of documents) that enable the historian to order the events it describes in a reliable sequence. The historical data embedded in oral narratives carry no such anchors to specific points in the past, but oral narrators often structure the clichés in their tales in epochs that suggest to unwary literate historians that the data are so anchored.

The creation of 'epochs' by oral historians resembles 'structuring' in that narrators collect clichés (and thereby appear to associate with each other the events the clichés represent) together according to nontemporal criteria: cultural preferences, cosmological tenets, or the unconscious tendencies of the human memory. In practice, such structuring affects clichés denoting events from long ago more strongly than it does those associated with recent times. The temporal epochs of the recent past commonly correspond to periods of duration in real time, as experienced by the people who structure their personal reminiscences in such epochs. But the absence of some unambiguous link, like a date on a document, between an event and the temporal epoch in which it occurred allows later tellers of tales, once they have become transformed into clichés, unintentionally to begin to find new ways to associate the two. They commonly, for example, collect stories about victorious battles led by different monarchs into a single epoch denoted as the reign of a conquering king. Or, oral historians handling clichés based on events in the distant past may move them from one epoch to another in order to create stereotyped good kings and bad kings who follow one another in line with some broad cosmological model, as Berg describes here for the Merina. At the extreme, the oral narrators may group clichés (still including some drawn originally from some event in the temporal past) in purely notional epochs bearing no relationship to anything that a literate historian would accept as a past period of time: a 'golden age' or an inverted world. The temporal epochs of the personal reminiscences thus merge gradually into the notional epochs of pure speculative thought, with clichés of historical origin possibly present in both.

Anachronisms, the basic problem facing historians who work with oral traditions, result from the separability of cliché from epoch, or the weak connection in the oral narrator's mind between the logical constructs representing historical events and the periods in which they occurred. Anachronisms are historical events represented as having taken place in an order other than that in which they in fact followed one another. The absolute lack of dates in African oral traditions is less significant than is the occasional lack of sequence thus produced. Sequence, even without reference to years, is the indispensable preliminary to establishing the before/after relationships between events on which rest all historical explanation and understanding. The tendency of oral historians to structure events according to epochs defined by nontemporal criteria causes them to lose all track of which events actually came before others.[35] Their narratives of such events therefore are weak foundations for the superstructure of sequence that literate historians must erect on them.

Anachronistic disordering of events in oral traditions arises from two distinct sources: lack of sequence within the set of epochs employed, and movement of clichés from one epoch to another even when the epochs exist in an established order corresponding to a historical past. In the former (probably rare) case, oral historians maintain no sequence among the epochs even though they may link each cliché unvaryingly to a single epoch. Anachronisms in such instances technically occur only when a literate historian imposes an incorrect order on the events recalled. The latter case is much more common, since often substantial parts of epochal systems closely reflect periods of the temporal past, even though oral narrators may sometimes misplace events in relation to them. Here the oral narrators introduce the anachronisms. The cases lacking sequence of epochs approximate in historian's terms what anthropologists have sometimes called 'mythical time', while those with firmer epochal series resemble 'historical time' whether events in them are positioned correctly or not. Both tendencies are present in most sets of oral traditions, though in different parts of the corpus. Clichés referring to ancient events tend to cluster in the epochs of 'mythical time', and more recent occurrences normally, though not always, linger in the more temporally structured epochs.

Anachronisms that occur when oral historians misplace events within a relatively firmly ordered sequence of epochs may be divided into two categories: ascending and descending.[36] Each results from a distinct kind of structuring. Ascending anachronisms, probably the better known of the two types, are those in which an event 'ascends' in the telling of the traditions from the epoch in which it belongs into a preceding epoch. Such ascents commonly result from a widespread nonliterate notion holding that change takes place in major isolated transformations (like the arrival of a culture hero) separated by periods of stasis, rather than in such gradual increments as the cumulative achievements of an entire dynasty of innovating rulers. Thus founders of dynasties tend to receive credit in oral traditions not only for their own deeds but also for the notable achievements of their successors.[37] The accomplishments of later rulers then 'ascend' to the epoch of the founder. This accumulation of later events around a 'time of origins' has sometimes been termed the 'lightning rod effect' in reference to the apparently invisible attractive force exerted by the figure of the founding king.

'Descending anachronisms' occur when oral historians transfer an event from an earlier to a later epoch. Such descending transpositions follow less predictable patterns than ascending anachronisms, but they may result often when oral narrators attribute changes dating from very remote, nearly forgotten times to periods well within the range of clearer memory. In such cases, they in effect move a cliché that has lost its original epoch to an epoch that has remained more clearly conceptualized, almost 'available' for such purposes. Anachronisms of the descending type would occur, for example, if a founding hero of a recent dynasty were given credit for the accomplishments of earlier lines of kings, as if the Babito kings analyzed by Berger (*infra*) were to be acclaimed for events that had in fact taken place under the earlier Abacwezi. Sigwalt's informant Mpara threatened to create a descending anachronism when he attempted to combine the early political autonomy of an ancient Shi chief, the NaRhana, with his later position as a minor official in the recent main Shi state. Mpara attached the memory of the earlier cliché to more recent events he held more clearly in his mind. Either descending or ascending anachronisms may result from narrators' efforts to clarify the significance of kings' reigns, so that a ruler

16

typed as a warrior may receive credit for battles fought by predecessors or successors stereotyped as 'pacific'.

The literate historian seeking to place such disordered events in their correct order must first spell out the logic of the epochal structure of the traditional corpus, then determine its stability, and finally examine each event in relation to the epoch(s) with which it is associated. The only effective means of identifying anachronisms, except in the rare coincidence of encountering dated confirming documentation, is an inferential technique analogous to the archeologists' methodology of seriation. Events, like objects, may be placed in a hypothetical order determined by logical analysis of which ones must necessarily have preceded others or according to some such long-term trend as increasing complexity or greater size.[38] For example, the reported conquest of a province must have preceded a revolt against the conquerers. In certain cases, the historian may establish a synchronic baseline at some time in the past and then array reported occurrences along a hypothetical continuum connecting that baseline to known present circumstances. Thus, if one can confidently assert an early period of small-scale polities and can also observe a recent period of large-scale political organization, events referred to in the traditions may fall into a rough but logically necessary sequence according to an assumed general increase in scale over time.[39]

Viewing narrators' conceptualizations of the past in terms of epochs forces literate historians to see as a special form of structuring a feature of traditions commonly cited as *'telescoping'*.[40] The notion of telescoping implies that oral historians maintain a set sequence, a list, of epochs denoted as 'kings' reigns'. If oral narrators lost track of some of the rulers in a lengthening historical dynasty, the list of kings' names rather than growing would collapse into a shortened sequence much as a telescope collapses within itself. Henige's essay in this collection on Ganda and Nyoro 'king-lists' cites new anthropological studies that argue that lists of any sort occur only in societies with writing. It therefore implies that the Ganda and Nyoro originally viewed their pasts in terms of relatively unsequenced sets of conceptual fields, the epochs denoted as 'kings' reigns'. They would have had no extended 'list' to collapse, only a set of epochs, some of which disappeared with the passage of time.

'Structuring' is also a process of selecting. Oral historians structure in part by selecting a limited number of aspects of their past experiences for emphasis, and the standards for selection are very stringent in a society reliant on oral modes of preserving information.

17

They therefore tend to discard, or forget, rulers so remote in time that descent from them, or the political parties once associated with them, no longer requires an accounting in the present. Thus the epochal system tends constantly to lose the rulers that move into an unperceived conceptual gap between the more temporal epochs referring to the recent past and the more cosmological epochs of the time of origins. The oral narrators cannot indicate this gap to literate historians, since they cannot array their epochs in the same unvarying sequence as the years of literate history. As time passes, more remote or insignificant rulers simply disappear into the void, producing the impression of 'telescoping' to historians who perceive them as ranked in a set list.

Both ascending and descending anachronisms result from the ensuing process of restructuring clichés once associated with the lost epochs. The most memorable deeds of such forgotten rulers (either events with consequences that remain distinguishable in the present, or those encapsulated in particularly arresting clichés and thus worth telling for their own sake) may survive. The narrators ascribe some to a single, increasingly composite, eponymous monarch, thus creating ascending anachronisms. Others descend anachronistically to the epochs denoted by more recent kings. This redistribution of deeds proceeds entirely unconsciously. Since the names are also epochs in the perception of the oral historian, an oral narrator working with epochs defined by kings' reigns can no more imagine an event not associated with a monarch he or she recalls than a literate historian can conceive of something happening outside the comprehensive sequence of calendar years, say, between the years 1640 and 1641. Such restructuring thus results at least in part from the strong historical sense of such persons, as they attempt to depict remote times as accurately as they can with the limited resources of memory, conceptions of time, and evidence available to them. In the absence of a measured baseline like the literate calendar, their conceptual means do not equip them to notice the gaps.

Genealogical relationships are among the most prominent clichés of narrative oral traditions. Oral historians customarily spin their stories in terms of parents, children, siblings, spouses, and other sorts of close relative. Historians have often taken these relationships as elements of ramifying genealogical trees, interpreting them as literally true, and seizing on them with a faint trace of desperation as ways of inferring clear sequences and possibly even dates by means of attributing average human lifespans to the human figures in them. In doing so, they ignored the possibility that they were

18

imputing formal genealogies to sets of relationships that oral narrators did not connect in such comprehensive structures. Recent work with oral traditions has shown that the apparent simplicity of these purported genealogies is deceptive. The individual figures forming the lines of descent in them turn out to be personifications of social groups, as Berger's chapter in this volume argues for the 'kings', 'sons and brothers', of the Abacwezi.[41] Recognition of the social referents of the characters in these genealogies has destroyed all chronologies based on human lifespans imputed to them. Among the contributors to this collection, Berg finds that the genealogical links reported between the Vazimba 'kings and queens' in Madagascar have primarily structural significance, and Yoder implicitly treats the figures in his Kanyok traditions as representing Luba chiefdoms and communities.

Judging from the ubiquity of genealogical relationships in oral traditions, it is possible to infer that oral historians personalize their narratives as a way of lending them concreteness and hence memorability for their audiences. Once having selected individuals to represent more abstract events, oral narrators then use genealogical clichés owing to the strong and multiple connotations of kin relationships, especially in small-scale, descent-structured societies. Genealogical clichés of this sort probably underlie the alleged father-to-son connection between rulers in many kinglists, a trait that has recently become highly suspect among historians.[42] Such descent would be a means of saying no more than that the kings followed upon one another in the order reported.

Variation in the narrative content of oral traditions that allegedly refer to the same events has been another of their most troublesome characteristics. The term 'variation' refers to the differences nearly always encountered when literate historians identify the multiple accounts present in the historical corpus of an oral society. It has afforded critics the opportunity to cite such differences as support for their doubts that the traditions could be historical. Historians who have retained their faith in the capacity of tradition to convey literal descriptions of the past have dismissed variation as the result of faulty transmission. The creativity with which oral narrators construct their tales about the past suggests rather that variation in detail is more a result of positive value placed upon individual elaboration of historical clichés than a failure in the handing down of some literal description of events. Historians who reconstructed lines of transmission did so in an attempt to eliminate variation, on the assumption that points on which all narrators could be shown to have agreed must have passed down unchanged from an original prototestimony and would thus be historical. This method tended to accept as accurate whatever minimal core narrative it could detect in all variants, a kind of historical lowest common denominator. If oral historians invent detail and structure along the lines of cultural consensus, however, it is easy to conceive of later convergences that could produce widespread unanimity on aspects of an episode that did not descend from a single original and that had no direct relationship to the event purportedly described.[43] If the narrator constructs his tradition out of materials readily at hand, like Lévi-Strauss's *bricoleur*, then it is not the convergence but rather the variation, the elements from which the narrative is made, that command the attention of the historian. Differences, not agreement, allow the historian to decipher the ways in which narrators have composed their traditions, and in analyzing variation the historian locates where the history may lie. The analysis of changes introduced in the past replaces the study of variants existing in the present. Variation that once seemed a weakness in traditions emerges as one of their greatest strengths for the elucidation of their historical content.

Readers who have followed the discussion historians and anthropologists have conducted on the historicity of traditions will recognize that many of the features described in this section—clichés, structuring, telescoping, and variation—resemble closely those elsewhere characterized as 'myth' and thereby dismissed as 'history'. It is now clear that 'myth' and 'history' are not mutually exclusive in the sense that 'history' relates to (or describes in some direct way) the past while 'myth' is unrelated to events in the real world. Rather, 'myth' designates a presentistic and communal *style* of reasoning and exposition in nonliterate cultures that oral historians may apply to recollecting the past. It is often filled with causation and change that appear 'magical' to the literate eye. It contains events not securely fixed in relation to a single cumulative time line. It involves immediate, concrete, and often personal images and characters. It is, finally, susceptible to structural analysis. If 'myth' is a style, 'history' is less a matter of style than of whether or not the narrative contains elements that descend from the past in ways that allow a person trained in literate historical techniques to work back from them to infer something about the way things used to be. One ought not to expect narrators in oral cultures to present information about the past in the western style, and the fact that they do not ought not to deter the search for other ways in which they do preserve valid historical evidence. History and myth are thus two entirely different orders of phenomenon, and as a result much history, in literate as well as oral contexts, seems mythical because of the style in which it is written, or spoken as the case may be. Myth, as this volume demonstrates, is by the same token susceptible to historical analysis if the historian only listens with sufficient care to how the oral narrator is working as well as to what he or she superficially seems to be saying.

How Traditions Develop

Over time, oral narrators transform the shape and historical content of personal reminiscences of an historical event, creating oral traditions that exhibit the distinctive features described in the preceding section.[44] In the beginning, individuals observe and remember what they have seen about an occurrence: let us say, a partisan victory in a succession struggle in an African kingdom. The victory, in reality an exceedingly complex series of individual strategies and multiple influences, may involve a phase of armed conflict, perhaps even a decisive battle that later people recognize as the moment at which the tide of the contest turned. Such an 'event' would generate a large number of highly selective personal reminiscences that for the most part would survive for no more than the lifetimes of those who were present. Some of the better told and more noteworthy experiences might pass on as extended recollections into a second or even a third lifetime. The victory would also generate, as soon as its significance was recognized, perhaps immediately, a generally agreed upon explanation that would emphasize a very few, or even only a single aspect of the complex reality. Perhaps the explanation would hinge on the victor's reputed use of a particular charm, and responsibility for the triumph would tend to fall to the leader, the new king, rather than to subordinates. The charm in the narration of the battle stands in relation to the event in precisely the same way that an abstract explanation for a military victory gained by a modern army might involve 'morale', 'training', 'fitness', 'discipline', or any of a number of other elusive concepts obvious to the participants. No doubt the leader would employ rumor and other methods to generate the story that explained the victory to his own credit, but he would encounter definite limitations on his ability to play with what people for their own reasons chose to believe. In addition, opposing factions would circulate their own public or

21

collective versions of the event. The two sorts of recollection, private impressions and the communal judgments on the meaning of the event, might coexist for a long time, typically four or five generations, or 120 to 150 years.[45]

Transformation of the narrative of the victory would then continue as individual historians vied with one another, working with their listeners to establish a history of the event satisfactory to all. The key influence on the content and structure of these maturing narratives would be the number of direct impressions available to the men of memory, and the quantity of these would decrease as time passed and as participants died. The concrete details composing the 'event' would yield to the force of collective memory, sooner for sensitive matters like the hypothetical battle in this example, somewhat later for less highly charged events. As a result, oral historians would stress the explanatory aspect of their narratives, giving greater and greater prominence to the charm at the expense of the contribution of individual warriors. The more skilled among them would invent details that fit the general pattern of expectations about such a battle, thus making the explanation more lucid and rendering the significance of the event clearer. Assuming that the victorious faction remained an important party in the politics of the kingdom, tracing its later influence back to that key triumph, the story would be told frequently and would crystallize in the form of a few basic narratives. Each might be stylized differently, perhaps employ various clichés, but all would converge on a single central point. After a very long time, if the party of the victor had dispersed, the story would be cast loose from its social and political moorings and might begin to drift about the epochs of the past, as perceived variously by people wherever the story was told. Eventually, the victorious king's deeds might be assimilated to those of a composite dynastic founder. The specific political significance of the original event and the first traditions about it, no longer evident once the heirs of its beneficiaries had left the scene, might begin to reflect cosmological assumptions and finally take its place, or become absorbed, as part of a highly structured 'origins myth'.

At a maximum, judging from common estimates of the time depths at which traditions at each of these stages refer to historical events, what began as historical descriptions become highly structured narratives after three hundred years or so. The examples of the structured kinglists of Buganda,[46] the Kuba traditions of origin,[47] the Lunda and Luba foundation myths,[48] and other widely known African traditions suggest this rough guideline in a relatively stable political environment. But it is by no means a firm rule. Intervening political upheavals, local historical canons, and other factors could foreshorten the process, speeding up the process of transformation. On the other hand, instances are known of accurate oral historical records, highly stylized and sometimes fragmentary, that reach back to the early sixteenth century or before.[49]

This pattern of transformation, as oral historians work initial perceptions of the past into the stylized performances here labeled 'traditions', is therefore a characteristic that those who wish to recover western-style history must understand. The fact that such changes occur has been recognized since the first serious work on traditions as historical sources,[50] but methodological emphasis has often fallen on negating the effects of change, reconstructing an original testimony rather than deriving historical inferences from the implications of change. A series of advances in dealing with traditions where individual elaboration is a primary rather than a secondary feature,[51] and as shown in the studies contained in this volume, now seem to offer ways of utilizing change, or the consequences of change as manifested in the historical narratives, as a major diagnostic feature of the traditions. By recognizing the residue of past changes, the historian uses these in positive ways to reconstruct more about what happened in the past than the older style might have permitted, even had the earlier method of reading literally the cognitive level of the traditions proved itself valid.

Analysis of transformations broadens the historical yield of oral traditions beyond the narrowly political preoccupations of the cognitive level of most oral narratives. Interpretations like those offered in this collection show that oral traditions thus have a distinct sociological dimension,[52] as Harms' analysis of the Bobangi story of Botoke illustrates. Behind the legendary phrasing Harms finds a metaphorical analysis of the sociology of Bobangi village fission. Cohen has used a different sort of oral historical material to reconstruct a social history of nineteenth-century marriages, residence patterns, and potentially even family structures in Busoga that is strikingly similar to the social history normally done from literate sources. Sigwalt's discussion of the Shi origin stories suggests how these traditions bear the 'scars' of their intellectual history during a period when the locus of Shi political power shifted from one chiefdom to another. Yoder's treatment of the Kanyok myth of Citend is very much a reconstruction of the intellectual preoccupations of several generations of ideologues who rationalized the Kanyok break with the Luba sources from which their kings derived their ideology of rule. Something very close to economic history emerges when Packard joins oral traditions to ethnographic evidence to depict the settlement of herding lords from the low plains along the Semliki river as cultivating chiefs in the Mitumba mountains. Harms' work on the Bobangi is also economic history in its reconstruction of the commercial development of the Bobangi trading system on the middle Zaire river.

Biography seems elusive, because the traditions tend to concentrate on social aggregates rather than on individuals and because they usually downplay motivation and perceptions in favor of a socially conditioned consensus, even though Cohen has elsewhere made strides toward biography from oral sources.[53] Vansina's essay on memory explains why Cohen finds that oral traditions do not provide descriptions of the way people actually behaved with respect to norms governing repetitive, relatively undifferentiated events like marriages and changes of residence. The norms and values concerning behavior of this sort cited in Bunafu traditions failed dismally to represent the historical reality. Otherwise, the genres of social, economic, intellectual, and even biographical history seem to hold potential for development to a degree until now only dimly perceived—even though each will undoubtedly continue to bear the distinctive marks of its oral sources, equally as do the comparable styles of history based on written sources.[54]

Meaning in Historical Clichés

If oral narrators use clichés to preserve memories from the past, as they appear to do, then historians must define a methodology by which they can interpret their meaning with respect to past events if they are to justify their use of oral traditions as historical sources. Several of the contributors profess to treat clichés 'symbolically' or 'metaphorically', inferring historical processes, often on a grand scale, from narratives ostensibly concerned with much less momentous developments. In doing so, they expose themselves to the objection that what they may individually sense as historical in the traditions would not so strike another analyst in possession of the same data. How does Packard, for example, know that Muhiyi's transformation from pastoralist to cultivator 'stands for' or 'represents' the advance of cattlekeeping chiefs into the highland domains of the Bashu, the eventual segmentation of the lowland-based polities, and the final settlement of scions of the noble herding

24

families as heads of agriculturally based states? Or how did Harms come to understand the Bobangi distinction between village founders who came downriver with Botoke, the civilizing hero, and others who encountered Botoke under different circumstances? To him, it means that Botoke's alleged companions had in fact moved downriver from the Bobangi nuclear region at the Ubangi-Zaire confluence while the others had joined the Bobangi commercial system later. Schecter understands that when the Kanongesha Lunda speak of adultery on the part of a king's 'wife' they mean that a descent group symbolized by the 'woman' changed its allegiance from the chief to whom it had been 'married' to a new overlord. But would another historian hearing the same tale reach a similar conclusion?[55] Without the ability to specify the logical processes of inference that lead them from symbol to meaning, historians open themselves to the criticism leveled against structuralist anthropologists: that their solutions to the puzzles of myths, however elegant, lack scientific status unless they can be confirmed by replication.

The historians' first solution to this dilemma, really a manifestation of the classic enigma of the relationship of the '-emic' to the '-etic', is empirical rather than theoretical. The major justification for accepting meaning comes from independent confirmation of the events to which the cliché is believed to refer and from evidence of consistency in the way oral narrators seem to use it. If the historian repeatedly, even uniformly, finds a cliché used to designate a class of events that he or she can independently establish from other sources, the case for the interpretation adopted is very firm. The historian also relies heavily on general ethnographic knowledge to infer past realities from clichés. The interpretation of the cliché recited in the present must be consistent with the way he or she understands people in the society to think and behave. In addition, the interpretation usually conforms to general knowledge about how oral historians seem to develop and to employ clichés.

The pattern most evident with respect to oral narrators' use of clichés is that they use them to refer in a general manner to repetitive events that are relatively common in their historical experience. Among the Imbangala of Angola, for example, prominent clichés refer to apparently standard processes by which title-holding nobles established or confirmed political ties with dependent descent groups, to the extinction of noble titles, and to other events that occurred again and again in Imbangala political history.[56] Harms has found that the central cliché of the Bobangi tradition of origin,

the story of how Botoke left Bobangi Esanga, analyses sociologi-
cally a similarly familiar pattern of village fission along the middle
Zaire river. Schecter's and Yoder's analyses of the political traditions of the Luba and Lunda both show how the well-known foreign
hunter cliché of the southern savanna accurately describes what
must have been a common occurrence as Luba- and Lunda-derived
political titles spread throughout the region. Oral narrators among
the Bashu, as Packard shows, expressed the repeated settlement of
cattle-chiefs among the farming people of the mountains in the
myth of Muhiyi, a pastoralist-turned-cultivator *par excellence*. Vansina's new study of Kuba history is based in part on using clichés to
describe generalized processes in the Kuba past.[57]

If meaning in historical clichés refers, however accurately and
perceptively, to broad classes of events in the past, in what sense
ought it to be taken as historical rather than, say, sociological? It
could be argued, for example, that the failure of such generalized
clichés to deal with the specifics of an event, the significance of
which they may illuminate only in universal terms, disqualifies them
as 'history' which, after all, is proclaimed as the study of the particular. In fact, historians of any kind use particular circumstances to
study the general. Literate historians use preserved details to allude
to the theme that they introduce into the past (although they may
claim that the theme emerges of its own accord from their data).
Oral historians, on the other hand, work the other way around.
They have at hand the preserved theme and introduce the details
that illustrate it effectively.

Harms' treatment of the Bobangi traditions, which parallels the
argument offered in more general terms by Schecter, suggests the
sense in which even the generalized clichés acquire a kind of
specificity when applied to particular circumstances. Harms divides
the Bobangi corpus of narrative traditions into three categories of
episode: traditions referring to historical origins, migrations, and
settlements, each defined by its characteristic cliché. For the
Bobangi tradition of origin, historical narrators emphasize the general process of village fission that in their opinion provokes movement, as in the cliché of Botoke. They express the migration
episodes in stereotyped terms of movement down the river. Settlement tales are built around some sort of cliché that accounts for the
relationships prevailing between the newcomers and the original
land owners. The specific content of each, as opposed to its allusion
to the usual course of events at such times, turns out to be an
elementary binary statement of the form 'With regard to historical

process X (fission, movement, settlement), the group telling this story either did it or did not do it.' A village did or did not come from Bobangi Esanga, it has moved or it has not, and it did or did not acquire particular rights in its present location.

The historical meaning of the clichés at the heart of oral narratives thus assumes the form of a binary contrast reminiscent of the paired oppositions detected by structuralist anthropologists on the narrative level of such tales in other cultures. This structured narrative level consists of details consciously invented in large part by the oral historian and therefore not related directly to the past. Yet the emergence of a similarly structured logic with respect to the historical content of the clichés, which presumably relate to the past, seems to confirm that oral narrators consciously embodied history, a record of the past, at the core of the traditions they tell. If, as Lévi-Strauss and Leach and other structuralists have argued, there is something about the thinking process of the human mind that shapes thought in terms of paired contrasts, particularly in oral cultures, the appearance of just such an opposition in the historical content of the traditions speaks in favor of the deliberate intentions of the tellers of the traditions to preserve an accurate memory of the past. Harms and others writing in this volume are therefore justified in interpreting the clichés in the narratives as the results of a conscious effort to describe historical processes and specific circumstances.

Meaning may also emerge from inaccurate but expressive details that oral narrators mix with generalized summaries of historical circumstances to deliver the intended judgment with greater force than the abstractions might do alone. There may thus be a sense in which even the invented detail approximates real circumstances. Returning for an example to Harms' analysis of the Bobangi cliché of Botoke's expulsion from Bobangi Esanga, one may surmise that skilled oral historians have developed a version of the events that accurately typifies the circumstances of village fission, employing details that are entirely descriptive and even historically correct in a generalized way. One ought never to attribute the specific circumstances described to any particular instance of village fission, but there is a good chance that the cliché transmits an exact impression of how Bobangi perceived the immediate events that sociologists abstract as 'village fission'. On the other hand, the fishing weir in which Bobangi men of memory say Botoke was ordered to transport water conveys historical meaning of a different sort. It is an image of obvious metaphorical content, added by the tellers of the

27

tradition to express not the way in which events took place but to render the tellers' judgment about the meaning of the events. The judgment in turn reveals something specific about who formulated the cliché, in this case presumably those who left, feeling wronged.

Distinctions of this type between the historical clichés of the narrative and aspects deriving from the style of the narrators' telling of them help to explain why historians accept some parts of an oral narrative as historical and reject other elements as having little or no relationship to the past. Identification of other aspects of the clichés may further diminish the formerly broad areas within which historians relied on instinct rather than explicit method and thus meet more fully the charge that historians have been unsystematic, even intuitive, in the way they have handled oral traditions as history.[58]

The contributors to this volume use several kinds of internal criticism of the corpus of tradition in which clichés appear to assess their meaning as distilled perceptions of events in the past. One method relates the extent of agreement among oral narrators on the concrete images they choose to the complexity or simplicity of the event, or class of events, described. Sigwalt discusses at length the structural factors that may constrain the oral historian's freedom in his choice of images and core narratives. Relatively simple historical points, like the Shi basic assertion that political legitimacy derives from a given location at Lwindi, are capable of expression in numerous ways, while the complex relationships within a political charter almost impose uniformity at the narrative level of that sort of tradition.

Judging from the analyses presented in this volume, more frequent instances of the process the cliché denotes also seem to increase the degree of uniformity in their representation. In practice, oral historians agreed on a single cliché to represent the almost routine 'marriages' of descent groups to political titles among the Imbangala, the common village fissions of the Bobangi, or the repeated formation of small states around 'Luba hunters' among the Kanyok. The Lunda political processes analyzed by Schecter and the emergence of *vazimba* spirits from water among the Merina, as Berg explains, are also connected with everyday events in those cultures. Conversely, less frequent events, or happenings whose significance is a matter of less universal agreement, ought to find expression in more widely varied clichés. Some historical events, particularly those connected with political disputes that are still alive, give rise to such divergent opinions at the time of their occurrence that the first descriptions of them are discrepant in ways that later oral traditions would preserve in varying clichés. Even in this case, the resultant clichés ought to converge on a unified agreement as to 'what happened', or in extreme cases only on the fact that 'something happened', even as they fan out into an array of varying judgments about what it meant to the parties affected by it. The very divergence of opinion ought to serve the historian as a first hypothesis for a more complex and nuanced reconstruction of the event that gave rise to deviant clichés than unanimity on the part of oral narrators might allow.

In the instance of an extremely well-established cliché like the Luba hunter legend of the Kanyok, as Yoder shows (and for that matter, among the Lunda studied by Schecter), the very regularity of the structure offers the opportunity to infer meaning from the pattern of deviations from the standard plot. Yoder applies this method by first defining the regular properties of the standard Luba hunter myth and then noting the idiosyncrasies of the Kanyok version of it focusing on Citend a Mfumu, the Kanyok culture heroine. He goes on to note as well the unique properties of regional variants emanating from the chiefdoms of Ngoi and Mwamba Ciluu. From these, he infers as first hypotheses the circumstances under which such differences could have arisen and then seeks independent data to confirm them. Yoder's method of inferring history from local variations of general patterns has its anthropological precedents, since it parallels the logic of structuralist analyses of similar southern savanna traditions, though emphasizing the effects of political and social conditions rather than of the cosmological assumptions of those who told the tales.[59] Even the intellectual emphases of the structuralists have an implicit, though often unstressed, historical dimension. A good cliché like that of the Luba hunter story must have been invented somewhere, and its local variants must reflect intellectual changes wrought from the basic idea as local groups adopted and adapted it. A pan-savanna study of this particularly widespread motif, as Schecter suggests, might yield conclusions very close to an intellectual history of its development and florescence in varying cultures. It could even lead to comparisons with similar hunter legends in western and eastern Africa.

A historical explanation of how and why widely separated individuals might choose similar clichés to describe historical processes in their respective pasts would weaken the argument sometimes offered by anthropologists that broad distributions of key elements found in myths constitute proof of their ahistoricity. Both Yoder and Schecter write against a background of this sort of criticism by de Heusch, and Berger's study of the Abacwezi is in significant part a response to a similar structuralist dismissal of the history to be found in the lacustrine legends associated with what she shows to have been the earliest surviving political institutions of that area. The case that each tries to refute holds in essence that demonstration that an underlying abstraction (or 'structure') transcends the range of the particular myth embodying it proves that the myth forms part of a tale that is cosmological rather than historical.

The explanation for the close resemblances, when they in fact exist,[60] lies in the similarity of the historical processes that they may in fact describe. Schecter traces the cliché of the arriving hunter throughout the Lunda and Luba regions of the central southern savannas, in an area where, from every indication, larger political structures spread from one or two nuclei into regions organized in terms of broadly similar small-scale institutions. In addition, there is evidence to suggest that the people living in those areas have been in touch with one another for hundreds of years, certainly since the present political systems began to form early in the present millennium.[61] It should not surprise historians to find that so elegant and powerful a cliché as the story of the immigrant hunter would have spread widely as individuals gradually agreed over the years on the meaning of the crucial events attending the growth of their political systems.

If this explanation of the widespread occurrence of the myth of the immigrant hunter king is accurate, then the hypothesized tendencies of oral narrators to streamline and structure their tales increasingly over time[62] ought to render the oldest and most far-flung stories the most mythical in style, though still historical in origin if not in narrative content. The distribution of the Luba tale of Kongolo and Kalala Ilunga has precisely that appearance. It deals with the most remote phases of savanna political history and in some areas has nearly attained the status and form of a creation myth. Adaptations of the same clichés to slightly more recent events, as in the case of the central Lunda story of Cibinda Ilunga and Naweej, have proportionally greater historical content and can probably be counted on at least for a correct indication of the source of the ancestral political culture and perhaps for general indications of the course of its implantation in its new context.[63] Applications of the same clichés to still more recent events, like those occurring among the Kanongesha and Luapula Kazembe, both late expansions based on the Luba/Lunda political institutions, ought to be most historical and least structured. Schecter's description of them seems to confirm this hypothesis. In short, borrowing and modification of particularly expressive and relevant clichés ought to produce precisely the varying historicity that scholars have noted in the southern savanna. Structure decreases in tales about more recent events, and also details shift from a patrilineal to a matrilineal idiom.[64]

Once the historian recognizes clichés as the units in which oral narrators encode meaning from the past, demonstration that a cliché has found its way from external sources into the oral traditions of a particular culture need not invalidate it as evidence from which knowledge of the past may be inferred. Thus, even if it should turn out that the 'drunken king' and his disobedient sons, who stand at the head of so many southern savanna traditions, should derive from Christian missionary stories of Noah told in sixteenth-century Kongo, this fact would open up whole new areas of investigation to historians. In Sigwalt's story of Lwindi, the very fact of borrowing serves as confirmation of the narrative content of the story.

Borrowed clichés, according to the dynamics by which oral traditions seem to change as oral narrators work with them, should be most frequently associated with events remote in time. Localization of borrowing in these very old sections of the traditions, especially in traditions of origin, results in part from the fact that the absence of personal recollections from those remote times leaves clichés more prominent there as means of recalling them. The tenuousness of the links between the remote past and the mnemonics in the present on which oral historians key their narratives leaves them freer to borrow a good idea at will. The ease with which such origin clichés move about often brings several of them to the same culture, where their very plurality alerts the historian to the need to examine each critically to determine which contains historical referents to the real origins of the people who tell them.[65]

Migrations as Cliché

The essays in this volume generally confirm historians' recent and growing suspicions about the historicity of migration clichés in particular.[66] Vansina's reworking of the Kuba traditions acknowledged that clichés of migration there indicating origins in the west, perhaps from the vicinity of the Kongo, are false if taken literally. They state that the Kuba came from near the ocean, a plausible claim in view of the references in the same tales to Imbangala, people from Angola identified among literate historians with so-called 'Jaga' invaders documented in the Kongo in the sixteenth century. The mention of the Imbangala, taken as equivalent to the 'Jaga', seemed to put the Kuba ancestors in the right place at the right time, in the west where the stories of migration seemed to point. Demonstrable linguistic influences from Kongo on the Kuba, an apparent independent bit of evidence, seemed to confirm the historicity of the narrative level of these stories. A broad pattern of new evidence drawn from linguistics and other narrative traditions has since established the proximate origins of the bulk of the Kuba peoples in the north rather than the west. The alleged connections with Kongo turn out to express a quite different fact, no less histori-cal: later trading relations linked the Kuba region to the west through commercial networks leading toward the Kongo coast. Even the reference to the Imbangala (though not the 'Jaga', to whom they were unrelated) is correct, though it points to eighteenth- or nineteenth-century trading contacts rather than to the sixteenth-century period of population drift. The original misin-terpretation followed, ironically, as much from mistaken European identification of the 'Jaga' with the Imbangala[67] as from ambiguity in the Kuba oral traditions.[68]

Africans commonly tell migration traditions to link themselves to people living elsewhere, asserting the connection in the form of a narrative tracing a movement on foot, by canoe, through a wilder-ness from a distant location to the place where the tradition is told. In fact, these traditions might be more accurately understood abstractly as 'myths of transferal', in Sigwalt's terminology, and understood as clichés denoting a variety of different historical circumstances by means of the personalized images of movements of real people. Such a perceived unity, between oneselves and other people living elsewhere, logically implies 'movement' in such a conceptual system. The historian's task then becomes that of decid-ing the real historical circumstances that brought the two areas connected by the 'myth of transferal' into touch with one another.

Recent work suggests that mass population movements in Africa generally have taken the form of slow and unco-ordinated drifts of clan or lineage segments, villages, or individuals, none of them the sorts of unified migration that turn up recorded in oral traditions geared to the preservation of memories of more dramatic kinds of change.[69] Several of the contributors to this collection reconstruct population movements of the sort that actually brought people to their present residences in Africa, though in none of these cases did the traditions record the movement in the form of a 'myth of transferal'. Cohen's examples are the most striking. The inhabitants of Bunafu by the end of the nineteenth century had come from long distances and from highly various backgrounds, yet these pervasive individual migrations found no mention in the collective narrative traditions. Packard describes the drift of cattlekeeping chiefs out of lowland grazing areas and into the Mitumba mountains, but the cliché denoting this process was not a 'myth of transferal'. Similarly, Harms found population movements large in scale, taking place over long distances, and even involving corporate groupings of people—all conditions ostensibly depicted in migration clichés—that turned out to be represented in the oral traditions by an entirely different sort of story. In fact, those Bobangi who told explicit migration stories were found guilty of protesting too loudly, as they revealed the falsity of their literal claim to have moved downriver from Bobangi Esanga, the ancestral Bobangi village. The villages who actually had done so still counted themselves part of a spiritual nucleus of Bobangi settlement, whatever their present residence, and so told no migration stories to account for their modern geographical dispersal.

'Migration', if the Bobangi are typical of other African oral historians, often denotes social or political connections rather than those resulting from demographic movement. The myths of transferal may indicate transfers of ideology and identity. The famous story of the Lunda émigré prince, Kinguri, said to have left the Lunda court and to have marched westward until he met the Portuguese in Angola at the beginning of the seventeenth century, appears rather to represent the diffusion of a complex of Lunda political culture centered on the *kinguri* noble title throughout a broad area of what is now eastern and central Angola.[70] Yoder's essay in this collection offers a similar interpretation of the meaning of the Citend migration story among the Kanyok, whose political affinities with the Luba are undoubted but whose physical origins there are unlikely. Sigwalt's analysis of the Shi narrative about the migration of their kings from Lwindi implicitly takes its historical content as referring to kings, perhaps only political institutions in the abstract, rather than to people. The historical circumstances inferred in all these instances concern political ties or commercial contacts, and the actual geographical origins of the people are often shown to have been elsewhere, if not autochthonous in historical times.

The seductiveness of the migration cliché for Europeans is owing to the fortuitous convergence of nonliterate depictions of change with colonial stereotypes associated with the 'Hamitic hypothesis', whose specific effects in Uganda and Madagascar Berger and Berg discuss here. The tendency of oral historians to phrase these clichés in personal and concrete terms, in this case showing living individuals moving through a familiar landscape, is entirely consistent with the general properties of oral history. Further, an uncircumstantiated, or stereotypically explained, direct movement from a place of origins to a place of settlement logically parallels the dichotomous kinds of change that occur typically in oral narratives. Ironically, literate historians for a long time abandoned their own gradualist conceptions of change in favor of only slightly less simplistic explanations of change in precolonial Africa: population movements in terms of mass migrations, state formation by sudden conquest, and group identities mainly in the form of static 'tribes'. This European illogic sometimes overwhelmed more nuanced African visions of their own history, as Berg and Berger indicate, and led historians more generally, as in the case of the migration clichés, to take traditions entirely too literally on this point. In particular, the idea of 'tribes' as cohesive and territorially bounded groups predisposed historians to view these units as capable of drifting long distances over the map of Africa.[71] This sociology had no connection with the more subtle sociology of people like the Bobangi, whose conceptualizations of groups transcended space and time in ways that allowed their historians to take little notice of gradual population movements that occurred as matters of course.

Only Schecter's analysis of the Kanongesha implies a physical movement of people corresponding to the cognitive level of the migration tales. However, he is careful to cite confirming evidence of the historicity of these Lunda narratives, in the form of Lunda and Luba phonemes in the speech of southern Lunda courtiers and documentary confirmation for the Kazembe Lunda. The Lunda case need not invalidate the general point, which is that migration traditions accurately identify connections between people living in one place and others living in another. What they do not specify is the historical circumstances of the connection, which usually remain hidden beneath familiar and personalistic images and a good deal of recent ahistorical detail drawn from commercial routes followed in the nineteenth century.

34

Selection and Structuring

As examination of the migration clichés suggests, all historians select and structure their data in the process of presenting them. The rule holds whether they work from oral or written sources and whether they compose on paper or before an audience. Several authors in this collection call attention to the fact that the historical information preserved in oral traditions is highly selective and refers to only a limited segment of a much more varied and complex past. Although selectivity and structuring distinguish oral narratives from written history only to a degree rather than absolutely, oral modes in which narrators work cause them to introduce patterns that historians must take into account.

On the cognitive level—that is, on the level of what narrators consciously intend to communicate—selection occurs because they can preserve observations only about events that participants and informants were in a position to perceive.[72] For example, slow and relatively uneventful migratory drift of the sort usually attributed to the spread of the Bantu through central, eastern, and southern Africa ought to have left little imprint on traditions of origin. Such a gradual movement lies at the beginnings of the history of the Kuba in Zaire, and they have no explicit recollection of it. The historian must infer it from ethnographic evidence and from linguistics. Cohen's paper on Bunafu emphasizes that the public, collective narrative histories of the Soga do not record the details of daily life that have attracted his attention. The selectivity that Cohen notes, this analysis suggests, may result from the very diffuseness of the individual experiences that he documents. There has been no group experience sufficiently dramatic to attract notice and thereby allow men of memory to fabricate narrative traditions of the sort found elsewhere.

Part of the silence of the Soga traditions, a consequence of their selectivity, may result from the view that narrators in Busoga and elsewhere in Africa hold of change. Like their western counterparts, they are historians and as such are concerned with what they understand as change. Where they do not perceive change, or where they do not understand events as constituting change, oral historians do not create narrative traditions. The traditions are thus dependent on how people think of change. People in nonliterate environments often develop conceptions of change different from what persons trained in European cultural assumptions take for granted. Whereas western historians perceive change in terms of refined and lengthy series of gradual increments, the constraints of orality lead narrators to conceive of and to present change in the form of abrupt, dichotomous transformations. Their neglect of all the intermediary steps that western historians feel are necessary to describe change meaningfully sometimes lends their narratives a 'magical' quality, as transformations are noted and explained in sudden steps that are quite unbelievable to literate observers.[73] The normality of the rise of Womunafu, the lack of dramatic and visible transformations attending it meant that few, perhaps no one, on that hill top in Busoga had the opportunity to notice what had taken place, to pause, to reflect, and to begin the process of interpretation that would have culminated in the sort of oral tradition described in most other essays in this volume.

Oral narrators seem to require a crisis to initiate the process of composition, a sudden and visible shifting of fortunes, perhaps marked by a singular and notable event. In the absence of such circumstances, the sort of gradual change that Cohen documents cannot be phrased easily in the 'magical' rhetoric of the traditions. It does not make a good story, and so the narrative format is inappropriate for its preservation. In the absence of other forms of record, it is lost to history. Only literate methods capable of amassing large amounts of data for simultaneous analysis, from clan histories, extended personal recollections, and other sources taken, as Cohen puts it, from the private 'fabric of daily life' allow its reconstruction. Individual cultures obviously vary in the level at which their narrators set what might be called the threshold of noticeability, since Packard's Bashu and Harms' Bobangi both have clichés describing processes of population drift and village fission that might elsewhere escape preservation. Perhaps the reasons that these have given formal expression to such gradual processes is that individual instances were sufficiently dramatic to be marked by ritual and thus involved conscious transformations of the sort readily assimilated to the 'magical' traditions.

The oral historian's predilection for dichotomous transformations also contributes to, or at least is entirely consistent with, another form of selection, or structuring: the so-called 'hourglass' shape of many bodies of oral traditions. The description of traditions as shaped like an 'hourglass' refers to the narrators' tendency to locate a great deal of the information at their disposal in a single period of 'origins' and then to pass without comment through the succeeding 'middle period'. Literate historians instinctively want to emphasize this 'middle period' because it is there that they would find the gradual increments of change that they feel they must place between 'origins' and the recent past. Extended personal recollections expand the amount of information available from the recent past, so that the literate historian who does not distinguish between oral traditions and personal reminiscences perceives clusterings of information at the beginning and the end of the past, with a near void in the intervening years.

What has in fact happened to produce this pattern, apparent only to the literate outsider, is that the oral historians' conception of change as cataclysmic and total leads them to group all events dealing with change in a single period of universal transformation, thus accentuating the drama of the changes portrayed. Their pushing back to the period of 'origins' of many or most events seen as marking change leaves the vacuum in the middle period and creates an impression of stability at the narrow waist of the hourglass. In fact, it is at this period that clichés referring to process may occur, and the regularity, repetitiveness, and normalcy of these processes is entirely consistent with the oral narrator's evident perception that 'nothing happened' from the time of origins until the recent past. The oral historian thus uses clichés as logical devices very akin to 'process models' to link the baseline of the 'time of origins' to the recent past of personal reminiscences.

Designation of the traditions as 'hourglass'-shaped reflects how individual narrators rework the past with oral techniques but often misrepresents the history that a literate historian may reconstruct by drawing together more than one sort of oral evidence. Frequently, several discrete bodies of tradition coexist in oral cultures which are not juxtaposed by oral narrators, who are bound by their oral methodology, but which are open to combination and analysis by historians who use writing. The traditions of smaller groups—clans, clan segments, provincial chiefdoms, priests and other ritualists all appear in the essays presented in this volume, themselves individually also hourglass-shaped—fill in much of the void left in empty 'middle periods' of the larger-scale narratives. Cohen's technique fills lacunae in this way, as does that of Yoder for Kanyok history. Schecter's traditions for the southern Lunda fill in the vacuum of the oral narratives of the central Lunda dynasty, while the traditions of local subordinates plug a similar gap in the Kanongesha traditions and these finally overlap with extended personal recollections.[74] Combining all the sorts of oral narrative found in most cultures expands the narrow waist of the hourglass and

Joseph C Miller

allows literate historians, though not their oral colleagues, to produce a chronologically balanced history.

Cultural emphases, little different from what has also been
termed structuring, are perhaps the most powerful source of selectivity in oral traditions, because in the absence of literacy people
preserve only matters that they regard as vital. Berg's paper on the
vazimba traditions of the Merina shows most clearly of those presented here how collective preoccupations narrow the range of
aspects of the past selected for inclusion in an oral corpus. The
vazimba, as Berg has shown elsewhere,[75] were originally ancestral
spirits associated with Merina descent groups. The Merina are well
known for the stress they place on descent and on veneration of
ancestors who stand for the social groups to which the living belong.
It is therefore hardly surprising that the Merina chose to express
their cosmological speculations, as Berg illustrates in this paper, in
the form of genealogical formulae involving *vazimba* ancestral
spirits. The selective effect on the traditions resembles the cultural
tendency of the Luba to identify themselves in terms of their ancestors' political achievements.[76]

Structuring imperfectly accomplished leaves telltale signs that the
literate historian may use to tease out his counterparts' techniques
of construction and beyond those some of the real history concealed
in the oral narratives. All historians, literate and oral alike, select
and structure, but those who write can do these things better than
those who must depend on the techniques available in a nonliterate
culture. Literacy enables a historian to come closer to working out a
consistent structure, an interpretation that explains all the data,
leaving few unrationalized inconsistencies or contradictions in their
exposition. The oral historian, though he may strive toward the
same goal as his literate counterpart, works less efficiently and
leaves oral narratives filled with incompletely rationalized elements, often juxtaposed in ways hardly noticeable during a live
performance but that leap out as contradictions once the narrative is
written down and subjected to literate analytical procedures. It is
partly through structuring, the shifting of episodes from epoch to
epoch so that each makes better 'sense' or the assimilation of all
sorts of transformations into a single period of 'origins', that oral
historians create these inconsistencies.

Sigwalt's study of the Shi narrator, Mpara, is the most developed
analysis of this kind in the papers collected here. Sigwalt shows how
the Shi historian combined two incompatible stories about a titleholder, NaRhana, associated in apparently contradictory ways with

the court of one of the important Shi kings, Ngweshe. NaRhana according to Mpara, was both an independent chief and also a subordinate official conquered by the Ngweshe kings. Sigwalt attempts to resolve the contradiction by treating it in a complex structuralist vein that tolerates both roles simultaneously. He also gives a historical explanation of the contradiction, suggesting that the two elements of the narrative may refer to different periods in the development of the NaRhana position, an earlier time in which he was an independent chief and a later period after he had been conquered and become the subordinate official who also appears in the tradition. It is Mpara's inability to distinguish the different periods of the past to which these stories refer and his failure to work out completely all the inconsistencies in his narrative that allow Sigwalt to perceive the apparent contradiction. The paradox, when subjected to the more powerful analytical techniques of the literate historian, yields a historical hypothesis that could be confirmed by further data. The weaknesses of history in an oral mode thus constitute diagnostic strengths for the literate analyst of the traditions.

Structure as Layers: The Past in the Present

Oral narrators structure their visions of the past in ways that often produce an effect that may be termed 'layering'. This effect gives the past the appearance of a layered composite of elements, originating at various times but all existing together in the heterogeneous institutions of the present. This feature is particularly marked where larger-scale political institutions have succeeded older institutions of smaller size, as is the case for every essay presented here. As Berger and Sigwalt show, and as Yoder and Schecter assume, people in oral societies tend to conserve the primary institutions of former eras, though in altered, often reduced forms as subordinated layers in the present. Thus, the heirs of ancient Abacwezi kings lived on into times dominated by Babito dynasties, no longer as chiefs and kings but as 'priests', prophets, or spirit mediums. Several of Sigwalt's Shi 'ritualists' turn out to have once been independent political authorities in their own right. The significance of these tendencies for historians wishing to make use of traditions lies in the fact that they explain why people in oral societies conserve records of former times. The presentistic atmosphere of oral cultures thus need not imply lack of concern for the past.

A recent study of the Merina of Madagascar, discussed here in another respect by Berg, uses anthropological approaches to the study of hierarchy, ranking, and prestige to show how one culture systematically preserved a record of its past in order to justify the power of the rulers of the present. According to this analysis, new dynasties of rulers were common in Merina history down to the late eighteenth-century rise of Andrianampoinimerina, whose heirs dominated the entire Merina region for the whole nineteenth century. New dynasties had earlier achieved recognition of their superiority in power by receiving tribute from the heirs of the previous rulers. The legitimacy of the newcomers, however, depended on their recognizing those who paid tribute, the former rulers who were thereby declared subordinate, but also more prestigious than the kings. Public demonstrations of obeisance from those who were recognized as higher in status could only enhance the kings' grandeur and power. Thus the conquerers depended on the conquered for their legitimacy, and to express their legitimacy they had to preserve the record of those who had preceded them. Since those who had preceded the latest kings had in turn preserved records of their own predecessors, each Merina kingdom was composed of a series of ranked layers reflecting not only the politics of the present but also the history of the past.[77]

The primary implications of this analysis for historians are that the presentism of the traditions may, indeed must, preserve the memory of times gone by in order that the politics of the present might make sense. Sigwalt's informant Mpara might have made this argument in defense of his superficially contradictory juxtaposition of the two historical roles of NaRhana, both a ritualist dependent on the king Ngweshe but also his equal or even his predecessor. One can find traces of such a process operating among the eastern Mbundu of Angola, where 'priests' described in the seventeenth-century sources look very much like the descendants of earlier political authorities,[78] and where modern traditions explicitly stress the grandeur of presently inconsequential titles. The Mbwela lineages discussed by Schecter stand in precisely this same relationship of simultaneous superiority and inferiority to their Kanongesha overlords. This logic may explain the ubiquitous stress on conquest in oral traditions, since a formulation of 'origins' by conquest simultaneously identifies and honors as more ancient the predecessors of the present regime, while accounting for their subjugation to the temporal power of the new arrivals. Most African systems of ranking based on historical precedence seem to be relatively simple,

40

consisting of only two layers, and so the present rank order may probably be taken to reflect actual historical sequence. In the multilayered ranking system of the Merina, however, present rank order need not correspond to historical sequence, since the power most recently dominant can adjust the standing of the subordinate groups relative to each other in accordance with changing modern political realities.[79]

The principle that modern regimes need the memory of their predecessors in order to legitimate their claims to power means that there is no theoretical limit to the time-depth to which oral traditions may reach. The traditions ought to extend to the periods from which the earliest groups descend that have managed to preserve, or that have had preserved, their social identities. Fortunately for western historians, African societies seem commonly to have incorporated dialectical tensions between the earlier institutions of smaller scale and the later states and kingdoms. It is the coexistence of the larger- and smaller-scale units that gives rise to traditions, as Harms recognizes when he explicitly attributes the existence of the Bobangi narratives to the growth in scale that accompanied Bobangi commercial expansion along the Zaire river in the eighteenth and nineteenth centuries. Berger concludes specifically that such tensions—between rulers and ruled, in her phrasing—provide the key to the preservation of the traditions of the Abacwezi.

The time-depth that corresponds to the origins of the components—or layers—of the present regime may be called the 'present past', since it is the period that contributes to the reminders that fill the oral historians' present environment and thereby their recollections of the past. This present past corresponds to the more historical epochs of the oral traditions. The depth of the present past possesses no regularity in terms of calendar years, since its range depends on when the present regime came into being and the earlier institutions it incorporated. The establishment of a new dominant institution, or recognition of its establishment, casts loose from their moorings in the present all traditions about former times. Those stories then come to refer to what might be called the 'past past', or the 'absent past'. It is in the absent past that historical traditions may become highly structured and most mythical in their phrasing. The traditions dealing with the absent past become fragmentary, and the remembered elements drift uncertainly as narrators varyingly attempt to link them to unrelated landmarks in the present past.

Berg's *vazimba* traditions are the clearest examples in this set of

41

papers of oral traditions dealing with the absent past (although Sigwalt mentions some of these). Berg phrases the distinction between what I am here calling the absent past and the present past as one between traditions of the *vazimba* where structuring appears to have taken over and a more recent period of 'invariable history'. His analysis confirms the general point that cosmological categories emerge most clearly in traditions dealing with epochs separated from the present by profound structural changes in the society. The rise of the large and enduring kingdom under Andrianampoinimerina at the end of the eighteenth century constituted such a divide for the Merina. If that is true, guilt-ridden loyalists to the Merina descent groupings might well have initiated the shift from benevolent to evil spirits Berg traces in the character of the *vazimba* before the Europeans came. If so, the change in the nature of these spirits would have resulted from internal changes rather than external influences. European missionaries would have been more important for documenting it than for causing it, as Christianity merely intensified a transition already under way.

A Typology of Traditions as History

Looking at traditions through the eyes of African oral narrators thus yields a typology of narratives based on the distinction between absent past and present past that also demarcates the sorts of historical referent predominant in each category. The distinction between public traditions, which tend to be more structured in conception owing to the interaction between narrator and audience as they are repeated through time, and private reminiscences is also basic. The quantity of historical information that may be derived from each category generally increases from top to bottom on the chart, from the completely (or nearly) fictional creation myths to the direct descriptions of what people have witnessed in the category of personal reminiscences. Forms of tradition dealing with the absent past are generally historical in only limited senses useful to the historian, while those associated with the present past may contain significant amounts of accurate information bearing on times gone by. Their historicity results in large part from the mnemonic assistance that tangible remains of the past offer to oral narrators and from the multiplicity of groups whose interests these stories affect and who therefore defend their accuracy. Rare will be the consensus in a characteristically segmentary African society

Oral Traditions as History

TYPE OF PAST	CATEGORY OF TRADITION	SOCIAL ORIENTATION	CHARACTERISTICS AS HISTORY
Absent (past) past	Creation myths	Public	No historical content, or so obscure as to have little meaning. Universal in scope, cosmological in content, highly structured.
	Myths of ultimate origins		Single, simple statement of history; broadly societal in scope. Highly structured.
	Transferal myths		Historical relevance limited to the institution preserving the tale; migration cliché stands for processes not often described directly by the narrative. Details of geography usually drawn from recent experience of narrator and/or audience.
Present past	Fragmentary episodes from preceding epochs		Isolated facts embedded in highly structured language; narrow in scope relative to charter myth.
	Comprehensive charter myths		Composed of cliché-centered narrative episodes, each bearing on a historical process or event; tendency to aggregate all episodes in a single period of 'origins'; chronological content depends on elaboration of system of epochs (kings' reigns, etc.). Scope congruent with dimensions of largest recent political unit.
	Independent charter myths clan segments regional nobility related states		Similar in form and historical content to comprehensive charter myth, though may fill in void left by ascendant anachronisms in 'middle period' of the former.
	Extended personal recollections and personal reminiscences	Private	Individual experiences, not as extensively structured in language. Properly 'oral data' rather than 'oral tradition'.

sufficient to allow any single party to achieve a wholesale fabrication in stories dealing with the present past.

Beyond the horizon formed by the distinction between present and absent past, narratives have lost their anchor in present consequences of past actions, and so they change shape more readily in response to the artistic and cosmological tastes of the culture in which they are told. The broader their scope, the less constrained they are by competing interests. As a result, narrators hone them over time into complex distillations of artistry and logic. The typology thus turns on the interplay over time between narrator and society, culture and politics.

The Historians and the Anthropologists

A favorite sport of anthropologists and historians has been taking potshots at the others' position with respect to the uses and abuses of oral traditions for historical purposes. If the historians have sometimes been guilty of beating the nearly dead horse of classical functionalism, the anthropologists have also failed to direct their criticisms unerringly against the most recent and refined historical techniques. The best practitioners in both fields have, however, generally recognized the need to take account of the conclusions of the other.

Anthropologists' misunderstandings of historical method come in some part from their tendency to apply their own rules of evidence and inference to historians, who in fact apply quite different critical methodologies to their data. Modern anthropology has necessarily accorded absolute and total respect to ethnographic data reported by anthropologists from the field. Anthropologists roundly criticize each other's interpretations, but they rarely call into question the raw facts, the ethnographic reports. By the historians' standards, such respect for reported 'facts' (in reality complex mixtures of observation, inference, and reported action or thought) avoids the scholar's primary obligation, which is to criticize such reports, to examine the processes by which the 'facts' were collected, to search for additional, possibly contravening information. Hence, the historians' insistence on footnotes and documentation, two kinds of scholarly apparatus relatively rare in ethnographies. Hence also, the historians' constant return to the original sources, whereas few anthropologists have, until recently, returned to the ethnographic territory of a predecessor. Hence, finally, the acceptance by anthropologists of such compendia of data as the Ethnographic Atlas, which strikes historians as filled with data of such dubious standing as to vitiate conclusions drawn from analysis of them.

What the anthropologists do, and what they have sometimes assumed historians must do as well, is thus to take the received datum on its own terms, in the form in which it is received, without going through the processes of criticism and analysis of the fact that historians employ to move beyond the level of literal meaning to 'read between the lines'. By the anthropologists' standard, the historian would have to seek evidence only on the straightforward narrative level of a tradition, and by doing so the historian would indeed fall foul of the clearly structured features to which anthropologists point on this level of analysis. There was, to be sure, a time when amateur historians, missionaries and administrators for the most part, as well as a few early professionals, accepted oral traditions in this literal fashion. There was a longer period when professional historians were relatively unsystematic in their rejection of the historicity of the superficial cognitive aspect of oral traditions, but most historians for at least the last two decades have hardly practiced what the anthropologists have preached against: use of data in the uncritical style in which some anthropologists have accepted field reports.

The contributors to this volume uniformly show their scepticism about the historical value of the narrative content of most oral traditions, particularly those dealing with the absent past. They try to be explicit and systematic about the methodologies that they employ to criticize the traditions, to move beyond the level of literal meaning to other aspects of complex oral narratives that may relate to former times. In doing so, they openly acknowledge their debts to structuralist anthropologists for having pushed them to exercise what in other fields of history would constitute ordinary critical procedures with regard to their sources. They reject as history that which cannot be verified by confirmation from independent sources. They view the traditions as complex ethnographic documents in which the narrative aspects may be among the least important elements for inferring history. As Berger points out, the historical meaning of the Abacwezi stories comes less from what is told about those ancient and semi-legendary kings than from who does the telling. Harms is sensitive to the sociology of lying that is implicit in the resort to traditions of migration by only those Bobangi who did not migrate. Cohen emphasizes the disparities between norms and behavior in Bunafu, and each of the other authors is similarly sophisticated in his own way about the traditions he discusses. If functionalist anthropologists once encouraged historians to view traditions as tightly integrated mythical charters, these historians rather see them as complex, imperfectly composed products of human narrators working without the benefits of literate modes of communication.

One recent example of the sort of misunderstanding of historical methods common to some anthropologists' approaches to oral sources comes from a study of a seventeenth-century Inca chronicle. It was first written down by Felipe Guaman Poma de Ayala, an Inca intellectual skilled in Spanish letters but originally trained in the nonliterate conceptualizations of his Amerindian ancestors. The judgment of the anthropologist who studied Guaman Poma de Ayala's chronicle is that the document, while describing a past, is not historical. Surely it is not history in the modern sense, as it exhibits precisely the nonliterate notions of time and the past that emerge from recent studies of African oral traditions: discrete epochs rather than a sense of gradual, incremental and continuous time, incomplete and inaccurate details on even such recent events as the Spanish viceroys of the author's own time, leaps back and forth through calendrical time, structuring, and so forth.[80] The historian immediately senses in the anthropologist's discussion of these features the anachronism as well as the culturocentrism implicit in criticizing the work of a seventeenth-century Inca from the perspective of modern 'scientific history'. The historian, unlike the anthropologist, is not discouraged by the failure of the sources to present her or him with finished, sound history at the superficial cognitive level. Rather, the document provides an opportunity to separate the elements of which it is composed and to criticize it in such a way as to turn up indicators of past times, 'past signs' in the terminology of some modern French historians,[81] that he or she can combine with other sources to infer something about times gone by.

Part of the apparent disagreement between historians and anthropologists as to the historical value of oral traditions thus comes from the lack of knowledge on the part of each about the methodologies and standards of the other. Historians tend to react to the most extreme antihistorical positions taken by anthropologists, who in turn see history in a much more positivistic sense than do most historians who work with oral traditions in Africa. The anthropological critique often concludes, in effect, that a 'complete and accurate reconstruction of the past, as it really was' cannot be achieved through the study of oral tradition.[82] The historians contributing to this volume enthusiastically agree. For them, history is the study of the remnants of the past that happen to survive into the present, which they then use as bases for drawing probabilistic inferences about what the past may have been like. They make no pretense at comprehensiveness and would be reluctant to distinguish themselves on this basis from colleagues who work with standard written sources. They accept as 'history' the selective and tenuous reconstructions they can achieve, however 'mythical' these may appear by the standards of others. Said in other words, where the anthropologists would sometimes have the historians study the past itself, very much as the anthropologists claim to study an assumed reality in the present, most historians today would limit themselves to the examination of evidence from the past, examined in the present as signifying something about the past.

If anthropologists and historians agree, as they do, that history must depend on the use of time or chronology, the anthropologists have applied the strict standard of an absolute chronology based on the western calendrical system, while many historians have been willing to settle for mere sequence, indeterminate in terms of years. This introduction attempts to define nonliterate notions of time in terms of epochs that may in a limited way and in some instances serve the needs of the historian for sequence and ordering. It is ironic that the anthropologists' quest for western cumulative conceptions of time has often led them to a position that ignores indigenous discriminations of past epochs.[83] These epochs may be employed effectively, however crude they may be by the refined standards of the solar calendar, to trace change through time.

The anthropological literature, on the other hand, is far from devoid of initiatives useful to the historians seeking to distill history from oral tradition. The passing attention given by anthropologists to the processes by which people create myths is of obvious relevance to understanding how oral narrators produce history. Lévi-Strauss, for example, has seen the fabrication of structured myths in very much the same terms as this introduction describes the encoding of history in oral traditions. Anthropologists have long argued, like the historians in this volume, that myths, or oral traditions, are sociological models. Functionalists, whose method of analysis was biased toward understanding matters in static terms, expressed this notion as the 'mythical charter'. Structuralists, following Lévi-Strauss,[84] have spoken of a 'sociological level' of structure in myths and have occasionally interpreted this idea to include

47

process in a manner not greatly different from that developed here.[85] For Victor Turner, the same parallel was evident between history in Icelandic sagas and the 'social dramas' that he defined as 'crisis situations (that) tended to have a regular series of phases'.[86] The lineage fissions described here by Harms, the shifts in political bases of plains and mountain chiefs found by Packard among the Bashu, the arrival of Lunda chiefs noted by Schecter, and the awarding of political titles among the Imbangala were 'critical' in Turner's terms and therefore potentially as structured in practice as the Ndembu 'social dramas' described in Turner's many writings. The notion that a mythical cliché is very like a sociologist's model is implicit in a definition of myth quoted by Edmund Leach: 'the expression of unobservable realities in terms of observable phenomena'.[87] What would a western social science model be if it were not the expression in concrete terms of abstractions, or as Leach says, 'unobservable realities'? The notion that history and the anthropologists' study of myth are not so far removed from one another has gained currency on both sides of the disciplinary fence and is implicitly supported by the contributors of the essays presented here.[88]

Anthropological precedents also exist for the proposition developed in this introduction that nonliterate thinkers tend to conceive of change as abrupt transformations from one static state to another.[89] Structuralists, for example, distinguish between 'synchrony' and 'diachrony' when they analyse myth structures. Diachrony is the apparent sequence introduced by the need in an oral culture to realize the myth structure in narrative form, rather than, say, on a synchronous diagram which is possible only in a literate culture. With this secondary diachrony eliminated, all the elements in the myth structure coexist and any two may be juxtaposed as simultaneous contrasting pairs. This method renders the myth timeless and converts the apparent change in the narrative line into 'transformations' or 'transitions', opposing entities (e.g. person and nonperson, equal and nonequal), either of which may be transformed into the other, or then back again. Unlike change, such transformations have no direction and are not cumulative. The suddenness implied by the designation 'transformation' is entirely analogous to the dichotomous transitions and 'magical' causation of oral tradition. Creation, for example, is less a sequence than an abrupt transition from nonbeing to being.[90] The difference between mythical change and literate historical change is that between Genesis and the theory of evolution. In at least one African culture, that of the Kuba, the word for 'change' is a verb, the semantic field of which centers on the notion of 'to turn over' and which may mean 'to become' when applied to people and objects. The Kuba conception of change is that of an appearance, a putting-in-place in relation to other persons or objects.[91] Thus, time and space again collapse, with the organization chart of the present differing hardly at all from the record of its historical development. It is nonliterate history told in the present past.

Conclusion: Oral Traditions as History

The misunderstandings between historians and anthropologists have arisen in no small part from confusion between the multiple senses in which both disciplines use the terms 'history' and 'historical'. The issues become clearer if 'history' refers only to the discipline concerned with systematic examination of the evidential links between the present and the past. 'Evidence' is those things that survive, either relatively unchanged as in the case of a document or altered in ways that can be determined, like the memories expressed in narrative oral traditions. That which is 'historical' then becomes anything in the past that present evidence establishes as known, or at least highly probable. 'Histories' are what historians, literate or oral, compose to explain their understandings of the past to readers or listeners in their present. The major skill of the historian is the ability to recognize, understand, and render intelligible to others the evidence he or she collects from past times. In understanding and explaining the historian inevitably draws on concepts examined more systematically in the work of anthropologists, or for that matter sociologists, theologians, economists, or philosophers.

In presenting the evidence from the past, both oral and literate historians engage in structuring, each in accordance with the perceptual categories or cosmological assumptions of their own cultures. The literate historian, for example, conventionally defines a 'topic' that *ipso facto* forces a selection and reordering of a few bits of evidence from the masses of data available to achieve a comprehensible focus for what he or she writes. Oral narrators accomplish the same sort of selection and structuring when they choose the events and processes that they encode in clichés for preservation into the future. The literate historian's 'topic' must accord with the interests, assumptions, and perceptual categories of his or her culture if it is to make sense. In the same way, oral narrators tell their tales in terms that reflect the culture they share with their audiences. Thus the style of presentation in both cases tends toward what anthropologists have emphasized as 'myth' on the side of the oral narrators but ignored on the side of the literate historians.

The style of presentation in no way changes the fact that evidence, something surviving from the past, may occur in even the most highly structured narratives. 'History' does not stand in opposition to 'myth', nor even 'histories' to 'myths'. The historian must not only concede but also embrace as vitally important the structure of the tales heard in oral societies in order to identify the ways in which evidence from the past survives there without writing. This distinction between evidence and structure constitutes a first step toward breaking narratives down into the heterogeneous components from which oral historians fabricate them, some elements from the past (therefore 'evidence') and others from the present (and therefore not 'evidence').

Historians first turn to what may be historical, that is from the past, in the oral traditions. So far, they have identified the nuggets of meaning here termed 'clichés' as the principal form in which narrative traditions preserve parts of the past in the present. The terms and concepts defined and described in this introduction—cliché, episode, personal reminiscence, epochs, anachronism, genealogical relationships, personalizing, variation—represent a first attempt to sort through the components of an oral narrative in a way that distinguishes those which are 'historical' and those which are not.

The next step in analyzing traditions as sources for history examines how oral narrators combine the various elements into finished presentations. Here such processes as structuring and selection assume important roles. Structuring leads to the creation of epochs, and with a system of epochs established, to anachronisms. Variation in the choice or positioning of clichés may arise from the weak connection between a cliché and its epoch, more easily for clichés deriving from remote periods or those expressing simple points capable of expression in many ways. Variation in detail comes as oral narrators develop their imaginative artistry in composing episodes about the historical clichés. Nonliterate conceptions of time and change encourage narrators to find sudden and striking ways of describing transformations that impress literate historians as somehow 'magical'. They reduce the specific message they preserve about any particular event to an elementary binary form, 'X did or did not occur', and leave the circumstantial details to the imagination of their successors. These and other features of oral narratives sometimes characterized as 'myth' turn out to be products of narrators' entirely rational efforts to preserve as accurate as possible a record of the past in an oral environment.

The record of the past so created usually conceals the meaning of events for outsiders, even as it preserves their memory for insiders. It is at this point that the historian turns with relief to the theories of anthropologists who, under the heading of 'myth', have developed powerful tools for unlocking the significance of what the historian identifies as evidence. Structure is meaning, and so are social and political charters. The historical meaning of many narratives, on the basis of the present studies, centers on events of general public significance, particularly on those of frequent occurrence and others of striking aspect. Meaning is associated with the perceptions and interests of those who recognized such events, encoded them in clichés and preserved them in oral narratives. Correlation of inferred meanings with other sorts of evidence and internal criticism of the narratives are the historians' main methods of confirming their conclusions.

The features that distinguish history in oral traditions from literate history derive from the technological limitations of remembering the past in an environment lacking writing and reading. Oral historians turn to clichés to create evidence in a form that is easily remembered and therefore likely to persist in time. They select only those that are most vital, and memory of the past endures only so long as people survive who care enough to maintain it. In an oral culture the properties of the human memory that reshape perceptions accumulate and compound more rapidly than in societies with writing, so that structuring develops to a comparatively exaggerated degree. Narrators dramatize the past in personal images and striking 'magical' transformations to gain in memorability what they lose in resemblance to western/literate perceptions of the same events. Oral narrators are also—perhaps primarily—good storytellers, and the effectiveness of their presentations gains much from structuring, elaboration of clichés into episodes, enlivening sociological generalizations as people, and clothing change in 'magical' garb. They no doubt rely on the fact that a good story is also a memorable one.

The tellers of tales about the past in oral cultures are professional historians in the sense that they are conscious of history and evidence. They deliberately employ techniques based on the cliché in order to record accurately, if selectively, and to preserve a memory, if incomplete, of times gone by. Like historians in literate cultures, they work only with the evidence at hand. In the oral environment,

51

such evidence comes to them only in the form of clichés contrived as such and in the form of casual reminders of past times that surround the oral historian in the present: customs, institutions, conscious social groups that descend from earlier times, and other mnemonic aids. Their use of such present reminders of the past looks presentistic to literate anthropologists, but such practices hardly differ methodologically from techniques of evidence in literate cultures. Because the conscious selection and creation of verbal clichés is so difficult in the oral environment, they merely rely more heavily than do their literate counterparts on non-verbal sorts of data. In fact, the randomness by which habits and institutions survive into the present closely parallels the chance distribution, relative to the topics scrutinized, of the documentation used by historians who write.

Oral historians are thus no less conscious of the past than are historians in literate cultures. If hierarchy, as some anthropologists have recently argued, demands that superior groups must preserve a record of the terminated superiority of their inferiors, such historical consciousness should exist in all but the most egalitarian of societies. Neither historians nor anthropologists should therefore be surprised to hear the composers and performers of oral narratives preserving records of the past.

Notes

* Thanks are due to several colleagues who read an earlier version of this essay and offered comments that have led me to rewrite it in its present form: Robert Brugger, David Henige, Jeffrey Hoover, Jan Vansina, and Roy Willis. I hope my decision not to tackle some of the challenging points they raised will afford them the opportunity to explain where I have gone wrong. Responsibility for shortcomings in what follows is of course entirely my own. I wish to acknowledge with gratitude financial assistance from the University of Virginia that supported the writing of the essay and the technical expertise of Lottie McCauley and Ella Wood, who more than once turned my handwriting into elegant typescript.
1 The classic and still fundamental methodological study of oral traditions as history is Jan Vansina, *Oral Tradition: A Study in Historical Methodology* (Chicago: Aldine, 1965). Vansina has subsequently developed the approaches first set forth in *Oral Tradition* along lines followed in this collection (see n. 6).
2 Vansina, *Oral Tradition*, esp. pp. 19–46.
3 Emile Durkheim, *The Elementary Forms of Religious Life* (Glencoe, Ill., 1915) (first edition 1912), and with M. Mauss, *Primitive Classification* (London, 1963) (first edition 1903); Bronislaw Malinowski, 'Myth in

Listening for the African past

Primitive Psychology', in *Magic, Science, and Religion and Other Essays* (Glencoe, Ill., 1948).

4 The major exception among British and social anthropologists was E. E. Evans-Pritchard, who formally embraced the notion of the 'mythical charter' but believed that history was both possible and useful in the study of oral cultures. His essay on notions of time and history among the Nuer is seminal: 'Nuer Time-Reckoning', *Africa*, vol. 12, no. 2 (1939), pp. 189–216. He also wrote many historical essays, some collected as *The Azande: History and Political Institutions* (Oxford, 1971).

5 The structuralism that has inspired most critics of African oral traditions derives from the writings of Claude Lévi-Strauss, particularly the essays collected and translated in *The Savage Mind* (London, 1966). The most explicit British structuralist critic has been T. O. Beidelman, 'Myth, Legend, and Oral History', *Anthropos*, vol. 65, nos. 5–6 (1965), pp. 74–97. Others, notably Edmund Leach, have been more tolerant of the possibility of history lurking within myth: *Genesis as Myth* (London, 1969), p. 114, '. . . the distinction between myth and history is not necessarily clear cut. It need not be inconsistent to affirm that an historical record has mythical characteristics and functions'.

6 Interested readers may follow the development of these positions in several essays: Patrick Pender-Cutlip, 'Oral Traditions and Anthropological Analysis: Some Contemporary Myths', *Azania*, vol. 7 (1972), pp. 3–24; Jan Vansina, *La Légende du passé* (Tervuren, 1972); idem, 'L'influence du mode de compréhension historique d'une civilisation sur ses traditions d'origine: l'exemple Kuba', *Bulletin des Séances* (Académie royale des sciences d'outre-mer), vol. 2 (1973), pp. 220–40; idem, 'Comment: Traditions of Genesis', *Journal of African History*, vol. 15, no. 2 (1974), pp. 317–22; idem, *Children of Woot* (Madison, 1978). See also Steven Feierman, *The Shambaa Kingdom* (Madison, 1974), and Alain Delivré, *L'histoire des rois d'Imerina: Interprétation d'une tradition orale* (Paris, 1974). The individual essays mention the previous contributions of authors included in this volume.

Explicit contributions from the anthropological side include Wyatt MacGaffey, 'Oral Tradition in Central Africa', *International Journal of African Historical Studies*, vol. 7, no. 3 (1974), pp. 417–26, and 'African History, Anthropology, and the Rationality of Natives', *History in Africa*, vol. 5 (1978), pp. 101–20; Roy G. Willis, 'On Historical Reconstruction from Oral-Traditional Sources: A Structuralist Approach' (Twelfth Melville J. Herskovits Memorial Lecture, 16 February 1976, Northwestern University). Harold Scheub, *The Xhosa Ntsomi* (Oxford, 1975), has also been very influential in forming my own thinking. Anthropologists who have stimulated historians with respect to particular sets of oral traditions receive mention in the notes to the relevant chapters of this collection.

7 Vansina, 'Comment', p. 221, stresses the widespread appearance of self-conscious history in Africa and the deliberate preservation of the memory of the past.

8 One study of an oral historian of such professional stature appears in Gerald W. Hartwig, 'Oral Traditions Concerning the Early Iron Age in North-western Tanzania', *African Historical Studies*, vol. 4, no. 1 (1971),

Joseph C Miller

pp. 94–114. See also the ensuing discussion in Patrick Pender-Cutlip, 'Encyclopedic Informants and Early Interlacustrine History', *International Journal of African Historical Studies*, vol. 6, no. 2 (1973), pp. 198–210, and Hartwig, 'Oral Data and Its Historical Function in East Africa', *International Journal of African Historical Studies*, vol. 7, no. 3 (1974), pp. 468–79. Joseph C. Miller, *Kings and Kinsmen: Early Mbundu States in Angola* (Oxford, 1976), pp. viii–ix, refers briefly to similar historians among the Imbangala. See also Victor Turner, 'Muchona the Hornet, Interpreter of Religion', in J. Casagrande (ed.), *In the Company of Man* (New York, 1959), reprinted in *The Forest of Symbols* (Ithaca, 1967), pp. 131–50.

9 The development here is entirely in line with tendencies toward a focus on individuals in Scheub's work on the Xhosa, *Xhosa Ntsomi*, and in Terence D. Ranger, 'Personal Reminiscence and the Experience of the People in East Central Africa', in Bernardo Bernardi, C. Poni, and A. Triulzi (eds.), *Storia & Antropologia: Fonti Orali* (Milan, 1978), pp. 129–64.

10 Notably among the historians, David P. Henige, *The Chronology of Oral Tradition: Quest for a Chimera* (Oxford, 1974).

11 Joseph C. Miller, 'The Dynamics of Oral Tradition in Africa', in Bernardi, et al. (eds.), *Storia & Antropologia*, pp. 75–102.

12 There may well be other elements, as yet unrecognized.

13 Scheub, *Xhosa Ntsomi*, pp. 22–3, relates the response of a Xhosa praise-singer to the chiefs, who explained how he learned to perform: 'You notice the events that are happening during the time of the chief when he is ruling, or you begin to think about events that happened long ago. And then you just begin to join these things.' The rather inchoate methodology of the Xhosa praise-singer may approximate the techniques of many oral historians.

14 Delivré, *Histoire des rois*, pp. 74ff., finds that legal dicta act as the clichés of Merina royal traditions.

15 Scheub, *Xhosa Ntsomi*, contains the most developed discussion of the clichés in a single culture known to me. He employs the phrase 'core cliché', an elaboration on the word cliché introduced in Vansina, *Oral Tradition*. I have used the term 'nucleus' or 'nuclear image' (*Kings and Kinsmen*). Roy G. Willis, *The Making of a State: Myth, History, and Social Order in Precolonial Ufipa* (forthcoming), has them as 'symbolic images'.

16 Emphasis on clichés can be found in Bethwell A. Ogot, *A History of the Southern Luo: Migration and Settlement* (Nairobi, 1967); David W. Cohen, *The Historical Tradition of Busoga: Mukama and Kintu* (Oxford, 1972); and in several recent studies by Jan Vansina, most explicitly in *Légende du passé*, p. 20, and *Children of Woot*, p. 26.

17 Vansina, *Légende du passé*, pp. 23–6.

18 Vansina, *Légende du passé*, pp. 10–11.

19 Sigwalt, *infra*, discusses reasons why two Shi episodes differ in the degree of convergence in their telling. Delivré, *Histoire des rois*, p. 97, terms this contrast as one between 'parallel' and 'divergent' traditions but adds an evolutionist explanation that wrongly implies that greater age leads to greater agreement. While increasing remoteness in time may reduce the amount of real historical data present in the traditions, as Delivré seems to

imply, Sigwalt's discussion of the Shi materials shows that traditions dealing with more distant times may for that very reason exhibit greater diversity in the form in which historians realize them.

20 Vansina, *infra*.
21 Vansina, *infra*.
22 Cohen, *infra*.
23 The distinction between personal reminiscence, extended personal recollection, and oral tradition is similar but not identical to the classic distinction based on transmission offered by Vansina, *Oral Tradition*, pp. 19–20ff. The typology proposed here is based on the prominence of the cliché and the degree of mythologizing or structuring present. These features may occur in personal reminiscences or extended personal recollections as well as, though less commonly than, in oral traditions. The distinction based on degree of structuring is directly relevant to the historian's need to distinguish those elements in a historical performance that may relate to the past from those derived from the narrator's present. Concentration on analysis of the lines of transmission is useful but very rapidly becomes cumbersome and laborious relative to the anticipated historical yield of the exercise. This is particularly true of lines of transmission that terminate in a myth rather than in a personal reminiscence (Sigwalt, *infra*, and Vansina, *Légende du passé*, p. 68 *et passim*) or in cultures where historical stylistics tolerate, even demand, elaboration by individual men of memory. In such circumstances the line of transmission is not important to the historian. Confusion between the definition based on the fact of transmission and that proposed here in terms of structure has allowed anthropologists to criticize historians' uses of oral tradition by showing a high degree of structure and mythical imagery even in public versions of events held by eyewitnesses, where no transmission has occurred; see, for example, frequent and repetitive examples of this argument published in the journal *Africa* (International African Institute).
24 Scheub, *Xhosa Ntsomi*, stresses the performance as the key to understanding Xhosa tales; this aspect of his analysis strikes me as applicable also to historical narratives.
25 My intention is to acknowledge the dialectic between historian and culture, but my argument should not be confused with old-fashioned cultural determinism, in which individuals in oral cultures are seen as having only the most limited freedom from collective norms and perceptions. For a statement of the case for balance, see M. A. M. Ngal, 'Literary Creation in Oral Civilizations', *New Literary History*, vol. 8, no. 3 (1977), pp. 335–44. Delivré, *Histoire des rois*, part II, esp. p. 111, explores the way in which the Merina royal tradition combines facts with contemporaries' opinions about them.
26 The writings of Jack Goody are basic to the approach adopted here. See his most recent statements in *The Domestication of the Savage Mind* (Cambridge, 1977); also *Literacy in Traditional Societies* (Cambridge, 1968), which reprints the famous article with Ian Watt, 'The Consequences of Literacy', *Comparative Studies in Society and History*, vol. 5, no. 3 (1963), pp. 304–45. Also stimulating are the writings of Eric A. Havelock on literacy in classical antiquity: 'Prologue to Greek Literacy', *University of Cincinnati Classical Studies* (Lectures in Memory of Louise Taft Semple),

vol. 2 (1973), pp. 329–91; *Origins of Western Literacy* (Toronto, 1976); and 'The Preliteracy of the Greeks', *New Literary History,* vol. 8, no. 3 (1977), pp. 369–91.

27 The phrase is from Wyatt MacGaffey, 'African History, Anthropology, and the Rationality of Natives', op. cit.

28 A recent example: C. R. Hallpike, 'Is there a Primitive Mentality?' *Man*, n.s., vol. 11, no. 2 (1976), pp. 252–72.

29 One strong current flows from Lévi-Strauss, *The Savage Mind.* Others are to be found in Robin Horton, 'African Traditional Thought and Western Science', *Africa*, vol. 37, nos. 1–2 (1967), pp. 50–71, 155–87, and Robin Horton and Ruth Finnegan (eds.), *Modes of Thought* (London, 1973). See also John M. Janzen and Wyatt MacGaffey, *An Anthology of Kongo Religion* (Lawrence, Kansas, 1974), introduction.

30 Besides Beidelman, 'Myth, Legend, and Oral History', writings to which the papers in this volume react include those of Luc de Heusch, *Le roi ivre, ou l'origine de l'état* (Paris, 1972), and 'What Shall We Do with the Drunken King', *Africa*, vol. 45, no. 4 (1975), pp. 363–72. Historians who have argued against the historicity of oral traditions on the basis of the presence of structure include C. C. Wrigley, 'The Story of Rukidi', *Africa*, vol. 43, no. 3 (1973), pp. 219–34.

Africanist anthropologists who reconcile structure with history include Feierman, *Shambaa Kingdom*, and Willis, *Making of a State.*

31 MacGaffey, 'Oral Traditions', p. 421, although MacGaffey may here use the term 'historical' to refer to the narrative style in which myths are realized rather than to the sense in which 'historical' is employed here: elements of whatever sort in a tradition that may reveal something about past times.

32 Gordon D. Gibson, 'Himba Epochs', *History in Africa*, vol. 4 (1977), pp. 67–121. Another example of careful use of epochs in John Lamphear, *The Traditional History of the Jie of Uganda* (Oxford, 1976).

33 In addition to the Himba, note 32 *supra*, the kinglists of the Imbangala kingdom of Kasanje in Angola exhibit a high degree of regularity that may be partially documented: Joseph C. Miller, 'Kings, Lists and History in Kasanje', *History in Africa*, vol. 6 (1979), pp. 51–96.

34 The fullest critique is Henige, *Chronology of Oral Tradition.*

35 E.g. Mbundu historians tell a migration tale marked by several notable events that they sequence according to where each occurred, along the presumed (but false) line of migration, regardless of which took place before or after the others. See Miller, *Kings and Kinsmen*, pp. 98–103.

36 Delivré, *Histoire des rois*, part III.

37 A well-developed example is found in Vansina, *Children of Woot*, chs. 4, 7, and 8.

38 E.g. Delivré, *Histoire des rois*, pp. 180–1.

39 Vansina, *Children of Woot*, pp. 235–40, has termed this procedure a 'process model'. See also idem, 'The Use of Process Models in African History', in Jan Vansina, Raymond Mauny, and Louis Vincent Thomas (eds.), *The Historian in Tropical Africa* (London, 1964), pp. 375–89.

40 Henige, *Chronology of Oral Tradition*, esp. pp. 27–38.

41 See also Joseph C. Miller, 'The Imbangala and the Chronology of Early

Central African History', *Journal of African History*, vol. 13, no. 4 (1972), pp. 549–74, and *Kings and Kinsmen*, chs. 5–6.

42 Henige, *Chronology of Oral Tradition*, ch. 2.

43 Vansina, *Légende du passé,* pp. 21–6 *et passim*, for these influences on traditions in Burundi.

44 Documented case studies of such transformations may be found in Vansina, *Légende du passé*, pp. 32–46, and Claude-Hélène Perrot, 'Ano Asemã: mythe et histoire', *Journal of African History*, vol. 15, no. 2 (1974), pp. 199–222. See also Joseph C. Miller 'Kings and Kinsmen: The Imbangala Impact on the Mbundu of Angola' (PhD dissertation, University of Wisconsin, Madison, 1972), pp. 20–154, esp. pp. 59–60 and 148–52, for a comparison of personal reminiscences and narrative traditions with regard to the same event (in the 1850s).

45 Claude-Hélène Perrot, 'De la richesse au pouvoir: les origines d'une chefferie du Ndenye (Côte d'Ivoire)', *Cahiers d'études africaines*, vol. 16, nos. 1–2 (nos. 61–62) (1976), pp. 173–87, has coexisting literal and mythologized accounts at four to five generations (c. 150 years?) before the present.

46 R. R. Atkinson, 'The Traditions of the Early Kings of Buganda: Myth, History, and Structural Analysis', *History in Africa*, vol. 2 (1975), pp. 17–57.

47 Vansina, *Children of Woot*, chs. 3–4, 6–9.

48 De Heusch, *Le roi ivre*, and Thomas Q. Reefe, *The Rainbow and the Kings: A History of the Luba Empire to the 1880s* (forthcoming), ch. 3.

49 Berger, *infra*, and Miller, *Kings and Kinsmen*, chs. 3–4. Vansina, *Children of Woot*, pp. 227–31, describes a similar process of transformation with specific reference to the Kuba.

50 Vansina, *Oral Tradition*.

51 Vansina, *Légende du passé*, 'Mode de compréhension', and *Children of Woot*.

52 See also Willis, 'On Historical Reconstruction', and Miller, 'Dynamics of Change'.

53 David William Cohen, *Womunafu's Bunafu* (Princeton, 1977).

54 W. G. Clarence-Smith, 'For Braudel: A Note on the "Ecole des Annales" and the Historiography of Africa', *History in Africa*, vol. 4 (1977), pp. 276–81, criticizes history drawn from oral sources as inherently and narrowly political, charging that it thereby misses the longer-term social and economic changes that the *histoire événementielle* of political developments merely reflects. The contributions to this collection demonstrate that this failing is one of interpretation rather than an inherent flaw, as demonstrated in Vansina, *Children of Woot*, pp. 11, 235 *et passim*. See also Vansina's response to Clarence-Smith, 'For Oral Tradition (But Not Against Braudel)', *History in Africa*, vol. 5 (1978), pp. 351–6.

55 I have given similarly metaphorical readings to Mbundu clichés, for example, taking the reported 'death' of an ancient king to signify the ritual extinction of a noble title; Miller, *Kings and Kinsmen*, pp. 123–5, 169–74.

56 Miller, *Kings and Kinsmen*, pp. 23, 101, 139, 145, 169–74, 187–91, 200–1.

57 Vansina, *Children of Woot*, pp. 26, 119.

58 E.g. MacGaffey, 'Oral tradition', p. 420.

59 E.g. de Heusch, *Le roi ivre.*

60 Berger, *infra*, expresses her doubts about some of the argumentation required to draw out alleged parallels between Abacwezi myths in western Uganda and the stories in the Bible. J. Jeffrey Hoover, '*Mythe et remous historique*: A Lunda Response to de Heusch', *History in Africa*, vol. 5 (1978), pp. 63–80, offers similar reservations about the accuracy of de Heusch's use of data.

61 Jan Vansina, 'The Bells of Kings', *Journal of African History*, vol. 10, no. 2 (1969), pp. 187–98.

62 And, it may be added, over distance. The most structured versions of the Luba story of Kongolo and Ilunga Kalala are encountered unaccompanied by more specific versions only in remote regions of the Luba diaspora; compare de Heusch, *Le roi ivre*, which selectively stresses the highly structured versions, with Reefe, *Rainbow and Kings*, which discusses relatively specific and historical variants still to be encountered in the Luba heartland.

63 Miller, *Kings and Kinsmen*, ch. 5, esp. pp. 114–28, suggests a tentative interpretation along these lines of published Lunda traditions, revised and expanded by Jeffrey Hoover, 'The Seduction of Ruwej: Reconstructing Ruund History (The Nuclear Lunda: Zaire, Angola, Zambia)' (PhD dissertation, Yale University, 1978).

64 De Heusch, *Le roi ivre*, and for the Kuba, Vansina, *Children of Woot*, pp. 322–3, nn. 1 and 4 especially.

65 Miller, *Kings and Kinsmen*, pp. 55–6ff.

66 Vansina, 'Comment.'

67 Joseph C. Miller, 'Requiem for the "Jaga"', *Cahiers d'études africaines*, vol. 13, no. 1 (no. 43) (1973), pp. 121–49.

68 Vansina, *Children of Woot*, pp. 35ff., esp. 40–5.

69 Aside from the voluminous literature on the Nguni movements of the nineteenth century, see Vansina, *Légende du passé*, ch. 6, and *Children of Woot*, chs. 3, 6, 7, and essays in *African Historical Demography* (Centre of African Studies, University of Edinburgh) (Edinburgh, 1978), especially D. W. Phillipson, 'Population Movement and Interaction in African Prehistory: Some Examples from the Last Two Thousand Years in Eastern Zambia', pp. 122–30; Robin Derricourt, 'Invasion Models and Zonal Exploitation in Later South African Prehistory', pp. 131–8; and J. S. Birks, 'Migration, A Significant Factor in the Historical Demography of the Savannas: The Growth of the West African Population of Darfur, Sudan', pp. 195–210. Also see Cohen, *Womunafu's Bunafu*, and *infra*.

70 Miller, 'Chronology', and *Kings and Kinsmen*, pp. 128–61.

71 See David Newbury, 'Bushi and the Historians: Historiographical Themes in Eastern Kivu', *History in Africa*, vol. 5 (1978), pp. 131–51.

72 Vansina, *Children of Woot*, p. 45.

73 For a development of this notion, see Miller, 'Dynamics of Oral Tradition'.

74 Schecter gives this theme fuller development in his dissertation, 'History and Historiography on a Frontier of Lunda Expansion: The Origins and Early Development of the Kanongesha' (PhD dissertation, University of Wisconsin, Madison, 1976). Delivré, *Histoire des rois*, employs similar methods, as does Vansina, *Children of Woot*. So also, though less systema-

tically, do Sigwalt and Berger in the papers published in this volume.

75 Gerald M. Berg, 'The Myth of Racial Strife and Merina Kinglists: The Transformation of Texts', *History in Africa*, vol. 4 (1977), pp. 1–30.

76 De Heusch, *Le roi ivre*, Reefe, *Rainbow and Kings*, and evident implications in the Yoder and Schecter papers herein.

77 Maurice Bloch, 'The Disconnection Between Power and Rank as a Process: An Outline of the Development of Kingdoms in Central Madagascar', *Archives européennes de sociologie*, vol. 18, no. 1 (1977), pp. 107–48.

78 Miller, *Kings and Kinsmen*, p. 256n.

79 Bloch, 'Disconnection', pp. 142–3. David Henige, in a comment on an earlier draft of this paper, points out that the tellers of the traditions may collapse multiple layers into only two.

80 Juan M. Ossio, 'Myth and History: The Seventeenth-Century Chronicle of Guaman Poma de Ayala', in Ravindra K. Jain (ed.), *Text and Context: The Social Anthropology of Tradition* (Philadelphia, 1977), pp. 51–93.

81 Clarence-Smith, 'For Braudel'.

82 E.g. Edmund Leach, 'The Legitimacy of Solomon', in *Genesis as Myth and Other Essays* (London, 1969), p. 81. Historians have been abandoning this positivist goal since at least 1900.

83 I hasten to add that my present understanding of nonliterate epochs comes proximately from an anthropologist, Gordon Gibson, and through him from Evans-Pritchard.

84 See Eric Ten Raa, 'The Genealogical Method in the Analysis of Myth, and a Structural Model', in T. O. Beidelman (ed.), *The Translation of Culture* (London, 1971), pp. 334–5.

85 Ten Raa, 'Genealogical Method', and Willis, 'On Historical Reconstruction'.

86 'An Anthropological Approach to the Icelandic Saga', in Beidelman (ed.), *Translation of Culture*, p. 351.

87 Leach, 'Genesis', p. 7.

88 For the anthropologists' side, *inter alia*, MacGaffey, 'African History', Leach, 'Solomon', p. 42.

89 The anthropological study that started my thinking along these lines was Frederick Errington, 'Indigenous Ideas of Order, Time, and Transition in a New Guinea Cargo Movement', *American Ethnologist*, vol. 1, no. 2 (1974), pp. 255–67.

90 Ten Raa, 'Genealogical Method', p. 343.

91 Vansina, *Children of Woot*, pp. 19–20.

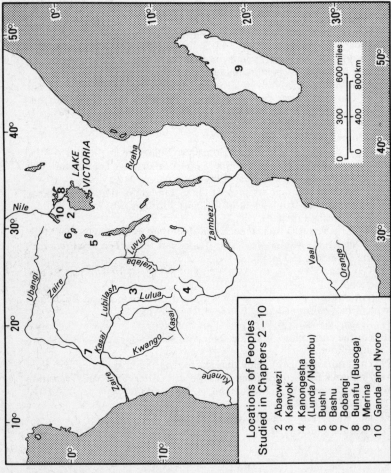

Locations of Peoples
Studied in Chapters 2 – 10

2 Abacwezi
3 Kanyok
4 Kanongesha
   (Lunda/Ndembu)
5 Bushi
6 Bashu
7 Bobangi
8 Bunafu (Busoga)
9 Merina
10 Ganda and Nyoro

General location map of East and Central Africa

2. Deities, Dynasties, and Oral Tradition: The History and Legend of the Abacwezi

IRIS BERGER

The complexity and highly symbolic content of many religious legends has placed them at the center of the debate between those who detect history in such myths and those who do not. Among some East African historians this conflict between historical and structural orientations has converged on the case of the Abacwezi, depicted variously as deities, religious specialists, and ancient kings in the historical traditions of western Uganda and parts of north-western Tanzania. While the religious significance of the Abacwezi as modern spirits and priests or mediums is undeniable, most twentieth-century historians also have accepted their portrayal as the historical rulers of a former vast empire whom later people deified in the wake of their sudden and mysterious departure from power. These writers then turned their analytical energies to the problem of identifying these mysterious and marvelous authorities which, in a colonial context, meant finding a suitable ethnic label for them. More recently, however, C. C. Wrigley, writing from a structuralist perspective, has tried to sever entirely the historical connection, arguing instead for the purely symbolic and cosmological significance of the Abacwezi place in oral tradition.

Also involved in this controversy is the question of the relationship between religion and history as reflected in the traditions. While Wrigley's approach simply ousts the historical dimension from the sphere of divinity, implicitly severing the connection between religion and history, others have formulated more historical approaches that may apply to the Abacwezi. Daniel McCall suggests two possible aspects of the interaction between deities and history, one by which important historical figures are elevated to godly status and another by which the identification of priests with their associated divinities has resulted in crediting the latter with the actions of the former. Thus, he explains, 'The conflicts of gods . . . may be the conflict of human groups who use these symbols'.[1]

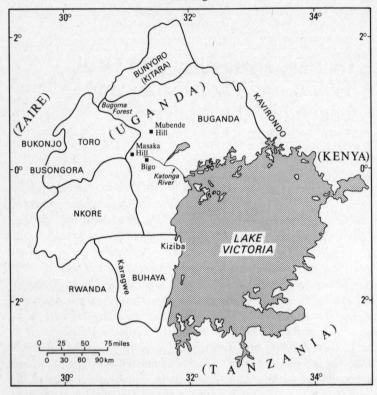

Map 2.1 Ethnic divisions of the Abacwezi and neighbouring zones (adapted from *Linguistic Survey of the Northern Bantu Borderland*, London, 1956)

Arguing from a broader historical perspective, Basil Davidson traces certain divinities to the newly emerging patterns of political and social stratification in the early Iron Age, explaining that during the reorganization and increased centralization of this period, which he locates in the millenium up to A.D. 1000, 'a new hierarchy of gods came to be modelled on a new hierarchy of rulers, although, of course appearances made it seem that the kings were an emanation of the gods and not the other way round'.[2] McCall's viewpoint implies that religious traditions may, indeed, depict the actions of particular individuals or human groups, while that of Davidson places emphasis more on their reflection of political patterns. Both, however, would insist on some correspondence between theology and history.

The Abacwezi legends form a vital part of the traditional histories

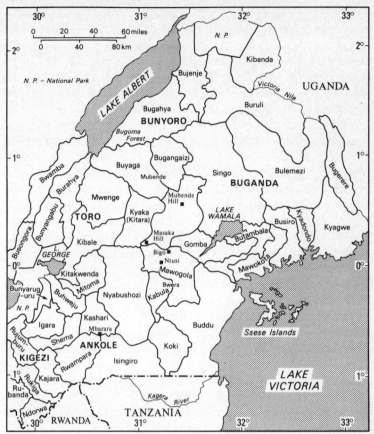

Map 2.2 Counties of Bunyoro, Toro, Buganda, Ankole, and Kigezi

of the former Kitara (Bunyoro) and Nkore kingdoms of western Uganda and of the smaller Buhaya states of northwestern Tanzania. All, by the late nineteenth century, were centralized political systems based, in varying ways, on the division between a ruling class and commoners and on a sometimes overlapping distinction between pastoralists (*abahuma, abahima*) and agriculturalists (*abairu*). In essence, the Bunyoro versions of the Abacwezi legend begin with the story of Isaza, the last of a line of Kitara kings known as Abatembuzi,[3] who angered Nyamiyonga, king of the underworld, by refusing to make a blood pact with him. Nyamiyonga secretly sent his beautiful daughter Nyamata to marry Isaza and upon returning to her father, she bore a son, Isimbwa. Then Nyamiyonga sent two magnificent head of cattle to Isaza; when they

63

disappeared accompanied by the latter's favorite cow, Isaza followed them into Nyamiyonga's kingdom, where he remained, and Bukuku, a royal servant, declared himself king of Kitara despite the ensuing rebellion of most local officials. Soon, however, Bukuku's daughter Nyinamwiru, defying her father's attempts to isolate her, received a visit from Isimbwa, the son of Isaza and Nyamata, and eventually gave birth to a baby boy, Ndahura.

Ndahura, great-grandson of the king of the underworld and grandson of the last king of Kitara, became the first of a short-lived dynasty of Abacwezi rulers. Although the baby was thrown into the river, a potter discovered and raised him. Ndahura grew up to be a quarrelsome young man who eventually killed his grandfather, the usurping Bukuku, and proclaimed himself king. The kingdom prospered under his rule and its territories expanded. In one version Mulindwa, a regent who took the drum while Ndahura went off to conquer foreign lands, succeeded him; in another, there were only two Abacwezi rulers, Ndahura and Wamara (the third king where Mulindwa is mentioned). According to tradition, the Abacwezi governed vast areas, in some obviously exaggerated accounts reaching from Tanzania in the south to Ethiopia in the north. New rulers from the north, also descendants of Isimbwa, soon precipitated the state's decline, however. Warned of imminent conquest by a succession of unfavorable omens, the Abacwezi bequeathed their realm graciously to the newcomers and then disappeared mysteriously into craters or underground. The new kings, the Ababito in Kitara led by Rukidi and the Abahinda to the south under Ruhinda, became the direct successors and heirs of Abacwezi rule.

Even this brief summary highlights the essence of the traditions—the explanation of the transition from one dynasty to the next in a framework that demonstrates each regime's legitimacy by virtue of genetic links with its predecessor and its successor. In Bunyoro Isimbwa is the key figure in establishing this connection as the son of the last Abatembuzi king, Isaza, the father of the first Omucwezi, Ndahura, and the grandfather of the first Omubito, Rukidi. The Buhaya and Nkore variants share this emphasis, but with local differences. The Nkore version, by contrast with the aesthetic integrity of that of Bunyoro, shows a thematic discontinuity which suggests that two, or perhaps more, separate traditions have been merged into one. This local variant combined the myths of the Abacwezi dynasty and the Ababito arrival (which there is no need to explain in Nkore), with legends linking the later Abahinda with the Abacwezi. In Buhaya the traditions of Kiziba, a state with an Ababito dynasty from Bunyoro, include the most widespread of the Abacwezi tales, while those of other Buhaya states without Ababito kings are much briefer with respect to the Abacwezi and often aim only at explaining worship of Abacwezi spirits rather than at legitimizing later rulers. Buhaya versions also commonly include a tale of purely local distribution presaging the Abacwezi downfall, a story about Kagoro, one of the Abacwezi, setting fire to the house of King Wamara. But everywhere, the Abacwezi filled a structural position in legend analogous to their role in Bunyoro, occupying the period between society's creation and the formation of the latest dynasty.

Wrigley, focusing on Bunyoro, has pioneered a sometimes fascinating structural interpretation of the Abacwezi legends that concentrates on universal mythical themes. In his most recent article he

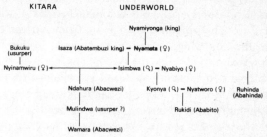

Figure 2.1 Genealogical chart of characters in Abaczewi legends

compares the tales not only with those of historically related societies, but also with the Tolkien trilogy *Lord of the Rings*, and chides former historians of the Abacwezi for accepting the reality of 'characters who have no more real substance than the prince of a European fairy tale'.[4] Yet his interpretation succeeds more fully in elucidating the richness and complexity of the traditions than it does in proving their lack of historical content. Thus Wrigley argues that they portray a transition not from one dynasty to the next, but from the rule of the gods to that of humans; that Wamara, the last Abacwezi ruler, symbolized not the death of an era but death in general; and that the three 'dynasties' represent not periods of time but three levels of a cosmological system including God (Abatembuzi), the spirits (Abacwezi), and the kings (Ababito). To assume, as Wrigley does, however, that analyzing the myths' philosophical dimension thereby demonstrates their historical poverty is only an assumption, apparently born in reaction to the writings of earlier historians, who tended to accept too literally the assertion that the

Abacwezi were individual kings who had ruled over a clearly defined territory. Knowing whether or not such a dynasty existed may, in fact, be impossible. But it is undeniable that, for local people, the Abacwezi inhabit historical as well as cosmological space and figure clearly in their own views of their societies' pasts. That the Abacwezi deal simultaneously with religious issues no more automatically denies their possible historical import than does the comparable dual significance of the Bible.

Nonetheless Wrigley is correct in implying that most previous analysis has focused too narrowly on the reality and identity of the Abacwezi rather than seeking broader interpretations of the traditions' historical or cosmological significance. And, in fact, he may be correct in denying the existence of a historical human dynasty called Abacwezi, since their reputation as historical figures developed as a result of European misinterpretations of African statements that happened to reinforce erroneous colonial theories of the African past. The European misconception arose from African characterizations of the first whites to arrive in Uganda in the nineteenth century as 'Abacwezi'.[5] While the Europeans involved understandably misinterpreted these attributions as evidence that the Abacwezi had been an ancient dynasty of light-skinned kings, the Africans undoubtedly were referring to the association of the color white with the world of spirits. The Bakongo, for example, believe that the skin color of the deceased changes to white after their arrival in the other world; and, much closer to Bunyoro, people in the Buhaya state of Kyamtwara who met the explorer Henry Stanley designated him and his European companions as *abaluga kuzima*, 'those from the dead'.[6] Stanley also reported the following conversation in Bukonjo, near Lake Katwe in western Uganda.

> Do you not know that we believe you to be of the Wanyavingi? (Followers of the goddess Nyabingi) Who but the Wanyavingi and Wachwezi are of your colour?
>
> What, are they white people like us?
>
> They have no clothes like you, nor do they wear anything on their feet like you, but they are tall big men, with long noses and a pale colour . . .[7]

The same misunderstanding of the Abacwezi as light-skinned outsiders assumed a new and more fully articulated form in the twentieth century. By then, the colonial setting was beginning not only to reshape the content of these histories but also to foster their transmission in written as well as oral forms. The new groups of literate historians, often Africans, drew on the legends in order to forge their own European-influenced conception of the Abacwezi. To complicate this situation further, recent writers, both African and European, have drawn freely, without acknowledgment, on each other's accounts and on the traditions of neighboring societies. As a result, it has become very difficult to decide the extent to which apparent correspondences between the available published traditions really mean that variants provide independent checks on each other.[8] This eclecticism may have created a misleading uniformity that has helped to obscure the colonial transformation of the Abacwezi.

The essence of this change involved a complete inversion of nineteenth-century European concepts about the Abacwezi, as the dark-skinned autochthonous religious specialists reported by the first explorers yielded to depiction as light-skinned immigrant rulers in the accounts of colonial historians. 'Wichwezi or Mbandwa' appear in the very first European reports from this part of East Africa as deep-hued people of local origin. Both John Speke's accounts of Karagwe, a Buhaya kingdom, in 1863 and James Grant's of Bunyoro in 1864 depict the Abacwezi as living persons they encountered, mendicants, often women, with religious functions. Grant adds in brief the essence of the later Abacwezi myth: that persons of this class called 'Wichwezee' once occupied the whole country and then, suddenly, disappeared underground.[9] Emin Pasha, the first European to speak Lunyoro, whose reports have been judged highly reliable in other respects, shared similar views. He wrote of the 'deep-black Wichwezi pariah', then living as beggars, gypsies, soothsayers, and amulet manufacturers, but gave them a historical dimension by adding that they 'appear to be the remainder of a distinct tribe'. He also drew a strong contrast in terms of color between the dark 'Wichwezi', as blacksmiths and bondsmen who comprised the remnants of a formerly dominant population of Bunyoro (and many neighboring areas), and the Wahuma (pastoralists) or Wawitu (the ruling dynasty), allegedly white-skinned herders and rulers from the north who displaced them. As the invading 'Wawitu' advanced, the indigenous 'Wichwezi' retired.[10] Here the Wawitu rulers of Bunyoro are identified with the pastoral *abahuma*, but neither group is ascribed any connection with the Abacwezi other than as conquerers. Gaetano Casati, writing on Ankole, similarly named the original part of the population 'Wichinesi' (Abacwezi) and credited their defeat to a pastoralist group called Wagassara.[11]

By the turn of the century, the idea of the Abacwezi as a superior immigrant racial minority was beginning to replace the European idea of them as wandering female religious specialists, survivors of a subordinated indigenous majority population. While many missionaries at this time remained interested in exploring the association of the term with historical specialists and deities, their concerns were mainly with the religious side of the double-sided 'Wichwezi' coin.[12] The historical Abacwezi became victims of the writings of a single British administrator in Uganda, Sir Harry Hamilton Johnston. Johnston ignored the stress of earlier writers on the local background of the Abacwezi and instead formulated the novel idea that they had been alien rulers from the north who had introduced their religious system to some other racially and culturally inferior indigenous population. His inversion of the older idea of the Abacwezi apparently arose not from any new African sources but from the pervasive influence of the entirely European notion that historians have called the 'Hamitic hypothesis'. This highly racist view credited all achievements of African civilizations to light-skinned northern outsiders whose pale complexion made them, if not quite European, at least closer to that august rank than their conquered subjects.

Whereas earlier writers had asserted without further elaboration that the ancestors of late precolonial Uganda's ruling families came from Ethiopia,[13] Johnston spelled out in detail his notion of 'superior races' from the north culturally leavening the 'totally savage Negro'. He identified Egypt as the source of African knowledge of plant domestication, iron smelting and working, music, 'in short all the civilization he possessed before the coming of the white man—Moslem or Christian—1,000 years ago'.[14] Within this context, Johnston observed that while in Nkore the pastoral *abahima* were the heirs to 'Hamitic' influence, in Bunyoro 'the traditional name of these Hamitic invaders is Bacwezi'.[15] Thus, although earlier writers had alluded to a theory of northern impact, Johnston was the first in this area to elaborate fully the racist assumptions underlying the idea and to identify these outside influences unequivocally, though without any evidence other than his own assumptions, with the Abacwezi. And since 'Hamitic' influence, according to his theories, permeated all areas of society, it naturally encompassed religion. He wrote, 'As regards religion, the Bairo have very little . . . Such beliefs as they have are subordinated to the practices of the Bahima witchdoctors . . .'[16] Johnston's derivation of the *abahima* from the 'Hamites' thus ascribed modern religious beliefs to his light-skinned invaders. Here then, resting squarely on the now discredited Hamitic hypothesis, lies the foundation for the compound image of the Abacwezi as both religious and historical figures that has pervaded twentieth-century scholarship.

Under the influence of Johnston's writings, supported by the colonial intellectual climate, Abacwezi came to be seen not only accurately as a generic term for priests and spirits, but also inaccurately as an ancient ruling dynasty from the north. From then on the early idea of groups of wandering female religious specialists disappeared from the literature[17] as did the nineteenth-century perception of the Abacwezi as the original inhabitants of the country. Coinciding with this shift came their change in color from black to white[18] and their transformation in status from serfs to rulers. While the earlier views recorded in travellers' accounts are not necessarily totally accurate either, they do at least reflect direct observations less subject than later ones to a systematically elaborated denigration of African societies.[19]

From then on, the concept of the Abacwezi as a group of historical rulers dominated the literature. But the legacy of earlier interpretations remained, as writers showed no unanimity about their origins and continued to invest them with divine characteristics. A. B. Lloyd, a British missionary in Uganda, described the Abacwezi as herdsmen from the south and termed Isimbwa, the first to arrive, as a 'strange God-man'. In the first detailed and thoroughly researched study of the legends, Ruth Fisher saw the Abacwezi as historical kings but also depicted them as 'semi-mythical' or as 'demi-gods'. To her account of the traditions she also added her own opinion that they 'evidently' were a migratory tribe from the north that subjugated the original inhabitants and taught them ironworking and perhaps also the rudiments of their religion.[20] The juxtaposition of the two inconsistent images of the Abacwezi, simultaneously humans and deities, shows the contradiction between them. Although the legends seemed to portray the dynasty as in some way mythical or supernatural, the Hamitic interpretation had transformed them into real human beings. Thus, while by 1923 John Roscoe still called the Abacwezi a 'misty and somewhat bewildering collection of beings regarded as immortal and almost divine', Julien Gorju, writing only a few years earlier, had already relied on the notion of their northern origins and their position as a ruling family to emphasize their human characteristics.[21]

The lingering doubts over these conflicting versions ceased after K. W. (Sir Tito Winyi IV, King of Bunyoro) published his own

version of the kingdom's history in 1933–4. Undoubtedly anxious
to render Bunyoro's past in every way equal to that of its arch-
antagonist Buganda and to prop up the kingdom's deflated morale
under British rule, he definitively crowned the Abacwezi as former
human rulers of Bunyoro-Kitara and vastly extended the terrain of
their power to include Kavirondo in western Kenya, parts of Tanzania and Zaire, and the entire expanse of East Africa northward to
Abyssinia.[22] Ignoring the racist implications underlying this theory
(whether unwittingly or from self-interest is unknown), his family,
the ruling Ababito dynasty, could only acquire prestige, not lose it,
as heirs to these exalted semi-European outsiders. Indeed the gains
in status were far greater than would have been the case had the
Ababito followed upon a rather nebulous, now low-ranking 'former
population'. In this situation the ideological prejudices of colonial
rulers coincided with the interests of the Bunyoro elite and the
racist-spawned myth of Bunyoro history received official African
endorsement.[23]

From this time on, the idea of the Abacwezi as an historical
dynasty, though still one with remarkable magical powers, held the
status of orthodoxy and writers began to focus heavily on the
question of who they were. In the colonial context this meant
finding some ethnic label—whether Lwoo, Hamitic, Abahima,
Abatutsi, or Portuguese[24]—to attach to them. For western historians the writings of a prominent British colleague, Roland
Oliver, defined the consensus that eventually emerged. He
identified the Abacwezi as a small immigrant pastoralist ruling clan
that had gained the prestige to dominate local populations mainly
through its members' supernatural knowledge and admirable skills,
thus neatly resolving the historical-religious conflict as a distinction
between identity and means.[25] This interpretation gained further
standing through the work of archaeologists who legitimized the
attachment of the Abacwezi to the area's major archaeological site
at Bigo, an extensive system of earthworks lying just south of the
Katonga River in modern Buganda. Thus from the mid-1930s on,
the Abacwezi metamorphosis from semi-divine to thoroughly
human was complete. Only John Beattie, the main anthropologist
of Bunyoro society, argued against the growing consensus that the
Abacwezi had been a human dynasty. In 1961 he pointed out the
incompatibility between two different views of the Abacwezi, one
as a 'wonderful race of people', the other as a small group of rulers
linked genealogically to the ruling Ababito.[26] But his failure to
analyze the historiographical origins of these notions or to spell out

more fully their political implications weakened his intended argument against the theory of the Abacwezi as an historical dynasty.

The preceding discussion, then, suggests that during the twentieth century, Europeans and their educated African allies took a generic term for 'spirit' that applied also to the former peoples of the area and gave it a third meaning—a ruling dynasty of conquerors from the north. Although this latest interpretation of 'Abacwezi' grew directly from colonial intellectual preoccupations, its invalidation does not necessarily negate the term's original historical significance. Rather it ascribes a relatively recent origin only to interpretations of the Abacwezi according to McCall's first hypothesis—that the spirits represent historical figures deified posthumously.

The Legends as History

But the historiographical evidence does not discredit McCall's second and equally historical theory—that religious legends may portray deities as symbols of associated historical human groups. From this perspective, discovering whether or not the Abacwezi existed is less important than knowing the identity of these groups, which might indicate who has preserved the memory of the Abacwezi and why. Both Wrigley's work and Peter Schmidt's study of Buhaya[27] deal with the latter question. They concur in tracing the recollection and transmission of the Abacwezi traditions before the colonial period not to representatives or members of the Ababito royal family, but to the priests and mediums of the Abacwezi deities. Ruth Fisher, who published the most detailed early account of the myths, attributed the ultimate sources of her material not to the newly literate kings of Bunyoro and Toro, who gathered it for her, but to the 'witch doctors' who were their sources; the kings, by contrast, 'had no very clear idea of the subject themselves.'[28] Although the identity of Fisher's 'witch doctors' is uncertain, Schmidt's study of Buhaya indirectly confirms the presumption that they were Abacwezi mediums, for he found that in pre-colonial times these religious specialists considered the Abacwezi myths a sacred validation of their form of spirit mediumship and recounted them regularly during possession ceremonies.[29]

With the colonial period, new groups developed an interest in these traditions—European writers (missionaries, administrators, anthropologists, and historians) and western-educated members of the Bunyoro elite, often with royal or governmental connections. For both groups, imbued until recently with variations of the Hamitic hypothesis, and for the second, concerned also with the low status of Bunyoro as compared with Buganda, transformation of spirits into kings offered a highly satisfying view of the past. Presumably the mediums, eclipsed and even outlawed by the joint opposition of Christian churches and colonial government to 'superstition', either acquiesced in the new orthodoxy or ignored its existence. Most probably, the new group of historians at first depended on the mediums as its sources of information. But soon the revisionists, through both English and vernacular publications, established themselves as founts of historical truth.

The earlier guardians of the Abacwezi traditions were not simply religious specialists, however. They also represented major ruling clans of the pre-Ababito period whose independence the new dynasty had usurped, but whose continuing political significance was never eclipsed. At least in Bunyoro, these older politico-religious figures still controlled a view of the past that made them, through their association with the Abacwezi, superior in certain respects to their overlords. Their traditions stress the idea of Abacwezi priority and supremacy in a number of ways. The Abacwezi period invariably precedes that of the Ababito in oral traditions, conveying the notion that the temporal power of the later Ababito depended on prior Abacwezi validation. Similarly the ancient deities' ability to reappear and possess people, even after their disappearance from earth, stressed their continuing influence on human affairs. The myths also imply Abacwezi primacy by connecting them symbolically with culture but relegating their Ababito successors to an association with nature. They portray Rukidi, the first king of the new dynasty, as a naked, hairy, wild man from the north who married not 'the daughter of men', as Wrigley's philosophical analysis wrongly claims, but two daughters of the Abacwezi. One of the Abacwezi women taught him to drink milk, the ideal food of pastoral culture and the mark of a civilized diet. The Abacwezi, then, not only preceded the Ababito but were a source of Ababito values and civilization.

The survival of the pre-Ababito clans' interpretation of the legends raises the question of why the ruling Ababito should have acquiesced in viewing their own ancestors as savage and inferior compared to the marvelous and civilized Abacwezi. While Wrigley simply acknowledges this as an anomaly, Beattie attempts to resolve the paradox by emphasizing that Rukidi, through his Abacwezi ancestry and his portrayal as half-white, was depicted as part Abacwezi. But a better explanation rests on the continuing political strength of the clans represented by the Abacwezi, which the Ababito had to acknowledge throughout the period of their rule.[30]

The Abacwezi myth's association with earlier ruling groups also emerges from its contradiction of the hierarchical and cattle-oriented social values that prevailed under the Ababito. In the legend, the union of the Abacwezi progenitors Isimbwa and Nyinamwiru fuses the commonly opposed symbolic categories of pastoral and agricultural, royal and nonroyal, and normal and abnormal. Isimbwa, who fathered the first Omucwezi, Ndahura, inherited distinct pastoral associations from both his parents; his mother introduced herself to her future mate as a pastoralist and bore the name Nyamata, 'of milk'. His father Isaza deeply loved cows. Yet Isimbwa impregnated Nyinamwiru whose name marks her status as a cultivator and whose father Bukuku was not accepted as king because he was an *omwiru*, a peasant. Similarly, while Isimbwa's ancestors possessed unquestioned royal rank, the legend portrays Nyinamwiru's father, Bukuku, as a palace official of commoner origin who usurped the royal position in the absence of the true king Isaza. Finally, although Isimbwa possessed no blemishes, Nyinamwiru suffered mutilation by her father resulting in the loss of an eye, a breast or both, depending on the variant. From this egalitarian union of opposites, Ndahura, the first Omucwezi, was born. The respect thus accorded cultivators descended from Bukuku and Nyinamwiru contradicts the status and power of the pastoralist Ababito kings.

Confirmation of the legends' association with pre-Ababito rulers comes not only from the tales' pro-Abacwezi bias, however, but also from the recorded political status of the descendants of these former rulers; many of them, in association with at least one major Abacwezi divinity, were able to maintain a high degree of political autonomy under Ababito rule. For the two Abacwezi 'kings' Ndahura and Wamara, evidence comes primarily from the major religious sites dedicated to them, located respectively at Mubende Hill in Mubende District and at Masaka Hill in Bwera. (By the late nineteenth century, both these areas of ancient Bunyoro had fallen under Bugandan rule.) The caretakers of the temples maintained a high level of privilege, respect, and semi-independence within the Ababito kingdom, and local traditions verify that their authority preceded that of the Ababito. The priestess of Ndahura's temple, from the Abasazima clan, played an important role in the royal accession ceremony and her domains were exempted from both Buganda and Bunyoro attack. The Abamoli clan official at Masaka Hill retained virtual political independence in Bwera and received pilgrims from all over western Uganda.

The traditional figures of Nyamiyonga, the 'king of the underworld', and Isaza, father of Nyamata, correspond to two other major ruling families whose political prominence spans a long historical period. Isaza clearly represents the Abasita, still the most numerous clan in Bunyoro and Toro, remembered in traditions both as rulers and as the majority population in the past. Nyakatura's account of them indirectly implies their ancient political importance by observing that the royal drums the Ababito received from their predecessors had not belonged originally to the Abacwezi, but to Isaza, the grandfather of the first Omucwezi, Ndahura. He identifies their caretaker as an Omusita.[31] Johnston suggests the Abasita connection of Isaza himself in the tale of an Omusita queen, Nyamwengi, who ruled over most of western Uganda and was succeeded by her son Saza (Isaza).[32] Legend also affirms the political importance of the Abasita in the pre-Ababito period through the tradition of Mulindwa, sometimes identified as a second Omucwezi ruler, whose descendants later held political and religious authority in the northwestern Bunyoro district of Buyaga. An alternative tradition on the transfer of authority to Rukidi, usually incorporated into the main one, makes the same point, alleging that Rukidi arrived in Kitara during a famine and gained the drum directly from Abasita women in exchange for millet. Furthermore, traditions closely connect the Abacwezi with the Abasita clan's taboo (called *obusito* or *obusita*), the milk of a cow within four days after mating. The taboo appears in Bunyoro as an avoidance of the modern Abacwezi clan and in Nkore as the taboo both of the ruling Abahinda clan and of the Abacwezi in historical legends.

Nyamiyonga's modern heirs are more difficult to identify, but he may represent a ruling family of the Abasonga clan (in Buganda, *nsenene,* grasshopper) whose political center lay in Kisozi, now in the Gomba district of Buganda. Both Abasonga and Abacwezi traditions associate the names Ruyonga (Nyamiyonga) and Ndahura with the area of Kisozi, while Nkore myths identify Nyamiyonga of the Kitara traditions as Ruyonga, ruler of Kisozi (Kishozi).[33] In both versions, the Kisozi area remains the capital of the domains of Isimbwa, Ruyonga's grandson, and the traditions of the *nsenene* clan in Buganda verify this association by identifying Kisozi as their chief ancestral land and an ancient 'important gov-

Deities, dynasties, and oral tradition

ernment center' whose leader Ruyonga was 'a king in his own right'.[34] The testimony that Sir Apolo Kaggwa collected in western Toro from among the oldest senior clansmen in Busongora spells out this history more fully, tracing the Abasonga back to a pastoralist named Kirobozi who ruled in Busongora and died leaving behind him a succession struggle among his children.

> Whereupon Ruyonga, Kalibbala and their sister Nandawula separated and emigrated with their herds of cattle towards Buganda. When they reached the district of Bwera, which was in the Province of Buddu, they settled there. On leaving Bwera they settled at Kakubansiri which was in the (modern) county of Gomba. Thence they settled at Nakanoni village and after that they settled permanently at Kisozi which was also in the county of Gomba . . .[35]

Gorju, who also identified Kisozi as the family center, listed Sendahura and Nandahura (variants of Ndahura) among the important clan names.[36] The coincidence of the ruler Ruyonga centered at Kisozi and the forms of Ndahura as locally prominent clan names points strongly to an Abasonga identity for the family of Ruyonga (Nyamiyonga) in the Abacwezi legends.

Combining this knowledge of the clans to which the primary figures in Abacwezi myth refer with an analysis of its themes suggests that the historical dimension of the first section of the Kitara and Nkore traditions concerns a conflict between two kingdoms, with the one centered in Kitara eventually taking over the other based in Kisozi.[37] The traditional motif of the king (Isaza) who follows an animal underground or into a cave until he arrives in the kingdom of another ruler (in this case Ruyonga) usually ends with the death of the former,[38] indicating that Ruyonga of Kisozi either killed or captured Isaza, king of Kitara. Meanwhile a royal servant, Bukuku, a peasant, seized power in the confusion of Isaza's defeat and attempted to establish his authority over the land despite the ensuing rebellion of most local officials.

The next motif is that of a king's daughter, isolated because of a physical defect, who becomes pregnant and bears a son who kills his grandfather and usurps the drum. In the Abacwezi myth, the daughter is Nyinamwiru, daughter of Bukuku, her suitor is Isimbwa, born to Isaza and Nyamiyonga's daughter Nyamata, and the son is Ndahura, the first Abacwezi king. A similar tradition in Rwanda describes the process by which new pastoralist rulers there assumed power from an older dynasty known as Abarenge. Both instances seek to mask a change of dynasties and to link the new with the old, in the Abacwezi tradition by adding the conventional lacustrine

75

theme of the king (also Ndahura) raised outside the royal family (in this case by a potter) who returns to take over the kingdom. Ndahura in the tradition achieved power over the former realm of Isaza by killing his grandfather Bukuku. Then, according to Nkore legend, he merged Isaza's kingdom with that of Ruyonga,[39] moved his capital to Mubende Hill, and left his relatives to rule in Kisozi. When Ndahura went to fight rebellious chiefs, 'Isimbwa, his father stayed at Kisozi and did not go anywhere else'.[40] Thus, rather than uniting the whole of western Uganda as some modern interpretations assert, the traditions suggest an historical period in which a strong king joined only Kisozi and Kitara into a single domain.

Early History

Analysis of the groups represented by the traditions, then, also supports McCall's supposition that people may use the deities as symbols representing the historical actions and relationships of human groups. In this case, both the content of the myths and the semi-independent positions that the representatives of the major Abacwezi divinities maintained after the imposition of new kingdoms suggest that the legends deal with actual historical relationships between competing states of the pre-Ababito and pre-Abahinda periods. Schmidt points to a lengthy duration for this era of small-scale kingdoms by connecting Abacwezi worship and myths with ironworking clans that date back to roughly 500 B.C.–A.D. 200.

Some of the ruling families of this period apparently based their authority on an economic surplus obtained through their control of iron production. The oral traditions of Buhaya, for example, stress that in ancient times local rulers were the heads of ironworking clans,[41] and for Kiamtwana Schmidt was able to document that the later Abahinda rulers eventually assumed power by wresting control of the ironworking centers from earlier ruling clans associated with both iron production and Abacwezi worship. The fragmentary written evidence for western Uganda also supports a connection between Abacwezi deities, their associated traditions, and early ironworking communities; Emin Pasha called the 'Wichwezi' of historical tradition blacksmiths as well as bondsmen,[42] while Nyakatura relates that before the Abacwezi King Wamara departed, he left Bwera region to a member of the Abamoli clan named Baralemwa Kihesantoni, 'he who works iron with his fist'.[43]

The Abamoli, as noted earlier, remained responsible for the ceremonies and temples dedicated to Wamara, the most prominent
deity in the northern lacustrine region.

Perhaps, then, the Abacwezi traditions known in recent times
reflect and document, albeit in a sometimes symbolic and obscure
form, a major political, social, and economic transformation. This
change involved the supplanting of small-scale states based on
control of ironworking with kingdoms whose rulers depended
essentially on a surplus drawn from control of cattle. Prior to the
Ababito and Abahinda assumption of power, new groups of pastoralists apparently had been infiltrating into the lacustrine area,
and their cattle became a new resource on which to base the
economic foundation of political structures. Nyakatura, no doubt in
response to the tendency of some historians to mislabel the Abacwezi as pastoralists, firmly asserts the distinction between the
Abacwezi and the *abahuma*, observing that during the reign of
Ndahura a group of people called *abahuma* appeared bearing great
numbers of cattle not only larger and taller than those already in the
country, but long-horned as well.[44] And the Abacwezi traditions, in
fact, far from portraying this 'dynasty' as purely pastoralist, clearly
depict them as a merger between cattlekeepers and agriculturalists.

This correlation of the Abacwezi with early ruling groups raises
questions about the usual tendency to identify as 'Abacwezi' the
earthworks that stretch across Bunyoro, Toro, and modern
Buganda from the Bugoma forest north of Buyaga to the noted and
most extensive site of Bigo just south of the Katonga River. Their
construction clearly presumed some form of centralized political
organization in the fifteenth and perhaps sixteenth centuries, they
lie roughly in the same area with which the traditions deal, and they
date from a time probably just before the Ababito assumed
power.[45] Archaeologists also have tended to label their extensive
cattle remains and distinctive hearths as evidence of pastoralist
occupation. Although no definitive conclusion on these sites is
possible, it is important to note that the evidence formerly thought
to link them with an 'Abacwezi' dynasty was purely hypothetical.
But the local designation of the largest site as Bigo bya Mugenyi,
'the forts of the stranger', may suggest a tentative connection with
those pastoralists who were arriving by the end of the Abacwezi
period.

The legends of the Ababito epoch also fit Davidson's presentation of the early Iron Age as a period not only of intensified social
and political stratification but also of religious innovation, although

the traditions themselves neither confirm nor disprove his theory that new hierarchies of divinities were modelled on new hierarchies of rulers. The Abacwezi myths concentrate instead on the dynasties of the later Iron Age, some of whose descendants were able to preserve their semi-independent power by maintaining control both of the worship of ancient deities and of legends that made the kings seem to emanate from their gods. The twentieth century produced major changes in these traditions with a colonial ruling class indirectly legitimizing its domination by formulating a theory of a previous dynasty of white-skinned outsiders, while Europeans and their African allies in government supplanted earlier politico-religious officials as the controllers of historical knowledge. This new class of Africans, by contributing to and accepting this historical revisionism, added to its own status under the new regime in much the same way as its Abacwezi predecessors had done under the earlier overlordship of the Ababito.

Rather, then, than invalidating the historical significance of the Abacwezi legends, the attention of structuralist criticism to a detailed analysis of the symbolic content of myth helps to enrich our understanding of its historical dimension. It also clarifies the fact that, although anthropological critics of historians have emphasized the function of these traditions in legitimizing new dynasties by tying them genealogically to the Abacwezi, the legends' viewpoint also strongly, though more subtly, has justified the continuing importance of political figures, traditions, and deities descended from the early Iron Age. This conclusion may suggest a new explanation for the greater elaboration of historical traditions in centralized than in decentralized societies. They may not only document and legitimate the authority of the dominant classes, as historians have agreed, but they may also, as in the Abacwezi legends, record and protect the remaining rights of the dominated.

Notes

1 Daniel McCall, *Africa in Time Perspective: A Discussion of Historical Reconstruction from Unwritten Sources* (Boston and Legon, 1964), p. 43.
2 Basil Davidson, *Africa in History* (New York, 1968), p. 78.
3 The term comes from *okutembura*, 'to build a new place'. According to tradition, this was the first Kitara dynasty and includes mainly names of an obviously legendary character.
4 C. C. Wrigley, 'The Story of Rukidi'. *Africa*, vol. 43, no. 3 (1973), p. 220.

5 J. W. Nyakatura, *Anatomy of an African Kingdom: A History of Bunyoro-Kitara*, ed. Godfrey N. Uzoigwe (Garden City, New York, 1973), p. 44.

6 Wyatt MacGaffey, 'Oral Tradition in Central Africa', *International Journal of African Historical Studies*, vol. 7, no. 3 (1975), p. 418; Frederick J. Kaijage, 'Kyamutwara', *Journal of World History*, vol. 13, no. 3 (1971), p. 43.

7 Henry Stanley, *In Darkest Africa* (2 vols., New York, 1891), vol. 2, p. 345.

8 Carole Buchanan's review article, 'Of Kings and Traditions: The Case of Bunyoro-Kitara', *International Journal of African Historical Studies,* vol. 7, no. 3 (1975), pp. 516–27, deals with some of these questions.

9 John Speke, *Journal of the Discovery of the Sources of the Nile* (Edinburgh and London, 1863), pp. 292–3; James Grant, *A Walk Across Africa* (London, 1864), pp. 266–7.

10 G. Schweinfurth et al., *Emin Pasha in Central Africa: Being a Collection of His Letters and Journals* (London, 1888), pp. 84, 92. He does, however, acknowledge Speke as well as local conversations as the sources of his material.

11 Gaetano Casati, *Ten Years in Equatoria and the Return of Emin Pasha* (London, 1891) vol. 2, p. 273. Much later, in 1939, B. Musoke Zimbe still described the population in neighboring Buganda when the kingdom's legendary founder Kintu arrived as 'aborigines called Bashwezi'.

12 See, for example, Diaries of A. B. Fisher, Church Missionary Society Archives, Acc. 84, pp. 11, 48, and Church Missionary Society Archives, Uganda Mission, 1903, G 3 A/70.

13 See Robert Felkin's appendix to Emin Pasha's letters and journals, Schweinfurth, *Emin Pasha,* p. 517, and Speke, *Discovery*, pp. 246–51.

14 Sir Harry Johnston, *The Uganda Protectorate* (London, 1902), vol. 2, p. 486.

15 Johnston, *Uganda Protectorate,* vol. 2, pp. 592, 614.

16 Johnston, *Uganda Protectorate,* vol. 2, p. 610.

17 In the new context of repression of Abacwezi religious observances, they probably disappeared in practice as well.

18 There is some ambiguity on the extent of the change, since they sometimes were identified in the nineteenth century as 'white', that is, as spirits.

19 This is not to argue that Johnston's attitudes were necessarily more racist than those of the early travellers, but that their comments on the Abacwezi in particular did not connect to explicit historical theories reflecting such attitudes.

20 Albert B. Lloyd, *Uganda to Khartoum* (London, 1906), p. 63; Mrs. A. B. Fisher [Ruth], *Twilight Tales of the Black Baganda* (London, 1970), p. 39.

21 John Roscoe, *The Bakitara or Banyoro* (London, 1923), p. 21; Julien Gorju, *Entre le Victoria, l'Albert et l'Edouard* (Rennes, 1920), pp. 42–5, 157.

22 K. W., 'The Kings of Bunyoro-Kitara', *Uganda Journal*, vol. 3, no. 2 (1935), p. 158.

23 K. W.'s basic perspective reappears in the later published writings of John Nyakatura.

24 J. P. Crazzolara, 'The Lwoo People', *Uganda Journal,* vol. 5, no. 1 (1937), pp. 12–18; Julien Gorju et al., *Face au royaume hamite du Ruanda: le royaume frère de l'Urundi* (Bruxelles, 1938), p. 8; Hans Cory and M. M. Hartnoll, *Customary Law of the Haya Tribe* (London, 1945), p. 259; Roland Oliver, 'A Question about the Bachwezi', *Uganda Journal,* vol. 17, no. 2 (1953), p. 137; J. Nicolet, 'The History of the Abacwezi', typewritten, Mbarara, Uganda, 1953, p. 2. Nyakatura, *African Kingdom,* p. 17, also argues in favor of the hypothesis of Portuguese origins.
25 Roland Oliver, 'Bachwezi', p. 136.
26 John Beattie, 'Group Aspects of the Nyoro Spirit Mediumship Cult', *Human Problems in British Central Africa,* vol. 30 (1961), p. 12.
27 Peter Ridgway Schmidt, *Historical Archaeology: A Structural Approach in an African Culture* (Westport, Conn., 1978).
28 Fisher, *Twilight Tales,* p. xli. More work on this hypothesis needs to be done for Bunyoro and Nkore focusing on identifying precisely the precolonial keepers of the Abacwezi traditions, the context in which they were preserved, and the later changes in both.
29 Schmidt, *Historical Archaeology*, pp. 53, 122.
30 John Beattie, 'Aspects of Nyoro Symbolism', *Africa*, vol. 38, no. 4 (1968), p. 430. This trend did not occur everywhere, however. In Kiziba where the ruling dynasty was able to formulate alternative religious ceremonies to oppose those of the Abacwezi mediums, they also were able to control historical traditions which identified the Abacwezi with nature and the kings with culture.
31 Nyakatura, *African Kingdom*, pp. 54–5.
32 Johnston, *Uganda Protectorate*, vol. 2, p. 594. In this account Saza died without heirs and his cook (a highly respected position) seized the throne, founding a line of kings whose third descendant was Bukuku. Some variants, however, identify Isaza as an Omugabo. See Gorju, *Entre le Victoria*, pp. 42–3.
33 A. G. Katate and L. Kamugungunu, *Abagabe b' Ankole* (Kampala, 1955), trans. Samwiri Karugire, 'The Emergence and Growth of the Kingdom of Nkore in Western Uganda, c. 1500–1896' (PhD dissertation, University of London, 1969), Appendix A, p. 477.
34 M. S. M. Kiwanuka, 'The Evolution of Chieftainship in Buganda, ca. 1400–1900', History Paper, Social Sciences Conference, University of East Africa, 1968–9, p. 112.
35 M. S. M. Kiwanuka, *A History of Buganda: From the Foundation of the Kingdom to 1900* (New York, 1972), pp. 39–40.
36 Gorju, *Entre le Victoria,* p. 193.
37 Kitara usually is identified as the modern district of Kyaka, while Kisozi has been placed directly east of this in Gomba, Mubende, or, less precisely, 'near Mubende'.
38 In one Kiziba tale, for example, the first king throws himself into a well after the emissary of the second has cast his favorite cow into it, while in another, a king named Igaba conquered Wamara by poisoning the well water, first killing Wamara's favorite cow and then him and his followers. In Fisher's version of the Bunyoro myth, Nyamiyonga captures Isaza. See *Twilight Tales*, p. 82.
39 Katate and Kamugungunu, *Kings of Ankole,* p. 496.

40 H. K. Kárubanga, 'Bukya Nibwira', trans. Rev. Anatasi Katurama, mimeographed, History Department, Makerere University College, 1969, p. 2.

41 Schmidt, *Historical Archaeology*, p. 41.

42 Schweinfurth, *Emin Pasha*, p. 92.

43 Nyakatura, *African Kingdom*, p. 61.

44 Nyakatura, *African Kingdom*, p.61. Carole Buchanan's work shares this interpretation of the social transformation occurring at this time. See 'The Kitara Complex: The Historical Tradition of Western Uganda to the 16th Century' (PhD dissertation, Indiana University, 1974), pp. 134–43.

45 The interpretation of these archaeological remains has been complicated by the tendency to identify them with the Abacwezi and thus to extend their occupancy back to the 1300's, when the radiocarbon dates for Bigo in fact center on the sixteenth century and perhaps extend back into the fifteenth and forward into the seventeenth. (The two most important dates are 1505 ± 70 and 1570 ± 90.) The reason for this backward projection has been the dual inclination to see the site as having predated the Ababito and the Ababito as having come to power by roughly 1500. David Henige's questioning of the accuracy of the Bunyoro kinglists, however, might point to a shorter time span for this dynasty. (See 'K. W.'s Nyoro Kinglist: Oral Tradition or the Result of Applied Research?' Paper presented to the African Studies Association, 1972.) Another possibility is that the Abamoli rulers of Bwera, associated with Wamara, continued to occupy the site of Bigo after the Ababito kingdom was established. An early tradition that Johnston collected suggests this by observing that after the Abacwezi left Kitara, 'They then went to Bwera, where they became the dominant race'. See *Uganda Protectorate*, vol. 2, p. 596. Taken together, these observations suggest that any conclusions drawn on the basis of archaeology remain provisional.

3. The Historical Study of a Kanyok Genesis Myth: The Tale of Citend a Mfumu

JOHN C YODER

Introduction

Recent structural analyses of genesis tales from the southern savanna region have led many scholars to conclude that these stories are in fact myths which have little value for historical purposes. As religious constructs, social paradigms, or ritual charters, genesis legends seem to reflect current influences rather than chronologically related events from the past. To the despair of ethnohistorians, even the tales' supposed factual kernel—names, places, accounts of wars, and migrations—melts into the realm of fanciful imagery when analyzed by a perceptive scholar like Luc de Heusch.[1]

While the structuralist critique is a powerful corrective of a simplistic and literalistic approach to African oral traditions, knowledge that the form and content of genesis stories are mythical in nature should not be cause to overlook the fact that these very intellectual constructs can become the objects of fruitful historical inquiry. Intellectual statements may be synchronic in content, but they are not immutable or static through time. Precisely because legends of origins are normative statements justifying a people's religious, social, economic, and political practices, the legends must be expected to change as norms change, either marginally or radically.

Because structuralist anthropologists stress the susceptibility of origin legends to change, they may underestimate the degree to which modern revised legends may retain recognizable fragments of older tales. Even Claude Lévi-Strauss concedes that legends are not invented *ex nihilo* but that they are formed by modifying existing information and tales.[2] Thus, a structuralist position could provide support for Jan Vansina's view that legends of origin resemble palimpsests composed of layers of meaning reflecting earlier times

82

and circumstances. According to Vansina, if the development of these layers of legend can be chronicled in a convincing manner, then the historical evolution of cultural norms and practices can be portrayed.[3]

The logic of the structuralist approach does not undermine the usefulness of genesis myths for historical purposes, although structuralism does suggest that the content of origin tales may prove more instructive about periods later in time than the era they claim to describe. Nevertheless, structuralist findings do present great methodological obstacles for historical research. The historian must discover a means to unravel the successive mythological levels and to order these levels in an approximate temporal sequence. Because the content of the myths cannot be relied on to supply that context, the problem is very difficult. However, the pattern of the varying structures of competing stories found in different regions provides a means of devising such a chronicle.

Since the development of mythological constructs is comparable to the evolution of languages in that both mythology and language are influenced by such similar forces as cultural conservatism, borrowings of content, migrations and other forms of population change, and political innovation, the broad assumptions and general techniques of historical linguistics are perhaps suitable analogs for examining the structure of genesis stories. While nineteenth-century optimism about the applicability of the principles of historical linguistics to the study of myths and legends proved unrealistic, several basic linguistic concepts seem useful for guiding the historical analysis of the development of legends of origin. The following propositions outline some of the relevant implications of certain analogies between languages and myths.[4]

(1) Languages and myths can be arranged into categories of family groups and subgroups. This analysis can be based on direct historical evidence or reconstructed indirectly from a careful comparison of current data. Fortunately, much of this work has already been done by Stephen Lucas and Luc de Heusch for the myths of the southern savanna.[5]

(2) Languages and myths diffuse and diverge from an original parent language or myth. These changes may be internally generated readjustments or externally stimulated innovations.

(3) Features shared by distinct later languages or myths must have been present in their common antecedent stage. There are, of course, exceptions caused by borrowings.

(4) Although the sequential development of language and myth systems may be reconstructed hypothetically without the benefit of independent confirmation, a much more satisfying and convincing analysis

results when the rudimentary historical background for this development is known independently.

The following essay will attempt to describe the historical development of the Kanyok myth of Citend a Mfumu (Citend the daughter of the chief). It will seek to demonstrate that, like modern languages, present-day Kanyok stories about the past contain identifiable elements from much earlier time periods. Furthermore, it will be argued, these older and often archaic elements can be placed within approximate time settings[6] enabling one to trace the general evolution of the genesis tale and to infer ideals and culture at remote periods in the Kanyok past.

The methodologies employed in this task are those of the historian who searches for independent, corroborating data, the historical linguist who determines familial relationships between languages and the sequential patterns of their development, and of the structuralist anthropologist who studies internal symbols. First, oral traditions from Kanyok lineages and regions, entirely distinct from material found in the legends of origin, stories from neighboring peoples, and occasional evidence from written sources provide a skeletal outline of Kanyok economic, political, and military developments going back to the early 1700s. Second, the analogy of historical linguistics suggests that it is possible to identify the basic components of legends of origin and to propose probable developmental sequences for these elements. Third, structuralist techniques illuminate the meaning of these various symbolic layers. Finally, the historian can correlate this sequence of changing symbols with outstanding features in the basic chronological record. Thus, legends of origin, as intellectual constructs, complement and complete the more narrowly focused political, economic, and military record.

The goal of this study is less to discover which descriptive elements of Kanyok tales of origin are literally true than to determine what these elements meant and why they were significant at different times. However, legends of origin may contain accurate descriptive data from very early times. Place names and titles are unusually resistant to change and can be very old. Incomplete and dimly understood descriptions of institutions which no longer function can reflect practices from previous periods. Contemporary ethnographic studies can at times clarify the meaning of titles, names, and institutions, although present-day evidence must be used extremely cautiously with reference to the past. While factual information embedded in legendary accounts of origins is both difficult to identify and hard to interpret, the scattered bits of data that can be found shed valuable light on life several centuries ago.

Kanyok Legends of Luba Hunter Rulers[7]

The Kanyok have never been a powerful or widely known people. Before January 1891, when Paul Le Marinel passed through the Kanyok capital at Mulundu, the Kanyok had no known direct contact with Europeans.[8] Thus, primary written records describing the Kanyok date from no earlier than the late nineteenth century. Furthermore, even neighboring peoples preserve few references to the Kanyok in their oral traditions.

The Kanyok, a small ethnic group of about 75,000 people living between the Mbuji-Mayi and the Lubilash rivers in the southeastern corner of Zaire's Kasai province, were organized into a single state under a leader entitled the Mwena Kanyok (ruler of the Kanyok) when visited by Le Marinel. According to Kanyok tradition, however, the development of this state structure came after a prior period of consolidation of the people in the area into intermediate-sized regional chiefdoms. Following the emergence of state structures in the late 1700s, the Kanyok polity was at times torn by schisms that divided the land between two or more competing individuals, each claiming the title of Mwena Kanyok.

Today, as in 1891, the Kanyok state is subdivided into about fifteen regional chiefdoms, each covering approximately 500 to 1,000 square kilometers and inhabited by several thousand people. The chiefs of these regions hold themselves above the petty Kanyok headmen who rule only single villages, who oversee only their own lineage of perhaps 100 people, and who trace their ancestry to the Basangal (autochthonous) peoples, whom they believe to have always lived in the area between the Lubilash and Mbuji Mayi rivers. According to their own traditions of origin, Kanyok regional chiefs are descendants of Luba hunters, who entered the land in search of game many generations ago. These Luba hunters, supposedly finding empty lands or lands inhabited by the politically and militarily weaker Basangal, established villages and organized the local inhabitants into larger political units. Kanyok informants say the first Luba hunter to establish his rule was Kazadi a Mwanang (Kazadi the son of Mwanang), who governed the region of Ngoi just west of the Luilu river in the center of Kanyok territory. Today the

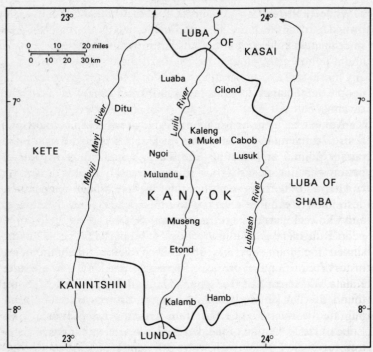

Map 3.1 Early Kanyok regional chiefdoms

chiefs of Ngoi hold the title Mwena Ngoi, and they claim descent from Kazadi a Mwanang. Northeast of Ngoi, near the present-day town of Luputa, another regional chief ruled an area known as Kaleng a Mukel. Supposedly, the first Luba hunter to settle at Kaleng a Mukel was Mwamba Ciluu (Mwamba the hunter). Other important regional chiefdoms, not described in this essay, existed at Museng, Etond, Cilong, Luaba, Ditu, Kalamb, and Hamb.

After the Luba hunter chiefs' initial settlement of the new land, their successors allegedly continued to pay tribute and to seek investiture at the Luba *mulopwe*'s capital in their old homeland. This practice, known as *kuyi ku mulopwe muluba* (to go to the Luba *mulopwe*) was institutionalized in a ceremony during which candidates for office submitted to a series of rigorous trials. The tests undergone there by the candidates included cutting down and completely burning a large tree, eating poisoned food, drinking prodigious quantities of palm oil, dancing on a booby trap, and collecting all their excrement in baskets so that none remained on Luba soil.

86

While oral traditions, linguistic studies, and ethnographic data provide strong evidence that regional chiefs have ruled the area since the seventeenth century,[9] there is no proof that modern stories about hunter chiefs depict the origins of the regional chiefdoms in any literal sense. Comparative studies of legends from neighboring people demonstrate that the details of these tales reflect a common savanna cultural heritage rather than specific events from the Kanyok past. Furthermore, internal analysis of these accounts suggests that the hunter chief stories are intimately linked to contemporary politics and thus susceptible to modification as political patterns change.

Although chiefs of every important Kanyok village claim to have descended from Luba hunters who entered the land many years ago and who established the present forms of government, many other people throughout southeastern Zaire trace their origins to very similar immigrant ancestors. The Luba of Shaba explain their early history by recounting the tale of Kongolo and his nephew, Ilunga Kalala, who came from the east.[10] The Lunda recall their state was founded when Ilunga Kalala's hunter nephew, Cibind Yirung, migrated westward and married the Lunda princess Rweej.[11] The Luba of Kasai, living north of the Kanyok, believe that their ancestors, too, were Luba hunters who settled the area many generations ago.[12] The Kete and the Sala Mpasu to the west of the Kanyok and the Kanintshin to the southwest all claim to have originated similarly from the eastern immigrants.[13]

Although the individual stories from unrelated Kanyok villages are distinct—the geographical details and the protagonists are not the same—analysis of accounts from villages throughout the land reveal a striking structural similarity among the separate Kanyok narratives. Each village's legend contains six basic components which describe first, the land before the hunter's coming, second, the hunter's arrival from his Luba homeland, third, the hunter's rise to power, fourth, the legitimization of the hunter's power, fifth, the hunter's exercise of power, and sixth, a genealogy of the hunter's descendants who are eligible to rule in the village.

Stephen Lucas, who has studied stories about immigrant hunter ancestors in southeastern Zaire, cogently argues that such hunter legends are understood best in their cultural settings as the literary analogues of political interregna. Viewing the tales as expressions of the classical *rites de passage* first described by van Gennep, Lucas contends that the legends' sixfold structure faithfully replicates the events and rituals of an interregnum. Therefore, Lucas believes, such hunter stories should be interpreted as mythological accounts providing stability in time of national crisis.[14]

Such an analysis neatly explains much about Kanyok legends of Luba hunters. These stories are recounted at the installation of every regional chief to insure that the protocols of the ceremony are identical to those performed when the 'original' Luba hunter was invested. Furthermore, the new chief is linked explicitly to the ancient hunter immigrant, since only patrilineal descendants of the hunter are eligible to hold office and because the newly elected chief is ritually identified with the hunter ancestor. Prior to his installation in office, the candidate recreates the original long journey by eating only uncooked food and drinking only palm wine. Similarly imitating the first hunter, he remains in a small grass hut named after the hunter, where he sleeps with a woman given by the minor local chief whose own ancestor supposedly gave a wife to the ancestral hunter. The new chief completes the investiture with a ritual bathing by descendants of the same local chiefs who installed his hunter forefather by an identical ceremonial washing.[15]

Although legends of Luba hunter chiefs have obvious current significance, the basic structure of the tales must have originated well before 1800. Much of the evidence for this assertion cannot be presented here, but the fact that *kuyi ku mulopwe muluba*, investiture at the Luba homeland, has been defunct since a major series of Kanyok-Luba wars in the early 1800s indicates that the legends must predate the nineteenth century. *Kuyi ku mulopwe muluba* is described in the tales of Luba hunters, but the institution has been abandoned for so long that most Kanyok people, whose perception has been dimmed by time and colored by tales of recent harsh Luba imperialism, no longer understand the original purpose of the ceremonies at the Luba capital. Not realizing that *kuyi ku mulopwe muluba* was once actually a political process, people today view it only as an ancient punishment inflicted by the Luba on their oppressed Kanyok ancestors. However, parallel examples from other savanna peoples and the accounts of a few older informants make it clear the *kuyi ku mulopwe muluba*, which figures so prominently in most Kanyok Luba hunter legends, was once a ceremony for selecting and installing pre-nineteenth century regional chiefs.[16]

Thus, the Luba hunter legends are important for understanding the status, sources of legitimization, and the practices of Kanyok ruling families over a long period in time. By claiming Luba origins, these families distinguished and elevated themselves from the rest of society. By seeking investiture at the Luba capital, they gained special ritual sanction for their monopoly of high office. By re-enacting their 'original ancestors' accession to power in *rites de passage* held at each subsequent succession, they reinforced in the minds of the entire population the rights of a few to rule. While some of these actions have continued into the twentieth century, all these customs were important components of Kanyok political, social, and economic life in the period before 1800. Although the origins of these practices cannot be dated precisely, one may be certain that they were current in the 1700s and one can posit that they probably existed in the 1600s.[17]

The Historical Meaning of the Citend Myth[18]

Although much of the historical background for the Luba hunter legends is speculative, the past context for the Citend myth is much more securely known. In the early 1700s, the regional chief from the Kaleng a Mukel area attempted to gain control over all the other regional rulers who claimed Luba ancestry. Thus he claimed the title Mwena Kanyok (ruler of the Kanyok). Unlike his regional counterparts, the Mwena Kanyok said he descended from a female, a Kanyok princess born at the Luba court after her mother had been sent to the *mulopwe* (ruler) as a slave. Throughout the eighteenth century, the Mwena Kanyok encouraged or forced the neighboring regional chiefs to offer him tribute and to seek investiture at his capital instead of traveling to the Luba empire for recognition. This policy resulted in frequent battles between the Mwena Kanyok and the regional chiefs who tried to defend their independence.

During the late 1700s, as the Mwena Kanyok's power increased, the incumbent Shimat dynasty and the emerging Kanyok state encountered especially grave dangers. At the death of one Mwena Kanyok, armed competition broke out among the numerous paternal relatives eligible to succeed to the chief's chair. Gathering the support of their maternal kin and relying on the help of dissident regional chiefs who had been conquered by previous Mwena Kanyoks, rival pretenders threw the land into frequent civil war. No sooner was Mwena Kanyok Cibang a Ciband (c. 1770–1790)[19] able to institute measures repressing this internal strife than a foreign war erupted between the Kanyok and the Luba. As the office of Mwena Kanyok gained power and prestige, its incumbents had become increasingly hostile to the Luba *mulopwe*. Finally, Mwena Kanyok Ilung a Cibang (c. 1790–1820) left Kanyok excrement in the Luba capital during the ceremony of *kuyi ku mulopwe muluba*, vowed that he would no longer recognize Luba sovereignty over the Kanyok, and asserted that he would cease taking tribute to the Luba chief. When the Luba *mulopwe* learned of Ilung a Cibang's insubordination, he retaliated by sending warriors to punish the Kanyok. Ilung a Cibang, however, had made careful preparations for war by constructing two extensive dry moat fortifications (*ihak*) near the capital Mulundu. After several years of bitter fighting, the Luba admitted failure and retreated from the Kanyok lands in defeat. Kanyok oral traditions claim that the Luba never again collected tribute or interfered in Kanyok politics.[20]

The period of Kanyok-Luba wars was a major turning point in Kanyok history and remains a crucial touchstone for Kanyok chronology. The approximate dates for this war can be determined by comparing Kanyok genealogies and historical anecdotes with independent data from Luba oral traditions. Kanyok records point to a birth date in the late 1700s for Ilung a Cibang, who lived three generations earlier than Mwena Kanyok Kabw Muzemb who died in 1893. Ilung a Cibang also ruled early in the lifetime of an extremely long-lived fraternal uncle who probably died in the mid 1850s.[21] In addition, several Luba sources report that the Kanyok threw excrement in the streets of the Luba royal village and stopped paying tribute late in the reign of *mulopwe* Ilungu Sungu (c. 1770–1810).[22]

Thus, Kanyok and Luba records converge to place the Kanyok-Luba tensions and wars early in the 1800s. The two *ihak*, whose moats are now overgrown with grass and filled with massive living trees, are proof that the Kanyok built elaborate fortifications to protect the region near the Mwena Kanyok's capital well before the twentieth century. Although imprecise, oral testimony from other Kanyok villages indicates that the Kanyok-Luba wars took place years before even the oldest informants' grandparents were small children.

Very complex but mutually consistent genealogies from separate Kanyok families indicate that Ilung a Cibang was born in the fourth generation of rulers who held the title of Mwena Kanyok. Thus if 25–30 years is used as a rough measure of generational lengths, the Kanyok state itself appears to have emerged by the early 1700s. Since Kanyok traditions, including those supportive of the Mwena Kanyok, agree that Ngoi and several other regional chiefdoms were already established when the first Mwena Kanyok took power, it is likely that the process of regional political consolidation took place in the 1600s if not before.[23]

The Luba hunter legends and the history of the Shimat dynasty at Mulundu provide the background for elucidating the history to be found in a remarkable Kanyok genesis tale: the story of Citend a Mfumu (Citend the daughter of the chief). The Citend story is the most powerful, poignant, and perplexing tale in Kanyok oral tradition. With the exception of the people living in the extreme southern part of the land, every Kanyok adult can recite the essentials of the Citend account, which describes the suffering of a Kanyok princess at the Luba court and details her glad return to rule her own people. So great is the emotional appeal of the Citend narrative that it has become a kind of national epic serving as a focus of ethnic unity, glorifying the past sufferings of the people, expressing Kanyok antipathy towards the Luba of Shaba, and justifying the political claims of the Shimat dynasty.

Unlike the Luba hunter legends, which are similar to tales recited throughout southeastern Zaire, the Citend myth is a unique expression of the Kanyok oral heritage. Nevertheless, the structure and content of the myth betray an obvious dependence on Luba hunter legends, and this relationship provides the key to chronicling the development and uses of the distinctively Kanyok variant of these accounts. The following discussion asserts that the Citend narrative grew out of pre-eighteenth century prototype hunter legend which had described a now defunct regional chiefdom of Mwamba Ciluu at Kaleng a Mukel in the northeastern part of the Kanyok territory. It is further contended that in the eighteenth century, narrators at the Mwena Kanyok's capital at Mulundu conspicuously modified the tale by incorporating elements from the hunter legend of the Mwena Ngoi regional chiefdom and by exaggerating the role of a previously minor female figure named Citend. This recasting probably reflected and facilitated political transformations affecting first the Kaleng a Mukel area, later the Shimat dynasty, and finally the entire Kanyok people.

Except for dramatic embellishments, local insertions, or unintentional omissions, the Citend story varies little from village to village. The following text is a composite summary of many accounts collected during my field work in 1975 and of others recorded by Father André Casteleyn, who lived in the region between 1947 and 1952.[24]

The Myth of Citend a Mfumu

Mwena Ngoi came here from the Luba *mulopwe's* land to found the village of Ngoi ya Yanda just west of the Luilu river. The hunting people living there recognized the newcomer as their chief even though he was not a member of the Luba royal family. As chief, Mwena Ngoi went to the Luba court with the people's annual tribute. Unfortunately, when he was at the Luba capital, a *citend* [calabash] from which he was drinking broke. Perhaps this was because of Mwena Ngoi's carelessness; perhaps this was because the Luba had secretly cracked the cup beforehand. Angered by the destruction of royal property, the *mulopwe* ordered Mwena Ngoi to bring him a woman as payment for the damage.

While at the Luba capital, Mwena Ngoi again incurred the wrath of the *mulopwe* who ordered the Kanyok chief to cut down and burn a great hardwood tree. The Luba ruler also stipulated that neither Ngoi nor his men could defecate on Luba soil; instead they were commanded to save their feces in baskets and carry these containers home with them after the other task had been completed. When Mwena Ngoi had disposed of the entire tree, a ceremony was arranged in which he would dance before the Luba chief. Plotting to kill Mwena Ngoi, the Luba chief treacherously had dug a pit which was then filled with upright spears and knives. Afterwards, the pit was hidden by a mat on which Mwena Ngoi was to dance. Several times in the course of the dance, Mwena Ngoi, who had been warned of the trick by a Luba notable, approached the mat. Then, at the conclusion of the dance, Mwena Ngoi advanced, hurled his spear into the mat, and exposed the trap. All the spectators applauded and Mwena Ngoi returned to his own land.

Mwena Ngoi's daughter Bond or Buman, the woman sent to the *mulopwe* as restitution for Ngoi's misdeed, became one of the Luba sovereign's many wives and soon gave birth to a baby girl whom the *mulopwe* named Citend as a reminder of the broken calabash. When Citend grew older, her siblings mocked her saying she was not the true daughter of the great Luba *mulopwe*, but only a slave since the name Citend referred to an object and not a royal child. Angered and saddened by these taunts, Citend confided in her mother Bond who then related the story of Mwena Ngoi and the broken calabash. Learning for the first time that her maternal grandfather Mwena Ngoi still lived west of the Luilu, Citend resolved to leave the Luba capital and return to her own family living in the land of the Kanyok.

In the course of her long and arduous westward journey home, Citend crossed the Luembe and the Lubilash rivers before arriving during the night at Ibol near the modern town of Luputa. Having met no one along the way, she stopped to rest at a fire left by someone manufacturing salt from burning palm branches. When the woman who was making the salt returned, she found Citend warming herself by the fire. Amazed at the great beauty and royal clothes of the girl, the woman ran to fetch the local chief Mwena Ibol who in turn called a neighboring chief Mwena Kabanda. Mwena Kabanda, remembering the affair of Mwena Ngoi, recognized the girl and told everyone her history. A third ruler Bandamai planned a test to determine if Citend was a true chief. Placing eggs and a mortar in a basket, he broke the eggs in front of her so that if she was not actually a chief she would die. Citend survived the trial and Bandamai said, 'Mother, we come to welcome you, enter into the house to warm yourself.' Bandamai then played the talking drum and called the people to come and behold the beautiful woman. Cilond, Mwena Katubi, Mwena Bihumba, Mwena Cikol, Mwena Cihemba, and Mwena Kabiji were among those who came. Overjoyed to have a person of Luba royal blood in their midst, the people all accepted Citend as their chief.

As the various local rulers presented gifts or performed favors for Citend, she gave them appropriate names. Mwena Ibol received his name because he came with a tribute of wet or rotten meat [*nyam ibol*; *ibol* can mean either wet or rotten]. Another person brought cooked beans and Citend, having no plate, asked for some leaves to hold the food. A man took leaves from a *Cifumba* tree and was known thereafter as Mwena Mafumba. Mwena Kabiji, a fisherman, obtained his name when he offered Citend some fish wrapped in leaves [*mabiji*]. Chief Mwamba, who furnished a white chicken [*nzool mutok*] was then named Mwamba Nzool Matok. Wanting to braid her hair, Citend asked someone to bring her the sharp barbs [sing. *cikol*, pl. *ikol*] of a palm branch to use as pins. The man bringing the barbs was called Mwena Cikol while the person who braided [*kubanda*] her hair was known as Mwena Kabanda. At that time Citend ruled from her capital at Kaleng a Mukel which is just south of the modern Luputa.

Before leaving the Luba capital, Citend had engaged in sexual relations with a Luba hunter named Mwamba Ciluu [*Mwamba the hunter*]. When Mwamba learned that Citend had returned to her maternal relatives, he decided to follow her to the land of the Kanyok. Arriving at Kaleng a Mukel, he found her living in a house carefully guarded by several old women. Citend welcomed Mwamba and together they entered the house as man and wife. [Some other accounts claim that in Mwamba's absence Citend had slept with another man named Mukadi Mut and that Mukadi Mut was the father of Citend's son Shimat.] Soon Citend gave birth to a son who was named Shimat or Tuba Shimat [to sit firmly or we sit firmly] which signified security and independence. Because there was now a fixed capital and a male heir, the people felt safe and secure.

Although Citend lived at Kaleng a Mukel for a time, eventually her hut fell down and she decided to move south. The people around Kaleng a Mukel, unhappy to see her leave and hoping to prevent her departure, used force to oblige Citend to remain. However, Citend prevailed and relocated her capital southwards across the Luilu river.

All went well until it came time for Citend to offer a feast for her people. *Bidias* [cassava] and *nyam* [meat] were cooked in great quantities; many calabashes of a palm wine were carried to the capital. Then, after all the preparations had been made and all the people were assembled, Citend began her menstrual period and became ritually unclean. During her time of impurity, which lasted six days, Citend had to remove her clothes and hide herself in the forest. Since she could not offer the feast, it was decided that her infant son Shimat, who, unlike Mwamba Ciluu, was also of royal blood, should distribute the food. Seated on a leopard skin and aided by his father Mwamba Ciluu, Shimat called out each person's name and gave him food. Realizing that a woman could not serve as an effective chief, the people deposed Citend and installed

Shimat in her place. Thus, Shimat became the Mwena Kanyok and Citend became the Inamwan or mother of the chief. Mwamba Ciluu became the Tat a Mukaleng or father of the chief and went to live at Cilond north of Luputa.

Today, only the descendants of Shimat are eligible for the office of Mwena Kanyok. [At this point, most informants list the descendants of Shimat.]

The story of Citend is unique because its central figure is the only female in Kanyok traditions exalted to such a degree as to over-shadow every other character in the narrative. The story's structure, however, is not new, since Citend is actually the female counterpart to the male Luba hunter; every incident in her life parallels a common motif in the hunter legend typical elsewhere. Because Citend's tale is so unusual a variant of such a standardized literary genre, it would seem that her story resulted from modifying already existing hunter legends.

In fact, the Citend myth can be separated into three distinct accounts attributable to three separate recensions: the two hunter legends of the regional chiefdoms of Mwena Ngoi and Mwamba Ciluu, which together provide a background framework for the story, and the tale of Mwamba's wife, Citend, which comprises the central core of the narrative. Because the story can be divided into three parts, one must examine the segments individually, seeking to determine the particular history and setting of each.

The prologue of the Citend myth appears to be literarily dependent upon themes from a Luba hunter legend best known in the region of Ngoi. In the region of Ngoi, informants refer to the first Mwena Ngoi's origins, travels, territories, wars, rivals, relatives, subordinates, government, and descendants. Ngoi region inhabitants identify the original Mwena Ngoi as a man named Kazadi a Mwanang and they assert that his son Kazadi a Kazadi was the first Mwena Ngoi to seek investiture by going to the Luba court (*kuyi ku mulopwe muluba*). Also the legend of Mwena Ngoi Kazadi a Mwanang unambiguously identifies exactly which descendants of the first ruler at Ngoi are eligible to succeed to office.[25]

An abbreviated version of Mwena Ngoi's arrival, rise to power, and legitimization introduces the Citend story everywhere among the Kanyok. Mwena Ngoi is linked to Citend by the claim that she was actually his granddaughter, born at the Luba court after Mwena Ngoi's calabash broke during *kuyi ku mulopwe muluba*. Because the Citend myth contains only a short synopsis of a much fuller Ngoi hunter legend and because there is disagreement among different versions of the Citend myth about which specific Mwena Ngoi actually gave a daughter to the Luba chief, one must conclude that the prologue of the Citend story grew from the summarizing and subsequent embellishing of an established hunter legend initially developed in Ngoi to portray the political development of that region. Location of the original legend at Ngoi is supported by the fact that oral traditions from every other Kanyok area agree that Ngoi was the first regional chiefdom to have emerged in the land.[26]

The material for the middle section of the Citend myth is provided by a hunter legend of Mwamba Ciluu, the regional chief who once lived at Kaleng a Mukel. Considering the remarkably uniform structure of all the other Kanyok hunter legends, it is unlikely that the original story of Mwamba Ciluu differed greatly from the common parent source of immigrant hunter legends. In spite of Citend's position of dominance within the myth, the figure of Mwamba Ciluu can easily be identified as a typical Luba hunter whose legend probably once was structurally and symbolically parallel to other hunter tales developed before 1800. Four of the six common Luba hunter motifs—local chiefs inhabiting the land before the hunter's arrival, the hunter's journey from Luba territory, the legitimization of the hunter's position through marriage to a local woman, and a genealogy of the hunter's descendants—still cluster around Mwamba Ciluu. The remaining two themes—the rise to political power and the exercise of authority over a multiplicity of local chiefs—are here attributed to the hunter's wife, Citend. They likely once were part of the Mwamba Ciluu story, since tying the other four motifs to Mwamba Ciluu makes little sense if he was never revered as the founding hunter chief at Kaleng a Mukel. In every other Kanyok oral tradition, immigrant Luba hunters who married a local woman and whose descendants ruled as important Kanyok chiefs are always identified as the first rulers of their region.[27]

Current ceremonial practices support the inferences drawn from literary structure to identify Mwamba Ciluu as a typical Luba hunter type chief. Mwamba Ciluu is celebrated by the Mwena Kanyok, just as the Luba hunter ancestors are honored during the installation and the reign of regional chiefs throughout the Kanyok land. At the investiture of regional chiefs, as of the Mwena Kanyok, the newly elected chief imitates the legitimization of his hunter paragon by having ritual intercourse with the daughter of a local 'Basangal' ruler. At regional chiefdoms, the small hut where this takes place and where the new officeholder is confined for several days is named after the hunter ancestor; at Mulundu where the

Mwena Kanyok is installed, the hut is called the *Mwamba nzub* (Mwamba's house). This type of hut, devoted to the memory of the original hunter, remains a permanent fixture in the compound of all regional chiefs and of the Mwena Kanyok.[28]

These literary themes and the ritual observances persisting into the present seem to demonstrate that Mwamba Ciluu was once the simulacrum of every other Luba hunter. It is probable, therefore, that Mwamba Ciluu was at some time in the past the hero of a Luba hunter legend justifying incumbent officeholders at Kaleng a Mukel. The original setting for the story was undoubtedly this northeastern Kanyok region sometime before c. 1700. Since it is extremely unlikely that the Shimat dynasty, which ousted the ruling family at Kaleng a Mukel in about 1700, would have fostered the development of a legend glorifying a deposed ruler or his ancestors, the Mwamba Ciluu tale must have matured as a typical hunter legend before the Shimat lineage seized the already functioning political system at Kaleng a Mukel.

Apart from judgments about the historicity of specific historical individuals, one may assume that an early chiefdom, which was associated with the memory of Mwamba Ciluu and his wife, Citend, was once located at Kaleng a Mukel.[29] Not only is the Citend myth best known in this region, but most versions identify Kaleng a Mukel as the capital of a polity whose subordinate villages included Ibol, Kabanda, Mafumba, Cikol, Bandamai, Cihemba, Bihumba, Katubi, Mwamba Nzool Mutok, and Kabiji, names listed as chiefs attending the legendary Citend upon her arrival in Kanyok lands. The extent of this domain was not large, for with the exception of Kabiji all these villages are located within a fifteen-kilometer radius of Kaleng a Mukel. Kabiji, a territory located thirty kilometers south of Kaleng a Mukel, was almost certainly inserted into the story at a later date when the capital was transferred after 1725 to Mulundu in Kabiji territory.[30] Thus, the realm of Kaleng a Mukel covered no more than 500 square kilometers and probably contained only about 1,500 to 2,000 people.[31]

Besides reconstructing the geographical extent of the chiefdom, one can characterize political relationships and rituals of seventeenth-century Kaleng a Mukel on the basis of the Citend legend. Unmistakable tendencies towards centralization and consolidation can be observed. Outlying villages described in the tale were subordinated to Kaleng a Mukel, whose chief supposedly named them and received gifts of tribute. The assertion that Mwamba or Citend named chiefs does not necessarily indicate that local chiefs were selected by the ruler at Kaleng a Mukel, but it does reveal that they were subject to his authority. The hierarchical nature of this arrangement was manifested through the gifts of tribute offered to the chief at Kaleng a Mukel. Although the Kaleng a Mukel ruler had more prestige and power than local authorities, he may not have been independent of them. The ceremonies performed by the local chief, Bandamai, in which he used eggs, a mortar, and a basket could suggest that each new chief had to submit to ritual trials before being recognized by neighboring villages. Since the ritual was performed by a 'Basangal' chief, it might be assumed that candidates unacceptable to local villagers could not have passed the test.

The stimulus for political development at Kaleng a Mukel may have been the manufacture and distribution of salt since the name Kaleng signifies grass while Mukel means salt. Before the higher quality marsh salt from Kabamba a Ngomb near the modern Gandajika entered the Kanyok territory in the early 1800s, the Kanyok people obtained salt from the ash of grass and palm branches. The area around Kaleng a Mukel, which abounds in palm trees and where even today old women manufacture and sell ash salt, was well known as an important salt producing region. Significantly, the first person encountered by Citend upon her arrival was an old woman tending a fire to prepare salt. Because of this story, one suspects that economic forces may have been responsible for the chiefdom's development. Possibly, the chief at Kaleng a Mukel was able to profit from the production and sale of salt, which he could exchange for such products as the meat, beans, fish, and chickens described in the Citend myth.[32]

The full version of the myth includes, in addition to the two hunter legends, a third source consisting of interpretative or speculative material about Mwamba's wife Citend. Extracting the independently recited and recorded Mwena Ngoi account and the hypothetically reconstructed Mwamba Ciluu legend reveals that this third segment of materials contains only statements of sentiment and imagination. The poignant descriptions of Citend's unhappiness at the Luba court characterize her emotions and attitudes but provide no information about actual ceremonies such as *kuyi ku mulopwe muluba* beyond what was contained in the Mwena Ngoi story. Similarly, only the strain and fatigue rather than specific facts or events are remembered from the long trip home from the Luba court. Although the narratives mention several rivers Citend crossed, these rivers are conventionally noted in

97

Kanyok stories about journeys from the Luba empire.[33] Citend's homecoming, which seems to reflect the historical consolidation of small Basangal rulers into a larger polity, fits the hypothesized structure of the legend of Mwamba Ciluu and was therefore probably borrowed from it. Citend's marriage to Mwamba Ciluu seems to be an obvious expansion on the theme common in the hunter legends depicting the legitimization of the hunter's rule by marriage to a local woman. Citend's menstrual cycle and abdication probably symbolize the loss of power by Mwamba Ciluu to the more powerful Shimat dynasty.

Because the Citend tale integrates themes from several distinct stories, it could only have arisen as a unified myth after its components, the Ngoi and Mwamba Ciluu legends, had developed. Furthermore, this integration could have been accomplished only by narrators and listeners familiar with both hunter legends, a familiarity which assumes some sort of association between the regions of Ngoi and Kaleng a Mukel where the two legends grew up. Although both legends probably were complete by the 1600s,[34] the Citend materials probably could not have been linked with the two hunter narratives before the early 1700s when Kabw a Shimat, who ruled at Kaleng a Mukel, expanded his domain through conquest of his southeastern neighbor, Ngoi. Moving his capital to Mulundu on the savanna of Kabiji, Kabw or his immediate descendants consolidated Ngoi and Kaleng a Mukel into a confederated chiefdom. Certainly by 1750 people there would have had occasion to learn and recite the hunter legends from both areas.

A more precise dating may be proposed after examining the strong anti-Luba viewpoint of the story. In sharp contrast to the typical Luba hunter legends, which emphasize the hunters' positively valued ties of blood and ritual to the Luba people, the Citend myth accuses the Luba of punishing Mwena Ngoi, mistreating and rejecting Citend, and extracting heavy tribute from the Kanyok. Downplaying Citend's Luba heritage, the story explicitly reports that Citend was actually a woman of Kanyok descent. These details suggest the myth actually evolved in the final decades of the 1700s or in the early years of the 1800s when the Luba of Shaba regularly raided the Kanyok territory and when Ilung a Cibang was beginning to resist Luba dominance.

Labeling the Mwena Ngoi legend N, the Mwamba Ciluu legend M, and the Citend modification C, the literary evolution of the Citend myth is schematically portrayed in Figure 3.1. The discontinuous horizontal line in the N recension represents the early

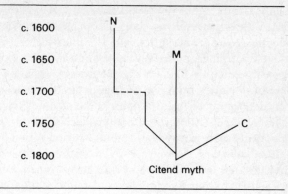

Figure 3.1 Literary evolution of the Citend myth

eighteenth-century consolidation of previously separate hunter legends.

Because the Citend myth has existed as a unified narrative since the early 1800s, it is important to study the text as a single literary composition as well as to examine its separate sources. In the villages where the Citend myth is known, the following six themes recur in every recitation: Mwena Ngoi's punishment at the Luba court, Citend's suffering at the Luba court, Citend's return to rule her own people, Citend's marriage to Mwamba Ciluu, Citend's menstruation and loss of political power, and the location of Citend's capital.

Using common techniques of literary explication, relying on current ethnographical observations, drawing on information about the main lines of Kanyok history, and accepting some of the explicit statements of the tale, one can discover a fourfold meaning embodied within the Citend myth. First, the myth serves as a symbol of ethnic unity. Secondly, it evokes the memory of suffering which the Kanyok people have experienced at the hands of outsiders. Thirdly, it expresses hostility against the Luba of Shaba, and fourthly, it justifies the political rights of the dynasty occupying the chair of the Mwena Kanyok.

The Citend myth has become a symbol of unity transcending the divisions separating families, villages, and regions among the Kanyok. Whereas the *Sitz in Leben* of every Luba hunter legend is limited to a single region, the Citend myth is known by people from almost every area. The integrative power of the Citend narrative can be explained partially because the main protagonist is both a female and a mother. Since the Kanyok trace all descent, inheritance, land rights, and political privileges according to strict patrilineal patterns, male ancestors become partisan symbols dividing one lineage from another. A man's political rights are restricted to his own patrilineage, and no one can claim rights in more than one descent group. Although special ceremonies allow a man to transfer his loyalties from one lineage to another, once integrated into the new family he loses all rights in the old one. Since maternal descent is less important from a political, economic, or social point of view, women are not symbols of lineage opposition in the same sense that men are. Moving easily from one descent group to another through the institution of marriage, women develop close ties with their husband's kin while at the same time maintaining loyalties to their own paternal family. Because women integrate separate lineages while men divide them, a female can unify, but a male would only polarize.[35]

The Citend myth also unifies by recalling the suffering the Kanyok people have experienced at the hands of outsiders. In many variants of the story, the theme of suffering is introduced even before the birth of Citend since her 'maternal grandfather' Mwena Ngoi is often depicted as a suffering hero, punished by his Luba master and bereaved by his own daughter.[36] Citend, the paragon of innocent suffering, is described as a mistreated outcast who arrives in her homeland bewildered and fatigued after her long journey.

Instead of falling into despondency because of suffering, the Citend myth reaffirms the Kanyok conviction that, in the end, suffering will be vindicated in triumph. Although Citend was mocked and berated by the Luba, who scorned her as a slave, her own people later honored her as a princess and revered her as a chief. The girl rejected by the Luba received homage from the Kanyok. Just as Citend was ultimately victorious, the Kanyok boast they have consistently expelled their foreign oppressors, no matter how powerful. Almost certainly, the Citend myth has supplied some of the hope and perseverance exhibited by the Kanyok and enabling them to defeat powerful, aggressive enemies.

Unlike the immigrant hunter legends which affirm a biological and political unity between the Luba of Shaba and the Kanyok, the Citend myth expresses sentiments of hostility towards the Luba. Kanyok troubles described in the myth were experienced at the hands of the Luba who punished Mwena Ngoi, enslaved his daughter Bond, and scorned Citend. Although recognizing that Kanyok political authority was derived from the Luba *mulopwe*, the tale of Citend bitterly details the cost of this association. By portraying

Mwena Ngoi as a mistreated visitor rather than as an office seeker at the Luba court, *kuyi ku mulopwe muluba* is depicted as an oppressive institution enabling the Luba to extract wealth from the Kanyok and to punish them arbitrarily for minor or contrived misdeeds. The payment of female slaves is described as the loss of Kanyok daughters who were forced to suffer indignities at the Luba court. The scepticism and condescension with which the Luba viewed the Kanyok rulers, even those claiming Luba ancestry and seeking investiture from a Luba *mulopwe*, are recalled perceptively in the details of Citend's life at the imperial capital, where she is said to have been treated as a slave rather than a princess. Seemingly, the Citend myth, focusing on Luba oppression, categorically rejects fundamental assumptions embodied in the immigrant hunter legends.

While the hunter legends glorify regional rulers' bonds to the Luba *mulopwe* from whose land they came, the Citend story characterizes these relations as detrimental and degrading. While the hunter legends attempt to legitimize regional rulers by describing their election and installation through the institution of *kuyi ku mulopwe muluba*, the Citend account argues that legitimacy is achieved in obtaining the blessing of local Kanyok leaders. These oppositions between the two traditions are striking enough to suggest that the Citend narrative developed not only in a context of hostility towards the Luba of Shaba, but also in an atmosphere of antipathy against regional Kanyok rulers who boasted of close ties to these eastern neighbors. The unsympathetic portrayal of Mwena Ngoi by some versions of the Citend myth may identify the object of this opprobrium.

The Citend myth serves as an instrument of support for the Shimat dynasty. Although the story is known by Kanyok people in all but the extreme southern regions of the land,[37] it is associated most closely with the descendants of Shimat who have occupied the Mwena Kanyok's chair for almost three centuries. Just as every regional chief claims descent from an immigrant Luba hunter, the Mwena Kanyok identifies Mwamba Ciluu, Citend a Mfumu, and Shimat a Citend as his ancestors. Presumably, because the Citend myth has a more powerful emotional appeal and because it has a wider geographical distribution than any regional hunter story, it is a more effective endorsement for an incumbent chief than the typical hunter narrative.

Within the myth, the most explicit statement of support for the Shimat dynasty is found in the story of Shimat's accession to power

following Citend's menstrual cycle. Arguing that Citend, as a
female, was unable to rule and asserting that Shimat, as her son, was
the legitimate heir to power, the tale sanctions the authority of any
Mwena Kanyok who claims direct descent from Shimat. The elaborate account of the feast and of Citend's inability to perform essential governmental functions probably reveals an early change of
dynasty, but it certainly supports the right of Shimat's children to
exercise political power.

The four primary meanings contained in the Citend myth are
closely interrelated in the cohesion and strength they give to the
Kanyok people. Sentiments of ethnic solidarity, faith in triumphant
suffering, feelings of xenophobic hostility, and a sense of loyalty to
an incumbent dynasty all contribute to this sense of unity. In the
process of transmission, two ordinary hunter stories were transformed into an account expressing the emotions, beliefs, and
allegiances of those people who know and retell the tale. The
content of the myth suggests that it reached mature form during a
time of severe crisis precipitated by the Luba of Shaba, a crisis
resolved by the Shimat dynasty.

Conclusions

Concealed like the original script on a palimpsest, an older legend of
Mwamba Ciluu is embedded within the Citend myth. The legend
describes Kaleng a Mukel as a typical Kanyok region, which had
been consolidated by innovative 'Luba hunter' chiefs sometime
before c. 1700 when the Shimat dynasty began to rule. After the
accession of the first Shimat ruler, the Kaleng a Mukel chiefdom he
headed emerged as the dominant power in the area. However, by
the mid-eighteenth century, serious problems threatened the
Mwena Kanyok. Subordinate chiefs from within his enlarged
sphere of influence revolted, ambitious rivals from within his own
family contested his right to rule, and aggressive neighbors from
within the Luba empire raided his territory. The Luba hunter symbols of fictive kinship, migration myths, and *kuyi ku mulopwe
muluba*, which had earlier helped individual regional chiefs in their
drive for increased authority, were of little help to a centralizing
dynasty opposing neighboring chiefs also claiming Luba forebears.
Nor could the Luba symbols assist incumbents threatened by
brothers, sons, or nephews drawing on the same sources of

extralineage support to revolt. Kanyok leaders facing Luba warriors coming to punish ungrateful subordinates similarly found the old ideology of small value.

Thus, kings at the Kanyok capital at Mulundu in the late 1700s needed the new symbology provided by the Citend myth. The inclusion of Ngoi within the Kaleng a Mukel chiefdom had allowed the people to become familiar and identify with the traditions of both Mwena Ngoi and Mwamba Ciluu. The unsettled political and military situation provided an ideal climate for the incubation of a tale stressing national unity, dynastic loyalty, triumph in adversity, and anti-Luba sentiments. Although the reign of Ilung a Cibang in the early 1800s provided the most probable setting for the Citend myth's final consolidation, the materials and the need for such a story were present already during the lifetime of Ilung's father Cibang a Ciband in the late 1700s.

The evidence for the birth of the Citend myth is admittedly inferential. No informant ever recounted stories about the evolution or modification of Kanyok traditions. Indeed, all informants considered the stories to be immutable and accurate records from the past. However, just as a lawyer can build a valid case from indirect evidence and hypothetical reconstructions, the historian can legitimately reconstruct past events which are not described directly by living informants. For a prosecutor's case three things are crucial: motive, material, and opportunity. Proof that a defendant had all three generally constitutes sufficient grounds for conviction. A parallel case can be argued for the transformation of the Mwamba legend into the Citend myth. The motive was real; members of the Shimat dynasty wanted to gain an advantage over other regional chiefs, to solidify their own hold on power, to unify the people, and to prepare for war against the Luba. The new mythical symbol met all four needs. The material was also at hand: two hunter legends which were both well known at Mulundu. The opportunity existed: the Mwamba Ciluu legend was outmoded since it glorified a defunct chiefdom while the Mwena Ngoi legend was the story of a subordinate ruler. Thus, radical modification of either story would not have aroused resistance from the people or even have threatened the legitimacy of the Mwena Kanyok so long as his genealogy remained an integral part of the narrative. Although the Mwena Kanyok or his henchmen at Mulundu may consciously or deliberately have changed the hunter legends, it is more likely that in a climate of regional rivalry, dynastic instability, military unrest, and ethnic conflict, certain elements and motifs

103

John C Yoder

gradually received more and more emphasis until a totally new story
had evolved.

Notes

1 Luc de Heusch, *Le roi ivre ou l'origine de l'état* (Paris, 1972).
2 Claude Lévi-Strauss, *The Savage Mind* (Chicago, 1966).
3 Jan Vansina, 'Comment: Traditions of Genesis', *Journal of African History*, vol. 15, no. 2 (1974), pp. 317–22.
4 For example see Theodora Bynon, *Historical Linguistics* (Cambridge, 1977), pp. 63–75.
5 Luc de Heusch, *Le roi ivre*, and Stephen Lucas, 'Baluba et Aruund: Étude comparative des structures socio-politiques' (Thèse de Troisième Cycle, École Pratique des Hautes Études: VIe Section: Sciences Economiques et Sociales) (Paris, 1968).
6 For the Kanyok, the basic chronological sequences can be determined by examining oral traditions and by comparing this information with scattered data from the following written records: Rev. S. W. Koelle, *Polyglotta Africana* (London, 1854); Joaquim Rodriques Graça, 'Expedição ao Muatayanvua', *Boletim da Sociedade de Geografia de Lisboa*, vol. 9 (1890), pp. 365–468; David Livingstone, *The Last Journals* (London, 1875) and *Missionary Travels and Researches in South Africa* (New York, 1858); Verney L. Cameron, *Across Africa* (London, 1877).
7 The following information is based on my field research among the Kanyok in 1975. For a fuller account providing more complete evidence see John C. Yoder, 'A People on the Edge of Empires: A History of the Kanyok of Central Zaire' (PhD dissertation, Northwestern University, 1977). Unless otherwise stated, all the data in this chapter are drawn from this thesis.
8 An account of the Le Marinel expedition is contained in Edgar Verdick, 'Cahier-premier séjour au Congo 1890, journal de route', Archives Verdick, Musée royale d'Afrique centrale (Tervuren, Belgium), section historique. A somewhat abbreviated description of the journey is recorded in Verdick's published journals, *Les premiers jours au Katanga (1890–1903)* (Brussels, 1952).
9 See Yoder, 'A People on the Edge of Empires', ch. 2, 'The Legend of the Luba Hunter and the Genesis of the Kanyok People', pp. 40–97.
10 D'Orjo de Marchovelette, 'Notes sur les funérailles des chefs Ilunga Kabale et Kabongo Kumwimba', *Bulletin des juridictions indigènes et du droit coutumier congolais (BJIDCC)*, vol. 18, no. 12 (1950), pp. 354–5; A. van der Nott, 'Quelques éléments historiques sur l'empire luba, son organization et sa direction', *BJIDCC*, vol. 4, no. 7 (1936), pp. 141–9; Edmond Verhulpen, *Baluba et balubaisés* (Antwerp, 1936), p. 91; W. F. P. Burton, *Luba Religion and Magic in Custom and Belief* (Brussels, 1961), p. 7.
11 Leon Duysters, 'Histoire des Aluunda', *Problèmes d'Afrique centrale*, no. 40 (1958), pp. 82–3; M. van den Byvang, 'Notice historique sur les Balunda', *Congo,* vol. 1, no. 4 (1937), pp. 426–38; Henrique Augusto Dias de Carvalho, *Ethnographia e historia tradicional dos povos da Lunda*

(Lisbon, 1890), pp. 521–665; V. W. Turner, 'A Lunda love story and its consequences', *Rhodes Livingstone Journal*, vol. 19 (1955), pp. 1–26.

12 Kalonji-Mashinda, 'La dynastie de Mutombo-Katshi et le concept du pouvoir chez les Baluba-Lubilanji' (Mémoire en histoire, UNAZA, Lubumbashi, 1973), pp. 22–3; Malengu Mubaya wa Kayemba Mpinda, 'Histoire des Bena Mulenge' (Mémoire en histoire, UNAZA, Lubumbashi, 1975), pp. 31–3; Frère Lazare M. Mpoyi, *Histoire wa Baluba* (Mbuji Mayi, 1966), pp. 34–6.

13 William Pruitt, 'An Independent People: A History of the Sala Mpasu of Zaire and Their Neighbors' (PhD dissertation, Northwestern University, 1973), pp. 47–8; Musasa Samal-Mwinkatim Dizez, 'Histoire des Kanintshini: Quelques perspectives sur l'histoire ancienne des États-Lunda' (Mémoire en histoire, UNAZA, Lubumbashi, 1974), p. 40.

14 Lucas, 'Baluba et Aruund', p. 31. See also Arnold van Gennep, *The Rites of Passage* (Chicago, 1960).

15 This information, which I collected in 1975, is also contained in a 1953 administrative report by Hugo van Beeck, 'Étude sur les notables kanyokas', Kanda Kanda, 1953, Archives du Territoire de Mwena Ditu. A copy of this document was supplied to me by William Pruit.

16 See Yoder, 'A People on the Edge of Empires', pp. 56–62. For the Luba of Shaba see D'Orjo de Marchovelette, 'Notes', pp. 355–8. For the Bena Mulenge north of the Kanyok see Malengu Mubaya, 'Histoire des Bena Mulenge', p. 81. Recent research among the Bahemb living east of the Luba capital reveals that they recall practices and ceremonies almost identical to those that the Kanyok describe (Personal communication from Pam and Tom Blakely, 15 September 1975).

17 My thesis argues that legends of Luba hunters probably arose during the time when the Kanyok population was being consolidated into regional chiefdoms. Since the Kanyok state, which emerged after regional consolidation, began to develop about 1700, regional chiefdoms and their supporting Luba hunter legends likely appeared in the 1600s. See Yoder, 'A People on the Edge of Empires', ch. 2 and appendix I, 'A Chronology of the Shimat Dynasty', pp. 396–429.

18 Information for this section is drawn from Yoder, 'A People on the Edge of Empires', ch. 3, 'The Myth of Citend and the Genesis of the Kanyok State', pp. 98–153.

19 Kanyok chronology is discussed in Yoder, 'A People on the Edge of Empires', appendix I.

20 For an account of the wars and diagrams and descriptions of the two great *ihak*, see Yoder, 'A People on the Edge of Empires', ch. 4. 'The Age of Ilung a Cibang and the Struggle for Kanyok Independence (c. 1790–1830)', pp. 154–218.

21 See Yoder, 'A People on the Edge of Empires', appendix I.

22 Harold Womersely, 'Legends and History of the Baluba', unfinished manuscript, p. 60. Womersely, a long-time missionary in Luba territory, spent many hours collecting Luba oral traditions. Thomas Q. Reefe recorded the same basic information during an interview with *Kyoni* Ngoye at Kimbokoke village, 29 March 1973. This information and Womersely's reference were given to me in a personal communication from Thomas Q. Reefe, 6 June 1976.

23 Yoder, 'A People on the Edge of Empires', appendix I.

24 Father Casteleyn, a Scheut missionary, based his writings on numerous oral interviews with Kanyok informants. His history, *Uit de Geschiedenis van de Bena Kanyoka* (Tielen Sint-Jaak, 1952), was written to aid new missionaries coming to the field. Casteleyn's history was supplied to me by Father Marcel Storme.

25 For the entire Kazadi a Mwanang legend see Yoder, 'A People on the Edge of Empires', pp. 43–4.

26 Unless specifically asked to supply details about Citend, Ngoi informants reciting the legend of the 'original' hunter ancestors, Kazadi a Mwanang and Kazadi a Kazadi, do not refer to Citend. They see the Citend story as an aside or as a separate episode which is not essential to their basic legend.

27 See Yoder, 'A People on the Edge of Empires', ch. 2.

28 The best description of this ceremony is contained in Hugo van Beeck, 'Étude sur les notables kanyokas'. The current Mwena Kanyok Kabamba Kabuluk gave me a very similar account.

29 Modern informants say the chief of Kaleng a Mukel lived near the present-day airstrip at Luputa.

30 Oral tradition from Kabiji supports this hypothesis. The people at Kabiji say the earliest members of the Shimat dynasty did not control the Kabiji region. If that is correct, the chiefs who ruled Kaleng a Mukel would have had no power over Kabiji.

31 These population estimates are based on current demographic statistics which place the density of Kanyok population at about three inhabitants per square kilometer. Léon de Saint Moulin, *Carte de la densité de la population du Zaïre établie pour le Service du Plan de la Présidence* (Kinshasa, 1973). Reprinted in Léon de Saint Moulin, s.j., 'La répartition de la population du Zaïre en 1970', *Cultures et Développement*, vol. 2 (1974). There is no reason to assume the population in earlier times was significantly denser than today.

32 The ability of a chief to dominate an important article of trade frequently has been cited by historians to explain tendencies toward political centralization and state formation. The ancient empires of Ghana, Mali, and Songhai were built on their monopolies of salt and gold. In the southern savanna area, Thomas Reefe has pointed out that Luba state arose near important deposits of salt: Thomas Q. Reefe, 'A History of the Luba Empire to c. 1885' (PhD dissertation, University of California, Berkeley, 1975), pp. 160–2.

33 For example, when describing the Luba invasions in the late 1700s and early 1800s, the Kanyok always mention that the warriors crossed the Luembe and Lubilash rivers.

34 Since the Shimat dynasty arose in the early 1700s, the Mwamba Ciluu tale justifying the Kaleng a Mukel rulers must have been fully developed before that time. Because the region of Ngoi is unanimously regarded as the first Kanyok area to have been consolidated, the Ngoi hunter legend would have arisen no later than 1600. More important than dates, however, are the sequential relationships.

35 While these remarks are based on modern observations, there is no reason to believe that the Kanyok have been matrilineal in the last several

hundred years described in this essay. Kanyok oral history and folk tales consistently reflect a patrilineal society.

36 In stories told in the region of Ngoi, the original setting for the legend of Mwena Ngoi Kazadi a Mwanang, the theme of Mwena Ngoi's suffering is not prominent. The emphasis on punishment and suffering apparently was introduced by storytellers outside the region of Ngoi.

37 For a table of the geographical distribution of themes and variants from the Citend myth see Yoder, 'A People on the Edge of Empires', p. 112.

4. A Propos the Drunken King: Cosmology and History

ROBERT E SCHECTER

Introduction

The recent evaluation of state origin traditions from the southern savanna by Luc de Heusch once again highlights scholarly disagreement about the historicity of these famous tales, once taken as straightforward descriptions of the African past. De Heusch represents a view common to structuralist anthropologists, and recently shared by some historians, that the various versions of a single stereotyped story, best known as the Lunda saga of Cibinda Ilunga and in Luba accounts of the adventures of Nkongolo and Mbidi Kiluwe/Kalala Ilunga, are essentially myths, purely symbolic statements of local world views clothed in pseudohistorical dress. Similarities between different versions of the tale, de Heusch says, may well indicate cultural borrowing, or historical contact, between peoples who recite it, but no variant, whatever its purport, really recounts the genesis of a particular state.[1]

Yet many historians, and some anthropologists, incline toward Jan Vansina's approach: they renounce unsophisticated literal readings of these tales but treat the traditions as representations, however distorted to the western eye, of real historical events and processes. Joseph Miller, in the best recent example of this type of analysis, traces the development and diffusion of Lunda political styles over a very wide area between the Kasai and western Angola in a new reading of the Lunda, Cokwe, and Imbangala versions of the story.[2]

Still other interested parties, although deeply impressed like Luc de Heusch with the undoubted cosmological significance of the tales, nonetheless reserve final judgment. Wyatt MacGaffey, for one, asks in a friendly but firm way for proof of historicity. He notes that while the traditions may well reflect real events or processes, historical interpretations have typically not sufficiently confirmed inferences drawn from the tales alone with other kinds of evidence.

He notes, in this regard, that we are not yet able to establish clear enough structural similarities between states in the region to conclude, as the traditions argue, that sometime in the remote past one polity influenced greatly the growth of another. For him, ethnographic data of this sort might verify the narrative traditions.

Professor MacGaffey also feels that we do not understand the local world views well enough to be able to distinguish historical descriptions from narratives fabricated to articulate cosmological universals. For example, the only reason that he can see why Kongo traditions stress an east to west migration of Kongo founding heroes is that such a movement follows the passage of the sun, thus conforming to the tendency in Kongo ritual and literature to contrast opposed concepts like night and day, life and death, masculine (east) and feminine (west), and so forth.

Luba versions of the state origin tale also seem mythical to him because they are so similar to those of the Kongo. In both, a founding hunter crosses a great river, marries a local princess, sweeps away the old wicked rulers, and founds the new kingdom. The only real difference between the two stories is that the Kongo variant highlights and justifies a matrilineal descent system, while the Luba account does the same for a patrilineal one. Despite these doubts, however, and without endorsing structuralist interpretations to the exclusion of historical analysis, MacGaffey is willing to be convinced that the state origin traditions are more historical than Luc de Heusch would allow.[3]

The surest way to meet this challenge is, as MacGaffey says, to seek other kinds of evidence to confirm inferences drawn up to now from these national epics alone. This is an exercise which, if there is anything to the notion that the tales are not merely myths, will also reveal the historiographical logic of the traditions. Miller, in his work on Lunda-connected versions of the story, has explicitly defined the historical meanings of several recurrent images, and his conclusions here echo the less explicit deductions of other scholars working elsewhere in the savanna.[4] But although these historians, especially Miller, provide some independent evidence that certain symbols and metaphors refer to specific kinds and even instances of events or processes, the generality of the essential historicity of the tales still needs further and more systematic confirmation. I certainly cannot provide general confirmation here, but I can show fairly conclusively that a Kanongesha derivative of the state origin tale, one framed by themes and images common to all of the presumably archetypal variants of the pan-savanna myth, refers to historical events among the Southern Lunda. My conclusions suggest that the data in these traditions are not ahistorical simply because they are expressed in stereotyped form, that traditional historical literature may only twist the facts—rather than fabricating them out of whole cloth—in order to make the past conform more closely to accepted cosmological categories, and that the effort needed to evaluate historically other versions of the tale may also pay off with some reasonable measure of historical truth. I begin with a brief sketch of features common to variant narratives from the Luba and Lunda areas, the apparently archetypal versions upon which Luc de Heusch concentrates, pass on to a presentation and analysis of the Southern Lunda account, and then conclude with evidence about its historicity of the sort that MacGaffey presumably would welcome.

Features of Lunda State Origin Traditions

These traditions develop a theme of socio-political change from barbaric to civilized in two very similar but somewhat differently detailed acts. The following summary, in the interest of economy, is highly selective of the many and diverse images used in variant versions to make what often appear to be the same general points.[5] The opening act presents a very troubled society. Among the Lunda, two besotted problem sons (Cinguli and Cinyama) kill their kingly father (variously Iyala, Mwaku, Kondi, or combinations of these names) after assuming that he used palm wine rather than water to soften his basket-weaving materials. They then institute a reign of terror in order to wrest control of the polity from their sister (Lweji), upon whom the old king conferred the succession with his dying breath because she had helped him in his distress. The Luba version begins by dealing at length with the reign of Nkongolo, a similarly troubled time dominated by a loud, tyrannical leader, careless of his peoples' lives, who is even married to his own sister.

The second act in both cases opens with the arrival of foreign hunters, the Luba prince Cibinda Ilunga in Lunda, and Mbidi Kiluwe, a nobleman from somewhere to the east, in Lubaland. These hunters introduce new and more civilized ways to their hosts, but they are especially distinguished from Nkongolo and his Lunda analogues by a personal refinement which extends to a refusal to eat and drink in public. The appealing Cibinda eventually weds Lweji, takes power, and defeats her brothers, who flee. Lweji proves

110

sterile, but with a woman whom she gives him Cibinda sires the Mwaant Yaav dynasty that subsequently ruled the mature Lunda empire. Mbidi Kiluwe in Luba fails to reform Nkongolo and departs, but his son Kalala Ilunga, born of one of the boorish king's sisters, escapes a pit trap set by the tyrant, kills him, and establishes the new order there.

Contrasting Interpretations

For Luc de Heusch, Nkongolo is a fictional character whose ways represent traits common to the profane, 'natural' order of things in Luba cosmology. He is the cruel, loud, drunken, and incestuous leader of a politically, socially, and materially backward people. His eating and drinking in public highlight the absence of attributes possessed by true kings. By contrast, Mbidi Kiluwe/Kalala Ilunga is the personification of the 'cultured' order, a reserved, exogamous, bow-hunting thrower of spears who eats and drinks in ritual seclusion, as befits a sacred king. Other images in the tradition further detail the contrast de Heusch perceives. Nkongolo's raucous open mouth parallels his frequent association in the tale with holes and caves, especially with the trap he sets for Kalala, the challenge of culture. All of these openings can be identified in Luba thought, like Nkongolo's incest, with death and sterility. Kalala, on the other hand, is associated with the hard, visible, pointed weapon, a mark of the fabricated and advanced cultural order. This symbol of virility, like the arrows Kalala uses in other contexts, is the means by which this close-mouthed hunter detects the hidden pit, eliminates the personification of the old order, and establishes the new one with his local wife.

De Heusch interprets the Lunda tale in much the same way, and for him it reveals essentially the same world view. Most of the characters and other symbols are clearly analogous to the Luba ones. Lweji's sterility, for example, stands as a metaphor for the deadening sameness of society without culture and is the equivalent of Nkongolo's incestuous relations with his sister. Cibinda's victory, associated in the story with what appear to be Lunda symbols for fecundity, civilization, and other cultural values, is a reprise of Kalala's. In this fashion, then, and using proverbs, conjectured color symbolism, and other cultural data to support his conclusions, de Heusch decides that the tales are not historical chronicles at all but rather symbolic dramas which express fundamental values in the idiom of traditional historiography. The conflict between the virtuous hunter and the backward old leader does not reflect a real power struggle. It is part of a philosophical discourse. Any differences between versions of the tale told in one region or another can be explained by cultural variations between the societies in which it is told, or to the variety of ways in which the same points can be symbolized.[6]

Miller, who is looking for history, sees things quite differently. For him, the actors in the tale represent political titles and groups which actually existed, and the plot of the story reflects their historic interaction. Thus, Iyala Mwaku and his 'children' were respectively the senior and subordinate political authorities, the titled heads of lineages, which constituted the earliest remembered Lunda polity. The upshot of their conflict mirrors a process of historic realignment between the forces they represented. Similarly, Cibinda's life and works represent material and political innovations subsequently introduced from Lubaland, probably by conquest, which were combined with the revised old regime to form the basis of the present Lunda state. He traces some of the results of this sort of interaction among the Lunda in the Imbangala kingdom of Kasanje (Cinguli did not 'die', but the title drifted west and was eventually established there in the Kwango river valley), as well as in various Cokwe and Mbundu based polities which lay before the advance of Lunda political culture across the savanna.

Although Miller does not try to define an explicit Lunda historiography, his inferences rest in great part on assumptions that constitute one. He assumes that some of the symbols in the tale are part of a traditional system of notation used for recording historical events. The names of its characters therefore represent historical political authorities not only because some of them still exist as political titles in Lunda and elsewhere in the savanna, but also because it is commonplace in the historiography of the region to refer to whole groups by the perpetual title at their head and to rank or relate title systems by analogy with the biological family. Similarly, the palm wine which set off the conflict in this 'political' family appears to be a recurrent symbol of the political authority which was the real bone of contention. Finally, Miller infers a strong Luba influence on the Lunda at a particular period because marriages like the one between Cibinda and Lweji are one way in which historical accounts from elsewhere in the region record permanent alliances and conquests, events which in any case usually involve intermarriage at all levels.[7]

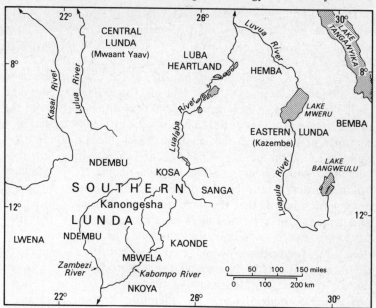

Map 4.1 The Lunda in the southern savannas, *c*. 1800

Although each of these interpretations is appealing in its own way, it would be unreasonable yet to accept either of them exclusively or with finality. Luc de Heusch, in order to get on with his cosmological analysis, has been much too cursory in his dismissal of the possibly historical aspects of the tales. Miller's hypothesis about the Luba-Lunda connection, on the other hand, still needs more confirmation from nontestimonial evidence and from a systematic collection and evaluation of historical looking symbols and metaphors in traditional literature. The following discussion of a Southern Lunda variant of the state origin tale reconciles some of the apparent differences between the two by suggesting that both scholars really only stress different aspects of the same truth about the traditions, namely that peoples in the savanna do indeed share a system of historical notation, and that this system is based in part on the images provided by equally shared cosmological categories.

A Southern Lunda Version of the Tale

Various versions of the pan-savanna tradition come from people attached to the Kanongesha, one of a number of senior titleholders

of the Ndembu, who reside near the source of the Zambezi. The
sum of the evidence shows that the early Kanongesha led one of
several statebuilding endeavors that developed on the southern
fringes of Lunda imperial expansion in the mid-eighteenth century.
Like the better known, related founders of the Luapula Kazembe
dynasty, the Kanongesha used typically Lunda institutions and
methods to create a new center of political diffusion beyond the
direct influence of the central Lunda state. The tradition cited here
purports first to sketch the situation which the would-be state-
builders found on the upper Zambezi and then to trace how they
combined with the pre-existing Mbwela people to form a new
political order. It must be noted that in doing this local historians
employ for a second time the same stereotyped formula, with form
and content similar to the Lunda tales discussed above, that they
have earlier used to describe the foundation of the 'mother' kingdom itself. The testimony comes from people of the Kanongesha's
subordinate titleholder Nsanganyi, the self-proclaimed and unanimously recognized descendants of those who lived in the area
before the Kanongesha and his Ndembu followers, including a
certain Mukangala, arrived. Versions told by descendants of the
Lunda immigrants are virtually the same save that these stress more
the defects of the older Mbwela order.[8]

The only one who lived here was Nsanganyi. After many years, Chifwanakeni [Kanongesha] came. Kanongesha was only a nick-name. He
had heard about the Mbwela, and their area, and especially about
Nsanganyi. First, Kanongesha sent his war leader, Chibwakata Kambanji, who passed this way and went to Kasanjiko. Kanongesha was
suspicious of the foolish Mbwela, so he sent his surveyor Ifota Nylamba
to follow Kambanji. Ikelengi was Kalula, who took away the chief's
mats.

So when everybody had arrived, they found old Nsanganyi living here.
It annoyed Chifwanakeni a great deal, so he began a bloody war. Nsanganyi was terribly afraid, and hid in a cave. He had thought that they
would live in peace. Most of Nsanganyi's people were killed.

There was a man of Musokantanda called Chikanga Kanakamweni.
Chikanga said: 'Chifwanakeni has killed everyone, so who is living in
that place near the river from which the smoke is rising?' The smoke was
coming from the cave in which Nsanganyi had hid. Chikanga was a
hunter. He went to the spot and reached the bank of the Lunga river.
Chikanga called to the ferryman, but Nsanganyi refused to have
Chikanga brought across. He said: 'You are the people who have killed
all of my relatives.' And Chikanga answered: 'I won't kill you.' So
Nsanganyi agreed to have him ferried across.

They greeted one another, and Chikanga said: 'I am a hunter come
from Luunda [the Lunda Center]. I have not come to kill you.' As he

looked around, Chikanga saw plenty of meat, fish, and honey. The only subordinate who had remained with Nsanganyi was Kabonzubonzu. Nsanganyi roasted meat on the fire and he ate, grossly and in public. There was no sign that Nsanganyi was the chief. Nsanganyi saw that the people who had come with Chikanga began to build a temporary house for him. The main foods were maize and millet, but they had a great deal of neither. They prepared porridge for Chikanga and put it into the temporary hut. Then, Chikanga entered. After a short while, he came out. His people then went into the house while Chikanga and Nsanganyi sat together conversing. They came out and snapped fingers to their chief. Chikanga then said to Nsanganyi: 'You are important, but you are not respected as a chief. When eating, all of you shout. Who, then, is the chief? Look here, Nsanganyi, you fool. My people have snapped fingers to me. This shows that I am a chief, and well respected.'

Chikanga spent the night at Nsanganyi's village. Next morning, he said: 'Your drawback is that you are not respected as a chief. When you go hunting, you all carry loads. So let me take you to Chifwanakeni.' Nsanganyi refused, thinking that he would be killed. But Chikanga forced Nsanganyi to go with him. Nsanganyi and his people all accompanied Chikanga, and they carried tribute to Kanongesha. Nsanganyi also carried a load.

Nsanganyi and his people gave the tribute to Kanongesha—honey, meat, and fish. They spent the night at the capital. Next morning, Chifwanakeni called Chikanga and said: 'I thank you very much for the visit, and I thank you again for bringing Nsanganyi. I will not harm him.' They remained at the capital for five days. Then Chifwanakeni told Nsanganyi: 'I will send my son to stay with you. You must stop carrying loads in the presence of your people.' Chifwanakeni told Mukangala to accompany Nsanganyi and live with him. 'Whatever Nsanganyi gives you as tribute, eat some and send the rest to me.' Mukangala agreed, and they both left. Chifwanakeni remained with Kalula, Ifota, and Nyakaseya in his capital.

The testimony thus concludes, having established the political relationships between the Kanongesha (king), Mukangala (his local deputy) and Nsanganyi (the tribute-paying Mbwela people). But the same informant, like many others, subsequently makes two further points about the Kanongesha-Mukangala-Nsanganyi link. The first is that Mukangala married a woman from Nsanganyi's family named Nyachintonga. Together they bore Nkatu, known as 'the child of the chief born while his father ruled' (*mwana wuta*, lit.: 'child of the bow'). The second point is that when the Kanongesha charged Mukangala with watching over Nsanganyi, he also told the Mbwela leader that he would thereafter be responsible for placing the bracelet of office upon the wrists of successive Mukangala.

Like Luba and Lunda tales of state origins, this tradition frames a series of contrasts between old and new, between 'primitive' and 'advanced' kinds of polity. Nsanganyi, the archetype of the 'natural' order in this essentially biased political philosophy, is the analogue of the boorish Nkongolo and some of the early Lunda rulers. Like them, he eats in public. He also carries loads, just as ordinary people do. Other variants of the story choose alternate means to stress the same point: Nsanganyi drank with the common people, or they did not defer to him in conversation. But the point is always the same, and in each case it represents an especially vivid and compelling example of the Ndembu traditions' general emphasis on Mbwela primitiveness. They point out in other contexts, for example, that the Mbwela lived in rude bark shelters, or in caves, and even that they were nomadic ('like the bushmen'), nonagricultural bow hunters who nonetheless ate meat raw, as if without knowledge of fire, and subsisted on wild fruit rather than on millet or cassava, the present cultivated staples. Politically, the image is as bleak: The Mbwela had no 'real' chiefs, with the result that these 'short tempered people' fought constantly with one another. If some views (especially those from the Nsanganyi group) admit that the Mbwela had leaders of a sort, most stress that such notables did not get tribute or respect from their people in the way the Kanongesha did. Chikanga, of course, is the measure of Mbidi, Kalala, and Cibinda Ilunga: a foreign hunter whose attitudes and attributes epitomize the new order which he helps to establish. He is a leader who eats and drinks in seclusion while his subordinates respectfully snap fingers after ministering to his special needs.

The story, however, is much more than a general contrast between 'natural' and 'cultural' orders, for the episode at the Kanongesha's capital, like Luba and Lunda accounts about what happened after the triumphs of Kalala and Cibinda, purports to show how the hierarchical ideals of the newcomers acquired the particular objective reality that exists today on the Zambezi. The Kanongesha directs Nsanganyi to pay regular tribute to a local governor, the Mukangala, who will then forward a portion to the Kanongesha himself. Today, this is the way Nsanganyi pays tribute. Nsanganyi is also obliged to give a woman of his lineage, a sister, to Mukangala, and she bears Mwana Wuta. Today, successors to the Mwana Wuta title are 'sons' of Mukangala and 'nephews' of Nsanganyi. In return for all this, but especially because he is the 'owner of the land', Nsanganyi gains a special ritual title, *chivwikankanu* ('he who dresses the chief with the bracelet of office'), responsible for installing future Mukangala. And in our time, the Nsanganyi installs the new Mukangala. This tradition, then, like Luba and Lunda

116

versions, offers both an explanation of and a justification for the
establishment of part of a new polity. Other Kanongesha traditions
detail similar linkages between the senior Kanongesha titleholder
and various other pre-existing and intrusive lineage heads. But the
question at hand is whether all of this really happened, or whether
the tale is only an etiological myth which employs the cosmological
images familiar from stories told elsewhere in the savanna.

Stereotypes and History

In looking to see if the tale reflects historical events, it ought first to
be emphasized that the data are not *ipso facto* ahistorical simply
because they are expressed in a clichéd form. The important distinction between various versions of the tale in this regard is that the
names of the characters, and of the places associated with them, are
in each case unique. True, Kalala, Cibinda, and Chikanga are all
hunters—the ideal men in regional culture and cosmology—and
the state 'founder' may often appear in this guise because the hunter
is a traveler who is therefore frequently an outsider who can sire a
dynasty that will appear to be 'above' local lineage politics. But each
of these hunters has his own name, or title, and each stems from and
operates within a different and distinctive cultural and political
setting: Cibinda Ilunga goes from Luba to Lunda; Mbidi Kiluwe
comes to Luba from somewhere to the east (some traditions suggest
that he was Hemba); and Chikanga stems from Lunda (after
Cibinda's triumph) and arrives on the Zambezi to work change
among the Mbwela.

These differences between versions of the tale do not prove that
each refers to real events any more than analogous distinctions
between stories about George Washington, Bolivar, and Frederick
the Great confirm the historicity of popular western traditions
which portray these heroes as thoroughly virtuous 'fathers' of their
nations. But it is clear that there exists in both central African and
European cultures a stereotyped shorthand used to express in
ideologically appropriate terms occurrences which are perceived to
be unique instances of a particular class of events. As for Washington, Bolivar, and Frederick, the similarity of the clichés used to
describe their lives (which were, in rough outline, similar), cannot
obscure their historical existence, or the reality of the separate
state-building processes which each represents, because we have
reliable evidence, apart from oral traditions, to confirm this. Here,

popular images, with cosmological import, reflect the truth, although in a limited way.

The same is true of Central African historiography, where at least some clichés with cosmological significance describe historically verifiable events. Kanongesha traditions, for example, use a cliché involving a concealed pit to indicate a conflict over political seniority between the established leader of the group, who sets the trap, and a pretender, who tries to avoid it. For at least one of the civil conflicts to which the image appears to refer, I have both written and oral genealogical evidence to show that a power struggle took place between the titleholding antagonists in the story. Another instance of the same cliché describes the genesis of a dynastic schism in the Kanongesha royal lineage which still informs local politics at least a century and a half later.

It may thus be true that the concealed pits in Luba and Central Lunda state origin traditions also refer to historical power struggles. Similarly, Miller has supported convincingly with other evidence his notion that epic tales of river crossings, replete with symbols of cosmological import, refer to significant social and political changes in a group of lineages during the course of a prolonged movement of Lunda titles toward Kasanje.[9] Indeed, events larger than life confounded the Kanongesha's own storied crossing of the river that now marks the political boundary between his domain and that of the Central Lunda, while the Luapula Kazembe's spirit-plagued crossing of the Lualaba, the original boundary between him and the Mwaant Yaav, is yet another indication that the clichéd river crossing is not ahistorical simply because of the mythic vestments which fix its historical importance. And we need translate only one among the multitude of perpetual political titles in the region—Mwaant Yaav, 'Lord of the Vipers'—to suggest that characters with cosmologically significant names once really walked the earth. Clichéd tales, then, which may well reveal a people's world view, can also refer to historical events. Certainly the Southern Lunda version of the state origin story which I collected appears to do this.

Evidence about Kanongesha History

It is easier at this stage of research in savanna history generally to infer the essential historicity of the Ndembu tradition than the truth of Luba or Lunda versions of the stereotype. This is so partly because on the Zambezi a certain cultural distance still separates

the indigenous Mbwela and intrusive Lunda elements which combined to form the present Kanongesha polity. If it is not yet clear
that the Central Lunda state similarly combines an older local
system with newer borrowed Luba institutions, the distinction between incompletely assimilated elements of the Ndembu-Mbwela
combination under the Kanongesha is still visible in aspects of the
local culture, in the structure of the polity itself, in popular notions,
and in the import of many other oral traditions, both local and
foreign. No one of these features taken alone could be totally

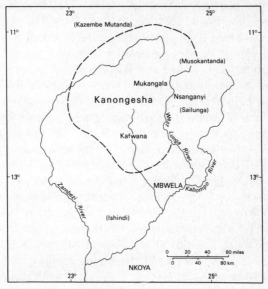

Map 4.2 Kanongesha, *c.* 1900

convincing, but together they conform to the purport of the Nsanganyi tradition to show that it reflects one instance of a widespread
process of political change on the periphery of the Central Lunda
kingdom.

Although sharp cultural contrasts no longer distinguish putative
Mbwela descendants from higher ranking Ndembu in the
Kanongesha area, an important local variation in dialect suggests
that the population as a whole may descend from a combination of
earlier residents and later arrivals. People in the southern part of the
area, where most of those self-proclaimed or alleged Mbwela
descendants live, regularly employ labial-dental 'v' phonemes in
place of the bilabial 'b' common in the north. This usage is shared by

119

Lwena and by various Nkoya groups, the latter including a section identified as 'Mbwela', all of whom reside immediately farther south or west. The linguistic difference may have arisen as a result of late nineteenth and twentieth century population movements bringing southerners into the northern area (for which there is some evidence), but another explanation would be that Ndembu who speak in this fashion are descendants of Mbwela incompletely assimilated by settlers (including the Kanongesha at some point) from the Lunda area. The basic linguistic work still has to be done in order to clarify whether or not the Ndembu language on the Zambezi represents a combination of pre-existing Mbwela with newcomers from the Lunda area.

But local traditions not parts of the general savanna myth support the hypothesis of Lunda immigration that the story of Nsanganyi proposes. Nsanganyi historians tell of the title's progressive retreat southward away from the encroachment of Ndembu leaders in the generation before their ancestors finally came to terms with the Kanongesha. Accounts about the same period from other Kanongesha subordinates trace a series of Ndembu contacts with the Mbwela which included demands for tribute and several battles. In addition, the traditions identify a number of marriages between Mbwela women and Ndembu titleholders, some of which are reflected today, as in the Nsanganyi-Mukangala case, by perpetual relations between lineage heads descended from the original couple. All informants, moreover, feel that local lineages known as Nkoya are today the closest relatives of the pre-Lunda peoples whom the early Kanongesha 'scattered like grains of millet'. They name a number of extant Nkoya titleholders when identifying the authorities who ruled the Mbwela before the Ndembu arrived. Indeed, the cave near the Lunga river in which Nsanganyi is said to have hidden is called Kahari, and this is the name of the Nkoya dynastic titleholder alleged by Nsanganyi and others to have been the senior Mbwela chief. There is a stream in the area called Kambwela, so named, people say, simply because the Mbwela used to live there. Finally, traditions from segments of the polity which seem to have been Ndembu from the first preserve accounts of similar linkages to the early Kanongesha in the same era. Their confirmation helps to place the Mbwela cases within a wider and more believable context of political engineering and change.[10]

Foreign traditions and other evidence from elsewhere support these conjectures by indicating that events on the Zambezi were parts of a wide-ranging and long-term process of mingling between

Lunda and peoples indigenous to the whole area south of the original Lunda kingdom. Lwena histories representing the earliest stage of the process, for example, have it that their senior titleholders stem from Lunda immigrants who fled from Cibinda with Cinyama, Cinguli's 'brother', and gained control of Mbwela lineages south and west of the present Kanongesha area. C. M. N. White, who has provided most of our knowledge of the Lwena, accounts for the differences between them and the Ndembu by suggesting that the Lunda newcomers among the latter were greater in number than among the former, and that this has obscured the Mbwela component and highlighted the Lunda ones in Ndembu culture.[11]

Traditions from north of the Zambezi—Lunda, Ndembu, Cokwe, Sanga, Luapula Lunda—trace the same kind of mingling, but sometimes with greater temporal dimension.[12] It would have begun, as in Lwena accounts, when Lunda who left the center during the Cibindan era joined with various outlying people, including the 'Mbwela' and Sanga who lived between the Kasai and the Lualaba. Appropriately, Ndembu and Sanga titleholders in that area join with the Kanongesha in claiming either to have originated in Lunda, or to have become part of the Lunda system when it expanded later, as we know it did, under the Mwaant Yaav.[13] It seems likely, then, that so far as the purport of the tradition is concerned, the Ndembu between the Kasai and the Lualaba, the area in which the early Kanongesha first appears convincingly in the historical record, were products of Lunda-Mbwela mixing even before the Kanongesha reached the Zambezi.

Luapula Kazembe history is actually the best documented example of how Lunda-inspired state-builders arose on this southern frontier of the Lunda kingdom. The Kazembe traditions, paralleling Lunda and Ndembu ones, say that the dynastic founder was a Lunda notable who fled Cibinda and married among the Kosa (today a mixed Ndembu-Lunda-Sanga group) near the Lualaba. Later, when the area came under Lunda control, the Kazembe moved on to the east and created the well-known state among the Bemba-speaking peoples of the Luapula.[14] That the ruling dynasty there is in fact an exotic import from the Lunda-influenced area to the west cannot be seriously questioned. Pinto, a visitor in 1799 at the Kazembe's capital, heard that the dynasty had come from the Lualaba about sixty years earlier. It is also reported that they then spoke some Lunda, a language yet found in the praise names of an aristocracy which otherwise discourses in the local Bemba.[15] The fact that some Kazembe praises also employ an apparently archaic form of Luba further suggests that the dynasty was founded by Lunda influenced by the Luba-related Sanga people (thus forming the Kosa) on the Lualaba.[16] Indeed, members of the Kazembe's Lunda aristocracy, who are quite distinct from various subject peoples on the Luapula, often visit the Lualaba and marry other Kosa, from whom they are now separated geographically by less closely related groups.[17] Kazembe history dovetails with Kanongesha and some other accounts about how both Lunda-inspired dynasties formed in the Lualaba area during the same era, and parallels the kind of political growth traced in Kanongesha traditions about the Zambezi.

But one can also see the exotic nature of the Kanongesha and related dynasties in a feature of their political systems created expressly to regulate relations between the Lunda newcomers and the older residents. This is the important post involving the installation of high Lunda political authorities. Nsanganyi, as we have seen, is the *chivwikankanu* of the Mukangala, the Kanongesha's local governor. Similarly, Kafwana, head of another lineage of putative Mbwela descent, is *chivwikankanu* of the Kanongesha himself. And people agree that the two 'Mbwela' leaders hold these positions because as descendants of the original 'owners' of the land they are best able through rituals involving the bracelet of high office to ensure the health and wellbeing of the whole community. Other Ndembu lineage heads have *chivwikankanu* of their own, but each of these installers heads only a fraction within the lineage, not a different lineage, and none of them is felt to have the power of an original 'owner' over a newcomer. The distinguishing attributes of the special *chivwikankanu* seem to point to the exotic character of those officials.

The special relationship in the Kanongesha polity between new and old populations, not at all uncommon in sub-saharan Africa, appears in fact to reflect what is emerging as a pan-Lunda political approach to subject populations. On the Luapula, the Kazembes' *kaninganankanu* (installer) is Mwinempanda, descendant of a local leader conquered while the dynasty was settled for a time near the Lualaba. Subordinates native to the Luapula hold other appropriate ritual positions.[18] Sailunga, the *chivwikankanu* of the Musokantanda, another Lunda-derived dynastic head living east of the Kanongesha, is said to be a descendant of the Mbwela who once controlled that area.[19] As yet inconclusive reports about the Ndembu senior titleholders Kazembe Mutanda (just north of the

Kanongesha) and Ishindi (to the southwest) have it that the ritual installers of both of these leaders are descendants of earlier residents.[20] The best known example of all of this, finally, would have been in the Lunda kingdom itself. There, the *tubungu,* conceived of as the original owners of the core area, and probably representing the political authorities subordinated to a new layer of political titles, play crucial roles in the installation of the Mwaant Yaav.[21] This mechanism of the Lunda ritual system certainly seems to say a great deal about their world view, as Luc de Heusch maintains, but the linkages which it continues to sustain are no less historical in origin for that.

Conclusions

Evidence from Kanongesha history shows that one variant of the stereotyped state origin tale of the southern savannas refers in some detail to historical events, and that certain of the cosmological universals in the tale form part of the historiographical shorthand. The Ndembu Chikanga is not the *deus ex machina* of an etiological myth, but rather an ideologically satisfying representation of the new political order established by the Kanongesha among some of the Mbwela of the upper Zambezi. Nsanganyi is not merely a personification of a deficient 'natural' order, but also the name of a lineage head who was drawn into the new polity after the general Lunda fashion. If Chikanga is portrayed like Kalala and Cibinda as a virtuous hunter who enjoys the respect due a sacred ruler, and Nsanganyi plays the familiar role of boorish leader ignorant of these proprieties, their similarity to other figures in the traditions only shows that history is often made to conform to appropriate cosmological categories. The results, of course, will often distort the truth, and sometimes what looks like history will be totally false. A whole class of etiological myths in the oral literature of central Africa, perhaps including the Kongo story of their own migration, falls into this category. But in a case like that of the Ndembu, the sum of the evidence indicates that the tradition does mirror seminal events. It clearly notes the historic titles of the groups involved. It discusses the linkages which helped to form the new polity. It provides enough data to allow us to infer the dynamics of these linkages. Cosmological images are set in a particular sociopolitical context and within a verifiable historical continuum. Doubts about the historicity of similar state origin tales may be likewise dispelled by further research. MacGaffey's unease about stereotypes may be allayed, and the historical 'residue' that de Heusch allows to Luba, Lunda, and some other versions of the tale may well prove greater than he thinks.

Notes

1 Luc de Heusch, *Le roi ivre ou l'origine de l'état* (Paris, 1972).

2 Joseph C. Miller, *Kings and Kinsmen—Early Mbundu States in Angola* (Oxford, 1976).

3 Wyatt MacGaffey, 'Oral Traditions in Central Africa', *International Journal of African Historical Studies*, vol. 8, no. 3 (1974), pp. 417–26.

4 Miller, *Kings and Kinsmen,* chs. 1, 5, 6.

5 In *Le roi ivre*, de Heusch summarizes most published versions of these tales. For the original texts, see the references in his bibliography and the appropriate citations in Jan Vansina, *Kingdoms of the Savanna* (Madison, 1966), esp. pp. 71–5. For some unpublished versions of the Lunda story see note 12 below.

6 De Heusch elaborates his interpretation of the Lunda story in 'What Shall we do with the Drunken King', *Africa*, vol. 45, no. 4 (1975), pp. 363–72.

7 Miller, *Kings and Kinsmen*, chs. 1, 5, 6.

8 Testimony of Nswana Kawewa, 13 February 1969, in Robert E. Schecter, 'History and Historiography on a Frontier of Lunda Expansion—The Origins and Early Development of the Kanongesha' (PhD dissertation, University of Wisconsin, Madison, 1976).

9 Miller, *Kings and Kinsmen*, ch. 6.

10 Schechter, 'History and Historiography', chs. 5–8.

11 C. M. N. White, 'The Balovale Peoples and their Historical Background', *Rhodes-Livingstone Journal*, vol. 8 (1949), pp. 28–30, 36; Vaughan Jones, 'The Tribes of the Balovale District and the History of Their Chieftaincies' (1936), Northwestern Province History File, Institute for African Studies, University of Zambia; Merran McCulloch, *The Southern Lunda and Related Peoples* (Ethnographic Survey of Africa. West Central Africa, Part I) (London, 1951), pp. 99–100, and references. Available on the Luvale ('Lwena') since the completion of this essay: Robert J. Papstein, 'The Upper Zambezi: A History of the Luvale People, 1000–1900' (PhD dissertation, University of California, Los Angeles, 1978).

12 For Sanga and Ndembu see: F. Grevisse, 'Notes ethnographiques relatives à quelques populations autochtones du Haut-Katanga industriel', *Bulletin du centre d'étude des problèmes sociaux indigènes,* no. 32 (1956), pp. 100–2; Dom Hadelin Roland, 'Résumé de l'histoire ancienne du Katanga', *Bulletin du centre d'étude des problèmes sociaux indigènes*, no. 61 (1963), pp. 24–32. For Lunda views see: D. Biebuyck, 'Fondements de l'organization politique des Luunda du Mwaantayaav en territoire de Katanga', *Zaïre*, vol. 11, no. 9 (1957), p. 802; B. Crine-Mavar, 'Histoire traditionelle du Shaba', *Cultures au Zaïre et en Afrique*, no. 4 (1974), p. 71;

H. Dias de Carvalho, *Ethnographia e historia tradicional dos povos da Lunda* (Lisbon, 1890), pp. 88–90; S. Chisol et al., *Ngand Yetu* (Cleveland, Transvaal, 1963), pp.13–14; Kabamb Kateng, 'Akarund' (unpublished MS, Institute Pédagogique Supérieur, Université nationale du Zaïre, Lubumbashi, n.d.), p. 3.

13 Roland, 'Résumé de l'histoire', pp. 20, 29, 33; Grevisse. 'Notes ethnographiques', pp. 93–7, 102; Kazembe XIV, *My Ancestors and My People* (Central Bantu Historical Texts: Rhodes Livingstone Institute Communications, no. 23) (Lusaka, 1962), p. 48.

14 Kazembe XIV, *My Ancestors*, chs. 1–3.

15 Personal communication from Jan Vansina regarding the use of Lunda at Kazembe's court. On Lunda praises, see Jacques Chiwale, *Royal Praises and Praise Names of the Luapula Kazembe of Northern Rhodesia, Their Meaning and Historical Background* (Central Bantu Historical Texts, Rhodes Livingstone Institute Communications, no. 25) (Lusaka, 1962).

16 Chiwale, *Praise Names,* for these praise names.

17 For the ethnic and political divisions on the Luapula see I. G. Cunnison, *The Luapula Peoples of Northern Rhodesia* (Manchester, 1959), chs. 6 and 7. Cunnison frequently notes the Kosa element in the Kazembe dynasty, for example in 'The Reigns of the Kazembes', *Northern Rhodesia Journal,* vol. 3, no. 2 (1956), pp. 131–9.

18 Kazembe XIV, *My Ancestors*, p. 22; field notes of I. G. Cunnison, vol. 1, Testimony of Kanyembo Musonda, 2 February 1949, Institute for African Studies, University of Zambia.

19 Testimony of Chief Sailunga, 9 June 1969, in Schecter, 'History and Historiography', p. 288. His story is confirmed by many informants from the Musokantanda area.

20 For Ishindi, see Thomas Chinyama, *Early History of the Balovale Lunda* (Lusaka, 1945), pp. 8–9.

21 Among the many independent sources which note the connection, see Biebuyck, 'Fondements de l'organisation politique', pp. 793, 801.

5. The Kings Left Lwindi; The Clans Divided at Luhunda: How Bushi's Dynastic Origin Myth Behaves

RICHARD SIGWALT*

Guided by the achievements of their own discipline and by the fruitful insights of structural anthropologists, Africanist historians have been engaged throughout this decade in redefining the relationship of genesis myths—stories explaining the origins of peoples, states, clans or dynasties—to history 'as it really happened'.[1] Although no systematic method has been formulated yet, three linked points of general agreement are among historians' working assumptions as a result of work done in the 1970s.

1. Origin traditions are *essentially* mythic, not historical—they are oral traditions but not historical ones. This means that if the original form of an origin tradition were correctly reconstructed, the reconstruction would be a myth, not the crystallized account agreed upon by a culture about a real historical event.[2] This being so, approaches useful for analyzing origin traditions for their historical worth will necessarily differ greatly from methods appropriate for studying historical traditions.

2. Because origin traditions are by nature mythic, the historian interested in using them in his work must become adept at using the tools developed by scholars of myth, and especially by the structural anthropologists. After a brief period of perhaps excessive infatuation, historians today would generally agree that it is useful to think in terms of a myth's 'structure' as something distinct from the 'contingent elements' which compose it. 'Structure' refers to an underlying pattern of symbols and interactions of symbols which makes a myth a coherent unit susceptible to analysis; 'contingent elements' are simply the concrete allusions constituting the context necessary to tell the tale: the language in which the tale is told, names and cultural idioms employed, the given social order of the tale's teller as it is reflected in the myth, and so forth. Contingent

*Chercheur associé de l'Institut de recherche scientifique, Kinshasa.

126

elements are, then, the context within which the structure's logic 'se parle', in the structuralist metaphysic.[3]

3. Indispensable though structural anthropology's insights and analytical categories are to historians, historians' concerns differ fundamentally from those of structural anthropologists. For the latter, myth itself is the object of study. By contrast historians aim at reconstructing real patterns of human change in the past and, in this undertaking, use origin myths as one source of data. These differing foci of interest imply that the historian must be more concrete—even prosaic—in applying the notions of 'structure' and 'contingent element'. Working out the internal logic of a myth helps the historian understand the culture under study, but it does not serve directly to recover the distant past. Most historians would agree that the commonplace definition of 'structure' as 'an arrangement of parts . . . the interrelation of parts as dominated by the general character of the whole'[4] is as good a starting point for historical analysis as any. By this definition 'parts' would take the place of the 'contingent elements' of the structuralist lexicon. This is as it should be, since for the historian these are likely to be precisely the source of historical data, in the sense that they have survived unchanged from some past time. 'Contingent', which implies ephemerality, is therefore seriously misleading. Few historians would object to using 'specific' in place of 'contingent' and 'specifics' in place of 'contingent elements'. This would correspond to the drift of present thinking about the potential importance for history of the apparent miscellany of concrete allusions in origin traditions.

These three points summarize, freely perhaps but not seriously inaccurately, the broad area of agreement within which historians are working at the moment. They do not constitute a theoretically coherent, practically applicable method of subjecting origin traditions to rigorous, systematic historical analysis. Developing just such a method is, or should be, one of Africanist historians' top priorities, for without it we can hardly approach either the distant past, or cultural and intellectual history. Until we have such a method, studies such as the present one will all be, to some degree, a groping in the dark. As much as they are gropings, however, one hopes they will contribute to an eventual reasoned methodology for myth analysis—*historical* myth analysis.

Richard Sigwalt

The Bushi Origin Myth

Taking the above points as given, the present essay begins by examining selected aspects of the origin tradition surrounding the Mwoca dynasty which rules Bushi, a lacustrine Bantu kingdom in eastern Zaire.[5] I argue that the myths which comprise this tradition can be made to yield firm, if limited, historical data. As I demonstrate how data can be extracted from the origin tradition I attempt to explain, in terms consonant with the above points, how certain

Map 5.1 The Mashi-speaking kingdoms (adapted from map by R. P. Tripsen, 1970, in the Archbishopric Archives, Bukavu)

'structural' and 'specific' elements 'behave', and why some have changed and others have remained fixed. In conclusion I venture a few observations about what the Bushi material seems to imply for the eventual elaboration of an historical method of origin tradition analysis.

When raconteurs in Bushi relate the origins of the ruling Mwoca dynasty they invariably begin by telling how the first NaBushi ('owner' or 'master' of Bushi), progenitor of a long line of kings bearing the same name and its associated title, *mwami,* was born in

128

Lwindi, an area just south of Bushi which the Bashi identify with the contemporary state of Bunyindu.[6] This opening episode, which I will refer to as the episode of 'ultimate origins', is followed by a linked but distinct story involving the departure from Lwindi of NaBushi's mother and all her children and the breakup of this royal entourage at Luhunda, in what is now southern Bushi. This second episode I will refer to as either the 'transferral episode' or by its Mashi title, *okugab' emilala*, 'the division of the clans'. Variants of these two episodes constitute the material I will analyze in this essay.[7]

The ultimate origins episode in the Bushi tradition of origins is remarkable for the range of variants extant. The range is in fact so wide that no single myth, in the structural sense of a single pattern of interrelationships between specifics, can be identified. Two examples are enough to demonstrate this.

One raconteur, Kakuja, opens in a Hobbesean past in which 'people killed one another and despoiled each other and danced at home, alone'.[8] In those chaotic times a subject of NaLwindi named Namuga had a palm tree (an *ibondo*) in his field. One day this tree burst open to reveal a man with no name who had with him a *murhwa* ('pygmy') and a dog, both of which symbolize kingship in Bushi. The intruder demanded a wife (*mukobwa*, a word seldom used in Bushi[9]) and *mubande*, referring to the royal Shi planting ritual performed annually by the king and his ritualists (*bajinji*, sing. *mujinji*). No one knew what the words *mubande* and *mukobwa* meant. Eventually, however, the king's daughter agreed to marry the anomalous stranger. The two married and had seven children. In naming them, Kakuja leads his listeners on into the second episode, that of the transferral of kingship from Lwindi to Bushi.

The account of Nyangaka is much longer than and very different from that of Kakuja.[10] Even where the same specifics occur in both stories the referents are entirely dissimilar: the most important example of this is that, where Kakuja considers 'Namuga' a cultivator subject to NaLwindi in whose field there was an *ibondo* (palm tree), Nyangaka amalgamates the separate syllables and gives 'Namugamubondo' as the given name of the *mwami* of Lwindi. Nyangaka tells how in Lwindi there was a large tree beside which mushrooms grew. People there were prevented from gathering these mushrooms by the presence of a large snake. A subject of Namugamubondo (i.e. NaLwindi), a trapper, one day heard a baby crying by the tree. He found a child there, its umbilical cord attached and the afterbirth spread about. He ran to tell the king what he had found. The latter, suspicious, twice sent servants to verify the story. The second time he asked to have the baby brought to him. When it was brought he decreed that it should be nursed by his own wife, who had just given birth to a girl, Nalubongolo. The adopted son, Karholwa ('The One Taken In'), grew up and was given a dog to hunt with. He presented Namugamubondo with a great deal of meat from his hunting. Eventually Karholwa asked his 'father' Namugamubondo to provide him with a wife. The king gave him 'his sister Nalubongolo'. The two had seven children whom Nyangaka lists, moving on to link the episode of ultimate origins to the transferral of kingship in the same way Kakuja does.

Other variants of the ultimate origins episode exhibit at least as much difference from one another as these two do from each other, so we clearly are dealing with different myths (i.e. entirely dissimilar structures) linked only by their common purpose: explaining the origins of NaBushi back in Lwindi. The individual myths are, in fact, independent reflections, not of several historical events vaguely remembered, but of a single cultural consensus among Bashi that their king, NaBushi, came from an agreed-upon place, Lwindi. Raconteurs work outwards from this core consensus and elaborate their own visions of the drama that must have occurred in Lwindi in the long ago. The historian is left with a collection of different myths which, when traced back, deadend at a single raconteur or, more accurately, at a local school of historical lore. Even if it were somehow possible to recreate accurately an original version (or original versions) of the ultimate origins tale, the reconstruction or reconstructions would be myth, not reflections of real past events: this is what is meant when we say these kinds of sources are myth traditions, not historical ones. Hence even the most detailed examination of the structures of these different myths would not bring us any nearer the real past. Only by examining the shared specifics might we possibly gain a limited access to what 'really happened'.

Comparing different ultimate origin myths I collected in Bushi revealed that the syllables alluded to above, *namuga* and *ibondo*, occurred in every variant of this episode. The hypothesis must be, then, that these syllables represent some fundamental agreement linked to the consensus that NaBushi 'came from Lwindi'.[11] As such, the sound cluster might have been transmitted across the generations via many different myth structures ever since the Banyamwoca came from Lwindi to Bushi. The way to test the hypothesis that these morphemes are a key to the historical

origins of the Mwoca dynasty is to look for the same verbal cluster in
the area from which the Bashi think the first NaBushi came. This
leads us to Bunyindu, the kingdom to the south of Bushi that the
Bashi equate with the 'Lwindi' of their origin traditions.

Dynastic origin traditions from Bunyindu prove to contain the
same cluster of sounds as those found in the Bushi core consensus.
The earliest Nyindu tradition recorded (in 1923 by a priest of the
White Fathers missionary order) gives the names of the first two
kings as 'Na Mubondwe, Na Muka (or Na muka mubondwe—
Namuka the son of Mubondwe)'.[12] Ten years later the Belgian
administrator of the area recorded his version of the tradition,
which speaks of the same 'Namuka Mubondwe' and a 'Kangere'
'leaving Itombwe with their subjects'.[13] Lastly, in 1972 I was able to
record a genealogical tradition at the Nyindu court which began
with 'Kangele Mubondwe' and claimed that this founder had two
sons, Kigonya Shunguti who ruled at Lwindi after Kangele had
established the dynasty there, and Namubondo who 'went on to
Itombwe'.[14] No one yet knows enough about the complicated history of the area south of Bushi to interpret these traditions, but they
certainly show beyond a doubt that the verbal specifics shared by all
Bushi variants of the ultimate origins episode occur as well in origin
traditions from the region where, according to Shi tradition, the
Mwoca dynasty had its beginnings.

It is practically certain that the shared verbal elements
namuga/ibondo went from Lwindi to Bushi and that the transfer
occurred a very long time ago, for any counter hypothesis is
implausible. Might the Banyindu have borrowed the syllables from
the Bashi? Hardly, without also having posited some genealogical
or ideological link between themselves and the Bashi, which they
have not done. Could the Bashi have borrowed the syllables in
recent, rather than ancient, times, long after the Mwoca regime
took root? No, given that basic features of the Nyindu version, such
as its genealogical format, do not occur in the Shi tradition. A last
distributional argument seems conclusive. The Nyindu myth is
apparently part of a pattern of myth and titles using the
namuga/ibondo morphemic complex which extends southwards,
away from Bushi, into the forest and onto the same Itombwe
plateau that turns up in the Nyindu traditions but not in those of
Bushi.[15] It is unreasonable to think that the Bashi in the north lent
specific verbal elements (which incidentally impress one as being
distinctly not native to the Mashi language) to a tradition stretching
to the south and pointing to the south as an ultimate point of royal

origin.[16] In sum, the probability that all the counterhypotheses are false is so very high that the only reasonable conclusion is that kingship in Bushi did come from Lwindi and brought with it *namuga* and *ibondo,* morphemes since retained by the many and varied Shi myths of ultimate royal origins.

The methodological inference from the above discussion of structure and specifics is that, contrary to the *de facto* working practices of many African historians, who have sometimes been rather too uncritical of structuralist assumptions, specific aspects of myth (as distinct from myth structures) can and do exhibit significant longevity independently of the particular structural 'vehicles' within which they are manifested. Specifics which can be shown to possess such longevity are of course potentially extremely useful sources of data for the recovery of truly ancient patterns of interaction and development when they confirm, as these do, the cognitive core consensus. We can only begin to understand why such long-lived specifics occur in the episode of ultimate origins, however, and therefore begin to use them confidently only if we contrast ultimate origins episodes with other parts of the Bashi origin tradition. For this reason we will examine briefly the Bushi transferral episode and then return to a comparative analysis of the 'behavior' of the two episodes.

The Bushi Myth of Transferral

Because a real historical link has now been established between Bushi's royal institution and its area of claimed provenance, the episode of transferral takes on real historical interest. This impression is heightened because the transferral story is always told according to a single myth structure. The single structure could result from a more rigorous system of transmission through time that has somehow preserved a literal description of real historical events. Prudence, nourished by the implications of recent thinking about origin myths, however, once again counsels us neither to search for nor to expect to find concrete historical personages or real past actions revealed directly in the episode—which is, after all, still a myth.

Bashi sometimes call the transferral episode *okugab'emilala* ('division of [or into] clans'). The story follows NaBushi, his mother and their supposed entourage from their point of origin in Lwindi to their arrival in Bushi. In striking contrast to the episode of ultimate

132

origins, which is recounted in many different ways, *okugab' emilala's* variants constitute a single myth structure with only slight differences in 'chord'. All who tell of the transfer tell the same tale and the occasional differences which do occur in specifics only serve to emphasize the singleness of the underlying structure. All agree that NaBushi's mother left Lwindi with her children and proceeded to Luhunda, a place in southern Bushi, where two of her sons left the entourage and went to become kings in the neighbouring countries of Burhinyi and Ninja. The mother died at Luhunda and was interred there by burialists who, because they violated funerary prohibitions (usually by eating raw meat which should have been cooked), were expelled from the Mwoca clan. The party then moved on to central Bushi.

Variation occurs in the specifics of the myth but does not affect its structural unity. Among the variants are some which have three kings instead of two in the first 'division' and others which include even 'NaLwanda' (king of Rwanda) and Nyibunga (putative mother of Nsibula, king of Buhavu, which lies north of Bushi) in the group which pushed on to Bushi after the mother's death and burial. There is also disagreement about the names of the burialists who were expelled from the Mwoca clan for violating funerary prohibitions.[17] Such differences in specifics are structurally inconsequential. As one reads texts of variants of the overall tradition side by side, the aesthetic contrast between the variability of the ultimate origins episode and the unitary *okugab'emilala* is impressive indeed. The former is always different, the latter always familiar, text after text.

The difference occurs, I think, because *okugab'emilala* is a complex political charter,[18] a depiction and explanation in historical idiom of NaBushi's relationship to several neighboring kings and to many royal ritualists in the kingdom without whom, in Shi thought, kingship could not exist.[19] The origins episode, by contrast, legitimates the kingship as an undifferentiated whole.

Identifying complexity as the key feature of the transferral episode helps explain why it is always a single highly structured myth in stark contrast to the free tradition (by which I mean that different myths occupy its 'slot' in the overall sequence of episodes) of the ultimate origins episode. A charter myth explains in allegedly historical terms a complex of sociopolitical relationships, which it thereby legitimates. By contrast, an ultimate origins episode refers to a simpler, but by no means less fundamental, verity: it affirms the essentiality of the institution explained by the charter myth (our 'transferral myth'). The consensus reflected in the ultimate origins episode is general and simple ('the *mwami* came from Lwindi'), but that reflected in *okugab'emilala* is elaborate, having to do with the interstatal context and the ritual order that a Mushi once described to me as *'une constitution vivante'*. It is logical that the complexity of the reality to which the transferral episode refers should limit the variations that individual raconteurs might work on its structure and thereby make *okugab'emilala* a single myth. To a considerable extent this explains the difference between the 'behavior' of the two episodes: in the main, the function of *okugab'emilala* explains its structure ('the interrelationship of its parts').

The story explains NaBushi's relationships (a) to neighboring kings the Bashi consider his 'brothers' and (b) to royal ritualists and the ritual system of which he himself is the center. There is no obvious reason these two different sets of relationships must be treated together in a single tradition; there could instead be two distinct episodes, as there are in many comparable etiological traditions. In the Bushi case, however, external interstate relationships and internal ritual ones are linked into a single structure by an overarching theme—another core consensus like the one affirming NaBushi's Lwindi origin—that all the kings and the ritualists share a common legitimacy, indeed were a single patrilineal group of kin before *emilala yagabir'eLuhunda*: 'The clans divided at Luhunda'. This simple consensus encapsulates agreement that the entire politico-ritual context, internal and external, of NaBushi's kingship is an integrated coherent whole, only lately and superficially divided, as would be explained by the splitting up of an original group. That this dispersal occurred at a given spot, Luhunda, and even, in a sense, at a given time—'in the beginning'—underlines the coherence that the Shi perceive in the whole.

Unlike the core consensus 'the kings came from Lwindi', which admits of vast numbers of different elaborations in the form of quite variant myths (with necessarily different structures), the complex consensual core of the transferral story produces a single myth structure. We are now ready to understand why this is so. The consensus in *okugab'emilala* not only includes a specific place as a core detail (as does 'the *mwami* came from Lwindi'), it also orders the relationships between the brother kings, who are equal, and between the other brothers who became subordinate ritualists because they violated burial proscriptions. The consensus 'the clans divided at Luhunda' imposes this comprehensive order by forcing the story of the breakaway and that of the pollution into a single linked set of related events forming a complex—and therefore single—myth. This can be diagramed as follows:

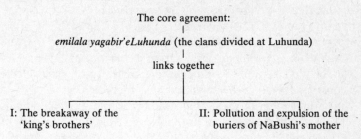

Thus is ordered the entire Shi political universe, internal and external.

My point is that by virtue of the relative complexity of the things the charter myth explains and because of the consensual framework within which Shi culture chooses to explain those things, a structure of myth emerges from the function, social and political, of the myth. NaBushi's royalty is located quite precisely within its broader cultural and political framework. The initial, ultimate origins, episode simply justifies royalty itself and can be fluid because the institution itself is depicted as unitary, not complex and plural, and exists almost outside the Shi cultural context—it is an abstraction, or nearly so. Kingship's disconnectedness from society in the first case—the ultimate origins story—and its embeddedness in the second—the episode of transferral—explain why the same storytellers, who disagree about what 'happened' at Lwindi in the long ago, are in apparent 'agreement' about what occurred at Luhunda, even though there is no reason to suspect the presence of formal methods of transmitting the second tradition and their absence in transmitting the first.

If this analysis has correctly identified the structure of the transferral tale, the details of different versions not related to the cores of royal hiving off and burialists' expulsion should exhibit a degree of variation similar to what we have already noted in the story of NaBushi's ultimate origins. Such variation in fact occurs in the royal division consensus of 'the clans divided at Luhunda', the story of the breakaway of NaBurhinyi and NaNinja (and occasionally of a king of one or another of the small states in what is now Kilega-speaking country). In the story of the kings' departures for their respective kingdoms, the individual raconteur is culturally supplied with the consensual 'fact' that the Burhinyi and Ninja dynasties began with the 'division' at Luhunda, and he must abide by it. Thereafter individual imagination can and does have free reign. Variations range from the typically prosaic to the highly fanciful and even—in one case at least—to the ingenious interweaving of folk etymologies of dynastic names.[20] The evidence from the breakaway theme of the transferral episode, then, seems to confirm my inference that the structure of *okugab'emilala* derives from its function as explanatory model for the entire Shi world centered on NaBushi, since *within that constricting structure* imagination has free reign.

The anthropologists' thesis that structure is fully explained by its function as myth charter does not, however, hold up in the case of the *okugab'emilala* story, since its core, the cliché of the ritual burial theme, can be shown to derive from outside Bushi and its political and cultural contexts. The burial sequence reflects a basic Shi practice—eating a cooked chicken called *lubaba* to mark the close of funerary rites—transgression of which (by eating the chicken uncooked) is abominable to a Mushi.[21] It is misleading, though, to think that this myth charter merely articulates a cultural assumption. That is involved, of course, but we are also dealing here with the transfer of the core notion of a myth from one culture to another. In that the burial theme has an extraneous origin, it in fact parallels the transfer of the syllables *namuga/ibondo* in the first episode. It differs only in that in the transferral episode the key is the core of the idea (a skeletal story) which has been transferred rather than the verbal elements somehow implying kingship.

The story originated in the neighboring southern kingdom of Bunyindu, where a senior ritualist bearing the name-title Namushungwe ('possessor of the royal diadem') claims an ancient link of kinship to the Tumu dynasty ruling there. To the Banyindu, practicing positional succession like the Bashi, Namushungwe's tie is ideologically that of a perpetual 'elder brother' of the Tumu king. As Namushungwe the ritualist (*mugingi* in Kinyindu, the Mashi *mujinji* a regular sound shift) related the story, 'he'—meaning his ancestor—lost the throne in the distant past because, when his mother died and the family quarrelled about who was to bury her, he eventually agreed to do the job. On his return from burying her in the bush he found that the others shunned him. He asked for a chicken to eat: 'This person [the mother] has made me stink. Do you lack even a single chicken . . . even a single goat to kill for me as meat?'[22] Eventually he got his chicken, but the declaration was made to him that 'you have now become a *munzoga* [burial ritualist; Mashi *munjoga*], you are no longer a king's child'. Reluctantly the expelled man selected someone else to be heir, for 'I am only one person and cannot bring an end to the Batumu'.[23]

Both the Shi and Nyindu burial stories elucidate the ritual order in the same explanatory idiom about violation of burial prohibitions leading to the expulsion of ritualists central to kingship. The Shi version differs from the Nyindu one in that it always cites a specific place, Luhunda, where the burial occurred, it includes more than one burialist, and it never in any way suggests that the expellers had been either kings or royal heirs. The specificity of the Luhunda reference among the Shi is owing to the incidental prominence of a mnemonic device in the area.[24] The plurality of Shi burialists is apparently due to the fact that in Bunyindu burialists are considered ritualists, while in Bushi the two categories are emphatically distinguished, by the tradition as well as in many other ways. The third difference, the original kingly status of the Nyindu character, cannot be explained with material presently available. Together the three differences are significant enough to preclude recent Shi borrowing of the story from the Nyindu. Once again, as in the case of the shared syllables in the ultimate origins episode, the improbability of the counterhypotheses leads to the conclusion that the original myth came from the south and has, over a considerable time, become 'naturalized' to the situation in Bushi.

Bushi's myth charter, the transferral episode of the tradition of origin, is, then, composed of a fixed structure imposed by the consensual idiom of patrilineal kin group division ('the clans divided at Luhunda') and containing two parts: (a) a logical, deductive part—the hiving off of the kings—and (b) a borrowed myth—the burial scene, which is simple enough to be transmitted easily but sufficient nevertheless to express the core truth being explained and legitimized. These two elements, linked by the ideology of patrilineality expressed in an historical idiom, emerge as a unified myth, *okugab'emilala*. A single myth constitutes the transferral episode (and I think it unquestionably does, by any reasonable definition of myth 'structure') because that myth's structure is forced on Shi raconteurs by the complexity of its legitimating function. All variations must satisfy that function, so the myth becomes unified without elaborate apparatus of transmission of formal mechanisms of consensus enforcement. The same set of circumstances occurs, I suspect, in many other African societies.

Some Interim Conclusions

If my argument thus far is sound, the historian can draw the following methodological conclusions from the discussion, which so far has dealt only with the contrasting stability of structure and specifics, not with how and why they change over time:

1. Origin traditions based on myth can be useful to historians. By approaching them as complex aspects of ethnography the historian can trace transfers of specifics or structures across what are today ethnic boundaries.

2. In practical terms this implies that anyone wishing to use origin myths as historical data must look beyond—perhaps well beyond—the confines of a single culture. If the Bushi case is typical, in fact, there is no point in examining a single people's origin tradition in isolation. The historian studying origin myths becomes, by that fact, a regional historian, not the historian of a single ethnic group. This is so, apparently, because mental units like myth themes and ritual fundamentals transcend political and cultural institutions in both time and space. This of course parallels an established trend in other areas of African history towards rejecting such simplistic concepts as 'ethnic group' or any of the other current crop of euphemisms for 'tribe'.

3. The historian can make no *a priori* assumptions about what is ephemeral and what is likely to be permanent in the origin tradition he or she is studying. Either structure or specifics may 'behave' in either way.

4. Although a structuralist anthropologist could successfully relate the several levels of the Bushi origin myth to each other, the historian must approach the material as a committed 'splitter', seeing the parts independently of each other and examining why they relate to each other as they do in terms of the different historical origins of each.

5. The concreteness of the sociopolitical reality reflected in an episode—the extent to which the episode is a charter myth—explains close structural resemblances between variants in the Bushi case. An analysis of function, in other words, resolves the puzzle of why the same presumed methods of transmission sometimes result in disaccord, as in Shi versions about what 'happened at Lwindi' to explain royal origins, but at other times in a high degree of accord, as when the Shi tell how 'the clans divided at Luhunda'.

6. Finally, the historian must grapple seriously with the history of

138

the oral document being examined for possible historical data. The history of the genesis tradition follows the history of the people or peoples who employ it in much the same way that a modern nation-state's constitution evolves along with the social world of the people living under it. Analyzing Shi traditions of dynastic origin has established that the Mwoca dynasty came from Lwindi, even though what 'really happened' in the past there is unrecoverable, given the mythic nature of the tradition.

In addition, the full value of such indirect evidence as myths can be neglected if we do not examine what 'scars' these myths bear from their encounters with history since their transferral to new ground. Modern myths resemble myths brought into Bushi long, long ago not because both categories describe the same past but because the modern tales resemble their parent myths and therefore their modern 'cousins' still told at the point of origin. By thinking in these terms we have looked beyond one veil, concrete descriptive elements, the 'specifics' of the myth. By penetrating the internal complexity of a myth in this way, we have used it as an historical document. We are now ready to turn to the second veil obscuring such aspects of the real past as the Shi origin traditions, properly read, can illuminate. I refer to the alterations tradition undergoes as the result of historical changes in the past, which can be recovered by using a different set of historical, rather than mythic, traditions.

The Impact of Historical Change on Genesis Traditions in Bushi

The rise of Ngweshe, a son by positional succession of NaBushi, dominates the reconstructable history of precolonial Bushi.[25] Today's Ngweshe, Ntatabaye, rules most of Bushi's historical heartland, the rolling plateau bounded to the south by the mountains of Kaziba, Luhwinja, and Burhinyi and, across the Ulindi River, by the low-lying Bunyindu kingdom. To the west rise the Ninja highlands and in the north and east lie the plains of Lake Kivu and the Ruzizi River. In theory the entire plateau region is still under sovereignty of NaBushi, but by 1800 Ngweshe had gained *de facto* autonomy from his nominal overlord, formalized by midcentury by public performance at the Ngweshe court of the royal seedtime ceremony called *mubande*—in effect Ngweshe's declaration of kingly rather than mere princely status (*bwami* as against *buluzi*) within the area he ruled. This formal declaration of kingly pretentions inaugurated

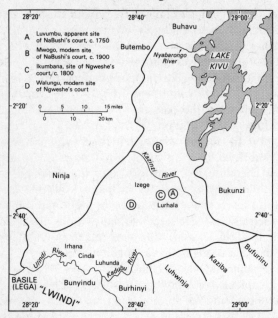

Map 5.2 Bushi

a state of permanent hostility between Ngweshe and NaBushi, but no Ngweshe has ever disclaimed his perpetual 'sonship' to NaBushi. Nevertheless, the last half of the nineteenth century saw bearers of the name Ngweshe unfilially drive their NaBushi 'fathers' to the northernmost extremity of the plateau, into an area which very likely had not even been a part of Bushi in 1800. Thus Ngweshe incorporated most of the old homeland, including NaBushi's old capital near Lurhala (see Map 5.2) and relegated the *de jure* supreme sovereign of Bushi to a region he had never before ruled, at least not directly.

On the northern rim of the plateau NaBushi established what was in effect a rump state, one which probably owed its very survival to its conquest of a good number of Bahavu people living along the lake shore. In the process of incorporating these Bahavu, NaBushi drove the old Havu king northwards into what is now Kalehe Zone. These events dramatically changed the identity of the population over whom NaBushi actually, as opposed to theoretically, held sway. In the eighteenth century his subjects had belonged to clans whose members inhabited mainly the plateau and the southern Mashi-speaking kingdoms of Burhinyi, Luhwinja, and Kaziba; by 1880 his real subjects were clansmen whose fellows inhabited areas

140

north, east, and west of Bushi: Buhavu, Rwanda, and Butembo.[26] This new situation poses the interesting methodological question of the effect NaBushi's northward displacement and expansion had on genesis traditions throughout the two areas over which NaBushi's *de jure* sovereignty was now recognized—in autonomous Ngweshe as well as in NaBushi's new kingdom.

Comparison of traditions from Ngweshe, from the environs of NaBushi's modern court, and from the formerly Havu areas conquered by NaBushi in the nineteenth century reveals that historically attested events have affected the ultimate origins episode of the genesis tradition in differing ways. The effect of the rise of Ngweshe can be seen in the proper names given the supposed first NaBushi in the different areas. Where NaBushi holds sway the variation in names attributed to the ultimate ancestor figure would madden a literalist, but the apparent 'disagreement' becomes entirely understandable once one recognizes that the origin tradition, a myth tradition, is normally 'penetrated' by truly historical data. The traditional Shi historian outside Ngweshe usually simply inserts the name of a king whose reign lies at, or just beyond, the threshold of his direct historical recall. A young man calls the first NaBushi 'Makombe', but an older man, whose recall extends further into the past, knows that Makombe, although he lived long, long ago (in fact about a century ago) was not the first NaBushi. After all, the older man would say, was it not Makombe who fought Cirhahongerwa (the Ngweshe of that time)? The older man then gives the name of a king further back than Makombe, one still attestable from the sources as being a late eighteenth or early nineteenth century figure. This variability according to the historian's threshold of recall is normal 'behavior' for oral traditions.[27]

In Ngweshe, however, when people choose or are asked to name the first king of the Mwoca dynasty, they call him 'Kabare' with striking invariability. Evidence from other historical traditions suggests that Kabare was in fact the name of the NaBushi under whom Ngweshe first asserted his autonomy. Ngweshe versions of the ultimate origins tradition have thus 'frozen' a single name into a universally accepted version of the story of Mwoca origin because of its importance to Ngweshe's early history. People actually subject to NaBushi (for whom the emergence of Ngweshe is of little theoretical—though great practical—significance) follow a kind of inherent logic of oral history in which myth structure is linked to and penetrated by a constantly changing corpus of specific lore from the remembered past.

141

Beyond this variation in specifics the rise of Ngweshe has not affected the ultimate origins episode. The structure is stable because *neither* Ngweshe *nor* NaBushi denies the sonship, by positional succession and perpetual kinship, of the former to the latter. Therefore the Shi perception that legitimacy derives fundamentally and originally from NaBushi's unique origins at Lwindi applies equally throughout Bushi, in the area ruled by Ngweshe no less forcefully than in that ruled by NaBushi himself. The core consensus of the general legitimating myth for all Banyamwoca has not undergone fundamental change because of the rise of one Mwoca prince (*muluzi*) over the king (*mwami*), however grand Ngweshe might have become.

Ngweshe's rise has, through the displacement of NaBushi's court, had a significant indirect impact on *okugab'emilala*, because it is a myth that explains and legitimates, not kingship in general, but the specific politico-ritual order which centers on NaBushi. That this is so is understandable. As earlier sections have demonstrated, *okugab'emilala* is a charter myth, and it must change so that what it says corresponds to the reality it legitimates, even, in the Shi case, at the occasional price of logical consistency. The clan identities of NaBushi's ritualists (*bajinji*) specified in different versions of this episode demonstrate how a charter myth's responses to historical changes reveal something about the past that has affected it.

The *okugab'emilala* charter myth relates the origins of NaBushi's entire ritual order, which focuses on the king but requires the active participation of ritualists (*bajinji*) who propitiate the royal ancestors as representatives of subject clans and perform individually specified ritual functions (*bikono*, sing. *cikono*) at the *mubande* seedtime ceremony. Because clan identity determines eligibility to ritual office, the charter story now told at NaBushi's new capital has had to adjust to the historical fact that NaBushi's present subjects, and therefore his present ritualists, have different clan (i.e. historical) identities than did his ancestors' subjects, and therefore their ritualists, a couple of centuries ago, when the Bushi capital was in the central plateau region near that of the present Ngweshe. NaBushi's modern domain is peopled mostly by members of clans which are absent or only sparsely represented on the plateau.[28] Although, owing to acculturation and in acknowledgment of NaBushi's sovereignty over them, these 'new' subjects today normally identify themselves collectively as Bashi, their individual clan traditions indicate origins in a little-known lakeside culture which flourished until the Bashi and Banyarwanda absorbed most of it, politically and in part culturally, in the nineteenth century.[29] That members of these northern clans have now taken positions in NaBushi's ritual order places a considerable strain on the logic of *okugab'emilala*, whose core consensus (*emilala yagabir'eLuhunda*, all 'the clans divided at Luhunda') implies that the *bajinji* once were Banyamwoca and therefore must have a Lwindi, that is to say southern, origin. Two examples of how the myth has adjusted to conditions in NaBushi's modern state illuminate the suppleness of one myth's structure in response to the demands history has imposed.

The simpler of the two examples concerns a *mujinji* ritualist called NaCahi. In versions of the charter tradition told in Ngweshe, NaCahi is depicted as a diviner, but in the version told by Mpara, a man acquainted with NaBushi's court ritual, NaCahi has become a maker of medicines instead of a diviner.[30] The duties of the NaCahi ritualist appear to have changed, and the reason for the change lies in the fact that the current incumbent belongs to the Ludaha clan, which traces its origins to southwestern Rwanda, where it is associated with medicine-making rather than divining. NaCahi's professional character has changed because the holder of the position changed from representing a plateau clan specializing in divination to representing a lakeside culture clan, the *bene Ludaha*, specializing in medicine-making.

This amalgamation and transformation process can be traced in somewhat greater detail in the story of a ritualist whom Mpara calls 'Namugakabene'. Mpara says this person came from Lwindi with Namugamubondo, the mother of the kings.[31] When Namugamubondo died, says Mpara, Namugakabene was sent by the kings to fetch wood to cook the meat for the mourning ritual. Namugakabene also gave the kings '*buntu* [stiff porridge] for which he had bartered his drum'.[32] Exchanging a drum, symbol of political authority, for *buntu* (literally 'human-ness') which the king then eats obviously suggests that the ritualist's putative ancestor at some point surrendered sovereignty to NaBushi, but this cannot yet be substantiated. More important for this argument is that the symbol of exchanging the drum for *buntu* links the 'Namugakabene' of Mpara's tale with a ritualist at the modern court of NaBushi called NaCigemwa, of the Mbiriri clan. The present NaCigemwa explained 'his' (ancestor's) acquisition of his ritual role in terms which implicitly identify it with the role of Namugakabene in Mpara's charter tradition:

143

We left Lwindi with the king [emphasis added]. We stayed at Luhunda, where NaBushi was gripped by hunger . . . NaCigemwa took his drum and bartered it for *buntu*, which the king ate.

The king said, 'I was hungry; when I reach my country I shall give you a country adjacent to it.'

NaCigemwa replied, 'I do not want that: I prefer the immunity (or protection) of a superior.'

'That I hereby grant you.'[33]

This is clearly a variant of Mpara's myth, its structure transferred from third to first person by one of the characters in the narrative. NaCigemwa's separate account of the origins of his clan, the Banyambiriri, however, conflicts with both his and Mpara's claim of a Lwindi origin for the character, for he traces Mbiriri origins to Nyundo in present-day Rwanda. Confronted by the blatant contradiction between the southern origin implied in his ritual position and explicitly stated in his recital of the transferral episode and the Rwanda origin he acknowledges elsewhere for his clan, he reconciles the two by affirming that his distant ancestor had gone (or must have gone?) south and established himself there, where NaBushi happened across him as he left Lwindi for Bushi. This facile reconciliation, besides its inherent implausibility, conflicts with data collected from the northern area beyond the effective intellectual reach of NaBushi's court. Banyambiriri there acknowledge that the NaCigemwa who now serves NaBushi as a ritualist (we would say his ancestor) was in fact once a governor and ritualist for the Havu king, who once ruled there before NaBushi pushed him farther north. NaCigemwa was also, in those days as he still is, head of the western, Bushi/Buhavu branch of the Banyambiriri.[34] His change from ritualist for NaBuhavu to ritualist for NaBushi signified the acceptance by Banyambiriri of NaBushi's overlordship. Owing, then, to the two distinct sources for NaCigemwa's present office, the present holder of the name is obliged to hold simultaneously two incompatible traditions of where 'he' came from—traditions he amalgamates with a singular, but understandable, lack of convincingness.

These examples of history's impact on the origin myth suggest that historians must not reject as valueless myth traditions which on their faces display glaring incongruities. These incongruities can, in fact, afford information about the relatively recent past that historical traditions ignore or conceal. The drama of the transfer of Mbiriri loyalty from Buhavu to Bushi a century or more ago is transmitted, obscurely but certainly, in inconsistencies between myth traditions; it goes unmentioned in the historical traditions that deal explicitly with these times. Theoretically, exhaustive comparison of myth variations within NaBushi's present domains and between that area and Ngweshe could yield an enormous amount of information that Shi historical traditions, dealing as they do solely with Mwoca history, ignore almost entirely. Because the ritual order reflects the sociopolitical order, albeit imperfectly, reconstructing changes in the ritual order by analyzing changes in the charter myth which reflects it (also imperfectly) can be of use in reconstructing recent, nineteenth-century changes in African systems of political organization. But what of deciphering the more ancient past?

Mpara's handling of another ritualist, NaRhana, shows that 'seams', or disjunctures like those in NaCigemwa's account of his own origin(s), can lead the researcher to ways of determining if the document he or she is studying is an 'overlaid' or 'palimpsest' tradition bearing historical evidence about a really ancient past.[35] Mpara introduces NaRhana as custodian of the royal regalia, to whom the dying royal mother, Namugamubondo, confides the mission of executing her last will and testament by bestowing the regalia on NaBushi. She is also shown wishing NaRhana well in the country he is to rule—an indication that his status at this point is not merely that of ritualist, but rather that of king and brother of NaBushi. The NaRhana figure next appears, together with NaCinda, a *munyamubira* by clan who can be identified with the petty kingdom of Cinda located to the southwest of central Bushi, and the funerary ritualist (*munjoga*) named Lukunjuka, burying the mother and then violating the funerary prohibition against eating the meat, breaking mourning, without cooking it.[36]

Suddenly, however, in the next sentence, the situation and indeed the very setting of the story change dramatically. NaRhana departs and goes to his enclosure—an incongruity, since up to this point the entire group, including NaBushi, Namugamubondo and NaRhana, has been depicted as being in a temporary hunting camp. Arriving at 'his' enclosure, 'home' to him, NaRhana finds a *mucuba* (playing board) outside its walls. The *mucuba* is supernatural, it seems, since its playing-pieces are in it, ready to be used. NaRhana and NaBushi play, and NaRhana wins but also curses NaBushi and in so doing recognizes NaBushi as his political superior. At this point in the narrative Mpara brusquely reverts to the hunting-camp setting, the scene of Namugamubondo's burial, and announces quite without warning that 'thereupon NaRhana became a Murhana [his clan—implication is that he had been a Munyamwoca up to this point], and NaCinda became a *munyamubira*, and Lukunjuka

145

became a *munjoga*, he who placed Namugamubondo in the here-after. They finished eating the *lubaba* chicken and playing *mucuba*' (lines 35–37, Appendix).

Mpara's narrative presents NaRhana in two entirely different roles, roles which can best be understood as myth themes with quite distinct clichés and equally distinct social referents. As burier of Namugamubondo NaRhana is the archetype for ritualist status at NaBushi's court, as is NaCinda the archetypal *munyamubira*. On the other hand, as is known from later episodes of the overall genesis tradition (not dealt with in this paper), the board game theme symbolizes a king who, though retaining kingly status, becomes a subject of NaBushi. Such a joint king/subject status (called *mwami mujinji*) is today held by only one direct subject of NaBushi, a man called NaLuniga. On the face of Mpara's narrative, however, is a mythic claim that NaRhana too shared—or shares—this royal status. Mpara thus deals with two different NaRhanas, whom he unites at the cost of the aesthetic unity of his narrative, which he destroys with two jarringly disconcerting transitions from the milieu and myth of one cliché to those of the other. The historian must try to understand why Mpara produced such a graceless testimony. To do this one must first try to establish the validity of the discordant general historical statements being made, mythically and implicitly: (a) that NaRhana, subordinate head of the Rhana clan (and perhaps NaCinda of the Mubiri clan) played a major ritual role within early Bushi and (b) that NaRhana was an independent king at some point brought under the political rule of NaBushi and obliged to surrender sovereignty to him. These two statements are, in fact, apparently contradictory, not merely discordant.

In order to identify NaRhana the burier, symbol of ancient ritual status, we must go beyond the kingdom whose traditions we are examining and compare Bushi's royal system with those of Kaziba, Luhwinja, and Burhinyi, the three Mashi-speaking states lying south of Bushi. The royal ritual systems of the four Mashi-speaking states are very similar. All have, at their centers, kings called *bami* (sing. *mwami*) who rule with colleges of *bajinji* ritualists who propitiate the *mwami*'s ancestors and perform the annual *mubande* seed-time ceremony. *Bajinji* are distinguished in all four systems from two other categories of persons who in English would also be called 'ritualists': *banjoga* burialists and *barhwa* ('pygmies') responsible for beating the royal drums on ceremonial occasions. In all four kingdoms *banjoga* and *barhwa* serve as the clan designations of the ritualists (and their kin) concerned.[37] These similarities are not due to the kingdoms' sharing a common dynasty which has divided and spread associated political culture throughout the area. Only one of the southern kingdoms, Burhinyi, shares Bushi's claim to a Lwindi origin for its ruling dynasty. Kaziba's ruling house is said to have come from Bufuriiru, a region near Lake Tanganyika ethnically very similar to Bunyindu, and Luhwinja sources claim a dynastic origin in Bukunzi, a pre-Tutsi state in southeastern Rwanda.[38] The common ritual order shared by the Mashi-speaking states must, therefore, predate the establishment of the present diverse dynastic regimes.

For this reason it is significant that, despite separate dynastic origins in the three southern kingdoms, the head ritualist in each carries the name NaRhana and belongs to and claims to head the Rhana clan. From distributional evidence alone it appears, then, that the Barhana preceded the present dynasties in the southern Mashi-speaking country and were absorbed into the new dynasties' royal ritual orders. This conclusion is supported further by the presence in all three of these kingdoms' origin myths of symbolic acts of Rhana subordination (drums changing hands, for instance) when the founders of the dynasties encountered earlier Rhana populations. We can conclude that in Burhinyi, Luhwinja, and Kaziba originally independent Rhana authorities were transformed into subordinate ritualists. The process is one with which Africanist historians are, of course, familiar.

In the modern court of NaBushi, so recently removed to a more northerly locale, we find no Rhana ritualist today. We do, however, find a respected historian, Mpara, who was born and raised in NaBushi's present domain, affirming what appears to be a Rhana role in a NaBushi kingdom where no Barhana live. Why does the NaRhana character play so prominent a role in a myth episode so obviously concerned with explaining a ritual office which today is *not* associated with the Rhana clan, even though NaRhana would elsewhere represent this position?

We have seen that, although there is no NaRhana at the head of NaBushi's college of *bajinji* ritualists, Bushi's court ritual system is conceptually and structurally very similar to those of the southern kingdoms, all of whose systems are headed by NaRhanas. It was argued earlier in this paper that the Mwoca regime in Bushi manifestly did, as the Bashi claim, originate in the south—in close proximity, it is worth noting at this juncture, to Burhinyi and in an area, southern Ngweshe, where there are large numbers of

Barhana. Together these points strongly suggest that in the past the Barhana played as prominent a role in Bushi's royal rituals as they do in the present rituals of Kaziba, Luhwinja, and Burhinyi. The presence of NaRhana in Mpara's burial story confirms this suggestion. It reflects a ritual arrangement now dead for at least a century, in Bushi.

NaBushi's nineteenth-century displacement left practically all Barhana beyond NaBushi's effective control; although many remain subject to Ngweshe and therefore ultimately under NaBushi's sovereignty, their relationship to NaBushi is hardly more than nominal. NaBushi understandably dropped the Rhana representative from his ritual college as its composition changed to accommodate the northern clans to which NaBushi's new subjects belonged. NaRhana the burialist appears in Mpara's narrative because the old man had a vague, though correct, idea, gained in his youth (before European conquest) that NaRhana was the 'first' *mujinji*. That idea is now apparently dead in the region which NaBushi actually rules; Mpara appears to have been the last to acknowledge it. Myth traditions, after all, like such historical traditions as kinglists and memories of kingly achievements, fade and disappear once their relevance disappears. However, because Mpara's narrative was his individually developed and ephemeral creation rather than a fixed, transmitted piece of historical wisdom, we cannot consider his retention of NaRhana-the-ritualist as a 'palimpsest' *tradition*. It is, however, a palimpsest *testimony* in which a more ancient stratum of reality than the present *status quo* coexists with a more modern stratum. The more modern stratum is that of NaRhana-the-*mucuba*-player, who represents a so-called '*mwami*' whose 'court' still exists in southern Ngweshe.

Mpara's synthetic testimony reflects contradictory sacred and profane aspects of NaRhana's present status. Until Ngweshe conquered the southern part of Bushi in the middle of the nineteenth century, the area was ruled by petty chiefs, most of whom are today remembered only vaguely, if at all. Mpara's *mucuba*-playing NaRhana represents the most successful of the petty kings whom Ngweshe overcame. (NaCinda seems not to have come under Ngweshe's control until colonial times.) Perhaps because of NaRhana's status as nominal head of the Rhana clan, which is very heavily represented in Ngweshe, he has retained a small 'state', Irhana, which he still rules from his own 'court', and he continues to wear an *ishungwe* symbol of royalty which his overlord, Ngweshe, a mere 'prince', dares not wear.[39] This modern NaRhana insists he is a

148

mwami mujinji, a ritualist by virtue of a kingship, the sovereign essence of which continues despite the reality of his present subjection to the Mwoca regime.

NaRhana's royal status means little in the context of Ngweshe politics, especially since clan organization is almost entirely absent there, making NaRhana's respected status as head of the Rhana clan meaningless in profane terms. Royal status implies only an annual appearance at Ngweshe's *mubande* (seedtime ritual) to acknowledge his *de facto* subjection to Ngweshe. However, NaRhana insists, his really important ritual act was his appearance at the *mubande* of NaBushi, to whom he had to bring a cow. This dual subjection, to both Ngweshe and NaBushi, is of course foreign to western notions of the sovereign equality of states. It is fairly simple, however, if one keeps in mind that Ngweshe, though a *mwami emwage* ('king in his own place') lacks an older and higher sovereignty which NaBushi and NaRhana both possess. NaRhana's political subjugation to Ngweshe is therefore qualitatively different from his ritual subjugation to NaBushi, Ngweshe's 'father' and, despite Ngweshe's centuries-old 'rebellion', still *mwami* of all Bushi.

Mpara's *okugab'emilala* episode deals primarily with an order of ritual reality centered on NaBushi, an order of reality in which any subordinate branch of the Mwoca clan, even that of Ngweshe, is profoundly irrelevant. Therefore, even though Mpara must acknowledge that NaRhana the *mucuba* player was brought under Mwoca authority, the fact that this was done by the profoundly irrelevant subordinate Ngweshe branch and thereby did not affect the order of ritual reality about which Mpara is speaking has the effect that Ngweshe as such need not figure in Mpara's *okugab'emilala*.

The historical link between the NaRhana who once played a key ritual role at NaBushi's court (the NaRhana represented mythically in Mpara's narrative as Namugamubondo's burialist) and the modern *mwami* of Irhana (represented by the *mucuba* player) is not clear. The second need not be the direct successor of the first, as the presence of three separate NaRhanas in the present ritual systems of Kaziba, Luhwinja, and Burhinyi strongly suggests. 'Rhana-ness' may have been divisible. However, the fact that even an autonomous *mwami* can be a *mujinji* of another—NaLuhwinja is a *mujinji* of NaBushi—suggests that they could have been one and the same. Furthermore, the place of NaCinda in Mpara's narrative parallels that of NaRhana. Since NaCinda was independent, perhaps

NaRhana was too—and both were also NaBushi's *bajinji*. The question cannot be decided with data available at the moment.

Nevertheless, this examination of Mpara's narrative shows that, by drawing evidence from outside the apparent scope of a charter myth, we can learn a good deal about how that myth 'behaves' in response to historical changes. Mpara's *okugab'emilala* narrative involves two *historically* distinct NaRhanas, and the tale's disjointedness results from the narrator's understandable and quite reasonable desire to combine into one story line all the explanations he had learned about 'NaRhana'—a character he clearly considered a single unique historical personage.

Conclusions

This analysis of the impact of the known past upon the Mwoca origin tradition suggests the following methodological points:

1. Each episode proves to be reducible to a core consensus ('the kings came from Lwindi' and 'the clans divided at Luhunda'). Most specifics must be thought of as reflecting contemporary or only recently disappeared arrangements and concepts—as witness the appearance of late eighteenth-century kings' names in the ultimate origins episode and the split personality of NaRhana in Mpara's version of the transferral story. Arguing a deep time-depth for any specific demands positive proof, such as has been presented earlier for *namuga/ibondo* and the mother's burial cliché, and has been put forth here for why Ngweshe people invariably call the first NaBushi 'Kabare'.

2. It is misleading to visualize mythic time as linear, since myth traditions contain evidence from several periods in the past. The case of the Mbiriri clan and its *mujinji* representative at NaBushi's court illustrates how a myth source describing ancient times can enrich our knowledge of recent events—in this case the process by which a large clan group came to acquiesce in Mwoca rule about a century ago. It says nothing about real events at the time in the long ago when its narrative is purported to have occurred.

3. The Mbiriri case and the Rhana case show the utility, indeed the indispensability, of using data from beyond the boundaries of the political unit under study. This is as true for the historian interested in what myth can tell about the more recent past as for the historian probing the distant past.

4. The distinction between a palimpsest *testimony* and a palimp-

sest *tradition* helps one's understanding of how traditions change. The former refers to an *individual's* combining strata of time references; this phenomenon is a result of the nature of verbal historical knowledge, which has a fixed lifespan in oral societies. The latter refers to a transmitted *corpus* which does so, mythic knowledge, which is learned and forgotten in a rhythm determined more by the relevance of the knowledge than by the passing of the generations. NaRhana the burialist is forgotten in NaBushi's domain now that Mpara is dead because NaRhana stopped playing a vital role in Bushi ritual about a century and a half ago—at just the same temporal threshold where the names of individual kings begin to disappear.

5. The profound irrelevance of Ngweshe in these sources underlines the truism that without understanding cultural categories—in this case the notion of *bwami*, 'kingship', as opposed to ritualist, political subordinate, etc.—one cannot begin to understand the history of a people.

Historians try to reconstruct past patterns of human reality and to chart the course of human change. Can genesis myths help in this undertaking? Certainly. The first step is to accept that such sources are in fact myths. In so doing we remove the illusion of a simple, direct historicity. Myths are sacral folklore, not historical representations. Using them demands the approach and skills of the comparative ethnographer, who can trace myth linkages along with linkages in royal regalia or vocabulary terms. Genesis myths should be analyzed with the assumption that their historical idiom is illusory—until the contrary is fully proven.

Once the ethnographic nature of the myth is nakedly exposed, it becomes perhaps the single most useful ethnographic body of evidence the historian has available. It can guide one in formulating hypotheses about the direction of historical change and, in conjunction with linguistic evidence, evidence from material culture, and archaeological evidence it can open a new door to the ancient past. It can also, however, help to understand better the recent past of the societies which transmit it. This said, however, we must admit that the contribution is limited. Myth alone told us no specific facts about what happened in Lwindi or at Luhunda. If it contributes to a chronology of events, that chronology can only be a relative one and one dealing only with general patterns, not specific facts.

Myth can help us make our understanding of the past richer, but only with the tools of comparative ethnography and only if we admit that our goals are not to recover historical personages and specific events, but to understand the broad currents of human change.

Notes

1 In no particular order, works appearing since 1970 which have been useful in preparing this essay include: G. S. Kirk, *Myth* (Berkeley, 1970); T. O. Beidelman, 'Myth, Legend, and Oral History', *Anthropos*, vol. 65, nos. 5–6 (1970), pp. 74–97; Patrick Pender-Cutlip, 'Oral Traditions and Anthropological Analysis', *Azania*, vol. 7 (1972), pp. 3–24; Luc de Heusch, *Le roi ivre* (Paris, 1972); Joseph C. Miller, *Kings and Kinsmen* (Oxford, 1976); David P. Henige, *The Chronology of Oral Tradition* (Oxford, 1974); David W. Cohen, *The Historical Tradition of Busoga* (Oxford, 1972); Steven Feierman, *The Shambaa Kingdom* (Madison, 1974), especially chs. 2 and 3; Jan Vansina, 'Comment: Traditions of Genesis', *Journal of African History*, vol. 15, no. 2 (1974), pp. 317–22, and 'L'influence du mode de compréhension historique d'une civilisation sur ses traditions d'origine: l'exemple Kuba', *Bulletin de l'Academie Royale des Sciences d'Outre-mer*, vol. 2 (1973), pp. 220–40; Frances Harwood, 'Myth, Memory and the Oral Tradition: Cicero in the Trobriands', *American Anthropologist*, vol. 78, no. 4 (1976), pp. 783–96. Indispensable older studies include: J. Vansina, *Oral Tradition: A Study in Historical Methodology* (London, 1965; first published 1961), and 'The Use of Ethnographic Data as Sources for History', in T. O. Ranger (ed.), *Emerging Themes of African History* (Nairobi, 1968), pp. 97–124; Edward Sapir, 'Time Perspective in Aboriginal American Culture: a Study in Method' (in several collections but originally Ottawa, 1916); R. E. Bradbury, 'The Historical Uses of Comparative Ethnography with Special Reference to Benin and the Yoruba', in J. Vansina et al. (eds.), *The Historian in Tropical Africa* (London, 1964), pp. 145–64; Bronislaw Malinowski, 'Myth in Primitive Psychology', in *Magic, Science and Religion and Other Essays* (Glencoe, 1948); Laura Bohannan, 'A Genealogical Charter', *Africa*, vol. 22, no. 4 (1952), pp. 301–15; and G. I. Jones, 'Time and Oral Tradition with Special Reference to Eastern Nigeria', *Journal of African History*, vol. 6, no. 2 (1965), pp. 153–60.

2 Vansina, *Oral Tradition*, part II.

3 Claude Lévi-Strauss, *Structural Anthropology* (Garden City, N. Y., 1967), especially ch. 11, 'The Structural Study of Myth.'

4 *Webster's New Collegiate Dictionary*, 2nd ed.

5 Scholarly work on the Bashi began with Pierre Colle: 'L'Organisation politique des Bashi', *Congo*, vol. 2, no. 5 (1921), pp. 657–84; 'Les clans au pays Bashi', *Congo*, vol. 3, no. 1 (1922), pp. 337–52; *Essai de monographie sur les Bashi* (2nd ed., stenciled, Bukavu, 1971). Three anthropologists have recently done significant work among the Bashi: J. B. Cuypers, 'Les Bantous interlacustres du Kivu', in J. Vansina (ed.), *Introduction à l'ethnographie du Congo* (Kinshasa, 1966) and *L'Alimentation chez les Shi* (Tervuren, 1970); Dikonda wa Lumanyisha, 'Les Rites chez les Bashi et les Bahavu' (PhD dissertation, Université libre de Bruxelles, 1974); and

Elinor Sosne, 'Kinship and Contract in Bushi, a Study in Village Level Politics' (PhD dissertation, University of Wisconsin, Madison, 1974). Historical works include Paul Masson, *Trois siècles chez les Bashi* (Tervuren, 1960), which is basically primary materials, and Richard Sigwalt, 'The Early History of Bushi, an Essay in the Historical Use of Genesis Traditions' (PhD dissertation, University of Wisconsin, Madison, 1975), which includes materials on recent history.

6 Geographically, the expression 'Lwindi' encompasses the Kilega-speaking Basile state as well as lacustrine-language Bunyindu. 'Lwindi' is also considered the point of origin of the Bafuriiru of the Tanganyika plain. Thus far no serious work has been done in Bunyindu itself, but its Lega neighbor now has a thorough ethnography: Mulyumba wa Mamba Itongwa, 'La Structure sociale des Balega-Basile' (2 vols., PhD dissertation, Université libre de Bruxelles, 1977).

7 Texts of variants of the origin myth are in appendices to Sigwalt, 'Early History of Bushi', pp. 192ff.

8 Sigwalt, 'Early History of Bushi', p. 239. Citations are to the English translations. Mashi originals are on the facing pages.

9 Professor Vansina points out that *mukobwa* is used for a wife in Kinyarwanda. This need not imply a borrowing from modern Kinyarwanda, however. Kinyindu is very similar to Kitembo (they may be dialects of the same language), a language linked to languages found in the past in western Rwanda. The complexities of deciphering the materials are suggested in Richard Sigwalt, 'Early Rwanda History: The Contribution of Comparative Ethnography', *History in Africa*, vol. 2 (1975), pp. 137–46.

10 Sigwalt, 'Early History of Bushi', pp. 246, 248, and 250.

11 The significance of the syllables *namuga* and *ibondo* emerged only in the course of later analysis of data collected while in Bushi from 1970 to 1973. I did not find out the meaning they held for the Bashi, but this failure on my part suggests that it is possible to reach at least valid conclusions, however limited, even without intimate knowledge of the cultures involved.

12 Untitled document by Father Feys, Archbishopric Archives, Bukavu.

13 F. Corbisier, 'Rapport Lwindi', Tervuren Ethnographic Archives, Dossier Territoire Kabare.

14 Interview with Ritualists, Kasika (Bunyindu), 7 July 1972.

15 F. Corbisier, 'Historique des Bashi', Tervuren Ethnographic Archives, Dossier Territoire Kabare.

16 Daniel Biebuyck, *Lega Culture* (Berkeley, 1973), pp. 69–70.

17 Dikonda, 'Les Rites', pp. 32–69 for examples.

18 Malinowski contributed the concept: 'Myth in Primitive Psychology.' See also Bohannan, 'A Genealogical Charter.'

19 For a fuller discussion of Bushi's royal rituals, see Sigwalt, 'Early History of Bushi', ch. 4, and Dikonda, 'Les Rites', ch. 4.

20 See especially the testimony of Nyangaka, Sigwalt, 'Early History of Bushi', p. 256.

21 Dikonda, 'Les Rites', p. 347, as *kababa*.

22 Sigwalt, 'Early History', p. 337. The original of this testimony is in Swahili of a special kind. Another testimony remains to be translated from Kinyindu; it probably is very close to this text.

23 ibid., p. 339.

24 Three large stones, known as *masiga ga Namuhoye* ('Namuhoye's cooking-stones') mark the point where the burial of the mother is supposed to have occurred, in southern Rhubimbi province, Ngweshe.

25 Sigwalt, 'Early History', ch. 3. This is a highly tentative reconstruction which is in the course of revision.

26 Colle, 'Les clans', deals exhaustively with clans, but fails to note that the clans he deals with are exclusive to the northern plains area. They are, in fact, Havu clans rather than Shi ones.

27 Henige, *Chronology of Oral Tradition*, especially pp. 27–38; Jones, 'Time and Oral Tradition'.

28 Colle, 'Les Clans.' No thorough study of clan distribution has ever been done, so this statement is impressionistic.

29 Sigwalt, 'Early Rwanda History'; Jan Vansina, *L'évolution du royaume rwanda des origines à 1900* (Brussels, 1961), especially ch. 5.

30 The two categories are, however, easily assimilated since to the Bashi they are aspects of the same thing. See Sigwalt, 'Early History', pp. 147–9.

31 Appendix, line 1.

32 ibid., lines 26–27.

33 Interview with NaCigemwa, 27 June 1973.

34 Sigwalt, 'Early History', p. 146.

35 For the notion of a 'palimpsest' tradition, see Vansina, 'Comment.'

36 Appendix, lines 21–22.

37 Confirmed in the course of field research in mid-1972.

38 Corbisier, 'Enquête-Luhwindja', Tervuren Ethnographic Archives, Dossier Territoire Kabare.

39 The item is an *ishungwe ly'olushembe*, a royal object which firmly corroborates by its distribution much of what this paper argues from purely mythic evidence.

Appendix
Mpara's *Okugab'emilala*

(Mpara's life history is still obscure. He was born and reared in northern Bushi, the plateau edge still ruled by NaBushi. He left that area for Ngweshe sometime after 1936, when NaBushi Rugema resigned his position and Mpara, like many loyalists, refused to recognize his European-named successor. He established himself in northern Ngweshe, where this testimony was transcribed by a court clerk in 1963 at the behest of the Ngweshe administration. Mpara had died when I arrived in Bushi in 1970.)

1 When [Namugamubondo] reached Ntondo she stopped and sent a servant

2 named Namugabakabene to go look for NaCahi and NaCinda; it was NaCahi

3 who made Namugamubondo *abasi* medicine. NaCahi and NaCinda
came and
4 found Namugamubondo at Ntondo, and they remained there. Later
the
5 princes went hunting at Izege and killed an *nshagarhi*. When they
6 returned with their game they found their mother ill with *musonga*.
7 She told them she was so ill they should refrain from going hunting
8 the next day, but they answered that they must go hunt, since the
9 game was so plentiful at Izege. Next day they left early to hunt,
10 and when they reached Bumbalali they killed a *njuzi*. When they
11 returned they found out their mother Namugamubondo had died.
12   When Namugamubondo was about to die she told NaRhana to
take
13 the drum Kalyamahugo and the spear Rutanigwa, the diadem Cidasa
14 and the chicken Nabunyunywe and give them to Ngabwe II,
NaBushi. He
15 should tell them to go on, each to the country he selected. Lastly
16 she gave NaRhana her benediction and wished him good fortune and
prowess
17 in hunting and in governing the country he would go to.
18   NaRhana—also called Karhalalwa—and Lukunjuka buried
Namu-
19 gamubondo with the help of NaCinda. As soon as they finished
burying
20 her, NaRhana went and cooked the meat of the *nshagarhi* which was
stored
21 above the fire; this became the meat of *ngusho*. NaRhana, NaCinda
and
22 Lukunjuka cut up the meat and ate it raw. When they told Ngabwe I
23 (NaBurhinyi) and Ngabwe II (Nabushi) and Kasabo (NaLwanda)
that they
24 too should eat of this meat raw, these latter refused categorically.
25 Instead they sent Namugabakabene and NaCahi to get wood.
NaBukuma
26 struck a fire. They roasted their meat, a leg, and Namugabakabene
27 gave them *buntu*, for which he had bartered his drum. And so they ate.
28   NaRhana then left. When he reached his enclosure he found a
29 *mucuba* there with playing-pieces in it, and he was astonished and
30 went to tell the others. They went and found it also and were as-
31 tonished as well to find playing-pieces with the board. They played
32 and NaRhana defeated them. NaRhana said, 'Listen, you foreigner
NaBushi,
33 from now on you shall fear no mortal, for there is neither man nor
34 beast whose cloth you shall not break.'
35   Thereupon NaRhana became a *murhana* and NaCinda became a
munyamubira
36 and Lukunjuka became a *munjoga*, he who placed Namugamubondo
in the
37 underworld. They finished eating the *lubaba* chicken and playing
mucuba.

38   Early next day each went into the country he had chosen. NaNinja
39   went to Ninja, and he too was a *munyamwoca*. Ngabwe I, Muganga
                                                              NaBurhinyi
40   went to Burhinyi and Ngabwe II NaBushi and Kasabo NaLwanda
                                                              went on with
41   their three subjects, Namugabakabene, NaCahi, and NaBukuma.

Notes

line 1 Ntondo lies between Luhunda and central Ngweshe. Mpara's is one
of the few accounts which does not mention Luhunda.

line 3 *Abasi* played a role in NaBushi's court rituals; its exact nature is
unknown. NaCinda is a petty *mwami* of the Mubiri clan whose territory was
incorporated into Ngweshe in the colonial period.

line 5 Izege is in northern Ngweshe. *Nshagarhi* is a large wild animal, no
longer extant in Bushi, that I have not been able to identify. It is equated
very consciously with the cow in rituals of kingship.

line 6 *Musonga* is a very general term for ailments involving the digestive
tract and spinal pain.

line 10 *Njuzi* is a serval.

line 13–14 This is a list of some of the more important ritual regalia of
NaBushi.

line 14 It is generally agreed that NaBurhinyi is NaBushi's senior. Therefore Mpara, who is attributing to the first NaBushi a past NaBushi's proper
name (Ngabwe), opts to call his mythic NaBurhinyi 'Ngabwe I' and his
mythic NaBushi 'Ngabwe II'. (See the text, lines 22–23)

line 18 'Karhalalwa' is usually given as the name of one of the kings of the
Kilega-speaking kingdoms south of Ngweshe. Is the name here attributed
to NaRhana by clerical error, or is Mpara, a man from NaBushi's area, not
as well-versed as people from Ngweshe about the lands that lie south of the
Ulindi?

line 21 *Ngusho* refers normally to the bull killed for NaBushi's succession
rites.

line 23 Kasabo (NaLwanda: *mwami* of Rwanda) is tacked on many traditions. In the next episode of the story he is depicted going across the Ruzizi
and becoming king of Rwanda. This appears to be entirely etiological.

line 25 NaBukuma is the *murhwa* 'pygmy'. The *murhwa* is responsible for
ritual fire at NaBushi's court.

line 32–34 The curse is obscene: to 'cut one's cloth' (*kutw'omushangi*) is a
euphemism for removing a dead enemy's genitalia.

6. The Study of Historical Process in African Traditions of Genesis: The Bashu Myth of Muhiyi

RANDALL M PACKARD

The publication of Jan Vansina's *Oral Tradition* in the early 1960s was clearly a watershed in the historiography of Africa.[1] It made the study of oral traditions a legitimate historical exercise and thereby allowed historians to expand greatly the scope and depth of their researches into the African past despite the handicap of an absence of written records.

By the early 1970s, however, the work of C. Lévi-Strauss, T. O. Beidelman, E. Leach, and others, on the the structural analysis of myth, was suggesting to a number of historians that oral traditions often reflect a society's present cultural values and ideas rather than aspects of its past.[2] Historical reconstructions based on a literal reading of such traditions, therefore, had to be reassessed. Thus C. C. Wrigley has recently argued that the story of Rukidi, a primary source of evidence for previous studies of Bunyoro history, is a mythical tale designed to explain why the Banyoro are ruled by men rather than gods and that the myth does not describe, even symbolically, actual historical events.[3] Similarly, Luc de Heusch has suggested that the story of Nkongolo and Ilunga, superficially a description of the foundation of the Luba state, in fact consists of a series of structural oppositions reflecting Luba cosmological speculations rather than their historical experience.[4] Finally, Vansina, reassessing his own earlier study of Kuba migration traditions, has concluded that purported migrations reflect Kuba ideas of cosmology expressed in terms of 'upstream' and 'downstream' and do not describe actual population movements.[5]

While these studies serve as a warning against historians' overly literal use of traditions of genesis, they do not negate entirely the historical value of such traditions. For, as Vansina concludes, traditions of genesis can contain elements of historical evidence despite their overwhelming cultural content. 'After all, the very tail end of

157

Kuba traditions of Genesis, when they talk about their last settlements, seems correct. They contribute something to our knowledge
about proto-Kuba culture in giving its location before 1600 and one
or two details about the body politic then.'[6] Similarly, Steven
Feierman, working with traditions of genesis from among the
Shambaa of northeastern Tanzania, shows that the Shambaa
genesis myth of Mbegha operates at several levels, giving expression to Shambaa cultural values, while at the same time providing
important information concerning the establishment of rule by the
Kilindi, the nineteenth-century dynasty in Shambala.[7]

The historian's task in working with traditions of genesis is therefore, to '. . . disentangle statements dealing with worldview from
elements which refer back to past events . . .'[8] Yet it is not a simple
task, for the distinction between what is historical and what merely
reflects later cultural values is often unclear. Even the episodes most
mythical in tone can contain elements of historical truth. This has
been demonstrated by Peter Schmidt's analysis of dynastic histories
in early Kaziba (northwestern Tanzania). These tales describe in
mythical terms the establishment of Babito rule in Kaziba and
appear to have little historical value. Schmidt shows, however, that
these traditions express tensions which existed between incoming
Babito kings and earlier Cwezi mediums and suggest symbolically
how the Babito overcame the resistance of these religious leaders by
developing their own Cwezi cult. Kaziba traditions of genesis are
thus important sources of historical evidence despite their mythical
form.[9] Traditions describing the establishment of the Bashu chiefdoms in eastern Zaire provide an even clearer example of how
apparently mythical traditions can provide important historical data.[10] Moreover, Bashu traditions suggest that while the specific
events described in traditions of genesis are often ahistorical, they
may in certain cases symbolize historical processes lasting over long
periods of time.

The Story of Muhiyi as Myth

The Bashu are primarily mountain cultivators who live in the
Mitumba mountains to the northwest of Lake Amin (ex. Edward) in
what is now the Kivu Region of Zaire. They are part of a larger
linguistic and cultural group known in Zaire as the Banande and in
Uganda as the Bakonjo. Politically the Bashu are divided into
several related chiefdoms. Each of these is ruled by a family of

chiefs who claim to be descended from a common ancestor named
Kavango, who is said to have come from Busongora in southwestern
Uganda in the early nineteenth century.

For the Bashu, the history of Kavango's arrival and the
establishment of their present chiefdoms begins with the story of
Muhiyi, a hunter who leaves his pastoral home in Uganda and
travels across the Semliki Valley in search of a buffalo. Muhiyi
discovers the Isale region of the Mitumba mountains and settles
there as a cultivator. He is later joined by his elder brother, or
father, Kavango, who establishes the first of the present Bashu
chiefdoms. While there is evidence to support the origins of
Kavango, or of the group he represents in Uganda, there is little
evidence to support the authenticity of the details told in the story of
Muhiyi's journey. Moreover, other aspects of the tale suggest that
this part of the Bashu genesis tradition may be mythical. First, the
story of Muhiyi is essentially a hunter-king myth, similar in content
to hunter-king myths found elsewhere in east and central Africa.
The name Muhiyi in fact means 'hunter' in Kinande. Secondly,
when analyzed structurally, the story of Muhiyi can be seen to be a
vehicle for elaborating Bashu social and political values. While I do
not intend to give a complete structural analysis of the Muhiyi story,
I will highlight some of the structural oppositions which occur
within it in order to demonstrate that the myth is at one level a

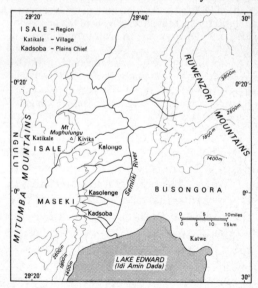

Map 6.1 Upper Semliki valley, *c.* 1900

159

cultural document and that the events described in it can be seen as expressing certain Bashu cultural values.

There are several major variants of the Muhiyi story, each told by a separate social group and each differing from the others in terms of its narrative arrangement. These variations reflect each group's attempt to rearrange the events of the story so that they will support their claim to first occupancy of the land and thus to the social privileges which this status entails. These alterations, however, do not affect the myth's underlying structure, which remains the same in all of the variants[11] The present analysis can therefore proceed on the basis of a single variant that illustrates the basic structure.

Muhiyi lived in Kitara with his father Kyavambe who owned many cattle which Muhiyi was in charge of herding. One day the milk which he had placed in a special hut for Kyavambe began to disappear. Muhiyi's older brother, Kavango, accused Muhiyi of stealing the milk. Muhiyi in his anger took his dogs and spear and left his father's home. After he had left, it was discovered that the milk continued to disappear and that it was being drunk by a serpent. Meanwhile Muhiyi had crossed the Semliki tracking a buffalo. When he reached the hill named Kaviro at the foot of the Mitumbas he succeeded in killing the buffalo. He then built a fire and began roasting its meat. At this time there was a man named Sine, of the Bito clan, living in the mountains above where Muhiyi was camped. Sine saw the smoke rising from the plains below and took some of his men to go and see who was there. He found Muhiyi eating meat alone. Since he and his men were hungry, Sine asked Muhiyi for some meat. Muhiyi distributed the meat from his kill and they all ate together. After they had eaten, Sine noticed that Muhiyi was living in the open without a hut. He therefore invited Muhiyi to come and stay in his village in the mountains. Muhiyi agreed and accompanied Sine to Vungwe. Muhiyi stayed with Sine for a long time and Sine gave him some land on which to grow crops. He also gave him one of his daughters for a wife. This daughter bore a son named Kisoro who was later invested chief of Bunyuka. Muhiyi was later joined by Kavango who settled at Kivika. Muhiyi recognized the authority of his older brother Kavango whose descendants established the other Bashu chiefdoms.

Analyzed structurally, the myth of Muhiyi describes a *rite de passage* in which the hero is separated from one status, that of a pastoralist, goes through a period of transition, and is then incorporated into a new status, that of a cultivator.[12] Muhiyi begins his transformation as a herder of cattle who is accused of stealing milk. As a result of this accusation, he flees from his father's home and crosses a river. In certain variants this river is called the Kalemba (Semliki), and the land from which Muhiyi comes is called Uganda or Kitara. In other variants no name is given to the river, and the land from which Muhiyi comes is called *Isiri. Isiri* literally means 'the land on the other side of the river'. However, it carries the connotation of a foreign land. This meaning reflects the role of rivers as political boundaries among the Bashu. By crossing the river, Muhiyi enters a new land. He moves from the world of the homestead, *eka*, to the world of the bush, *ekisoki*, from the world of the pastoralist to the world of the hunter.[13]

Muhiyi's entry into the world of the bush and hunters symbolizes his social death and transformation. The homestead and the bush are separate and opposite worlds in Bashu cosmological thought. The world of the bush is an extremely dangerous place which is associated with disorder, wild animals, ritual pollution and malevolent spirits. The homestead, on the other hand, is associated with order, domestic animals, ritual purity and benevolent spirits. These associations occur in a number of different ritual contexts.

All substances and beings which are viewed as ritually dangerous must be kept in the bush away from the homestead. Thus certain powerful medicines employed by *bakumu* (healers), as well as the rainstones used by Bashu rainmakers, are kept in the bush. The forge used for making iron tools, a ritually dangerous occupation, must be built in the bush away from the homestead. A man who kills another man and thus becomes ritually unclean (*erihala*) may not re-enter the homestead until he has been purified by a *mukumu*.

Similarly, spirits which are potentially dangerous to the homestead dwell in the bush. The most common of these malevolent spirits are Ndyoka and Lusenge. Ndyoka is said to attack or trap women who go into the bush to draw water from a stream. Lusenge traps women collecting firewood in the bush. Having trapped a woman these spirits can enter the homestead where they cause the death of children, in the case of Ndyoka, and the sterility of women in the case of Lusenge. In this way the creatures of the bush threaten the world of the homestead by preventing the production of children, who are essential to its continuity. The spirits of ancestors who were not accorded proper burial rites are also said to dwell in the bush and to 'whistle through the mountains like the wind', causing harm to anyone they meet. The spirits of ancestors who have been properly buried, on the other hand, dwell within the homestead and can be called upon for assistance.

Certain spirits which inhabit the bush are also called upon from time to time to assist the people of the homestead. *Kalisya*, who is the protector of animals, *Mulemberi*, the protector of children, and *Muhima*, who protects the village, are but a few of these. However, invocations to these spirits, unlike those to the ancestors, may not

161

be made within the homestead, for despite the potential good that these spirits can bring, they are viewed as creatures of the bush and must be kept away from the homestead itself. Sacrifices to these spirits are therefore performed in the banana plantation which surrounds the homestead. The banana plantation (*mboko*) is viewed as a liminal area between the *eka* and the *ekisoki* and thus as an appropriate place for communication between these two worlds.[14]

Since the bush is associated with death, disorder, and pollution in Bashu cosmology, the movement from the homestead to the bush in Bashu life crisis rituals symbolizes the shedding of a former social status, or social death. During ritual investiture ceremonies, a new chief (*mwami w'embita*) undergoes a ritual burial which marks the end of his former status and the beginning of his transition to the life of an invested chief. This ritual takes place in a special grove which has been left to grow wild and which is referred to as the bush (*ekisoki*).[15] Similarly, Bashu circumcision ceremonies, like those of many other societies, require the initiates to live in the bush for several months during which time they shed their boyhood and enter manhood. Muhiyi's entry into the world of the bush thus symbolizes the shedding of his former status as a pastoralist and the beginning of his transition to the status of agriculturalist.

Representing Muhiyi as a hunter emphasizes the transitional character of this stage in Muhiyi's development. The hunter is a man who frequently moves between the world of the homestead and the world of the bush. He is thus a liminal figure in Bashu thought and an ideal symbol for Muhiyi's transition.

When Muhiyi reaches the other side of the plains he kills the animal he has been chasing and roasts its meat. This leads to his being discovered by Sine and to his movement into the agricultural world of the mountains where Muhiyi's transformation from pastoralist to agriculturalist is completed.

Two symbolic oppositions are set up by Muhiyi's movements from the world of pastoralism to the world of agriculture. The first is between Muhiyi's life as a hunter and his life as an agriculturalist and signifies Muhiyi's humanization and socialization into the agricultural world. It also expresses an ambiguity inherent in the relationship of superiority and inferiority between chiefs and subjects in Bashu society. The second opposition is between Muhiyi's life as an agriculturalist and his life as a pastoralist. This contrast expresses a conflict between Bashu ideology of acquiring political power through the consent of the governed and the reality of frequent, sometimes violent usurpation.

162

Muhiyi the Hunter vs. Muhiyi the Agriculturalist

The opposition between Muhiyi's life as a hunter and his life as an agriculturalist takes several forms. First, while living in the plains Muhiyi is described as sleeping in the open without a hut. In one version he is said to have lived like a certain type of jackal. Sine observes that Muhiyi has no shelter and invites him to stay in his home. Thus we have the opposition: one who sleeps in the bush vs. one who sleeps in a hut. People who dwell in the bush are more like wild animals than people. They are extremely dangerous and often harm or even kill people they meet in the bush. Three types of people sleep in the bush: hunters, sorcerers, and *bakumbira*.[16] *Bakumbira* are people who have performed particularly abhorrent actions such as having sexual relations with their mother or full sister. As a result of these actions *bakumbira* are expelled from society and live in the forest like animals, letting their hair grow long and never bathing. Muhiyi, by sleeping in the bush, is associated with these wild and dangerous beings. By moving into Sine's homestead and sleeping in a hut, he leaves this wild state and conforms to the behavior associated with normal men.

Muhiyi lives alone in the bush and is self-sufficient. He hunts his food and eats by himself. His initiation into the agricultural world, on the other hand, begins with his sharing meat and involves a series of exchanges with Sine. In return for giving meat, Muhiyi receives shelter, land and a wife. In one version Muhiyi also gives Sine a hunting knife to be used in sacrifices for the wellbeing of the land. In another version Sine gives Muhiyi a hoe and seeds. Ultimately, Sine's people give Muhiyi, or his son Kisoro, political power. We thus have the following opposition: one who eats alone and is self-sufficient vs. one who shares food and engages in exchange.

This opposition expresses a basic problem for the Bashu, or any society: the conflict between individual and group action. Men must act in concert with each other, they must engage in exchange and cooperate in numerous activities if the society is to exist and not be reduced to anarchy. Yet men often act individually. The necessity of acting in concert with others and the dangers of acting alone are expressed in Bashu ideas about the performance of ritual. A man cannot make a sacrifice to his ancestors without the assistance of neighbors from other lineages. It is said that a sacrifice made without this cooperation will be unsuccessful. Moreover, it may offend the ancestor to whom the sacrifice is offered and result in the ancestor causing harm within the man's family.

Cooperation is also necessary in the performances of public ritual. Unilateral attempts to perform land rituals, like attempts to sacrifice to an ancestor without one's neighbors, can bring misfortune. Thus a rainmaker who acts alone can only bring damaging storms. Calling up the long soft rains needed for growing crops requires the cooperation of several rainmakers. In general, individual action brings famine, while cooperative action brings plenty.

By eating alone and not engaging in communal activity, Muhiyi is therefore a potential threat to the community of men. His actions are in fact those of a sorcerer (*muloyi*) in that they are antithetical to the values of society. Conversely, by sharing meat and entering into exchange with Sine's people, Muhiyi conforms to the values of society and contributes to the society's wellbeing.

Muhiyi's socialization is further defined by the nature of the exchanges in the which he engages.

Muhiyi gives Sine	*Sine gives Muhiyi*
meat	land
a hunting knife	a wife
	a hoe
	seeds
	shelter
	chiefship

Muhiyi offers the gifts of a hunter, while Sine's gifts are associated with the agricultural world. Wives perform most of the work involved in the cultivation of crops. The chiefship which Muhiyi or his son receives is ritual in nature and related to the fertility of the land and is thus directly tied to the growing of crops. Muhiyi thus exchanges his life as a hunter for a life as an agriculturalist. There are no references to Muhiyi hunting in the mountains. This exchange of statuses is paralleled by the transformation of Muhiyi's hunting knife into a knife used for making sacrifices for the land.

Up to this point the discussion has focused on Muhiyi's socialization as presented in the opposition between Muhiyi's life as a hunter and his life as an agriculturalist. However, Muhiyi's exchanges with Sine have an additional meaning which is independent of their role in defining Muhiyi's socialization. Muhiyi is shown to be a giver of meat, and meat givers are socially superior to meat receivers. At such localized lineage (*nda*) functions as sacrifices for the lineage's ancestors, the meat of the sacrificial animal, along with other meat, is distributed by the head of the lineage, the *mukulu,* who possesses the sacrificial knife *omuhamba w'ovuhere* and is responsible for the performance of these sacrifices. At functions requiring the attendance of several *nda* from the same clan, each *nda* eats together as a group separate from other clanmates. On such occasions it is the *mukulu* of the genealogically senior *nda* who distributes the meat to the *bakulu* of the other *nda.* Distributors of goods are in general superior to receivers of goods.[17] Thus the term *mughavi,* 'he who distributes', is used to describe a chief, *mwami w'embita*, while the term *avayhavirwa*, 'those who receive', describes his subjects.

Although Muhiyi is a giver of meat, he is a receiver of land, and land givers are superior to land receivers. Muhiyi also receives a wife from Sine, and wife givers are superior to wife receivers. A man accordingly shows great respect and deference to his father-in-law and avoids any action which might offend him. Muhiyi's exchanges thus create conflicting patterns of superior-inferior relations. Muhiyi as meat giver is superior to Sine as meat receiver, but Sine as land and wife giver is superior to Muhiyi as land and wife receiver. This conflict in role attribution gives expression to the relationship between Bashu chiefs and pre-existing leaders. Bashu chiefs are politically superior to pre-existing social groups, but they are also dependent upon these groups for the performance of certain local rituals related to the productivity of the land, as well as for their continued political support. Bashu chiefs exercise political control through consensus rather than force and thus the relationship between chiefs and subjects is inherently ambiguous. This ambiguity is expressed in Muhiyi's exchange of gifts.

Muhiyi the Agriculturalist vs. Muhiyi the Pastoralist

A second set of symbolic oppositions is set up by Muhiyi's transformation from cattlekeeping to farming. Muhiyi leaves his father's home after being accused of stealing milk. Conversely he is incorporated into the agricultural world of the mountains after distributing meat. This symbolic pair, one who steals milk as opposed to one who gives meat, symbolizes the conflict between the ideology that political authority is always given and the reality that it is often taken.

Stealing milk is a symbol for the usurpation of political authority, as indicated by the role of milk giving in Bashu royal ritual and in

165

certain historical traditions. Prior to the investiture of a *mwami w'embita*, the candidate for investiture or his representative must visit several families of former chiefs who were superseded by the present chiefs. These groups are called *basaghula*. The *mwami*-to-be asks each family for some milk to drink. By fulfilling this request each family acknowledges the political authority of the candidate. In principle, if the *basaghula* do not give the candidate milk, he cannot be invested.

The giving of milk also appears as an acknowledgment of political authority in the historical traditions of the Bashu chiefdom of Buhimba. Shortly after the *mwami* Kihimba arrived in Buhimba, he was visited by two hunters who were servants of a neighboring *mwami* of the Bamate, a related section of the Banande. The hunters asked Kihimba for some food for their dogs. Kihimba gave them squash. The hunters then returned to their master and reported that they had found a powerful *mwami* living in the land which bordered on their master's chiefdom. The Mumate *mwami* told the hunters to return to this *mwami* and ask him to give them some milk. The hunters followed these instructions but Kihimba did not wish to give them milk and so told them that he had none. The hunters, however, saw drops of milk on Kihimba's beard and knew that he had lied. They thus returned to their master and reported that Kihimba had refused to give them milk. This news enraged the Mumate *mwami* and caused him to send his hunters to Kihimba a third time, instructing them to kill Kihimba. The hunters followed their master's instructions and killed Kihimba with a spear. Following Kihimba's death the Bashu of Buhimba began paying tribute to the Bamate. The story clearly expresses a Bamate request for political submission by the Bahimba, Bahimba refusal, and their subsequent conquest, all told through the metaphor of giving—or failing to give—milk.

In Bashu royal ritual and in the story of Kihimba the giving of milk is equated with the recognition of political authority. Conversely, the refusal to give milk signifies a denial of political authority. It follows logically that the stealing of milk signifies the illegitimate acquisition of political authority. Thus the story of the pastoralist Muhiyi accuses him of having stolen political power.

Conversely, Muhiyi's life as an agriculturalist begins with an act of giving, when he gives meat to Sine and his men, rather than an act of theft. This action ultimately leads to his being given political authority. Muhiyi's attainment of power thus conforms to the Bashu ideal that political power should be given rather than taken. Men

166

who demonstrate their ability to provide meat, land, and above all good harvests are given political power. The idea that political power is *given* is expressed by the rituals and prohibitions associated with the investiture ceremony. Thus in the milk-giving ceremony each group of former chiefs must in principle acknowledge the new *mwami*'s right to rule before the *mwami* can be invested. The same ideal is also expressed by a sanction against members of the *mwami*'s family participating in the direction of the investiture ceremony. While many of the *mwami*'s relatives are assigned ritual roles related to the investiture ceremony, they must find individuals from other lineages who actually perform these duties. The net effect of these and other regulations is to give the impression that the *mwami* is being given chiefship by those he will rule.

The pastoralist-agriculturalist opposition therefore parallels the opposition of two models for the acquisition of political power. As a pastoralist Muhiyi steals or is accused of stealing power. As an agriculturalist he gives meat and is given political power. This opposition gives expression to the failure of Bashu ideology to reflect accurately how *bami* actually attain power. From an ideological perspective a *mwami* is always *given* power. In reality, however, *bami* frequently usurp political authority. They undermine the authority of existing chiefs by forming alliances with their subjects and on occasion even resort to political assassination.[18]

The Story of Muhiyi as Historical Process

To the extent that the story of Muhiyi's transformation is a vehicle for a number of Bashu social and political values, it reflects timeless cosmological ideals. Yet it is also a distillation of Bashu historical experience. The history of the Mitumba mountain region within which the Bashu live is one of the ascent of successive groups from the grasslands of the Semliki Valley up onto the forested slopes of the mountains and of the interaction between these groups in the higher elevations. While the Mitumbas rise sharply from the floor of the Semliki Valley to a mountain plateau with an average elevation of around 6,000 feet, river valleys transecting this escarpment provide channels of communication between the lowlands and the highlands. From the middle of the seventeenth century, seed-agriculturalists expanded their cultivation along these valleys by cutting back the heavy vegetation that covered them and came into contact with the forest Bantu who had preceded them into the mountains. Later, after the seed-agriculturalists had cleared away the forest cover, these same valleys provided avenues by which several groups of plains chiefs, whose wealth was in cattle and other livestock, expanded their influence and grazing activities into the mountains and eventually established themselves as chiefs over the mountains' agricultural inhabitants at the end of the eighteenth and beginning of the nineteenth century. Towards the middle of the nineteenth century, the chiefdoms established by these former plains chiefs, now mountain agriculturalists, were brought under the control of a single family of plains chiefs descended from a man named Kavango.

I suggest that the story of Muhiyi's transformation from a cattle herder to a cultivator represents a distillation in mythical terms of this last migration of cattle chiefs into the Mitumbas and their transformation into agriculturalists. It therefore describes long-term historical processes which led to the creation of the present Bashu chiefdoms and is more than a vehicle for Bashu cultural values.

The individual histories of several Bashu chiefly families confirm the historicity of the transformation symbolized by the story of Muhiyi. These traditions come from the descendants of Kavango, Mukumbwa, and Kadsoba, Bashu chiefs who are said to have been pastoral chiefs who settled to farm in the Mitumbas. However, these claims cannot be accepted without additional independent evidence, for they are consistent with Bashu cosmological ideas concerning 'east' and 'west', in which the 'east', and thus the direction of the Semliki Valley, is thought to be the appropriate direction for one's ancestors to have come. Moreover, these histories may have incorporated the structure of the central myth of Muhiyi. Fortunately, independent information comes from the traditions of the pastoral groups who formerly occupied the Semliki Valley. While these groups no longer inhabit the valley, having been forced to leave on account of sleeping sickness in 1932, their traditions were partially collected by Belgian agents who first found them in the valley in 1896.

When the Belgians first arrived on the west bank of the Semliki River they found the region controlled by several 'Hima' chiefs, who, in contrast to the farming chiefs of the Mitumba mountains, had large herds of cattle and other livestock.[19]

Chez le petit chef Makora, toute la population est de race Wahima, origine de Toro. Cette tribu s'occupe uniquement d'élevage de gros et de petits bétails. Aucune plantation ne se remontre dans leurs villages . . .[20]

These chiefs claimed to be related genealogically to a number of politically prominent mountain families. For example, the plains chief Kalongo, who also claimed to be related to the Babito rulers of Busongora, Toro and Bunyoro in Uganda, stated that he and Kavango's descendants were members of the same family, Kavango's branch having settled in the mountains, leaving Kalongo's ancestors to rule the plains.[21] The common historical origin of Kavango and Kalongo is further supported by similarities between the royal rituals and terminology of the present Bashu chiefdoms and those of the Babito states of western Uganda. Moreover, Kavango's descendants, like the Babito rulers of Busongora, Toro, and Bunyoro, sent representatives to Ntsinga Island in Lake George, the home of Ninyamwine, mother of the Cwezi king Ndahura, as part of their accession ceremonies.[22]

The plains chief Kasolenge also attested to the historical movement of cattlekeeping chiefs into the mountains, claiming that his ancestor, Isimbwa, had travelled from Uganda with the mountain chief Mukumbwa who ruled the Maseki region of the Mitumbas before the expansion of Kavango's descendants into the region. Isimbwa is said to have remained in the plains while Mukumbwa went on to settle in the mountains. The historical relationship between Isimbwa and Mukumbwa is supported by a Belgian report which states that during the early years of colonial administration Mukumbwa's descendants avoided compliance with Belgian administrative regulations by returning to the plains to live with their 'Hima' relatives there.[23]

References in early Belgian reports to the plains chief Molekela, whose family had political authority in both the plains and the mountains, provide further evidence connecting the chiefs in the mountains with those in the plains.

> La chefferie de Molekela comprend deux parties bien distinctes, l'une en plaine, l'autre en montagne. Dans la plaine sont les bétails et les sujets de race Wahima qui les gardent. Les sujets de la montagne sont de race Wanande . . .[24]

Among Molekela's mountain relatives were the chiefs Kyabinire and Kakuse. Thus traditions from the plains support those of the mountains in indicating that sections of several pastoral families settled in the Mitumba mountains and eventually became chiefs over the farmers living there. The myth of Muhiyi therefore accurately distills the historical process which led to the establishment of the present Bashu chiefdoms.

Yet the story of Muhiyi is not simply a migration myth. It is also the story of Muhiyi's transformation from herdsman to cultivator, and this contrast too captures Bashu historical experience. The colder, damper climate of the mountains is not suitable for cattle acclimated to the plains. Plains chiefs who settled in the mountains eventually abandoned pastoral activities in favor of agricultural practices, adopting ritual and political activities associated with the growing of crops and the fertility of the land. However, this transformation occurred gradually. Cattle thrive in the warmer lower slopes and foothills of the Mitumbas where these plains chiefs first settled. It was only later, when political expediency forced them to settle higher in the mountains, that they or their descendants found it necessary to leave their cattle with relatives who remained below and acclimate to the agricultural world of the mountains.

The initial settlement of pastoral families in the lower mountains and foothills was apparently stimulated by a desire to safeguard their access to important dry season pastures located there. These dry season pastures with their higher rainfall played an important role in the annual pattern of cattle movements by which the plains chiefs maximized grazing resources and maintained their herds.

The plains chiefs, however, were not the only people to use these lands. Mountain cultivators grew maize, groundnuts, and manioc in the lower mountain areas, which, while wetter than the plains, were drier than the upper mountain ridges upon which they lived and thus better suited for these crops. Because of the agricultural importance of these transitional lands mountain chiefs claimed authority over them. The joint use of the lower mountains by pastoralists and cultivators occasionally resulted in conflicts arising primarily from the destruction of crops by the herds of the pastoralists. By establishing more permanent settlements in the disputed area, the plains chiefs protected their access to them and defended them against the incursions of mountain chiefs and cultivators. At the same time, there is evidence that sleeping sickness and warfare in the Semliki Valley at the beginning of the nineteenth century may have stimulated further movements into the mountains that led to settlement on a more permanent basis. In the face of such misfortunes certain plains chiefs may have viewed the highland pastures as both more defensible and less infested with tsetse flies than the plains below.[25]

Having settled in the lower mountains the plains chiefs continued their cattleherding activities. Moreover, it is clear from their continued emphasis on marriage alliances with groups in the lowlands that their social and political orientation remained fixed on the world of the plains.

These historical alliances can be reconstructed from several types of data contained in Bashu oral traditions. First, the traditions of chiefly lineages normally contain the names of the localized lineages from which each chief took his senior wife, i.e. the mother of his successor; his *mombo*, a ritual wife who is ideologically, though never biologically, the mother of his successor; and other wives whose sons later held prominent positions within the chiefdom. These marriages are generally confirmed in the traditions of the local lineages involved. Secondly, the traditions of commoner lineages contain information concerning the ritual roles which their members played in the investitures or funerals of various former chiefs. Together, these types of data allow one to reconstruct former alliance patterns within Bashu society and to examine how these patterns changed over time. The amount of data of this type which is remembered obviously increases as one moves closer to the present. However, there is sufficient evidence for earlier periods to piece together some of the marriage alliances which the incoming plains chiefs established when they settled on the lower slopes of the Mitumbas. From this evidence it appears that these early alliances were primarily with other plains groups located in the Semliki Valley or in Busongora to the east. This indicates that the social and political perspective of these pastoral settlers was still oriented toward the plains. Kavango's successor, Mukunyu, for example, chose both the biological and ritual mothers of his successor from plains groups.

Despite their continued pastoral orientation the former plains chiefs who moved to the Mitumbas eventually found it necessary to secure their position in the mountains by using their wealth in livestock, especially goats, which were the basis of Bashu bridewealth, to establish alliances with influential mountain leaders.[26] These alliances involved them more deeply in mountain politics and led eventually to their incorporation into the mountain agricultural world. The family histories of two former plains chiefs, Kavango and Kadsoba, illustrate this process.

Kavango's family settled at Kivika on the lower slopes of Mt. Mughulungu in the Isale region of the Mitumbas sometime in the early decades of the nineteenth century. They initially accepted the political authority of the existing mountain chiefs in return for access to grazing land. Kavango's successor, Mukunyu, continued this practice but also began strengthening his family's position in the mountains by creating alliances with several other influential mountain leaders, while at the same time maintaining his ties with the plains through the important marriage alliances mentioned above.

The most important of Mukunyu's mountain alliances was with the Baswaga clan of Katikale, from whom he acquired a wife. The Baswaga of Katikale were recognized as the first occupants of a sizeable area of land west of Mt. Mughulungu and thus had considerable ritual influence within the region as a whole. They were also related to the powerful Baswaga chiefs of Ngulu to the west of Isale. Mukunyu's alliance with the Baswaga not only helped him secure his family's control over the lower slopes of Mt. Mughulungu by providing them with an influential ally, but it also produced a son, Luvango, who as an adult would greatly increase his family's involvement in mountain politics.

Luvango was raised among his mother's brothers, the Baswaga of Katikale, where he evidently learned a great deal about mountain politics, for he grew up to become a master at alliance building and subversion—the two pathways to political authority among the Bashu—and to become a major political figure in Isale.

Yet Luvango was not Mukunyu's immediate successor. Instead, Luvango's younger brother, Visalu, whose mother's brothers were the pastoral Banisanza of the Lisasa plains, was made chief, indicating the continued pastoral political orientation of Mukunyu and his advisors. Visalu, however, was still a young boy when his father died and Luvango was therefore appointed as regent. Luvango soon took advantage of this position and of his family's wealth in livestock to further his own political advancement by establishing an extensive network of alliances with influential mountain leaders throughout Isale. With the support of these allies Luvango established himself as a chief in the mountains by undermining the political authority of the mountain chiefs his predecessors had recognized and by usurping Visalu's position and driving him out of Isale.

Luvango legitimized his claim to political authority in the mountains by replacing his family ritual practices associated with pastoral chiefship with others associated with the fertility of the land and agricultural chiefship. This transformation was brought about in part by necessity. In usurping Visalu's authority, Luvango had alienated many of his father's former pastoral allies, who had supported Visalu and may have have regarded Luvango's involvement in agricultural politics with the contempt that their descendants now hold for cultivators. Among the pastoralists who refused to recognize Luvango were the family of royal ritualists who had invested Luvango's ancestors since the time they lived far to the east in Busongora. This group refused to participate in Luvango's investiture and thus denied him access to the traditional rituals associated with pastoral chiefship. Luvango was therefore forced to enlist the assistance of royal ritualists from the mountain chiefdoms of the Baswaga and Bamate to the west and south of Isale. In doing so, he accepted their rituals and the regalia associated with mountain chiefship.[27] Thus Luvango, the descendant of plains chiefs, established himself and his descendants as mountain chiefs whose power base lay in the mountains rather than the plains, with authority consecrated with agricultural rather than pastoral rituals.

The history of Kadsoba's family provides a second example of how pastoral groups became increasingly involved in mountain politics once they settled in the lower mountain pastures.[28] Kadsoba's family settled sometime between 1870 and 1880 with many cattle and other livestock in the plains and foothills which bordered the territory of the mountain chief Binga. Kadsoba's wealth in livestock is said to have attracted a large number of Binga's followers, mostly young men who settled in the plains and lower mountains in order to become his clients and thereby acquire goats for bridewealth payments. These clients grew crops in the nearby plains and foothills and exchanged them along with beer, pots, and arrowheads, for hides, milk, butter and livestock. In addition, each client was given several of Kadsoba's cattle to guard. When a cow gave birth, the client received a goat as a gift.

While this arrangement proved satisfactory for Kadsoba and his Bashu clients, it posed a threat to Binga, whose political power vis-à-vis other mountain chiefs was weakened by the movement of his subjects to the plains. Binga, therefore, attacked Kadsoba's settlements. Kadsoba, either unable to respond to these attacks militarily or perhaps concerned that a protracted conflict would endanger his herds, decided to placate Binga by sending him gifts of cattle. Binga accepted these gifts, perhaps interpreting them as tribute payments, and ceased his attacks. However, Kadsoba did not wish to see his herds reduced through continued payments to Binga, nor did he wish to abandon his settlements in the hills and the access to dry season pastures they provided. He therefore established a series of alliances with other mountain leaders who were Binga's subjects. Through these alliances Kadsoba slowly undermined Binga's chiefdom. Binga's death soon after his initial attack on Kadsoba's settlements and the succession of a young

173

inexperienced son to Binga's position, no doubt aided Kadsoba's incursions. By 1900, Kadsoba's influence extended into the mountains and his followers had begun to practice the agricultural rituals of their new subjects.

The histories of Luvango's and Kadsoba's families provide historical examples of the process described symbolically in the story of Muhiyi's transformation from a herder to a cultivator. Plains chiefs extended their political influence into the mountains and eventually became mountain chiefs. In addition, both Luvango's and Kadsoba's acquisitions of political authority in the mountains illustrate the conflict between the ideology and practice of acquiring political power in Bashu society symbolized in the myth of Muhiyi by the opposition between his life as a pastoralist and his life as a cultivator. From the perspective of Luvango's and Kadsoba's relationships with allies who chose to support them in return for political or economic favors or privileges, Luvango and Kadsoba were given political power and thus conform to the ideal pattern by which Bashu political authority is acquired. However, from the perspective of their relationships with the chiefs whom they replaced, they must be seen as usurpers who stole political power.

Thus the story of Muhiyi's journey from Kitara and his transformation from a herder of cattle to a cultivator, while not necessarily describing a specific series of historical events, symbolizes long-term historical processes by which cattle chiefs expanded their influence into the Mitumbas and became acculturated to the agricultural world of the mountains. The story of Muhiyi therefore accurately reconstructs the development of the present Bashu chiefdoms, even as it also reflects Bashu cultural values. Moreover, the myth of Muhiyi suggests that repetitive historical experience can over time affect the structure and content of traditions of genesis in much the same way that social and political values affect them. While further research needs to be carried out before we can determine whether the Bashu story of Muhiyi is a unique case or whether it exemplifies a more general phenomenon, this case should at the very least encourage historians working with similar traditions of genesis to re-examine the apparently ahistorical episodes they describe to see whether they too reflect long-term historical processes.

Notes

1 Jan Vansina, *Oral Tradition; A Study in Historical Methodology* (London, 1965).
2 See for example, Edmund Leach, *The Structural Study of Myth and Totemism* (London, 1967), and T. O. Beidelman, 'Myth, Legend and Oral History', *Anthropos*, vol. 65, nos. 5–6 (1970), pp. 74–97.
3 C. C. Wrigley, 'The Story of Rukidi', *Africa*, vol. 43, no. 3 (1973), pp. 219–34.
4 Luc de Heusch, *Le roi ivre ou l'origine de l'état* (Paris, 1972).
5 Vansina, 'L'influence du mode de compréhension historique d'une civilisation sur ses traditions d'origine: l'exemple Kuba', *Bulletin de l'Academie Royale des Sciences d'Outre-Mer*, vol. 2 (1973), pp. 220–40; 'Traditions of Genesis', Journal of African History, vol. 15, no. 2 (1974), pp. 317–22.
6 Vansina, 'Traditions of Genesis', p. 322.
7 Steven Feierman, *The Shambaa Kingdom* (Madison, 1974).
8 Vansina, 'Traditions of Genesis', p. 322.
9 Peter Schmidt, 'An Investigation of Early and Late Iron Age Cultures Through Oral Tradition and Archeology: An Interdisciplinary Case Study in Buhaya, Tanzania' (PhD dissertation, Northwestern University, 1974).
10 The present essay is based on research carried out among the Bashu during 1974–5, under grants from the Fulbright-Hays Dissertation Year Abroad Program and the University of Wisconsin, Madison.
11 See R. M. Packard, 'The Politics of Ritual Control Among the Bashu of Eastern Zaire During the 19th Century' (PhD dissertation, University of Wisconsin, Madison, 1976), pp. 91–103.
12 Professor Feierman has reached a similar conclusion about the structure of the Shambaa myth of Mbegha. My own analysis of the story of Muhiyi owes much to the insights provided by his study, as well as to his personal comments. See Feierman, *The Shambaa Kingdom*, pp. 45–53.
13 Arnold van Gennep, *The Rites of Passage* (London 1969), p. 13, discusses rituals of separation associated with river crossings. This definition of *isiri* may throw some light on the meaning of references to *Msiri* which appear in the origin traditions of a number of East African peoples. The term is often translated from Swahili as 'Egypt' but may have a meaning similar to the Kinande term *Isiri* and simply mean the land on the other side of the river.
14 The liminal nature of banana groves is indicated by the use of banana leaves in rites of transition. For example the widow(s) and children of a deceased man must put on clothes made of green banana leaves for the head shaving ceremony which marks the end of the mourning period. Once the head shaving is completed, these clothes are discarded and new ones of barkcloth are put on. It is also said that a man's spirit (*kirimu*) leaves his body at death and enters the banana grove. It is said to be in limbo between the world of the living and that of the dead. After the funeral rites are completed he enters the world of the ancestors and dwells again within the homestead.

15 When I began collecting data on the investiture ceremony I was told that it took place in the bush (*ekisoki*). It was only later in my research that I learned that this 'bush' referred to a special grove.

16 The Bashu view hunters as very dangerous people. I was warned on several occasions that I should be very careful when travelling in areas frequented by hunters, 'for a hunter can kill you in an instant'. A *mukumbira* can transfer his pollution to another person through sexual intercourse. They thus attempt to rape or seduce those they meet in the bush in order to free themselves.

17 This association occurs in a tradition which refers to the investiture of Mughashu s/o Vyogho, a descendant of Kavango. When Vyogho died, his son Kitawiti was designated as his successor. Kitawiti, however, died before he could be invested. Mbuanga, Vyogho's firstborn son, thought that he should be invested since Kitawiti had died. However, his younger brother Mughashu was chosen in his place. Mbuanga was infuriated by this decision and after Mughashu's investiture went to the shrine in which Vyogho's royal emblems were kept. Mbuanga desecrated the shrine by exposing the emblems to sunlight. At this time he was said to have cried, *Ingy'endwa mughavi mawere muyhavirwa*, 'I who was the distributor, became a receiver', Bashu Historical Texts (BHT) 29, Rutava, 19 June 1974. These texts are based on interviews carried out by the author in Zaire during 1974 and 1975 and are in the author's possession. An indexed edition of the collection is being prepared for deposit at the University of Wisconsin-Madison Memorial Library.

18 Discussing the structural elements of the Shambaa myth of Mbegha, Feierman suggests that the opposition between Mbegha's life in Ngulu and his life in Shambala present two opposing paradigms of the exercise of political power. Mbegha's life in Shambala represents the characteristics associated with the proper exercise of political power, while his life in Ngulu represents the misuse of political power (Feierman, *Shambaa Kingdom*, p. 64). Muhiyi's two roles, however, are not mutually exclusive, for Bashu chiefs are both stealers and receivers of political power.

19 Belgian use of the term 'Bahima' or 'Wahima' generally resembles the Bashu use of the term in that it refers to people who live primarily by cattlekeeping as opposed to cultivation. It does not necessarily imply the existence of any specific physical or racial characteristics, though many of the 'Bahima' in the Semliki Valley did exhibit the distinctive physical features generally associated with Bahima elsewhere.

20 Reconnaissance fait Octobre 1911, Registre des Renseignements Politiques-Kasindi 1908–13, Archives de Zone de Beni, p. 52.

21 The political and social relationship between Kalongo and the Babito princes of Busongora is supported by sources from both Uganda and Zaire: E. R. Kamuhangire, 'The States of the Southwestern Uganda Salt Lakes Region', paper presented to Department of History, Makerere University, Kampala, 1972, p. 13: Reconnaissance October 1911, Renseignements Politiques-Kasindi, p. 53. Political disruption in the upper Semliki Valley at the end of the nineteenth century left these west bank chiefs virtually independent of their overlords in Busongora. Registre des Renseignements Politiques-Semliki 1924–27, p. 44: Rapport d'enquête sur le Chefferie Bahema, Registre des Renseignements Politiques-Territoire de Beni:

1928–37, p. 334; BHT 165, Kalongo Mahombo, 2 February 1975.

22 For example the Bashu employ the term *mukama* as a chiefly title, *mubito* for the chief's eldest brother and head of the royal lineage and *ekikali* for the chief's homestead. These terms do not occur elsewhere in the Lacustrine region of Zaire but do occur in western Uganda where they are closely associated with Babito rule. Similarly, like the Babito of Bunyoro, the Bashu remove and preserve the lower jawbone of a deceased chief. While a number of Lacustrine Zaire groups remove their ruler's entire skull, the removal of just the lower jawbone occurs primarily to the east of the Bashu, among the Bakonjo chiefs of the western slopes of the Ruwenzoris who claim to be Babito, and among the Babito rulers of Bunyoro, Toro, Busongora, and Kaziba. The Baganda also preserve the king's lower jawbone, but like the Lacustrine Zaire states remove the whole skull. The practice thus appears to be associated with Babito culture. There is some evidence that Kavango's family are related to the chief Molekela of the Bamoli clan rather than to the Babito. This however was not confirmed by Molekela or his descendants and would not in any case alter the fact that Kavango's descendants trace their origins to the Semliki Valley and to pastoralism. See: Packard, 'Politics of Ritual Control', pp. 134–5, for a discussion of this evidence.

23 H. Daniels to M. Henne, Beni, 24 August 1927, Archives de Zone de Beni, Correspondance.

24 Reconnaissance June 1913, Renseignements Politiques-Kasindi, p. 61.

25 See Packard, 'Politics of Ritual Control', pp. 143–55, for a fuller discussion of these possible motivating factors.

26 The disparity between the livestock wealth of the plains dwellers and that of the mountain folk is attested to by numerous traditions which indicate that the plains were a reservoir from which the Bashu replenished their herds whenever they were decimated by disease or raiding. Thus one Muhima informant stated that the people of the plains used to call the people of the mountains *avai-ira*, 'because they were poor while in the plains we had many cattle and goats'. BHT 112, Kahembe, 28 October 1974.

27 Among the accession rituals apparently borrowed at this time were the mock burial of the *mwami*, the banging of hammers by the *omwamihesi* (literally chief blacksmith) and the smearing of the *mwami*'s body with red powder.

28 This description is based largely on traditions collected by early Belgian agents who visited Molekela. Reconnaissance October 1911, Renseignements Politiques-Kasindi, Archives de Beni.

7. Bobangi Oral Traditions: Indicators of Changing Perceptions*

ROBERT W HARMS

Since the early 1950s, when historians first began using oral traditions in writing the history of Africa, they have been searching for better methods to deal with the basic fact that oral traditions, as documents which are stored in the human mind and transmitted anew to each generation, change over time. Although some historians continue to treat them as more or less straightforward accounts of past events, many others have turned to newer approaches which take the dynamic element into account.

These approaches are predicated on the assumption that oral traditions are retained and passed down, not out of an idle curiosity about the past, but because they make significant statements about the present. Thus, some oral traditions serve as cultural charters which use the medium of the past to express symbolically and to legitimate the ideals of the present social order.[1] Other traditions justify the claims of incumbents or pretenders in the struggles of lineage, clan, or royal politics, and therefore may reflect present politics more than actual historical events.[2] Sometimes, of course, elements of both may be found in a single tradition.

The intimate relationship between oral traditions and the present order suggests that the traditions are slowly being altered as the society changes. These alterations come about primarily in two ways. In some cases, the individual narrator adjusts different parts of the tradition in an *ad hoc* manner much as the owner of an old house might update it one room at a time over a period of years.[3] In other cases, some traditions simply become irrelevant with the

*Some of the texts used in this chapter have been printed also in the *Journal of Interdisciplinary History*, 10 (1979), pp. 61–85, and are used here by permission of the *Journal of Interdisciplinary History* and the M.I.T. Press, Cambridge, Massachusetts. Copyright © 1979 by the Massachusetts Institute of Technology and the editors of the *Journal of Interdisciplinary History*.

passage of time, and cease to be passed on to succeeding generations. New traditions, which more accurately reflect current interests and perceptions, take their place.

This new understanding of the dynamics of oral traditions has
caused many historians to re-evaluate their uses of oral traditions as
historical sources. Instead of uncritically accepting the narratives as
given, they apply insights gained from anthropological fieldwork to
try to separate the kernel of unchanging historical narrative from
the changing symbolism and political posturing. While this
approach has proved successful in some cases, it has led to heated
debates in others. Some scholars have argued that anything that
symbolically reflects present realities must be rejected, while others
contend that symbolic significance does not necessarily make a story
untrue.[4]

While the problem of separating unchanging historical narrative
from changing cultural perceptions is difficult enough when working with a single oral tradition, it is compounded by the tendency of
different narrators to tell a story in different ways. The standard way
of dealing with this problem has been to compare the variants to find
the common threads. But, as Robin Horton has pointed out, there is
no reason why the common denominator should be any nearer to
historical truth than the variants.[5] Others have attempted to overcome the problem by trying to distinguish a 'true' version from the
'distorted' variants, but this is often impossible to do, if, indeed, a
'true' version does exist.

However, both the problem of change over time and the problem
of coexisting variants can be overcome in some cases by taking a
broader view of what constitutes historical truth. While many oral
traditions simply do not permit the reconstruction of a narrative
history, they can point to subtler processes of change over time. This
view stands much of the recent criticism on its head: if oral traditions are not simply narratives of past events, but rather changing
commentaries on cultural values, social structures, and political
relationships, then it follows that they may be useful tools to illuminate broader issues of African intellectual, social, and political
history.

The task, then, is not to separate the cultural elements from the
historical ones, but to search the oral traditions for evidence of
broadly based cultural, social, and political change. Sometimes, a
tradition makes a conscious symbolic statement about how the
present is different from the past, but usually the evidence must be
deduced from incongruities among the elements in a single tradition

or differences among variants. The incongruities and differences are crucial because they reveal how the traditions themselves have changed over time. These changes, in turn, point to underlying shifts in the cultural, social, and political realities that the traditions reflect. In sum, the very characteristics of oral traditions which frustrate the reconstruction of historical narratives can prove invaluable in providing clues to underlying processes of change.

Bobangi Society and Traditions

The oral traditions that I collected among the Bobangi of the Zaire (formerly Congo) River provide an excellent test case for this approach.[6] They not only exhibit the limitations inherent in all oral traditions, but also present special problems of interpretation stemming from certain features of Bobangi life.

Bobangi society is composed of highly individualistic and mobile people who make their living primarily by fishing and trade. The demands of commerce and the tendency of fish to congregate in different areas at different times of the year cause most individuals to travel frequently to markets or fishing camps. This emphasis on mobility is reflected in the bilateral kinship system, which prevents the formation of closely knit kin groups, and the Bobangi tendency to form fishing and trading parties on the basis of friendship and mutual interest rather than kinship. The Bobangi have never had any kind of centralized political organization. Rather, each village was governed by a headman who held office by virtue of being the most powerful trader in the village rather than through claims of ritual or genealogical legitimacy.

As a result of Bobangi social and political organization, the kinds of interest groups which retain and pass down oral traditions in most African societies simply did not exist. The absence of corporate kin groups prevented the formation of lineage or clan traditions. Even personal genealogies seldom went back more than four generations, and these were always sketchy. Informants knew the names of certain ancestors whom they had seen or heard about in specific contexts but had no systematic genealogical knowledge. Finally, the cultural similarities between the Bobangi and the other river peoples negated any necessity to maintain traditions stressing the uniqueness of Bobangi culture.

Despite these limitations, some oral traditions have been passed down among the Bobangi in the form of stories which were important to some segments of the society for one reason or another. They were not told by specialist historians in formal oral performances, but were simply recited around the night fires at a fishing camp or on a beach where a fleet of trading canoes stopped for the night. A story continued to be told as long as it was important to the listeners, but once its relevance faded, it ceased to be told and would be remembered only by a few people with exceptional memories. This system of transmission caused me much frustration during my research, for there was no way of knowing in advance who was likely to remember the old stories, especially the ones that were no longer being told. My best informants turned out to be people who occupied no special position in Bobangi society. Rather, they were people ordinary in all respects other than their possession of keen memories that helped them to recall stories they had not heard or told for many years.

Because of the rather special features of Bobangi social organization and oral transmission, it is not surprising that Bobangi oral traditions proved resistant to the standard interpretative approaches. Clearly, they could not be taken literally. In response to straightforward requests for information on the history of the Bobangi, I got stories about people crossing a ten-mile-wide river on a rope, a man trying to carry water in a fish basket, and people migrating down the river on raphia mats pulled by rats. This, it seemed, was hardly the stuff of which serious narrative history is made.

On the other hand, it was difficult to view these stories as cultural charters whose purpose was to legitimize existing cultural values. In the first place, they were known by only a handful of very old men. If they were to function as cultural charters, one could expect them to enjoy greater popularity. In the second place, there was no apparent pattern of relationships between the elements of the stories and past or present cultural values. It was equally difficult to view them as position papers in current political squabbles because the people who knew them were generally far removed from any current disputes, and because no direct link between the traditions and politics could be found.

Despite abundant grounds for doubting that these stories had any historical value at all, there remained one unshakeable fact that argued for giving them serious consideration: they were considered important enough to be handed down from at least one past generation and to be remembered by a few old men. Unlike literate societies, where a relatively unimportant bit of information may lie in an archive for hundreds of years, oral societies, which can pass down only a relatively restricted body of knowledge, generally hand down only those things regarded as important for one reason or another. Since the Bobangi traditions were regarded as important by some very knowledgeable elders, the first task of the analysis was to discover why.

Upon further reflection, it became clear that the purpose of these stories was neither to present a narrative history of the Bobangi nor to establish a cultural charter, but to put forth a certain definition of what it meant to be Bobangi in an area where ethnic identity is particularly vague and fluid. They did not affirm any specific cultural values. Rather, they outlined an arbitrary definition of Bobangi ethnic boundaries, including some groups that were culturally different from the Bobangi, while excluding others that were culturally similar.[7]

This does not mean that the stories have no historical value. On the contrary, the ethnic boundaries they define formed in a specific historical setting in the past and subsequently evolved in response to later historical circumstances. Therefore, by understanding how the Bobangi defined themselves at a particular point in the past and how this definition changed, it becomes possible both to trace a very subtle process of change in the oral traditions and to gain valuable insights into the historical circumstances that these changes reflected.

Fortunately, the reconstruction of Bobangi history does not rely on oral traditions alone. Bits of documentary evidence, plus linguistic and ethnographic studies of the area, have provided some needed background to understanding the traditions. Shortly after Portuguese explorers first arrived at the mouth of the Zaire river in the late fifteenth century, a lively trade developed in which Africans supplied slaves, ivory, and other products to the Portuguese in return for European goods. This trade spread inland, and by the 1780s it had reached all the way to the lower Ubangi river, where the Bobangi had become major suppliers of slaves to the coast.[8] During the nineteenth century, Bobangi traders branched out, migrating downstream and establishing villages at most of the key points along the Zaire river between the Equator and the Pool. Thereafter, they dominated this stretch of the river trade to such an extent that they exercised a near monopoly.

Since most of the riverbanks in this area consist of low floodplains that become inundated during the rainy season, the Bobangi and the other river peoples built their villages on the few spots where the riverbanks were high enough to provide protection from the flood-waters. The result was that each stretch of high banks housed a cluster of densely populated villages, while uninhabited stretches of up to 150 kilometers separated the clusters.

This settlement pattern caused widespread confusion among early explorers and ethnographers who were trying to map out the ethnic composition of the area. On the one hand, each cluster of villages was somewhat different, both culturally and linguistically, from every other, so some observers tended to look upon each cluster as a distinct ethnic group. On the other hand, all of the river peoples speak closely related languages, share similar cultural patterns, and mix freely at fishing camps. Because of this, some writers have tended to lump them all together as 'Bangala' north of the Equator, and 'Bobangi' south of the Equator.[9]

The confusion has persisted to the present day because the question of ethnic identity is not very important to the people themselves. For purposes of everyday life, identification with a certain village or village cluster usually suffices. Broader-scale ethnic identity becomes important only when some large-scale issue arises to make it important. This happened in the early 1960s, when all of the river people united under the ethnic name of 'Bangala' in order to gain political leverage against the inland peoples during the political conflicts of the first years of independence.

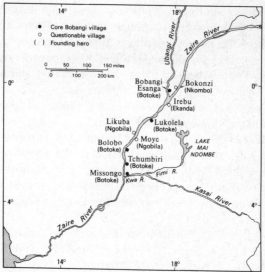

Map 7.1 Major village clusters of central Zaire basin

183

Despite the fluid nature of ethnic identity in the area, there are some village clusters that can be clearly identified as Bobangi. The main one is the cluster along the lower Ubangi river known as Bobangi Esanga. This is the historic homeland. Further down on the Zaire river are four other village clusters—Lukolela, Bolobo, Tchumbiri, Missongo—which were founded by immigrants from Bobangi Esanga. This link is confirmed not only by the inhabitants of all of these clusters, including Bobangi Esanga, but also by the fact that names of individual villages in the Bobangi Esanga cluster are sometimes duplicated in the downriver clusters. These five village clusters, then, can be called the core Bobangi clusters.

The other major village clusters along this stretch of the river—Bokonzi, Irebu, Likuba, Moye—are very similar both culturally and linguistically to the core Bobangi clusters, but their identity remains open to debate by both outside observers and the people themselves. Although they often claim to be Bobangi, they lack clear ties to the Bobangi homeland. In contrast to the core Bobangi clusters, which all claim the same founding hero, each of the questionable clusters has its own founding hero.

The oral traditions that I collected among the Bobangi were short narratives which took from ten minutes to half an hour to recite. Each narrative contained a series of distinct episodes. A comparison of the narratives showed enormous variation. Some narrators integrated all of the episodes into the framework of a single downriver migration, while others posited several migrations in order to fit in all of the episodes. Although certain episodes appeared in almost all of the narratives, others appeared in only one or two. Furthermore, the episodes appeared in different orders in different narratives. Soon it became clear that a narrative did not form a coherent whole. Rather, the performer created the narrative by stringing together whichever stories he happened to remember. One informant, Bomele, explained that he had indeed constructed his narrative in this fashion for my benefit. This explains the observation of John Whitehead, who noted in the 1890s that no two people would tell what they knew of any particular events in the same order.[10] Therefore, it seemed appropriate for me to divide the narratives into separate stories and treat each story as a separate tradition.

This done, I found that the stories could be divided into three types: traditions of origin, traditions of migration, and traditions of settlement. These types correspond roughly to the major divisions of a hypothetical composite narrative which would begin with the tradition of origin, trace the migrations, and end with the traditions of settlement. In practice, however, no single narrative that I collected contained all three types. The tradition of origin is known only at Bobangi Esanga; traditions of migration are known in all the village clusters; while the settlement traditions are known only at the villages nearest to the Pool. The significance of this distribution should become clear as the analysis proceeds.

Each type of tradition reflects a different type of reality and therefore requires a different interpretative approach. The tradition of origin refers to a process that resulted in the formation of Bobangi Esanga. This was a single 'event', which is reflected metaphorically in the tradition. Therefore, the 'event' can be recovered by interpreting the metaphor. The migration traditions reflect a gradual and broadly based process of change which covered a huge geographical area. This process can be recovered only by comparing all of the variants in order to distinguish the underlying pattern beneath the surface variation. The third type of tradition, settlement traditions, refers to specific contractual relationships which have been unilaterally altered by one party. Here, the key to the interpretation lies in exposing internal incongruities in the traditions themselves.

Origin Tradition of Botoke

The Bobangi tradition of origin is essentially a declaration of independence. Unlike many African traditions of genesis, it does not refer to the creation of the world or the origins of institutions, but to a split with another group. To tell the tradition of origin is to declare that 'we are no longer part of another group. We are now a separate and distinct people'.

The tradition of origin collected at Bobangi Esanga is a good example of this type.[11] This tradition is known in the lower Ubangi area, but not in the core Bobangi clusters along the Zaire River because the downriver villages stress their ties with their historic homeland, while the people of the homeland stress their distinctness from their neighbors farther up the Ubangi River. The story tells of Botoke, a simple fisherman who lived in a village somewhere up the Ubangi River. Botoke was caught sleeping with the wife of a local chief and sentenced to carry a certain quantity of water up from the river in an *ekete*, a fish weir with large holes. Finding the task impossible, Botoke began to fear for his life and fled downstream with a small group of kinsmen to found the village cluster of Bobangi Esanga, which then grew to become large and prosperous.

While the story obviously describes the rejection of a former social identity and the development of a new one, its significance goes deeper than that. The story is a metaphor for a general process of schism and migration that has been a central feature of Ubangi River culture for hundreds of years. Recent anthropological fieldwork in the area by Pierre Van Leynseele has shown that one of the most regular features of the river culture over the long term has been a cycle of incorporation, division, and migration which begins when a group of people locate some inhabitable land, settle, and become wealthy through fishing and local trade. Their prosperity attracts newcomers who affiliate themselves to the core group. Eventually, the growing population taxes the ability of the settlement to support it, and the affiliated members begin to be perceived as a threat to the prosperity of the core group, which closes ranks to protect its rights, creating conditions which force the affiliated members to move on to seek a place of their own. The immigrants then become the core group in the new location, and begin to attract affiliate members.[12]

The story of Botoke can be seen as a personalized metaphor for this sociological process. Since Botoke was not wealthy, he was clearly not a member of the core group. By sleeping with the chief's wife, he presented a challenge to this group, which responded by making his life so uncomfortable that he had to leave and seek a place of his own. Once established in the new homeland, his group began to prosper and attract immigrants from other areas. The key elements of the story thus correspond with the key elements of the process described by Van Leynseele. Although the main purpose of the story is to declare the distinct identity of the Bobangi, the insights of anthropological fieldwork allow the historian to reconstruct the process by which this distinct identity emerged.

Traditions of Migration

The second type of tradition, migration traditions, recounts episodes which allegedly took place after Botoke left Bobangi Esanga and went downstream to open trade in slaves and ivory with the Pool and establish trading settlements along the Zaire River. Taken as a group, these traditions describe the spread of Bobangi identity to encompass most of the river people between the Equator and the mouth of the Kwa.

This growth in the scale of Bobangi identity was a result of the enlarged scale of economic competition engendered by the slave and ivory trade. While rivalries in former times had been carried out among small groups of kinsmen who sought wealth through fishing and local trade, the new economic competition was carried out among alliances of village clusters which formed widespread commercial networks for purposes of monopolizing trade. Thus, the old process of incorporation and division was duplicated on a grand scale. A core group of allied village clusters became wealthy and attracted other village clusters which sought affiliation with the alliance. Some affiliates later challenged the pre-eminence of the core group and were expelled.

Bobangi identity spread in two ways. First, emigrants from Bobangi Esanga left their homeland to establish the settlements of Lukolela, Bolobo, Tchumbiri, and Missongo (core Bobangi villages) along the Zaire River in order to serve as way stations between the upriver sources of slaves and ivory and the markets at the Pool. These migrations did not indicate a split among the people of Bobangi Esanga, but rather an extension of their commercial reach because the downriver settlements maintained close ties with the homeland. Family genealogies show that these migrations continued over several generations. The newly established villages grew rapidly as a result of the massive incorporation of slaves into Bobangi kin groups. Thus, the name 'Bobangi', which originally referred only to the people of Bobangi Esanga, spread to encompass the homeland plus the four downriver village clusters.

But the migration traditions shed little light on the economics or demography of this process, either directly or metaphorically. Rather, they focus on its sociological aspects: the generalized spread of Bobangi identity to village clusters whose inhabitants had not come from Bobangi Esanga. Their purpose is to define the changing boundaries of Bobangi identity by explaining which village clusters were considered Bobangi and which were not.

This interpretation is partially confirmed by the geographical distribution of the events recounted in the traditions. The downriver village clusters which were founded by immigrants from Bobangi Esanga—Lukolela, Bolobo, Tchumbiri, Missongo—are not discussed in any detail in the migration traditions. Although the traditions state that Botoke founded these villages, they do not provide any details. Rather, the traditions focus on the questionable village clusters—Bokonzi, Irebu, Likuba, Moye—and seek to explain why each one should or should not be counted as Bobangi. Since the inhabitants of the core clusters did not question their Bobangi identity, there was no need for them to retain elaborate stories to justify it. The identity of the other village clusters, on the other hand, was open to question. Therefore, it became necessary to create and maintain a body of stories dealing with this issue.

Since under normal circumstances ethnic identity was not an important issue in that area, why was it so important to define who was Bobangi and who was not? The answer has been suggested by Abner Cohen and others who have noted that ethnicity is often a political phenomenon that becomes particularly important in situations of intense interaction in which groups are competing for scarce resources, or in which one group tries to maintain a monopoly on privilege and seeks a way of defining who is to be included and who is to be excluded.[13] Such a situation came into being in the early nineteenth century when the core Bobangi group gained a near monopoly over the river trade by capturing the narrow stretch of the river between Tchumbiri and Missongo, thus gaining the power to dictate who could or could not pass down to the markets at the Pool. Once the monopoly was established, it became important to define precisely who was Bobangi and who was not in order to determine who could participate in the trade.

Since many inhabitants of the core Bobangi village clusters were of slave origin, the key to Bobangi identity was not personal genealogical ties to the Bobangi homeland, but residence in a village cluster that was considered Bobangi. While at first this included only the core Bobangi village clusters, it later came to include any other village clusters which joined the alliance. Residents of village clusters which were considered Bobangi enjoyed full participation in the Bobangi trading alliance, while residents of non-Bobangi clusters did not.

The central symbol for this alliance was the mythical founding hero, Botoke. Although most of my informants insisted that Botoke was one man, others explained that Botoke was actually a chiefly title that had been created by the early inhabitants of Bobangi Esanga.[14] Therefore, 'Botoke' refers to a series of Botoke chiefs who governed during the eighteenth and early nineteenth centuries. By the late nineteenth century, however, the Botoke title had disappeared, but nobody remembers why.

Since the early inhabitants of Bobangi Esanga identified themselves as the followers of the Botoke chiefs, it is not surprising that

Botoke became enshrined in oral traditions as the symbol of the core Bobangi group. Thus, the inhabitants of the core Bobangi village clusters proclaimed their identity by claiming that their ancestors had migrated downstream with Botoke. Village clusters which joined the Bobangi alliance at a later date explained their new identity in terms of a meeting with Botoke. Exclusions from the trade network were justified in terms of a dispute between Botoke and the excluded group. So important was the Botoke symbol in the nineteenth century that the crew of every trading canoe that approached a Bobangi village was required to acknowledge the Bobangi monopoly over the trade by singing the following song:[15]

Every country has its master,
The master of the river is Botoke.

The first story illustrating the incorporation of a non-Bobangi community concerns the village cluster of Bokonzi, located along the Zaire River near the Equator.[16] These people do not claim that their ancestors came from Bobangi Esanga. Instead, they trace their origins to the Mongala River, an upriver tributary of the Zaire, and claim that they once spoke a language that resembles those of the Mongala area. The story, which is known both at Bobangi Esanga and Bokonzi, tells how Nkombo, the founding hero of Bokonzi, went on a trip down the river and met Botoke. At first, the two spoke to each other in sign language, but then Botoke performed a miracle and suddenly Nkombo began speaking Bobangi. He returned to Bokonzi and taught his people to speak Bobangi, which they speak to this day.

This story testifies to the incorporation of an alien group which gained recognition as Bobangi. Although it does not give the reason for this incorporation, an analysis of trade patterns in the area suggests an explanation. During the nineteenth century, the Bokonzi traders navigated the productive stretch of river between their ancestral homeland and the downriver Bobangi villages in search of trade. Since they funnelled a lot of wealth into the Bobangi trade network, it is small wonder that they gained full recognition as Bobangi, despite their alien origins.

The case of Irebu is more complicated; it shows incorporation followed by exclusion.[17] Like the people of Bokonzi, the people of Irebu speak the Bobangi language and claim an origin in the Mongala area. Traditions about Irebu are known both at Bokonzi and Irebu, but the two versions differ significantly. The Bokonzi version says that Ekinda, the founding hero of Irebu, met Botoke on a downriver trip. Botoke again performed a miracle, causing Ekinda to change from his former language to the Bobangi language. This implies that the Irebu people gained full participation in the trade network as Bobangi.

The version collected at Irebu, however, tells the story differently. It recounts how Ekinda came down from the Mongala area and began to trade, but omits any mention of a meeting with Botoke or a language change. In contrast to the version collected at Bokonzi, this one denies any present or historical identification with the Bobangi. Yet the denial is not totally convincing because it leaves unanswered the questions of why they adopted the Bobangi language, and why the Bokonzi people claim that the Irebu people were once Bobangi.

Insight as to why the Irebu people would deny their Bobangi connections is given by two other stories, one from Lukolela, the other from Irebu. The Lukolela story tells of a group of traders from Irebu who were traveling down to the Pool with a group of traders from Bobangi Esanga. On the first day out, the Irebu traders spotted a parrot and caught it. Since they had seen it first, they refused to share it with the Bobangi traders. The next day the Bobangi traders spotted a dead elephant on the bank, and went to get the tusks. When the Irebu traders demanded one of the tusks, they replied, 'You wouldn't share your parrot with us, so we won't share our ivory with you.' The Irebu traders got angry and started a fight in which several people were killed.

The story from Irebu says that the people of Bobangi Esanga once came to attack Irebu. They were driven off, but after that, the two groups fought whenever they met on trading trips. During the interview that followed the telling of this story, I asked the informant if the Bobangi and the Irebu people formed a single people. He replied, 'We are one person. We are divided because of those wars of long ago.'

By taking into account the points of view expressed by the different stories, it becomes possible to reconstruct the main lines of the changing relationship between the Irebu people and the Bobangi. After the Irebu people arrived from the Mongala area, they joined the Bobangi trade network and gained recognition as Bobangi, taking advantage of their ancestral ties to the Mongala area and their new ties to the Bobangi to carry on a lucrative trade. The cooperation between the two groups eventually disintegrated as they quarreled over trade rights. The Bobangi view of this quarrel, as illustrated by the Lukolela story, is that the Irebu traders sought certain advantages for themselves and refused to cooperate on an equal basis. The Irebu version does not explain the cause of the fight, but does associate the fighting with trade.

As a result of the quarrel, the Irebu traders lost their rights as Bobangi in the trade network but continued to trade independently. Oral testimony and documentary evidence have confirmed that although their access to the markets at the Pool was diminished, they maintained a lucrative trade on the upper river.[18] Because of this, they tried to disassociate themselves from the Bobangi.

Bobangi traditions about the Likuba and Moye illustrate cases of exclusion.[19] Not surprisingly, they are ambiguous about the nature of the relationship between these groups and the Bobangi before the exclusion took place. One variant states that Ngobila, the founding hero of the Likuba, and Ngobila, the founding hero of the Moye, both came from Bobangi Esanga, having been sent down the river by Botoke as advance scouts prior to the descent of the master of the river himself. Others, however, merely note that the two Ngobila were already in place when Botoke arrived. The Likuba and Moye themselves place their ancestral homeland vaguely in the area of the lower Ubangi without any specific reference to Bobangi Esanga. Although they do not claim to speak the Bobangi language, their own dialects are so closely related to Bobangi as to be almost indistinguishable from it.

The traditions state that when Botoke came down the river, he found the two Ngobila fighting with one another. He settled the affair to the satisfaction of all concerned, and then requested that each send some people down with him to help paddle and fight. They both refused, claiming that they needed all the available manpower for themselves. Botoke became angry and declared that he would go on without them, but that the Likuba and Moye should never again expect freedom of passage along the river.

In contrast to Bokonzi and Irebu, which had no historical connection with the Bobangi, the Likuba and Moye did have such ties, though their exact nature remains unclear. This, however, did not prevent the Bobangi from excluding them from the trade and refusing to recognize them as Bobangi. The Bobangi definition of themselves as a group was not based on historical or cultural criteria of ethnicity, but on the commercial and political realities of the river trade.

Confirmation that the purpose of the migration stories was to justify the inclusion or exclusion of these marginal groups comes from the story of Mokemo mo Bolanga, a Bobangi chief who lived at Missongo, the Bobangi village cluster closest to the markets at the Pool.[20] Some variants claim that he was the son of the founding hero, Botoke. Whether or not this is literally true, it shows that in the Bobangi view of their historical chronology the events associated with Mokemo mo Bolanga were the results of earlier decisions made by Botoke.

The story says that Mokemo mo Bolanga stretched a vine across the river so that nobody could pass without his knowledge. Everyone who wanted to pass had to stop and ask his permission. Bobangi were allowed to pass, but others were not. Most variants specifically mentioned that Likuba and Moye could not pass because they had refused to help Botoke when he needed them.

The migration stories have several serious shortcomings as historical sources. First, the heavy use of metaphors and symbols makes it impossible to reconstruct just how a certain inclusion or exclusion came about. But whether or not it came about in the manner described is beside the point, which is that it did take place, or there would have been no reason for preserving a story which justified it.

A second limitation is that they do not provide a basis for constructing a chronology. Except for the statement that Mokemo mo Bolanga was the son of Botoke, there are no clues as to the order in which the events took place, much less when they occurred. While the stories do reveal certain changes in the Bobangi definition of ethnic identity, they probably ignore others which have been forgotten. All that can be said is that the stories recounted here probably represent the ethnic definition current in the late nineteenth century, when the Bobangi were driven out of the river trade by the European colonizers.

Since that time, the stories are unlikely to have changed because there has been no reason to change them. They are survivals from another age, not living traditions. Evidence for this comes from the fact that the only people who know them are very old men who learned them long ago when memories of the river trade remained fresh. Younger men do not know these stories because they are not being passed down. The purpose they once served has disappeared, and the stories themselves will probably disappear with the passing of the few remaining people who know them.

Historical traditions told by the Moye provide an interesting contrast with the traditions of the Bobangi and show how the conflicting interests of the two groups have resulted in conflicting perceptions of history.[21] The Moye tell of a group of men who banded together to migrate downstream from the Ubangi river.

Whenever one of them saw a piece of riverbank suitable for settlement, he settled there while the others continued on. This story accounts for the origin of every major village cluster from the mouth of the Ubangi to the mouth of the Kwa. In it, Botoke was not the master of the river, but simply one of the group.

This story shows that the Moye defined the river people as a single large group in which all of the subgroups were equal. It denied that Botoke was the master of the river and proclaimed that all groups deserved equal rights on the river and equal status with the Bobangi. The contrast between the Bobangi stories and this one shows how the dominant group tried to be as exclusive as possible, while the Moye, an excluded group, proclaimed the brotherhood of man.

A comparison of the present distribution of Bobangi and Moye historical traditions reveals how changing situations have affected their transmission. At the same time that Bobangi traditions are dying out because they serve no purpose in the twentieth century, the Moye traditions are gaining popularity. Since 1960, two local historians have written histories of the river people which elaborate the Moye version of the traditions at great length.[22] These stories represent a plea for the river people to unite on the basis of supposed historical ties.

This call became especially strong in the early 1960s, when the river people united to form a special province that consisted mainly of the river and its banks.[23] Although it was subsequently disbanded by the central government, the sentiments that it embodied remain strong. Thus Moye traditions are becoming popular at a time when only the very old men still remember the song, 'The master of the river is Botoke'.

Although the perception of Bobangi identity expressed by that song is no longer significant to the river peoples of the Zaire basin, it is very significant to the historian, for it exerted a major influence on the history of the river trade during the eighteenth and nineteenth centuries. The Bobangi definition of ethnic identity was a political one. It was a way of rewarding friends, punishing enemies, and maintaining privilege. It did not correspond with any linguistic or cultural definition that might be proposed by an ethnographer.

But if an ethnographer were to try to place the Bobangi on an ethnographic map, he would have his choice of four definitions of the Bobangi as an ethnic group, each including a larger group of people than the last.

1. The genealogical definition: All those who can trace their ancestry, whether through slave or blood ties, to Bobangi Esanga.
2. The political definition: All those who participated in the Bobangi trade monopoly in the nineteenth century.
3. The linguistic definition: All those who speak the Bobangi language.
4. The cultural definition: All of the river people.

No single definition is the correct one in an absolute sense. Historically, the people have defined themselves differently in different situations. Originally, they probably used the genealogical definition, since the very name 'Bobangi' implies that they are the people from Bobangi Esanga. But with the growth of the river trade, definition number two became operative, though the exact composition of this group fluctuated with the vicissitudes of the trade. During the late colonial period, the unity of all the river people emerged as an important theme.

Settlement Traditions

The traditions of origin and migration illustrate perceptions of identity rather than the historical reality they seem to describe. Traditions of origin attest to a people's perception of themselves as a distinct group. Migration traditions define perceptions of who is Bobangi and who is not. There are no true or false traditions here, only differing perceptions. Thus, the Bobangi traditions and the Moye traditions can both be true in the sense that they accurately reflect the perceptions of the two groups, even though they give very different versions of the migration. Interpreted in this way, the traditions can be trusted, for there is no reason for a group to misrepresent its own perceptions.

But the third kind of traditions, settlement traditions, represent a different kind of reality. Their purpose is to define specific contractual relationships between the Bobangi of the river and their inland neighbors. Since contractual relationships involve an agreement between two parties, the terms of the contract constitute an objective reality that cannot be changed simply by altering one's own perceptions. A person who contracts a debt can change his perceptions and decide that he no longer wishes to pay it, but that does not change either the terms of the contract or his obligations. To claim that the obligation no longer exists is to lie.

While traditions which describe perceptions evolve in an almost organic fashion, changing slowly as the perceptions change, traditions involving contractual relationships must be deliberately altered and distorted when one of the parties breaks the contract. In the Bobangi settlement traditions, there is evidence of deliberate alteration in order to hide broken contractual relationships between the Bobangi and their inland neighbors.

The distribution of the settlement traditions provides insights into the nature of the relationships involved. The settlements north of Bolobo have not retained such traditions because in this area both the Bobangi and the peoples of the hinterland speak closely related Zone C languages and share many cultural traits that are common to all the people of the central river basin. For as long as people remember, the Bobangi have enjoyed excellent relations with the inland peoples. Intermarriage was common, and commerce between the river and the hinterland was carried on by individual traders who visited the inland villages, often staying with friends or affinal relatives.

In the region of the three downriver settlements—Bolobo, Tchumbiri, and Missongo—the situation was very different. The inland Tio lived on the high plateau overlooking the river and spoke a Zone B language which was unintelligible to the Bobangi. Relationships between the Bobangi and these neighbors have been tense for as long as anyone remembers. Trade in this area, for example, was carried out by means of formal markets located halfway between the river and the nearest inland villages. They met every four days under the supervision of a market chief who had the duty to keep peace between the two groups. There was little intermarriage between the two groups.

This hostility has persisted up to the present day. In the early 1960s the Bobangi and the Tio engaged in armed struggle over the question of whether the land on which the Bobangi were living actually belonged to the inland Tio chiefdoms. If so, according to the reigning administrative system, the Bobangi should be subject to the Tio chiefs. The Bobangi acknowledged that the Tio had settled the hinterlands long before they had settled on the riverbanks, but they argued that the Tio chiefs had never exercised jurisdiction over the land near the river. The Tio chiefs, on the other hand, argued that their jurisdiction had always reached all the way to the river.

The key to settling the dispute was to determine whether the Bobangi had ever symbolically recognized the inland chiefs as owners of the land by paying tribute to them. In pre-colonial times, a Tio chief was considered the owner of all the land in his chiefdom only in the sense that he controlled hunting rights. Every hunter who hunted on the chief's land had to send him one leg of every animal killed in symbolic recognition that the chief was the owner of the land. No other tribute was paid, and the chief had no other authority over the people living on his land. The colonial and post-colonial administrative systems, however, gave the owner of the land control over all the people who lived there. Therefore, a modern dispute over political power centered on the question of whether the Bobangi had ever acknowledged the hunting rights of the Tio chiefs by sending them a leg of every animal killed.

The Bobangi recount the Bolobo settlement tradition as follows:[24] When the Bobangi arrived, the riverbanks were empty. Shortly afterwards, a Bobangi hunter named Makwango Nsambo went hunting along the riverbank and killed seven hippopotami. He said to his companions, 'We have killed seven hippopotami, but who is their owner? There are no people living here.' One of the companions climbed a tree and looked around until he spotted three people, whom he called to come over. The three strangers explained that they had come from the inland village of Bwema and that the animals belonged to the Bwema chief. The two groups argued, and finally, to settle the argument, the hunter gave the strangers a portion of the meat to take to their chief as a sign of friendship. The strangers left. A short time later the inland chief arrived, bringing the hunters gifts of wives, bananas, sugar cane, sweet potatoes, and cassava. The Bobangi were so impressed at the bounty of the inland area that they began negotiations to set up a market between Bolobo and Bwema to facilitate the exchange of inland agricultural products for Bobangi fish. The market functioned until the early colonial period.

The Bobangi story stresses the cooperation of the two groups on a basis of equality. It concludes with the founding of the market, making no mention of any agreement by the Bobangi to send a leg of every animal killed to the inland chief. The Tio, of course, claim that such an agreement was made, and therein lies the heart of the dispute. In this case, the technique of comparing the variants yields nothing, for the two versions totally contradict each other on the key point.

The story of settlement told at Tchumbiri also stresses the equal and reciprocal nature of the Bobangi-Tio relationship.[25] This story tells of a certain hunter who went into the forest to hunt. There, he met some strangers who explained that they came from the inland villages behind the forest. The Bobangi gave the Tio strangers gifts of salt, fish, camwood, and oil. The visitors left and presented these to their chief, who reciprocated by sending sugar cane, beer, peanuts, and raphia mats to the Bobangi. This gift exchange led to the establishment of a market.

One day a representative of the Tio king arrived to ask the people of Tchumbiri to send tribute in fish to the king. The Bobangi refused, saying, 'Botoke is the master of the river. Why should I give you fish? If you want fish, bring some cassava and we will trade.' As a result, the two parties entered into an agreement in which the Bobangi sent fish to the Tio king in return for cassava.

Yet there is an incongruity in each of these stories which suggests that the versions told today are not the same as those told a hundred years ago. It seems strange that stories which purport to explain the establishment of a market should revolve around the central symbol of the hunter, which in local cosmology is intimately linked with the issues of tribute and ownership of land. Stories which sought merely to explain the beginning of trade could do so very well without using the hunter as a central figure. It appears likely, therefore, that at one time the stories explained why Bobangi hunters sent a leg of each animal they killed to the inland chief as well as the origins of the market.

Fortunately, this hypothesis can be supported by documentary evidence.[26] In George Grenfell's personal diary of 15 April 1888, he mentioned that the people of Bolobo sent one leg of every hippopotamus killed to the inland chief. This evidence not only proves that the Bobangi once paid tribute but also allows a reconstruction of how and why the traditions were transformed. When the Bobangi first settled on the riverbank, they made an agreement with the inland chiefs in which they promised to send them one leg of every animal killed on solid ground and to open up markets for mutual trade. They told the story of the hunter to explain both the origins of the tribute and the origins of the trade. But with the advent of the colonial period, they saw a chance to break loose from the inland chiefs. Accordingly, they altered the story to omit any mention of the tribute arrangements. The version that I collected at Tchumbiri has apparently changed more than the one collected at Bolobo, for it omits any mention of a dispute over rights to dead animals, while the Bolobo version retains this incident.

Conclusion

The Bobangi case illustrates the importance of treating oral traditions as living documents which alter over time in response to changing historical situations. They cannot be treated as isolated texts, but must be seen as stories told by specific people in specific places under specific conditions. Such an approach encourages analysis of symbols and metaphors, interpretation of the meaning underlying the variants, and the uncovering of incongruities within a single tradition. The dynamic elements of oral traditions, far from negating their value as historical sources, can open the way to a broader understanding of African intellectual, social, and political history.

Notes

1 See, for example, T. O. Beidelman, 'Myth, Legend, and Oral History: A Kaguru Traditional Text', *Anthropos*, vol. 65 (1970), pp. 74–97; Luc de Heusch, *Le roi ivre* (Paris, 1972); Jan Vansina, 'L'influence du mode de compréhension historique d'une civilisation sur ses traditions d'origine: l'exemple Kuba', *Bulletin des séances de l'Académie Royale des Sciences d'Outre-mer*, vol. 2 (1973), pp. 220–40; Wyatt MacGaffey, 'Oral Tradition in Central Africa', *International Journal of African Historical Studies*, vol. 7 (1974), pp. 417–26.

2 For a detailed discussion of this, see David Henige, *The Chronology of Oral Tradition* (Oxford, 1974), pp. 17–70.

3 Laura Bohannan, 'A Genealogical Charter', *Africa*, vol. 23 (1952), pp. 301–15; Jan Vansina, 'Comment: Traditions of Genesis', *Journal of African History*, vol. 15 (1974), p. 320.

4 For examples of successful applications of this approach, see Steven Feierman, *The Shambaa Kingdom* (Madison, 1974), pp. 64–5; Thomas Spear, 'Traditional Myths and Historians' Myths', *History in Africa*, vol. 1 (1974), pp. 67–84. For debates, see C. C. Wrigley, 'The Story of Rukidi', *Africa*, vol. 43 (1973), pp. 219–34; Beidelman, 'Myth, Legend and Oral History'; Vansina, 'Traditions of Genesis'.

5 Robin Horton, 'Stateless Societies in the History of West Africa', in J. F. Ade Ajayi and Michael Crowder (eds.), *History of West Africa* (New York, 1972), vol. 1, p. 79.

6 This fieldwork was done under a grant from the Social Science Research Council and the American Council of Learned Societies. Professors Jan Vansina and Steven Feierman made valuable comments on an earlier draft of this article. However, the opinions stated in this article are those of the author and not necessarily those of the Councils or the above-named professors.

In distinguishing Bobangi oral traditions from other categories of Bobangi verbal material, I followed the distinctions made by the Bobangi informants themselves. I would open the interviews by asking the informants to tell me anything they knew about the history of the Bobangi. In response, they generally gave me stories or songs about Botoke and other lesser figures of the past. They never gave me fables or proverbs, for example. In this article, I have limited my discussion to traditions which illuminate the history of the Bobangi group as a whole, omitting the numerous stories which refer to the internal history of a single village cluster.

7 This view supports the observation of Fredrik Barth that it is 'the ethnic boundary that defines the group, not the cultural stuff that it encloses'. Fredrik Barth, *Ethnic Groups and Boundaries* (Boston, 1969), p. 15.

8 Further details on the development of this trade network are given in Jan Vansina, *The Tio Kingdom of the Middle Congo, 1880–1892* (London, 1973), and Phyllis Martin, *The External Trade of the Loango Coast, 1576–1870* (Oxford, 1972). Before 1971, the Zaire River was called the Congo River.

9 To cite just a few examples of this confusion, Basile Tanghe argued that thirty-five groups usually considered distinct were all Bobangi in 'Les Mbangi et leurs apparentés dans l'ancien district de l'Ubangi', *Congo* (1934), vol. 1, pp. 654–6; Bernard Mambeke-Boucher claimed that the Likuba were actually Bobangi in 'Ce qui arriva du temps où regnait Boloundza, chef des Afouru', *Liaison*, no. 46 (1955), pp. 40–6; a 1904 political report from Irebu debated the question of whether the Irebu people were actually Bobangi, Archives africaines (Brussels), A.E. (346) 9; a report from the 1920s claimed that the Bobangi were actually Bangala, Archives d'Outre Mer (Aix-en-Provence), AEF 5D60.

10 John Whitehead, *The Bobangi Language* (London, 1899), p. v.

11 Variants of this tradition were told by Bongembele (Bobangi Esanga), 14 September 1975 and Mamadu Jalo (Bobangi Français), 26 September 1975.

12 Adam Kuper and Pierre Van Leynseele, 'Social Anthropology and the "Bantu Expansion"', *Africa*, vol. 48, no. 4 (1978), pp. 342–6.

13 Abner Cohen, *Custom and Politics in Urban Africa* (Berkeley, 1969), pp. 190–201. For a more recent elaboration of this theme, see Crawford Young, *The Politics of Cultural Pluralism* (Madison, 1976).

14 Bongembele (Bobangi Esanga), 13 September 1975; Mbianga Balimba (Bobangi Esanga), 9 September 1975.

15 Even in the early twentieth century, a canoe crew that passed Tchumbiri without singing this song risked being fired upon. Leland Wood, 'Bobangi Life and Christian Education' (PhD dissertation, University of Chicago, 1923), p. 94.

16 Variants of this tradition were recounted by Ianza (Bobangi Esanga), 14 September 1975 and Mokoko (Bokonzi), 16 September 1975.

17 The stories about Ekinda were told by Mokoko (Bokonzi), 16 September 1975; and Malanga (Irebu), 18 September 1975; the stories about the quarrel were told by Ibokiwa (Irebu), 19 September 1975; and Bomele (Lukolela), 25 September 1975.

18 Oral evidence comes from the above cited interviews with Malanga and Ibokiwa; documentary evidence comes from Camille Coquilhat, *Sur le Haut-Congo* (Paris, 1888), pp. 323–4.

19 Variants of this tradition were told by Ebaka (Bolobo), 15 June 1975; Wawa (Tchumbiri), 4 August 1975; Bomele (Lukolela), 25 September 1975; Mambula (Tchumbiri), 5 March 1976; Yangawa (Bolobo), 21 March 1976.

20 Ebaka, Wawa, Bomele, Yangawa, variants cited.

21 Variants of this tradition came from Losengo (Makasu), 10 December 1975; Eyongo (Boyanga), 12 December 1975; Nyangu (Pokolo), 12 December 1975; Limyo (Matende), 14 December 1975.

22 J. J. L. Lingwambe, *Histoire Banunu-Bobangi* (Mimeographed: Kinshasa, 1966); Vincent Bokono, *Monkama mo Mibembo mi Bankoko o Ebale e Congo* (Typescript with several carbon copies: Bolobo, 1960).

23 For more details, see J. C. Williams, *Les Provinces du Congo: Moyen Congo, Sankuru*, C.E.P. vol. 5 (Kinshasa: IRES, Université Lovanium, 1965).

24 Ebaka (Bolobo), 15 June 1975.

25 Wawa (Tchumbiri), 4 August 1975.

26 Diary of George Grenfell, 15 April 1888, Baptist Missionary Society Archives, London.

8. Reconstructing a Conflict in Bunafu: Seeking Evidence Outside the Narrative Tradition

DAVID WILLIAM COHEN

In about 1855, along the northern margins of the Luuka state in Uganda, an intense struggle opened between two centers of authority vying for pre-eminence on the *mutala*[1] that was to become known as Bunafu. At the outset, the enclosures of Nafa and Mukama Womunafu were both located on the upper hillslopes of Bunafu. At the conclusion, in the late 1860s, Nafa's estates had been reduced to an unattractive and nearly unpopulated angle of land along the edge of Nakaibaale swamp, the eastern boundary of the *mutala*. The old supporters of Nafa had fled, some had perhaps been killed. Some were brought quietly and firmly within Mukama Womunafu's community. By various methods and processes, the constituency of the lineage of Nafa had disappeared from Bunafu. Higher up on the *mutala*, Mukama Womunafu's sons had planted estates across the land and Mukama Womunafu was securely established in his second substantial enclosure built on Bunafu, this one close to the old center of Nafa's estates.

Of these two competing centers of authority around mid century, Nafa's was the older. This man Nafa was the descendant of a person who had, around the close of the eighteenth century, arrived from the Mpologoma River area some forty kilometers to the northeast. At that time, the lands that Nafa's ancestor settled lay beyond the northern frontier of the Luuka state, outside the region of regular Luuka administration, and, similarly, beyond the reach of other administrations in northern and central Busoga. Nafa's predecessors, like the midcentury Nafa himself, bore ritual qualities and powers that were translated into local influence, even domination, wherever they and their children and their brothers settled. It is not unlikely that this special capacity had been transferred across numerous generations and considerable space from settlements and experiences in the far north of Uganda. The particular means of

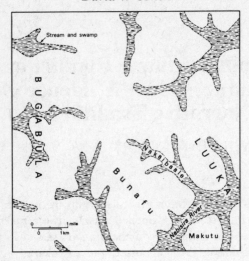

Map 8.1 Bunafu and environs

translation of ritual capacity into local domination appears to have
been the attraction and incorporation of a number of individuals
and groups within an affinal network focused on Nafa. Marriages
were contracted between these settlers and members of Nafa's
household, and thick patterns of service and obligation developed
around the Nafa figure. Today, we have data on the relations of
some ten households with Nafa and his kin in the early part of the
nineteenth century.[2]

The second, and newer, center of authority to develop in
nineteenth-century Bunafu was Mukama Womunafu's. Mukama
was born about 1820 on the southern or 'Luuka' bank of the
Nabisira River and just across the shallow, murky water from Nafa's
community. Mukama Womunafu was one of the eight sons of
Wambuzi, ruler of Luuka from the early nineteenth century until his
death in about 1841. Mukama Womunafu's mother was a woman
raised in Nafa's community (known more recently as 'Mukanni' or
'whose wife?'). Leaving her kin behind, she established herself as
maid and whore in the palace of Wambuzi and there her child by
Wambuzi was conceived.

Just before—or at, or just after—the birth of the child (who early
in his life was probably known simply as 'Mukama'), he was diag-
nosed as being possessed by the force of Mukama, deity and folk-
hero of the wider region who intermittently invaded the persons of
royal men and male children of the royal houses of northern and

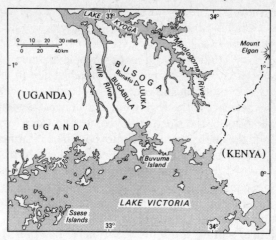

Map 8.2 The Busoga region

central Busoga. The diagnosis of possession was usually made through identification of some blemish, mark, or deformity of the body, or unusual speech, behavior, or sign, and the diagnosis was usually made by a priest or priestess.

Through the integration of royal status and spirit possession, the birth of a Mukama brought within a single concrete and worldly form ideas of diverse origin and composition. The birth of a Mukama created an environment in which ideas of superordination and possession were not only integrated, but also concentrated. Consequently, the birth of Mukama Womunafu attracted numbers of people to the camp where he was born, including priests who served the infant there and later in the first enclosure built for Mukama on the flatter land at the top of Bunafu *mutala*. Girls were 'married' to the child and were settled in homes in the enclosure. And refugees seeking a world protected from the political turmoil and persecution of Buganda, Luuka, and elsewhere joined the community forming about this exceptional person.

By mid century, people in Mukama's orbit were attempting to open a second front of expansion, as Mukama Womunafu's eldest sons were seeking for themselves worthy estates in the area of Bunafu. These pressures upon the resources of Mukama Womunafu and Bunafu raised the tension between Nafa and Womunafu and the tactics of competition in one phase were converted to those of subversion in the next and to those of more open conflict in still the next. The struggle was carried out spatially, as the

203

two parties moved to control the most attractive lands of the *mutala*, and it was carried out socially, as each sought to disengage supporters from the orbit of his adversary. By about 1870, the domination of the *mutala* by Mukama Womunafu's people had been achieved and most of the kin and old support of Nafa had fled to the west.[3]

This story of contention and eclipse is not, certainly, sensational, nor is such experience in this region unique. Yet, in less compressed, more detailed, fọrm, the story of the conflict between Womunafu and Nafa, and the depiction of the context of which it formed a part, reveals significant aspects of the political architecture of the precolonial Lakes Plateau region. The conflict unveils processes that from our perspective may seem benign, yet which are likely to have been fundamental in the formation of culture and in the organization of authority across the region.

The point of setting this brief scene here, however, is not to explore the political terrain of precolonial Uganda lighted by this microstudy, but rather to discuss the approaches to historical reconstruction taken which made this microstudy possible, and to consider more generally and theoretically the relationship between the sources of historical investigation of the precolonial African past and certain objectives of historical inquiry. It is a methodological excursus that connects a study completed with a work now comtemplated on general structure and process in the precolonial Lakes Plateau region.

Conscious and Unconscious Evidence

A starting point for this essay is simply that the story of the conflict between Womunafu and Nafa is *not* found within the narrative historical tradition spoken by the people of Busoga, or, for that matter, of the people of Bunafu. (Nor is it found in the notes of travellers, missionaries, or early Protectorate agents stationed in the area; nor in the written accounts produced by local historians in this century.) During interviews in 1971, the residents of Bunafu offered no testimony on Nafa, except to relate that there was once a spirit (*Muzimu* or *musambwa*) headquartered in a stone called by that name on the *mutala* or to offer the term as an alternative name for the Nakaibaale swamp (though a surviving member of Nafa's lineage referred briefly to the attacks Nafa's kinfolk suffered in earlier times). For the residents of Bunafu in 1971 and 1972, the community was Mukama Womunafu, Mukama Womunafu was the community. The tendency for authority and narrative tradition to coordinate, observed elsewhere by historians, was rather sharply reinforced in Bunafu by the fact that Mukama Womunafu, who died in 1906, was, by 1972, the progenitor of some 445 persons through the male line, or some 45 per cent of the population of the *mutala*.

In the narrative tradition of Womunafu's descendants, offered as marginally varied accounts, the long life of Womunafu is rather undifferentiated episodically. Greater clarity was brought to the Bunafu traditions when it was established that Mukama Womunafu occupied four enclosures serially (certain remains of which were still evident in 1972). The narrative tradition of Bunafu offered no testimony on the duration, intensity, and patterns of conflict between Mukama Womunafu and Nafa. Indeed, the narrative traditions left a rather uninteresting picture of another prince establishing royal domination over a new area, this domination simply a consequence of 'appearing', its legitimacy conferred to the present not by the carriage of detailed memories of the past but, rather simply, by the conclusive reality of a descent group's numerical and positional domination in the community.

Even before reading David Henige's 'History as Present Politics',[4] one should not have been terribly startled by this opaque quality of tradition noted in the narratives recorded in Bunafu. As a trained historian, I understood that the history of the Bunafu community that I would write would, for several reasons, fail to replicate Bunafu's own renderings of its past—referring here to both the narrative traditions that I recorded in notebooks or on tape and to the understandings of that past that may have informed, yet were hardly exposed, in the oral presentations of the past. Nor would the history that I would write be one that any person brought up in Bunafu would write. I also understood, from previous work on the traditions of Busoga, that narrative historical tradition was the modern product of 'the workings of individuals, groups, and institutions that affected, shaped, and reformed the shared history of a past'.[5] And though I was uncertain, and remain so today, of the nature of the complex processes of articulation and change in historical memory, I have sensed, or at least convinced myself, that these 'workings' are dense and infinite, that the formation of a popular historical tradition involves myriad social and political transactions as well as the transmittal of information over time.

As I have noted elsewhere, in recording oral documentation from some 2,000 informants in Busoga in 1966–67 and 1971–72, I found that neither in the present nor in the past were there officials charged with the responsibility for recording events, for the preservation of these records, or for the transmission of such records to future generations. There was, moreover, no written documentation until the 1890s. To some extent, everyone was involved in the preservation and transmission of historical information, though . . . not necessarily consciously . . . Information was not contained within fixed traditions or highly stylized testimonies. Tradition in Busoga was much less the arcane survivals of an oral past than the free tapping of the lively and ever-functioning intelligence upon which society and man rest. The transmission of historical information was not seen to rest upon orderly 'chains of transmission' but rather across and through the complex networks of relationship, association, and contact that constitute social life.[6]

While this writer recognizes the richness of certain categories of mythic and historical prose in African settings, he locates his own ethnohistorical focus upon the 'intelligence' of everyday life, transmitted through open social networks, often in non-specific situations, and most often by persons without specialized privilege, and passed to the historian-recorder in quite extraordinary aggregations, given the unique nature of the historian's inquiry. There is considerable work to be done in exploring further these unspecialized relays of crucial 'working information' and in 'mapping' more extensively the reservoirs of holdings of intelligence upon which social life is contingent. To ignore this enormous wealth of material in favor of formal, cogent, and important texts would be like a field anthropologist ignoring observations of what people are doing in favor of statements in which people say what they are doing.

This view—of the open locations and open modes of transmission of historical information—is, admittedly, different from the view offered by Jan Vansina in his volume *Oral Tradition* and carried forward in subsequent work.[7] In the earlier work, Vansina gave relatively little attention to the general processes of circulation of historical information in society, the processes which are not orderly, are not predictable, and are not reconstructable. In the present writer's view, the reality of Vansina's concepts of 'original' or 'proto-tradition' and the validity of his concept of 'chain of witnesses' should be questioned in terms of both conceptual logic and pertinence to historical inquiry (an empirical test in this case is not simple to operationalize). As I have argued elsewhere,

> While Vansina sees the 'original tradition' and the 'initial testimony' undergoing distortion through time until they are finally recorded by the historian or ethno-historian as a historical testimony, this writer sees the historical testimony as the *outcome* of a variety of processes that essentially constitute the modes of communication in society.[8]

Reconstructing a conflict in Bunafu

In a lovely piece of ethnolinguistic observation, Ben G. Blount has presented a portrait of the manner in which the construction of a historical testimony (in this case a lineage genealogy) is a rather undifferentiated aspect of social life, persons contributing detail and 'authenticating' constructions through complex weighting of individual and collective strategies.[9] In respect to such social constructions of historical texts by collections of individuals—whether over time or in one place and time as with Blount's subjects—it should be observed that the construction of a consensual or popular or purposive tradition may not thereby automatically close off (or tidy up) the substantial and often subtle realms of information from which such a tradition, in part, derives. Indeed, the significance of such social constructions in everyday life means that considerable value is placed upon the maintenance and use of what have been termed above 'the reservoirs of holdings of intelligence upon which social life is contingent'.

If the narrative tradition of Bunafu and on Bunafu is closed, opaque, perhaps the product of extensive negotiation, having the defects of 'history as present politics', and its formative process so complex as to defy the sort of transmissional analysis originally proposed by Vansina, how does one proceed from the memories of informants to the reconstruction of the past? To this writer the answer is not through the extension of symbolic and structural studies of tradition,[10] nor through the trait studies of particular genre, nor through the search for more pristine variants of particular traditions, though certainly some value may lie in furthering work along these lines. Rather, to place the response in terms of the study of Bunafu's past, one must recognize that

> Much of the information that Bunafu's past has left for the historian falls outside the knowledge of past that informs Bunafu's own presentations of history. The information the past has left for us . . . includes data on the environment, the locations of settlements, migrations, marriages, developments away from Bunafu, and the meanings of words and phenomena. This is not to say that the people of Bunafu are unaware of their environment, that they are ignorant of the locations of their compounds, or that they are without knowledge of where their antecedents may have lived before traveling to Bunafu. This is in fact crucial information in this society, and it is in part because of its significance that considerable information from the past is present for the historian to collect and use. The point is that such familiar, such parochial, information does not lie within the mental compartments from and through which the past is perceived, understood, and presented in the form of conscious history by the people of Bunafu.[11]

David W Cohen

What I am attempting to do here is discern the distinction between what may be evidence and textual materials of an intense purposive nature and evidence of a more unconscious quality. In simpler terms, nearly four decades ago, Marc Bloch distinguished between what he called 'narrative sources—accounts which are consciously intended to inform their readers' (which with the substitution of 'listeners' at the end would make a good working definition for the oral historian)—and a second category of material which he called the 'evidence of witnesses in spite of themselves'.[12] Bloch, his own spirit clearly on the side of the 'witnesses in spite of themselves', argued that the

> tracks which the past unwittingly leaves all along its trail do more than simply permit us to fill in the narrative where it is missing and to check it where its truthfulness is suspected. They protect our studies from a peril more deadly than either ignorance or inaccuracy; that of an incurable sclerosis. Indeed, without their aid, every time the historian turned his attention to the generations gone by, he would become the inevitable prey of the same prejudices, false inhibitions, and myopias which had plagued the visions of those same generations.[13]

For Bloch then, the non-narrative material held value beyond simply another, parallel, body of evidence. For the African historian, there has been little reaping of this non-narrative material, even in the simpler mode of just another body of evidence.

Unconscious Sources in Bunafu

Let us look at two sorts of 'evidence of witnesses in spite of themselves—some marriage data and some migrational data—that allow us a view of Bunafu's past that is absent from the narrative historical tradition. In respect to marriage, we note today that marriages are perceived in the Lakes Plateau region—indeed over much of Africa—as important means of engaging support and enlarging the social network within which one lives. These linkages among affines are called in Lusoga (as in Luganda) *buko* ties. Because of the play of feelings of how one should behave toward in-laws, including fulfilling duties and responsibilities, marriages are strategic elements in human behavior. The marriage contributes to the shaping of the status, mobility, and power of the lineages of both husband and wife. Each new marriage joins together young segments of kinship groups into broader relational networks.

There is considerable evidence from the present century that these networks, forged through *buko*, enlarge and refine the support that one calls upon in time of need, which one employs naturally in everyday affairs, and through which one defines his own identity and ambitions. What is also important about marriages is that, relative to other contractual bonds among social groups, the *buko* bond is long-enduring. Clientage ties may be instantly transformed or broken, friendship ties may erode as a result of substantial rates of geographical mobility in the population, but the deeper relations established through *buko* may survive the marriage itself in the networks formed through *buko* that overrun generational boundaries. At minimum they persist in the obligations placed upon the children of a marriage and the lineages of the immediate parties.

Because the marriage is a great social statement generating signals of status and ambition and because the *buko* relationship has a capacity to operate over distances and time, the marriage is approached with a strategic sense or interest, a knowing of circumstance, unparalleled in any other field of social and political activity. That this was largely true in the eighteenth and nineteenth centuries is suggested by the wide distribution across the region of shared understandings of the meaning of *buko*, by evidence on *baiwa* relations, by evidence on clientage arrangements, by evidence on royal marriages, and by evidence that locates previously undisclosed patterns of marriage avoidance.[14]

It is because this was a world in which marriages were the key institutions of social linkage that historical data on marriage hold the potential for unveiling the larger and sometimes less visible dimensions of social groups and networks, the 'working constituencies' of the past. Indeed, observations in the twentieth century suggest that marriages articulate the working networks of social activity rather than the residual categories of corporate social identity (clan, ethnic group, neighborhood, and so forth). The historiographical key to the collection and use of marriage data is that these data survive time and change because the relationships have a tendency to persist (in the requirements of descendants to know their forebears), because the 'mechanism' of retention of these data rests upon the memories of large numbers of persons rather than particular specialist informants, and because this sort of evidence lies outside the 'mental compartments from and through which the past is perceived, understood, and presented in the form of conscious history.'[15]

Aggregations of marriage data in a particular area, then, may offer a glimpse, admittedly faint, of the outer dimensions and internal arrangements of social networks and communities. To return to Bunafu, a study of nineteenth-century marriages locates a cleavage between the two organizing centers within this community—Nafa's and Mukama Womunafu's—between 1850 and 1875, to propose some outside dates. While the existence of the two centers was noted in other source material, an intense conflict in the field of social relations between these two proximate centers was not noted in the narrative material recorded in Bunafu or elsewhere.

Importantly, the marriage data expose more than simply a cleavage. The evidence shows that before about 1855, there was substantial energy imparted to the creation of *buko* ties between these two centers, Nafa's and Womunafu's. But between 1855 and 1870, no marriage relations were contracted between these two centers directly or indirectly (that is, through intermediate groups). Somewhat later, after the 1870s, there is again an indication of the formation of *buko* arrangements between the two centers, though by this time there were few of Nafa's people left on the *mutala*.[16] The marriage data, then, locate spatially, socially, and chronologically a significant boundary between two *buko* networks, or working communities. As one moves closer to the details of the marriages, an outline of the changing networks of support on both sides of the boundary emerges. What is critical, methodologically, is the way in which these data, of the nature of 'unconscious witnessing' of the past, offer images of the organization of a social world not otherwise exposed in official tradition of the Luuka state or in the more formal or fluent narrative accounts.

In respect to migrational data, the historiographical key to their collection and use is that these data tend to refer to actual and residual claims of lineage segments to certain offices and estates at various locations and that these data are by their nature particularistic, denoting persons and places by name. These are not, as they come into the historian's record, salvaged ephemera, but rather very important associative knowledge that help one locate one's social, political, and economic place. Because of the significance of this knowledge in this regional setting, the historian is provided with a thick, detailed matrix of statements referring to migration and settlement in the past. While the language of these statements—for example, 'Misango was born at Kabukye in Bugabula and later went to Kirimwa in Luuka where he received an estate'—is of the nature of narrative historical tradition, they may be distinguished from more general and popular narrative tradition in the high specificity of the references and in the narrowness of the reference group.

There is, in respect to Busoga, far more to the overall body of data on migration that permits the historian to bring sturdy tools of criticism to the material. First, the data on migration are held by dispersed segments associated with, or descended from, the migrant individuals in the past. As this material refers to, and is held by, relatively small groups, one is tempted, simply, to invoke John Lamphear's reasonable axiom that 'group traditions often tend to become progressively less reliable the larger the group'.[17] Here, fortunately, the dispersed nature of lineage segments allows the historian an opportunity to check, at distant and independent locations, migrational data already in hand. Second, because migrations in the past do not stand apart from other action, the historian has a larger body of data of a related or contingent nature along which to read the migrational data in view. Data on marriage and on office-holding may be useful in locating a particular person or kin group at a particular location in the past and may be useful in working out an approximate period or moment in which a particular migration occurred. Third, one has, in respect to Busoga, various confirming data on the nature of burial (the alignment of the head of graves in the direction from which the individual, or his or her patrilineal antecedents, came). One has, as well, toponymic evidence and the complex configurations of locations and names of shrines associated with particular clans, lineages, and sublineages, some of which may be indicative of migration in the past.

In the reconstruction of migrations in Busoga's past, this historian has passed over the general, consensual, and popular traditions of migration that circulate rather widely in the society in favor of focusing on the material referring to smaller groups. At this level of reconstruction, the particularistic narrative statement referring to a migration in the past was of considerable interest, though evaluations of such statements were made in light of other references, including the more unconscious evidence of toponymy, shrine names, and grave alignments, as well as ethnographic detail. In certain instances in the reconstruction of the past of both Busoga and Bunafu, particularly where greater time depth has seemed to be involved, or greater distance implied (and this was the case with the reconstruction of the migrations of Nafa's forebears, to cite one example), the reconstructions were based on the non-narrative material alone.

The migrational data were of considerable use in several ways, though here discussion will concentrate on the use of migrational data in the difficult reconstruction of the small social world of Nafa

which began to form in Bunafu around the beginning of the
nineteenth century. The reconstruction was difficult because the
community of Nafa had largely disbanded a century ago and
because the period of concern lies in the penumbra of the rise of
Mukama Womunafu's community. What the migrational evidence
reveals is that Nafa's community was formed, demographically,
within the compass of about two generations (or about fifty years)
by people arriving in the area from remarkably diverse 'origins'.
What I have noted elsewhere is that in respect to Nafa's community

> the complex tedious record of migration reveals that located close to one
> another on a hillslope above the Nabisira were, in 1830, individuals
> whose antecedents had resided on the floating papyrus islands of the
> Mpologoma River system, had fished in and traded across Lake Victoria
> waters, had managed an environment offering 140 centimeters of rain-
> fall per year and one providing but sixty, had carried the status of
> members of the ruling family of a small state, had participated in a
> movement to overthrow the king of Buganda, had crossed the Nile, had
> empowered charms and amulets for the rulers of the Bukono state, had
> resided immediately next to the courts of kings as well as in worlds
> without kings, and had experienced a loss of place amidst the expansion
> of the Luuka state.[18]

The general character of this young community (as opposed to
the old communities in which most residents were of lineages present for at least three generations) appeared suggestive of the
'broken network' model of community that Lloyd Fallers found in
Busoga in the 1950s,[19] which he associated with processes of modernization observed in the vicinity of new towns and in areas
resettled after sleeping sickness epidemics. The distinguishing
characteristics of the 'broken network' type, late appearance of the
population base of the community, demographic instability, and
exceptional styles of leadership, are noted in the early nineteenth
century community of Nafa, quite far removed from the forces of
world modernization. And one may suppose that Nafa's new community shared other qualities with Fallers' model, the heightened
importance of social as opposed to kin relations and the lessened
role of patrilineage in the organization of the household and in the
control of land.

The migrational evidence from and on Bunafu's past suggests
that migration, far from being merely a symbolic appurtenance of
narrative tradition, or the grist of corporate clan and lineage history,
is a historical *force,* a force to be studied, measured, and evaluated
in the reconstruction of the past. Equally important for precolonial
eastern and central Africa, migration appears to have been the

outstanding mode of social and cultural communication, the means by which knowledge flowed from one part of the continent to another, by which ideas filtered from community to community, by which the working information of social and political life was conveyed. At Mukama Womunafu's birth, migrants carried ideas concerning possession and the Mukama from diverse centers, and their arrival on the banks of the Nabisira River just to the south of Bunafu made possible the formation of a new center of prestige and authority organized around the possessed child of the royal house of Luuka. Even if we are unable to detail the moments and means by which such crucial information moved from place to place, the capturing and examination of such migrational data as that pertaining to Bunafu expose a significant section of cultural process that is not to be found in the narrative historical tradition of the region.

The above is only one limited consideration of the use of migrational data in the reconstruction of Bunafu's past. These data have also been used in forging a chronology for the nineteenth century,[20] in describing the changes in the composition of communities and of political followings,[21] in locating certain frontiers and centers evidently attractive to new settlement at particular moments in the century,[22] and in identifying spatial variations in organizational forms in the Busoga area.[23] Again, these data—circulating independently of the conscious frameworks of the narrative traditions—offer evidence on the past otherwise unavailable.

Human Behavior and Understanding the Past

Marc Bloch remarked that such evidence of the past—'of witnesses in spite of themselves'—may hold value beyond simply extending our coverage of the past into previously unvisited corners or offering us another means of evaluating the narrative material on hand. The extra dividend derives from such 'unconscious' data offering a view of the past that tends not to refer to, or emerge from, idealized 'constitutions' of a system of social and political relations in the past. In this, the marriage data and the migrational data share, as types of evidence, one very important quality: the data are generated by and refer to human action and human decision and tend toward independence of conscious, narrative tradition. If, in our close reconstructions of the pasts of various domains, we are in fact recovering forms of action in the past, then we may at the same time be isolating and capturing particular examples of *behavior*. It is the view here

213

that the study of action in the past within particular narrow fields may reveal patterns of behavior, choice, and orientation that are not revealed at an explicit level in narrative tradition, in which expressions of behavior and orientation tend to be normative—that is, reflecting the rules, styles, and expectations of present or recent eras.

To take an example, the narrative traditions of Busoga present stories that offer various lessons and remarks indicating that high value is placed upon dying and being buried upon the land where one was born, that permanent settlement or a return to one's home carries very high valuation. We, along with young Basoga, are informed through the narrative tradition that the principles of land tenure rest upon this value. But oral documentation of a non-narrative kind reveals that migration in Busoga in the nineteenth century was so extensive, and one-way in virtually all cases, that such a value of permanent settlement had little influence on actual behavior; and that, concomitantly, values concerning the prising of fortunes elsewhere came to have greater currency. Obviously, the conditions of land tenancy were far more complex under these conditions of intense migration than our narrative traditions would have us believe. In this case, the normative tradition is not merely off the mark but presents a completely contrary picture of the world than that offered through the study of inventories of action and decision culled from the migrational data.

This emphasis upon the observation of behavior—which is gaining an increasing place in this writer's work on the region's past—is not in itself novel, although the strict observation of behavior has as yet found little place within the work of reconstruction of the precolonial African past. Over the past thirty years, however, the social sciences have embarked upon a 'behavioral revolution'. Particularly germane to the African historian is that the literature of social anthropology has been deeply marked by a concern for the observation and comprehension of choice, decision, and behavior, and through this the concept of structure has greatly changed in the past twenty years. Raymond Firth, in his essay 'Social Organization and Social Change',[24] offered in 1954 a guide to future progress in the field of social anthropology. Firth gave considerable emphasis to the decisional element in his mapping of the terrain lying between a concept of social structure and his concept of social organization.

It is to the act of decision and its social consequences that we look primarily for our material. Studies in social organization demand attention to three criteria: the magnitude of the situation (as in men and materials); the alternatives open for choice and decision; and the time dimension.[25]

Among others, F. G. Bailey, Fredrik Barth, Maurice Bloch, Jeremy Boissevain, and Bruce Kapferer have extended and deepened the exploration of decisional terrain.[26]

In the view of this observer of both recent anthropological literature and data on marriage and migration, behavior is not merely a reflex of rules but a means of evoking, framing, maintaining, and redefining the meanings and understandings we gloss as culture. If something we may call 'structure' does indeed lie 'out there', we may ask where it lies and by what means it is maintained. The people who came to serve the young Mukama Womunafu in Bunafu were not merely recreating in a new place an old, archetype possession complex, but were also, in assembling ideas radiating from diverse centers, transferring ideas and ways of doing things from one era to another, at the same time creating a new source of generation of reformed or refined ideas about possession, authority, association, and service. It is the view here that it is in the calculus of just such decisional behavior as moving there, marrying this one, serving that one, binding one's future to this one, cutting ties with the other one, that the 'architecture' of social and political life gathers its form and is carried, in revised ways, from one era to another. Extending this point of view, it is in the observations of decisional behavior where one may find evidence on the processes of formation of society and culture.

This interest in the *formative* (and not merely regulative) potential of behavior implicit in the Firth-Barth-Bailey literature has, unfortunately, had little impact upon the study of the African past. This is rather paradoxical in that this literature stands as a branch of social anthropology particularly congenial to a recognition of the importance of a time dimension. Yet, in historical studies of Africa, the rendering of past has been in terms of structure and event, everyday decisional behavior being seen to be contained and regulated by—subordinate to—those two elements.

This subordination of what I call here 'everyday decisional behavior' entails difficulties for analysis and description in African historical writing in another way. To a considerable extent the rendering of the African past has been captive of an old and rather formal institutional analysis handed down through the pre-behavioral social sciences. We are inheritors of a shorthand social, political, and economic vocabulary that makes extensive use of such institutional concepts as clientship, kingship, feudality, clanship, bureaucracy, caste, and slavery. When we seek to understand how these 'institutions' have been identified and given analytical stress in the study of Africa, we recognize the play of one or another implicit criterion: (a) the identification of similarity between formations observed in Africa and those recognized as significant in European society ancient and modern, similarity implying significance; (b) the recognition that European colonial authority rested upon the manipulation of certain formations, the relevance to colonial management implying significance; and (c) the intimation that certain sets of behavior or certain formations had parallels elsewhere in Africa of interest in cross-cultural comparative studies, analytical utility implying significance.

The difficulty is that the organizing and simplifying concepts which have come to frame the analysis of past societies tend to derive from outside our collections of data. Perhaps because the narrative traditions tend to confirm a more recent or present normative view of the past, perhaps because they tend to provide for us a simplified view of process, it has been relatively easy to carry forward the routinized 'institutions'—clientship, kingship, clanship, bureaucracy, caste, and slavery—as shorthand devices in our analysis and description of the African past. Indeed, rather than devising and applying logical criteria of analytical significance, we have allowed 'prominence and visibility'[27] to determine for us the historical significance of forms, categories, and routines that we gloss as 'institutions'.[28]

Optimistically, the inventories of decisional behavior that African historians have already collected may allow us to reach beyond the routine analytical models and formations and beyond the normative descriptions of the narrative tradition to identify institution and structure in action and decision. The challenge at the outset is to establish the period, density, and significance of observed routines that we may choose to call institutions. Beyond this, there is hope that with the disaggregation of the behaviors that operate together as an 'institution', the processes of formation of particular routines or institutions will become more evident. Evidence of a relatively unconscious character referring to action in the past would seem to offer a promising means of identifying these behavioral components as well as suggesting the linkages among various ways of doing things through which institutions were generated or transformed.

The position taken here is a hopeful one, for among the vastness of texts recorded over the past two decades on the African past we have in hand far more data on the past than ever realized. The

Reconstructing a conflict in Bunafu

challenge rests in reading the documentation with a fresh eye for evidence of basic human action and decision and in seeking a more integrated and logical perspective of structure and change, of context and event. The elevation of strictures concerning the veracity of narrative historical accounts seems, from this point of view, of limited pertinence to the tasks and possibilities of reconstructing the African past, for the riches lie not so much in the formal accounts but in the information that ranges openly in the African community.

Notes

This paper was first presented to the African History Seminar at the School of Oriental and African Studies, London, on 30 November 1977. I am grateful to the members of the seminar for their comments. I am also grateful to colleagues and students in the Departments of Anthropology and History at The Johns Hopkins University whose patience and interest allowed a slow, but unimpeded, festering of some of the thoughts contained herein. I thank Richard Price in particular for his comments and suggestions made over several years of discussion. The John Simon Guggenheim Memorial Foundation and The Johns Hopkins University provided generous support for the field research undertaken in 1971 and 1972 and thereby made the microstudy of Bunafu possible. Johns Hopkins and the National Endowment for the Humanities have provided support for the period of study during which this paper was written.

1 The *mutala* (pl. *mitala*) is a raised section of land typically marked off by stream or swamp and which comes to constitute a residential unit and administrative area under conditions of occupation.

2 Though we have no text that relates, or conveys an impression, that an exceptional ritual capacity was shared by members of Nafa's lineage.

3 This exposition is a compression of book-length study of Bunafu: David William Cohen, *Womunafu's Bunafu: A Study of Authority in a Nineteenth-Century African Community* (Princeton, 1977).

4 In David P. Henige, *The Chronology of Oral Tradition: Quest for a Chimera* (Oxford, 1974), ch. 1.

5 Cohen, *Womunafu's Bunafu*, pp. 13–14.

6 Cohen, *Womunafu's Bunafu*, p. 8. The character of tradition in Busoga and the methods of interviewing and recording deployed there are also discussed at length in David William Cohen, *The Historical Tradition of Busoga: Mukama and Kintu* (Oxford, 1972), pp. 28–69.

7 Jan Vansina, *Oral Tradition: A Study in Historical Methodology,* trans. H. M. Wright (London, 1965); 'Once Upon a Time: Oral Traditions as History in Africa', *Daedalus*, Spring 1971, pp. 442–68; *La Légende du passé: traditions orales du Burundi* (Tervuren, Belgium, 1972); and 'Traditions of Genesis', *Journal of African History*, vol. 15 (1974), pp. 317–22. In Vansina's most recent major work, *Children of Woot* (Madison, 1978), he retains an approach to Kuba history that holds methodologically central

David W Cohen

what I have called the 'formal, cogent, and important texts'. This is not to say that Vansina has rested his analysis exclusively upon 'official' texts; indeed, he has utilized both boldly and brilliantly a very broad array of source material, particularly ethnographic and linguistic. However, the major accounts assume a central place in Vansina's reconstruction of the Kuba past because of his assumption that modern Kuba traditions have 'origins' in some ancestral setting and that what he recorded in modern times were variants of these proto-traditions, altered by processes of selection, distortion, and structural amnesia. Treating the modern traditions as reflexes of earlier historical texts leads him to devote considerable space in his volume to exploring variations among the major accounts and to showing how the Kuba have over time constructed their distinctive conception of the past. Vansina further holds that these types of tradition—particularly myths of origin—have had a pervasive effect upon all other types of Kuba oral historical performance, a 'pebble in the water' view of the formative processes of a people's historical corpus.

The present writer views the differences between what Vansina describes as the central role of the formal traditions in the shaping of Kuba historical knowledge and the absence of similar focal compositions in the Lakes Plateau Region not in terms of varying degrees of reference to the past in the two cases nor in terms of the question of 'how much history is contained by myth'. Rather he sees the difference at a level of implicit social theory, either the social theory of the Africans or that of the historians who study them. Vansina's sociology assumes some former 'ancestral society': 'In practice almost all my arguments rest on differences among features in societies that stem from a common ancestral society, or on similarities among features in societies that do not share a common ancestry.' (*Woot*, p. 82) For the Lakes Plateau Region of East and Central Africa, by contrast, it is difficult to reconstruct such an 'ancestral society' or even to imagine that one ever existed. If two such distinct modes of social formation in fact occurred among the Kuba and in the Lakes Plateau Region, then this difference would have colored in important ways the historical consciousness of each people and thereby explain why each constructed their portrayal of the past in such distinctive ways. If on the other hand we are talking about different historians' theories of the formation of societies that do not reflect real historical differences, then one or the other of these assumed theories may distort at a profound level how we represent the ways in which Africans construct historical knowledge.

8 Cohen, *Womunafu's Bunafu*, p. 189.
9 Ben G. Blount, 'Agreeing to Agree on Genealogy: A Luo Sociology of Knowledge', in Mary Sanches and Ben G. Blount (eds.), *Sociocultural Dimensions of Language Use* (New York, 1975), pp. 117–35.
10 So much of the existing literature utilizing symbolic and structural analysis is flawed by inadequate consideration of the origins and 'constituency' of the *text*.
11 Cohen, *Womunafu's Bunafu*, p. 14.
12 Marc Bloch, *The Historian's Craft*, trans. Peter Putnam (Manchester, 1954), p. 61.
13 Bloch, *Craft*, p. 62.
14 The *baiwa*, young affines, are recalled frequently by name in reference

218

to their assistance at a particular person's funeral celebrations. In reference to clientage, we have considerable examples from the data of affinal relations being established in advance of appointment to a lower level office. In reference to royal marriages, we have quite extensive data both on the marriages contracted between princes and distinguished commoner groups in the realm and on the service given by affines to princes during succession disputes. In reference to avoidance we note in the aggregate of data on marriage, though not from explicit remarks in the narrative tradition, that princes of the royal houses of northern Busoga carefully avoided marriage links with Lwo-speaking and once Lwo-speaking lineages—these royal houses were descended from Lwo speaking lineages.

15 Cohen, *Womunafu's Bunafu*, p. 14.

16 A figure summarizing these *buko* networks is to be found in Cohen, *Womunafu's Bunafu*, p. 126.

17 John Lamphear, *The Traditional History of the Jie of Uganda* (Oxford, 1976), p. 30.

18 Cohen, *Womunafu's Bunafu*, pp. 67–8.

19 Lloyd A. Fallers, *Bantu Bureaucracy* (Chicago, 1965), pp. 113–25.

20 Henige, *Chronology of Oral Tradition*, has ignored this very dense sort of evidence of the working data of social life in favor of formal chronicles and dynastic lists. These latter are highly ratified forms of tradition and hardly represent the bodies of data available to the historian concerned with the construction of chronology. In an appendix to *Womunafu's Bunafu*, pp. 166–86, I have attempted to construct, out of these denser data, a chronological framework for the representation of Bunafu's past.

21 In *Womunafu's Bunafu*, extensive use of migrational data is made in estimating the period and scale of enlargement of the following of Womunafu.

22 In several papers in process of revision for publication in the form of a history of Busoga 1700–1900, I have used dense data on migration to identify zones in the Busoga area that become, in certain periods, more attractive to settlement.

23 Migrations—in a sense voting with the feet—have revealed previously undisclosed distinctions between states on the eastern side of Busoga, in which commoners were given short shrift and in which princes had the run of offices from top to bottom, and states on the western side of Busoga in which commoners were given, in the eighteenth and nineteenth centuries, responsibility for curbing the excesses of princes. This is not strictly or solely a geographical delineation. For example, in Luuka, the extent of discipline exerted upon the princes varied with the period and fluctuated back and forth. The point here is that these variations, temporal and geographical, in the nature of political life are revealed in the migrational data and are undisclosed in the narrative tradition.

24 *Journal of the Royal Anthropological Institute*, vol. 84 (1954), pp. 1–20.

25 Ibid.

26 F. G. Bailey, *Stratagems and Spoils: A Social Anthropology of Politics* (Oxford, 1969); Fredrik Barth, *Models of Social Organization* (London, 1966); Maurice Bloch, 'Introduction', in Bloch (ed.), *Political Language and Oratory in Traditional Society* (New York, 1975); Jeremy Boissevain,

Friends of Friends: Networks, Manipulators and Coalitions (Oxford, 1974); and Bruce Kapferer, 'Norms and the Manipulation of Relationships in a Work Context', in J. C. Mitchell (ed.), *Social Networks in Urban Situations* (Manchester, 1969), pp. 181–244.

27 This phrase is drawn from the 'second law' laid down by a colleague, Jack P. Greene: 'Prominence and visibility no longer constitute a prima facie case of historical significance. On the contrary, the value of every subject depends entirely upon how much it reveals about larger historical processes', 'The New History: From Top to Bottom', *New York Times,* 8 June, 1975, p. 37. Elsewhere, I have phrased Greene's law in different terms. 'It is unlikely that the past will be revivified, its meanings discerned, its lessons conveyed, its portent disclosed, through observations filtered through the frames most conveniently at hand', 'The Convulsions of Devolution', *Times Literary Supplement,* 18 February 1977, p. 194.

28 With the noteworthy and splendid exception of Marcel d'Hertefelt's *Les Clans du Rwanda ancien: éléments d'ethnosociologie et d'ethnohistoire* (Tervuren, Belgium, 1971). D'Hertefelt saw the significance for social and historical analysis of an institution of extremely low visibility and importance in colonial and postcolonial Rwanda—the *ubwooko*—the close study of which has thrown very bright light across the more extensively studied institutions of precolonial and colonial Rwanda. For an exception in another region of Africa, see Joseph C. Miller, *Kings and Kinsmen: Early Mbundu States in Angola* (Oxford, 1976). Miller finds patterns of political formation revealed in the close study of certain symbolic regalia.

9. Some Words about Merina Historical Literature

GERALD M BERG

The early history of Imerina rests on interpretations of a large corpus of oral literature written by local historians and collected and edited by Europeans and Malagasy in the nineteenth century. The most remarkable of many compilations, the *Tantara ny Andriana eto Madagascar*, collected by Father François Callet, printed about a century ago, and reprinted in a 1,200-page reference edition in 1908, has only recently been subject to the scrutiny of a trained linguist.[1] The principal task presented to historians by such documents is to determine what they tell of real historical events. In Imerina, the task is made difficult by the lack of independent sources, such as explorer accounts or archeological records, which could balance the conclusions derived from oral literature. History, therefore, must be culled from the oral testimony alone. The first step is to understand what historical testimonies meant to the people who transmitted them. Ideally, 'each word of every testimony must be understood in terms of its own perceptual field'.[2] This essay has a more modest aim.

I intend to define some words and phrases which appear often in Merina historical testimonies about the remote past, and which express central historical concepts. One such word is *vazimba*, taken incorrectly by European-influenced historians to mean a racial group consisting of Imerina's original inhabitants. Stories about *vazimba* are frequently embroidered with the image of beautiful women arising from and descending into pools of water, and this image will be discussed. Finally, most narratives about the remote past are presented in the form of a genealogy, and so I will consider what it meant to say 'someone gave birth to (*niteraka*) another'.

In many cases the literary context of these words and phrases provides their meanings. But since meaning is given to words by an audience as well, it is necessary to consider the social environment which enveloped historical testimony. I will therefore note dynamic

221

tensions in nineteenth-century Merina society from which new historical perspectives emerged. Whether or not nineteenth-century historical testimonies accurately depict much earlier events remains to be seen. Here I attempt only the first step: to see the remote past as nineteenth-century Merina saw it, and to suggest how that view of the past changed later in the century.

Becoming *Vazimba*

The term *vazimba* pervades Merina oral literature. First, in an historical sense, *vazimba* denoted the original inhabitants of Imerina (*tompon'tany*) who preceded or opposed monarchy. Second, in a didactic sense, *vazimba* described the objects of a contemporary cult called ancestor worship by early European observers. Merina revered the spirits of long-dead ancestors who, if neglected, returned in a grotesque form to wreak havoc among living kin. Though *vazimba* had many other meanings, European-educated savants combined only these two, and in re-editing and interpreting early Merina texts they gave the term *vazimba* a new meaning.[3] Thus, by the end of the nineteenth century, *vazimba*, as it appeared in European and Merina historical works, implied that Imerina's first inhabitants were racially distinct from the current population.[4] Moreover, since revenge-seeking spirits came to epitomize in the minds of European and Merina Christians the barbarism of traditional Malagasy religion, the *vazimba* of antiquity were seen not only as racially distinct but inferior and abhorrent as well.[5] The new meaning of *vazimba* was used as evidence for a theory that racial conflict accompanied the founding of Merina monarchy some centuries earlier. According to the theory, there were two groups in ancient Imerina, indigenous *vazimba* and immigrant *hova*. Second, race defined these groups. Third, *hova* were superior to *vazimba*, and in conformity with prevailing Merina and Victorian racial stereotypes, *vazimba* were short and black with kinky hair and *hova* were robust and light-skinned with supple hair. Finally, *hova* conquered the backward *vazimba* and established monarchy in Imerina.[6]

This interpretation appealed not only to Europeans influenced by Spencerian social theory, but also to *hova*. *Hova,* defined in Merina terms as a status group of the freeborn, modified history to depict themselves as a superior race. By claiming that they had established monarchy amidst an inferior population, *hova* hoped to support their requests for elevated status and major posts in a royal bureaucracy where Europeans set intellectual fashions. In remaking history both Europeans and *hova* narrowed the meaning of *vazimba* to include only those ideas and images which served well their political aspiration or philosophical persuasion.[7]

Nevertheless, the original field of meaning surrounding the term *vazimba*, which may be reconstructed from a wide range of traditional testimonies, indicates that *vazimba* did not initially refer to a racially distinct group. For one thing, many sources speak of ancient ancestors 'becoming' *vazimba*. The *Tantara ny Andriana eto Madagascar* refer to Razanahary who 'is buried at the summit of Ambohijanahary where she *became vazimba*' [my emphasis].[8] The Vig Manuscript, which is completely independent of the *Tantara*, speaks of Ranoro who '*became vazimba* though she was of noble rank and the descendant of nobles' [my emphasis].[9] The idea that a person can become *vazimba* shows that the word did not apply to race and requires a definition of the term which does not imply racial distinctiveness.

Moreover, many oral sources portray *vazimba* as extraordinarily beautiful women when telling of group origins. Thus, Ranoro, the 'mother' of an Antehiroka group, was a beautiful water creature with long supple hair as was Rasoalavavolo who, according to some tales, gave birth to all Malagasy. Likewise it was a charming mermaid who was the genetrix of the Zafimarano.[10] The physical form of *vazimba*, then, differs according to the purpose of the tale. They are attractive women in stories intended to recount the origins of social groups, and they are grotesque dwarfs in tales which reminded living kin of unfulfilled obligations toward long-dead ancestors.

The two images express different aspects of the nineteenth-century attitude toward ancient ancestors which is often associated in the literature with another striking image: women *vazimba* arising from and then descending into pools of water. To return to the above examples, Ranoro came from the Mamba River and upon her death was drawn into a lake: 'She was never seen again and so she is *vazimba* there'.[11] Rasoalavavolo, also a female *vazimba*, lived in water, and her two sons died in water;[12] and the Betsimisaraka of the northeastern littoral tell of a mermaid who arises and descended into water.[13] All these water-dwelling figures are considered the originators of their descent groups: Ranoro, of the Antehiroka; Rasoalavavolo, of the inhabitants of Madagascar; the mermaid, of the Zafimarano. In literature, water surrounds group origins, and in

Merina rituals, water is the primary medium of ancestral will.[14] Rising from water connotes group origins and transmission of ancestral will, while dying in water connotes entrance into the sacred realm of the most ancient ancestors.

Moreover, since social organization depends on territories delimited by tomb sites, dying in water conveys a sense of loss and danger because such a death leaves no tomb to which living kin can come to fulfill the many obligations to the dead. Since *vazimba* are not ordinary ancestors but 'sacred', 'famous', and 'holy' genitors of modern social groups,[15] absence of a tomb is especially disturbing.

The importance of the tomb in Merina cosmology should not be underestimated. As Bloch has shown,[16] the tomb and surrounding area (*tanin'drazana*, ancestral lands) symbolize the strong tie between social groups and their territories. The ultimate criterion for membership in a kin group is territorial, hence the use of the word, deme, to describe Merina kin groups. Bloch notes that 'a Merina finds his place in a complex segmentary system by where he is going to be buried, since association with a village in old Imerina is an indication of membership in a whole set of groups including district, larger deme, and smaller deme'.[17] Bloch calls the group associated with a particular tomb, the 'tomb family', and ties to it are explained in theory by Merina in terms of genealogy, though in practice there is considerable irregularity. *Vazimba*, though they are important ancestors, do not have natural tomb families, and this is an anomaly which yields the grotesque image of *vazimba*.

To be *vazimba* is to belong to the era of genitors with whom direct genealogical connections have been blurred by segmentation, mobility, and the passage of time. Since hoary ancestors must receive attention and yet by the nineteenth century there were no tombs upon which to focus loyalty, surrogate tombs have been established, though the impossibility of direct connection with *vazimba* remained vexing. Legend expressed the desire to re-establish direct connection to group genitors by employing the image of descent into water, the medium which transmits ancestral will and beneficence. So it is that females Rafohy and Rangita, the last rulers before monarchy, are said to be buried in water though tombs of recent creation dedicated to them stand today at Alasora and Merimanjaka.[18] Returning to Ranoro, one finds a variant in *Firaketana ny Fiteny sy ny Zavatra malagasy* which illustrates the symbolic meaning of descent into water. Ranoro, the mother of the Antehiroka, was betrayed by her husband. She took her only child and 'descended into the water', never to be seen again. The key to understanding this metaphor lies in the evocative use of *varina* to express entering the water. *Varina* usually means descent, but it may be used figuratively in a phrase which indicates a special burial (*varina aman-tany*, precipitated to earth) accorded to the poor without relatives. This burial leaves no tomb, nor *lamba mena*, the customary silk winding sheet.[19] By saying that Ranoro was buried in water, the tale means that sacred obligations to her can never quite be fulfilled. Her descendants, though able to remember their earliest ancestor, cannot establish direct links to her. This inaccessibility is the essential component of the term *vazimba*.

Water unites sacredness with a sense of loss arising from the absence of tombs and the lack of direct genealogical connection with original ancestors. Emergence from water evokes the sacredness of birth while descent (*varina*) into it, implying burial without tombs, expresses a rupture with the past.[20] A didactic passage from the *Tantara* presents this discontinuity by distinguishing ancient ancestors who are forgotten by their descendants from recent ancestors who are properly remembered:[21] 'And of the tombs already ancient, they became *vazimba* as well as friends of *vazimba*: —although they were formerly simply people they nowadays become *vazimba* for they died long ago when people were yet few and so they were not associated with the population that followed . . . And now people may no longer become *vazimba* for there are many people nowadays, so the dead simply become ancestors.' Tomb families of recent ancestors are intact but those of the ancient ones no longer remain. While recent ancestors receive their due, the ancients, *vazimba*, are neglected, and they possess their descendants who attempt to placate them: 'When people prayed they came to call upon their ancestors because they considered their ancestors the same as *Vazimba*: and the ancestors possess their kin when those kin displease them. And thus throughout the land grew the worship of the *Vazimba* and of the ancestors. They are alike—one is considered the same as the other.'[22]

The living are haunted by their inability to pay respects to genitors of a lost era. That era of lost ancestors, the *vazimba* epoch, appears in historical literature as the epitome of chaos—reminiscent of the Genesis story before light was separated from darkness:[23] 'There was still neither rice nor manioc nor sweet potatoes and people were few. They were still *Vazimba*, isolated from one another, and a dark forest completely covered the world.' It is easy to see how the word *vazimba* was transformed and came to signify the complete absence of culture so that the preceding passage, if taken literally, could mean that *vazimba* had no communities and cultivated nothing. But when Merina attitudes towards ancestors, tombs, and tomb families are considered, a more figurative interpretation appears appropriate. To be 'isolated from one another' in a dark forest is currently perceived as the epitome of an undesirable state in which society's genitors are not precisely connected with their descendants through tomb sites. It expresses a rupture in time between past and present generations, and it may well be that as the time of genitors receded into the past and knowledge of their original tomb sites was lost, traditions about Imerina's first inhabitants increasingly accumulated images of void and grotesqueness.

In many didactic stories, therefore, *vazimba* appear as the archetype of evil. They come from a dark chaotic world to remind living kin of their obligations to the genitors—obligations which can never be completely fulfilled. In this context, *vazimba* are described as dark dwarfs, and many observers have misunderstood this image as a racial description of Imerina's earliest inhabitants. But, as Rasamuël had observed fifty years ago, the grotesque image of the avenging *vazimba*—short, dark skin, oddly shaped head, long teeth, and unkempt hair—is the archetypical image of evil in Merina literature.[24] The dark dwarf is a metaphor for evil and it applies not only to avenging *vazimba* but to a host of such evil spirits as the *kokolampo* dwarfs with small heads and the *angalampona* who, according to one mid nineteenth-century missionary, were the size of ten-year-old children.[25]

The *vazimba* owe their grotesqueness not only to the passing of time but also to increased anxieties over unfulfilled obligations to ancestors that accompanied the spread of Christianity through nineteenth-century Imerina. The existing cult which attempted to placate *vazimba* and to ask their favor[26] came under severe attack by missionaries and converts who saw these beliefs as a form of idolatry. In popular mission schools where Christian worship was taught, grotesque *vazimba* frequently appeared to students as a result of Merina fears about the consequences of embracing an alien religion. From students' descriptions of these *vazimba* visions, European missionaries constructed a new view of Imerina's first inhabitants. Far from the original image of beautiful women and heroic giants which represented a system of ideas about holy ancestors, *vazimba* depicted as grotesque dwarfs now stood for primitiveness. *Hova* and Europeans alike used the new image to remold history according to the conventions of the day. *Vazimba* became racially unique and inferior.[27]

The Nature of Genealogy

Stories about *vazimba* appear at the beginning of almost every modern group's history. They are presented in the form of a genealogy, and like the physical images of *vazimba*, the genealogical link, expressed as 'one gives birth to another', denotes something other than biological fact. How else can one explain that the names and their sequence in the *vazimba* section of a group's history vary greatly from version to version as illustrated by the Antehiroka case?[28] Moreover, despite substantial variation in names and their sequence, the Antehiroka lists all present eight generations of *vazimba* beginning and ending with the group's eponym[29] which suggests that *vazimba* are remembered only as a category without name-specific content. What appears to be genealogy, then, says little about biological generation.

Genealogy nevertheless presents a sequence of large historical categories beginning with the eight-generation *vazimba* section. After this period of genitors, Antehiroka histories insert a transition category characterized by an elaboration of descendants and, most significantly, images of women in water.[30] The final category is a modern history of the group in which symbolic images are absent and names and their sequence do not vary. In a wider sense then, genealogy is the idiom of historical cosmology beginning with the remote era of creation, continuing with a transition to modernity which symbolically depicts the origins of the group, and finally modern history itself. In this context, the phrase 'one gives birth to another' represents a procession through time toward increasing social coherence.

'Progress' of this sort appears when looking at the group's history as a whole so that large historical categories connected together by genealogy can be seen. Yet within each section, the genealogical link has added meaning which I wish to consider by narrowing the focus of the discussion to include only the *vazimba* section of Merina royalty. By way of illustration I have chosen the third royal genealogy (TA III) in Callet's collection, *Tantara ny Andriana eto Madagascar* (see Fig. 9.1).[31] It is often used by scholars, and unlike less elaborate forms, it speaks of Merina political institutions. Moreover, the provenance of TA III, Ambohijanahary, can be

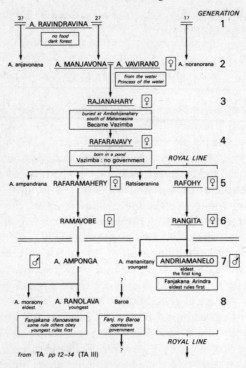

Figure 9.1 A Vazimba genealogy, TA III

reasonably asserted and will facilitate analysis.[32] Of the scores of versions available, nine have been selected to provide comparative material because they incorporate all derivative versions.[33] Like the Antehiroka case, *vazimba* names and their sequence in several versions vary considerably; only Andriamanelo, the first kind of the new monarchy is found consistently in the same place, at the very end.[34] Here again, the *vazimba* category lacks specific content and sequence.

Specific sequence, the basis of history, is ignored in favor of expressing moral relationships between the list's various components (see Fig. 9.1).[35] But before elucidating these relationships, one should define the principal components, in the case of TA III, the forms of rule. The first is *fanjakana ifanoavana* which means government by succession (rotation): 'some rule while others obey'. It was introduced by two brothers, Andriandranolava and Andriamoraony, and the latter also created the *kabary*, a communal assembly central to Merina politics. Even though *fanjakana ifanoavana* is essential to social order, it is not quite ideal. The younger son, represented by Andriandranolava, rules before the eldest, Andriamoraony, and thus contradicts 'proper' succession in which the eldest son rules first. This is why *fanjakana ifanoavana* is designated as a junior branch of the genealogy. The generational position of *fanjakana ifanoavana* in the sequence of names and events appears to be of little concern to the authors of the lists under consideration. Though all versions present *fanjakana ifanoavana* as the creation of two brothers, Andriandranolava, the youngest who ruled first, and Andriamoraony, the eldest who served, there is no agreement about the brothers' joint generational position relative to the other names in the lists,[36] and second, there is no agreement on the names of the brothers' kin.[37] The only data which do not vary are the names and relative ages of the two brothers and their association with *fanjakana ifanoavana*.[38] The brothers, then, jointly symbolize a type of rule rather than a stage in an historical sequence.

The second form of rule, and a major component in TA III, is *fanjakana arindra* (see Fig. 9.1). *Fanjakana arindra*, 'proper government', like *fanjakana ifanoavana*, maintained order, but the former is considered the ideal form of rule. Whereas *fanjakana ifanoavana* placed the youngest son in power before the eldest, *fanjakana arindra* placed the eldest son, represented by Andriamanelo, in power before the youngest son, represented by Andriamananitany.

Thus TA III defines two types of succession, but beyond that it conveys moral sentiment about them by means of genealogical links. Since the two types of succession have in common the ability to maintain order the genealogy links them together through a common ancestor, Rafaravavy (fourth generation). Thus it may be said that the two are morally 'related'. And, since Merina considered *fanjakana arindra* superior to *fanjakana ifanoavana*, genealogical links connect *fanjakana arindra* to the royal line and *fanjakana ifanoavana* to a junior line. In contrast to the two desirable forms of rule, *fanjakan'i Baroa,* the symbol of oppressive government, bears no genealogical connection to any part of the table because evil does not partake of genealogy. A genealogical link, on the other hand, expresses positive moral judgment by connecting good forms of government to the sacred period of *vazimba*. Moreover, all three forms of government appear simultaneously without any indication of historical relation. Relation, here expressed by the genealogical link, should be seen to have a moral, rather than sequential or biological, sense as even the modern Merina term for kin (*havana*) includes ideas of moral value without connoting descent.[39]

Yet just as the narrative as a whole is a kind of history, the *vazimba* section contains within it a sequence of historical categories. They are presented schematically in Figure 9.2. It begins with Andriandravindravina and evokes a sense of void befitting the era before Creation. There were no food crops, very few people, and a dark forest covered the earth. In the next generation, the creation symbol appears in the form of a union between Andriamanjavona[40] and Andriambavirano, Princess of the Water, a title often attributed to such female originators as Ranoro of the Antehiroka.[41] And like Ranoro, Andriambavirano, arisen from water and returned to it, is considered by TA III a genetrix, in this case, of the royal line. Each of the ancestors following her is female and bears some relation to water, the symbol par excellence of generation and group coherence. The offspring of Andriamanjavona and Andriambavirano is Rajanahary, the Creator, a woman who 'became *vazimba*' as her descendants multiplied. Rafaravavy follows her and unites the two lines representing *fanjakana arindra* and *fanjakana ifanoavana*, making her the genetrix of social order. As such she is quite naturally born in a pond. Finally, the originators of 'proper' government by primogeniture (*fanjakana arindra*), Rafohy and Rangita, were buried in the lake. They give rise to Andriamenelo, the first king. Thus a general historical sequence emerges within the *vazimba* section: void, creation of the world, creation of order, and the creation of succession leading to the transition section. Each creation category is portrayed by women in water.

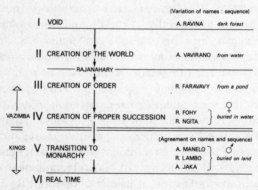

Figure 9.2 Historical structure of TA III

Names and their sequence vary from version to version, and yet one name in the TA III version, Rajanahary, does have specific meaning with regard to the group that produced the document. As mother of Rafaravavy and daughter of Andriambavirano, Rajanahary assumes a central position in TA III. She is placed between the symbols of creation before her and of the founding of social order after her. In this context, knowledge of TA III's provenance adds to its meaning. It comes from Ambohijanahary (Place of the Creator) and it is at Ambohijanahary that Rajanahary has her tomb shrine and is worshipped as *vazimba*. TA III, then, reflects the perspective of Ambohijanahary's inhabitants who claim Rajanahary as their founding ancestor and insert her name, as group eponym, at the very center of evolution between the creation of the world and the creation of social order. Though the name and exact position of an intermediary figure such as Rajanahary, or of the figure which unites *fanjakana arindra* with *fanjakana ifanoavana*, varies from version to version, the structure of the list is similar.

The final category in TA III, real historical time, begins at the close of the *vazimba* epoch, and the names and events which follow the *vazimba* section do not vary from list to list. Unlike figures in the *vazimba* section, the rulers who appear in the epoch of historical time have tombs on land and hence are properly remembered by their modern descendants. Those who belong to the era of origins are *vazimba*, and those who follow are modern, though both groups contain revered ancestors. A symbol of transition, which concludes the *vazimba* section and opens the historical section, marks the connection and the distinction between the two groups of ancestors who appear in the genealogies. In royal genealogies, the transition symbol consists of the first three kings, Andriamanelo, Ralambo, and Andrianjaka.[42] Unlike their female predecessors, they are male.[43] Whereas females and descent into water represent the era of generation, males form the bridge to the historical era characterized by the efficacy of rule. Since the era of generation is lost to memory, the female *vazimba* are buried in water, whereas the male kings of historical time have tombs on land.[44] Merina groups thus begin historical time from the point at which proper social relations based on tomb families and effective order are remembered.

Between the categories of creation and of historical time a shift takes place from female to male, from *vazimba* to royalty, and from water to land burial. This shift from nature to culture has become a subject of considerable elaboration as illustrated by stories about the conquest and renaming of Antananarivo, the capital of the new kingdom.[45] According to royal versions, Ralambo, son of Andriamanelo, came from Ambohitrabiby, and his son, Andrianjaka, conquered Alamanga and renamed it Antananarivo. Ambohitrabiby means 'the place of wild animals' and contrasts vividly with Antananarivo, the town of human strength. The capital's former name, Alamanga, means 'powerful forest'[46] and connotes, as does Ambohitrabiby, untamed nature. Thus, the narrative moves its focus from the chaos of the wilds to the order of human rule as power passes from Ralambo to Andrianjaka, Master of the *jaka* offering. The *jaka* is cooked or smoked meat. It is an offering through which the Merina expressed status distinctions between individuals or groups. The *jaka*, therefore, symbolizes social order and directly opposes Ralambo's birthplace, 'the place of wild animals'. In addition the move to order is reflected in the parts of these stories that tell of the renaming of cattle from wild cattle (*jamoka*) to domesticated cattle (*omby*).[47] Taken together, these stories elaborate upon the transitional component of Merina kinglists. They describe the passage from nature to culture and mediate between the *vazimba* era of holy originators and the profane era of historical time.

Transition, then, occurs in three stages. First, Andriamanelo, as first king and son of the last *vazimba*, connects historical time to its mythic female antecedents. Second, Ralambo moves from the wilds to the center of the new order, the capital. Finally, Andrianjaka completes the transition. He rules the *jaka* cattle offering, creating a system of status as the basis of order. The conclusion of the transitional era and the rupture between the remembered and the forgotten past are signified by Andrianjaka's 'expulsion' of *vazimba*. Historical time begins when the memory of original ancestors is lost. In this context, the meaning as well as the form of the term *vazimba* bears striking similarity to the Swahili *ku-zimu* (from *zimu*, to die or disappear), people of the tomb; the Central African *vadzimu*, ancestors; and the Common Bantu *-dímù*, spirit.[48]

The preceding quest for definition yields a more precise understanding of key historical concepts embedded in Merina narratives about the remote past. *Vazimba* in its widest sense means sacred genitor, and physical forms attributed to them convey moral attitudes which, until the end of the nineteenth century, were devoid of racial connotations. Moreover, the era of genitors symbolized by images of women in water presents a system of moral relations expressed in terms of genealogy. The genealogy as a whole, though containing large historical categories, lacks specific content. Yet historical categories such as void and creation do have a meaningful sequence. It remains to be seen, however, whether the procession of such broad historical categories that these narratives provide should be called history or cosmology.

In any case, Merina cosmology changed in the nineteenth century as time and an alien religion pried Merina from their ancestors. Genealogies of the remote past assumed increased moral significance by elaborating the rewards of reverence to ancestors with images of beauty and the punishments which could result from their neglect with images of ugliness. Later in the century, as politics dictated, Merina narrowed the meaning of *vazimba* by using only the image of ugliness to support a racial interpretation of the past which accorded well with Victorian sensibilities.

Notes

Preparation of this paper was made possible by generous grants from Sweet Briar College, The Mednik Foundation, The Mabelle McLeod Lewis Memorial Fund, and the Regents of the University of California. I wish to thank Maurice Bloch, Joseph C. Miller, Catherine Payne, Raymond K. Kent, Margaret Mooney, Elizabeth Colson, John Savarese, Erica Gienapp, and Gina Blythe for commenting on an earlier draft, though I alone am responsible for what appears here.

1 Callet's first edition was published in Tananarive in five volumes from 1873 to 1902. All citations in this paper unless otherwise indicated refer to the reference edition in two volumes, *Tantara ny Andriana eto Madagascar* (Tananarive, 1908), henceforth TA. For the major study of Callet's work, see Alain Delivré, *L'Histoire des rois de l'Imerina* (Paris, 1974).

2 Joseph C. Miller, Review of Janzen and MacGaffey, *An Anthology of Kongo Religion, Journal of African History*, vol. 18, no. 1 (1977), p. 140.

3 On the impact of printing and editing on Merina oral literature see Berg, 'The Myth of Racial Strife and Merina Kinglists', *History in Africa*, vol. 4 (1977), pp. 1–30.

4 The notion of racial discontinuity still plagues current accounts of the monarchy's foundation. For examples, see: A. Dandouau and G. S. Chapus, *Histoire des populations de Madagascar* (Paris, 1952), pp. 10–11, 96–7; H. Deschamps, *Histoire de Madagascar*, 4th ed. (Paris, 1972), pp. 26 n. 1, 56–8, 114–16; P. Vérin, 'L'origine indonésienne des Malgaches', *Bulletin de Madagascar*, no. 259 (1967), pp. 958–61; E. Ralaimihoatra, *Histoire de Madagascar*, 2nd ed. (Tananarive, 1969), p. 6; R. K. Kent, *Early Kingdoms in Madagascar* (New York, 1970), pp. 227–34, 239; N. Heseltine, *Madagascar* (New York, 1971), pp. 54–7; Delivré, *Histoire des rois,* pp. 101 et seq.; P. Mutibwa, *The Malagasy and the Europeans* (Oxford, 1974), pp. 5–7; A. Southall, 'The Problem of Malgasy Origins', in H. N. Chittick and R. I. Rotberg (eds.), *East Africa and the Orient* (New

Gerald M Berg

York, 1975), pp. 193–206; P. Vérin, 'Austronesian Contribution to Madagascar', in ibid., pp. 175–6; H. Neville Chittick, 'The East Coast, Madagascar, and the Indian Ocean', in Roland Oliver (ed.), *The Cambridge History of Africa*, vol. 3 *From c.1050 to c.1600* (London, 1975), p. 222.

J. Dez has recently sought to minimize the theme of racial conflict in his 'Essai sur le concept de Vazimba', *Bulletin de l'Académie Malgache*, vol. 49, no. 2 (1971), pp. 11–20.

5 On the transference of Vazimba images see Gerald M. Berg, 'Historical Traditions and the Foundations of Monarchy in Imerina' (PhD dissertation, University of California, Berkeley, 1975), pp. 25–37.

6 For the classic statement of this myth, see A. Grandidier, *Ethnographie de Madagascar*, vol. 1 (Paris, 1908), fasc. 1, pp. 72, 78–85, 234–5, and fasc. 2, pp. 627–8. Derivative versions are discussed in Berg, 'Historical Traditions', pp. 38–59. For an alternative view of the monarchy's foundation see ibid., pp. 92–221.

J. C. Miller has shown in the case of the Jaga that invaders are seen incorrectly as the racial opposite of the indigenous population. See his 'Requiem for the Jaga', *Cahiers d'études africaines*, vol. 13, no. 1 (no. 49) (1973), p. 130. Wyatt MacGaffey, in his *Custom and Government in the Lower Congo* (Berkeley, 1970), p. 30, suggests that the view of the indigenous population as dwarfs is a religious concept that has nothing to do with historical dwarfs. Unkempt long hair is often attributed to Vazimba, and this as well may have spiritual rather than physical connotations. Marc Bloch notes that long hair attributed to the founders of the Frankish dynasty 'had certainly been at the beginning a symbol of a supernatural nature'. See his *The Royal Touch* (London, 1973), p. 33.

7 For an expanded treatment of this topic see Berg, 'Historical Traditions', pp. 2–63, and 'The Myth of Racial Strife'.

8 TA, p. 13: 'Ary milevina ao an-tampon'Ambohijanahary Razanahary, *tonga vazimba* ao.' (My emphasis.)

9 Vig MS., Norske Misjonsskolen, Boky VIII: 'Ranoro dia olona *nanjary Vazimba*, nefa izy io dia zanak' Andriana ka aloha sady taranak' Andriana' (my emphasis). The manuscript referred to is Lars Vig, coll., Manuscript Notebooks, I–X, Archives of the Norske Misjonsskolen, Stavanger, Norway, under *Madagassisk Afguder*, RUM. C. Avd. VIII–1, nos. 10, 275–10, 284. The tale of Ranoro, which forms the substance of Boky VIII, was probably told to Vig between 1875 and 1887. The translation as a whole is extremely valuable since it was made during the same time as Callet's though it is completely independent of the latter.

All notebooks with the exception of Boky VIII have been recently translated into French by J.-P. Domenichini under the title, *Histoire des palladium de l'Imerina*, Musée d'Art et d'Archéologie de l'Université de Madagascar, Travaux et Documents, VIII (Tananarive, 1971), mimeograph, 719 pp. Domenichini attributes authorship of the manuscript to Rainibao and Ramboa (pp. x–xi). All references to Boky VIII, Ranoro, will be to the manuscript at Stavanger, henceforth Vig MS., Boky VIII.

10 Berg, 'Historical Traditions', pp. 70–9.

11 TA, p. 240: '. . . ka tsy hita intsony: dia vazimba ao izy.' In R. Vally-Samat, *Contes et légendes de Madagascar* (Paris, 1954), Ranoro is called

Some words about Merina historical literature

'daughter-of-the-water' (*zazavavindrano*) and is a *vazimba* with long hair. In addition to TA and Vig MS., the following Ranoro versions are used:

(a) *Firaketana ny Fiteny sy ny Zavatra Malagasy*, no. 37 (1940), pp. 14–15. *Firaketana* usually relies heavily upon TA for its oral traditions, but often, as in the case of Ranoro, it includes variants found nowhere else.

(b) Vally-Samat, *Contes et légendes de Madagascar*, pp. 67–71, contains some unusual elaboration. It is a French translation possibly taken from G. Ferrand, *Contes populaires malgaches* (Paris, 1893).

(c) T . . . [Rainitiary], 'Andriambodilova, Andriantsimandafika, Ranoro', *Mpanolo Tsaina*, 7 (1909), pp. 193–200, is a check on other sources. It contains no unique variations.

12 Lars Dahle, *Specimens of Malagasy Folk-lore* (Tananarive, 1877), p. 301: 'Ary dia notsofiny rano, hono, izy [Rasoalavavolo] mianadahy . . .'

13 Ferrand, *Contes populaires*, pp. 91–2, 'L'Ondine'.

14 Various rituals use the sprinkling of water, *safo-rano*, or *tsitsika*, including circumcision, *fora* (see TA, p. 307), the royal bath, *fandroana* (see G. Razafimino, *La Signification religieuse du Fandroana*, Tananarive, 1924, pp. 14–17, and David Griffiths, Journal, entry of 19 June 1822, London Missionary Society, Journals, Madagascar, I/4), and talisman benedictions, *sampy* (see Callet, Letter, 8 September 1875, *Ann. St. Enfance*, 18, 1877, pp. 179–94, and Griffiths and Baker to Clayton, 2 December 1831, London Missionary Society, Letters received, IV/1/C). I wish to thank Maurice Bloch for his comments on water rituals used currently in circumcision ritual.

15 TA, p. 309: Ranoro was a 'holy vazimba' (*vazimba masina*) and a 'famous ancestor' (*razana malaza*) of the Antehiroka. In many cases, the phrase 'holy person' (*olo'masina*) replaces *vazimba* so that TA, p. 12, refers to Andriandravindravina, a noted *vazimba*, as a 'holy person who had long been worshipped' (*olo'masina izany nivavahany ny tato aoriana*).

16 Maurice Bloch, *Placing the Dead* (London, 1971), pp. 43–5, 106–22.

17 Ibid., p. 111.

18 Fieldnotes, 1973, and TA, p. 16.

19 J. Richardson, *A New Malagasy-English Dictionary* (Antananarivo, 1885), pp. 739–40, and A. Abinal and V. Malzac, *Dictionnaire malgache-français* (Tananarive, 1888), p. 814, 'mivarina aman-tany'. *Varina* also includes in its field of meaning ideas of exile and shame.

20 See Berg, 'Historical Traditions', pp. 67, 75.

21 TA, pp. 239–40: '. . . ary ny fasana efa ela, misy tonga vazimba, koa tonga namany ny Vazimba, kanjo olona hiany tany aloha ary ankehitriny tonga Vazimba fa ela ny nahafatesan'ny fony ny olona mbola vitsy, fa tsy mba nikambana tamy ny be tato aoriana . . . ary izao tsy mba misy tonga vazimba intsony fa be ny olona ankehitriny, ka tonga razana hiany ny maty.'

22 TA, p. 239: '. . . tonga miantso ny razana indray izy ivavahana: satria fa atao ny sahala amy ny Vazimba ny razana: ary tonga misy razana manindry ny hava'ny kosa raha misy mampalahelo azy. Koa ity tany tonga maniry ny fivavahana amy ny Vazimba sy ny razana: zavatra ifanarahana izany ka ny iray no angalana tahaka amy ny iray.'

23 TA, p. 12: 'Tsy mbola nisy vary, tsy mbola nisy mangahazo ambany vomanga, mbola vitsy ny olona aty ambony, mbola vazimba tsirairay, ala maizina avokoa izao tontolo izao.'

24 M. Rasamuël, 'Ny Vazimba', *Mpanolo Tsaina*, 24 (1927), p. 50.
25 C. Renel, 'Anciennes religions de Madagascar', *Bulletin de l'Academie malgache*, n.s. 5 (1920–21), pp. 60–6. See L. Dahle, *Specimens*, pp. 99, 294 et seq. in which Angalampona are 'tsy lehibe tahaka ny olona . . . dia lehibe kokoa noho ny zaza mingodongodona'. For more on Angalampona, see L. Vig, 30 December 1877, in *Norske Missions Tidende*, no. 43 (1888), pp. 276–7. In *Firaketana*, no. 53 (1941), p. 241, Angalampona are similar to 'Kinaoly': 'madinika hoatra ny zazakely'. Renel, in 'Anciennes religions', no. 2, p. 68, derives the term Angalampona from *angatra*, meaning 'ésprits malfaisants', and *lampy*, the large flat stones under which they live. In addition, Renel gives descriptions (pp. 66–8) of other legendary beings similar to Vazimba. *Firaketana*, op. cit., pp. 241ff, gives a comprehensive survey of mythical spirit beings related to Angalampona. For Kinaoly dwarf spirits, see *Firaketana*, no. 232 (1962), pp. 222–3. In *Firaketana*, no. 238 (1963), p. 314, Kokolampy appear as 'madinika sady fohy, ny lohany kely', which is very close to Dahle's description of Vazimba (p. 294): 'olona madinidinika izy ary kelikely loha'.
26 Rainandriamampandry, Tantarany Madagascar, first redaction, 1875–1880, Archives de la République malgache, SS. 22, fol. 3v: 'Fa rehefa resy sy lao izy [vazimba], dia nataony ny olona ho masina ny fasana izay nilevenany ny Vazimba, ka dia nivavahany . . . Fa nataon'ny razana ho masina sy mahay nitaky ny Vazimba maty, ka dia nivavahany . . .'
27 Berg, 'Historical Traditions', pp. 19–21.
28 In the following discussion, three versions of the *vazimba* portion of Antehiroka lists are used:

A. IV. TA, p. 308
A. VIa. Rainandriamampandry, Tantarany, fols. 7r–v.
A. VIb. Rainandriamampandry, Tantarany, fols. 7v–8r.

The lists below give generation, name, and burial site.

Version A. VIa	*Versions A. IV and A. VIb*
1 ANDRIANDROKA—Vodivato	1 ANDRIANDROKA—Ambohidratrimo E.
2 Ramoraony—Ambohidratrimo E.	2 Ratsitakondrazana—
3 Randranovola—Ambohimahatakatra	3 Razevozevo—Ambohimahatakatra
4 Andriantsitakondrazana—Fanongoavana	4 Razevomanana—Fanongoavana
5 Razevomanana and Raonimianjeva—Ampandrana	5 Ramasinanjoma—Ambohipaniry
6 Rasambomanoro and Ramasinanjoma—Merimanjaka	6 Rasambomanoro—Tananarive
7 Ramasinamparihy—Alasora	7 Ramasinamparihy—Alasora
8 ANDRIANDROKA—Ambohidrabiby	8 ANDRIANDROKA—Ambohidrabiby

The order of burial sites in versions A. IV and A. VIb are the same, although A. VIb leaves out the site for the second generation. All lists end with Ambohidrabiby which is also a sacred site of Ralambo, the second Merina king.

29 In Ganda lists as well, it is the eighth ruler who ends the nonhistorical section. See R. R. Atkinson, 'Traditions of the Early Kings of Buganda', *History in Africa*, vol. 2 (1975), pp. 20–1.

30 In TA, pp. 238, 308, Andriandroka engenders Andriampirokana who fathers Andriambodilova and Ratsimandafika by the same women. In Rainandriamampandry, Tantarany, fol. 8r, Andriampirokana, the eldest, Andriambodilova, and Andrianstimandafika are the sons of Andriandroka. Most versions support TA, though in *Firaketana*, no. 35, (1935), p. 552, Ramasinamparihy is Andriampirokana's father. All versions end with three names: Andriampirokana, Andriambodilova, and Ratsimandafika.

   Even Andriambodilova's name lends itself to this interpretation. The name comprises *andriana* (ruler), *vody*, and *lova*. *Vody*, meaning summit or crest, often combines with other words to denote sacred power. Thus, the *vodihena* is the zebu hump which belongs to the ruler and is an emblem of respect for authority. Genealogies, both royal and nonroyal, often give Vodivato (rocky summit) as the place of *vazimba* origin. *Lova* means inheritance or hereditary property, and so the combination, *vodilova*, signifies sacred origin and corporate inheritance. Andriambodilova, then, means ruler of the sacred origin/inheritance.

31 TA, pp. 12–14.

32 Provenance has been determined by a method suggested by A. Delivré in *Histoire des rois*, pp. 47–8. Malagasy, he notes, has a number of prepositions which indicate the distance between the speaker and the object or place spoken of. Thus, toponyms preceded by *eto* are places where the speaker is when telling or writing the story or where he was when he learned it. Delivré's method, however, has severe limitations. In much, perhaps most, of the oral literature set down in writing, confusion arises from inconsistent application of these prepositions and in the case of most royal genealogies it seems that *eto* precedes most toponyms. In the version selected here (TA III), however, use of the preposition is consistent and unambiguous. *Eto*, indicating the presence of the speaker, appears twice before Ambohijanahary south of Mahamasina, and before no other toponym. According to coordinates developed by the Institut géographique de Madagascar, Ambohijanahary is located at 807.2/511.2.

33 They are:
   TA, pp. 8–9, called TA I.
   TA, pp. 11–12, called TA II.
   David Jones, coll., Ancestry of the Kings of Imerina, MS., 1836, in the library of Rev. J. H. Hardyman. I wish to thank Prof. Simon Ayache for allowing me to consult his translation, and to Rev. Hardyman for permission to consult the original.
   William Ellis, *History of Madagascar* (London, 1838), vol. 2, p. 115.
   Rabetrano, Ny tantarany Razan'Andriana tao aloha nolazaindRabetrano borozano avy ery Ankadivoribe, 3 alahotsy 1844, MS. (Copy), Archives de la République malgache, PP. 35, fols. 31r–39v.
   Raombana, Histoires de Madagascar, MS., 3 vols., 1853–1856, Archives de l'Académie malgache 413. Typescript edition of Simon Ayache, pp. 106–14.

Gerald M Berg

Rainandriamampandry, Tantarany, fols. 40r–52r.

Firaketana, no. 41 (1940), p. 105, 'Andriamboninolona'.

Firaketana, no. 185 (1956), pp. 44–6, 'Ifanongoavana'.

34 Lists agree on nearly all points after Andriamanelo, though Delivré (op. cit., p. 97) believes that royal traditions become more varied as they speak of events close to the present. Michael Twaddle in 'On Ganda Historiography', *History in Africa*, vol. 1 (1974), pp. 85–100, suggests that Ganda traditions became less diverse with the development of indigenous historical writing. In Imerina, however, indigenous historical writing has preserved much of the variety in lists which was overlooked by many late nineteenth-century and early twentieth-century observers.

35 The original takes the form of a story about political history. The emphasis on politics, however, is not readily apparent in the illustration presented here which is a schematic representation intended to simplify the original.

36 TA III places the brothers in the eighth generation of father-to-son succession. TA I, Jones, Rabetrano, and Rainandriamampandry place them in the third generation; *Firaketana* (1956) in the second generation; and TA II in the fourth.

37 TA III makes Andrianamponga of Sampazana the brothers' father. In *Firaketana* (1956) the father is Andrianamponga of Ifanoavana; in Jones, Raombana, and Rainandriamampandry the father is Andriamboniravina of Ambatondrakorika; and in TA I the father is Andriamboniravina of Beravina. Moreover, the offspring of the ruling brother, Andriandranolava, are not mentioned in some versions, while others (TA I, Jones, Rabetrano, and Rainandriamampandry) name Rafandrandava, and yet others (TA II, *Firaketana* 1956) mention Andriaboniravina.

38 Rainandriamampandry, in addition to the standard version, presents another that names Andriandranolava, not Andriamoraony, as the inventor of the *kabary*. He notes, moreover, that Andriandranolava and Andriandranovola are the same.

39 Bloch has shown that modern Merina use the term kin (*havana*) to include not only ideas of descent but of moral value which is not tied to descent. See Maurice Bloch, 'L'extension de la notion de *havana* dans la société merina rurale', *Bulletin de l'Académie Malgache*, n.s. 45 (1967), pp. 15–16.

40 This name and another like it, Andriananjavonana, appear at or near the beginning of most *vazimba* lists. It derives from the root *zavona*, literally fog or mist, and figuratively, numerous or innumerable. See Richardson, *Dictionary*, p. 798.

41 For a summary of the Ranoro theme, see Berg, 'Historical Traditions', pp. 85–6; *Firaketana*, no. 38 (1940), p. 48; and TA, no. 1, pp. 12–13. Another variant appears in L. Dahle and J. Sims (eds.), *Angonon'ny ntaolo* (Tananarive, 1930), p. 181, 'Ny Vady amanjanaka fanaraka.'

42 TA I; TA II; TA III; Rainandriamampandry, fols. 51r–52r; Jones, p. 2; Raombana, pp. 113–14; Rabetrano, fol. 31v; Merina manuscripts, collected by A. Grandidier, II (1869–1870), pp. 345–6, in the Musée de l'Homme, Paris. In Ganda lists, the eighth ruler, Nakibinge, is the transition figure mediating between historical and nonhistorical time. See Atkinson, 'Traditions', pp. 20–1. The second portion of the Merina lists, consisting of

names after Andriamanelo, takes on a decidedly historical tone and so requires a different method than used here.

43 Rafohy and Rangita precede Andriamanelo, though there is considerable disagreement about the order of the two queens. Rafohy precedes Rangita in TA III, *Firaketana* (1956), and Ellis, *History*, p. 115. Ellis calls Rafohy *ravady fohy* (short woman) and in his version neither woman gives birth to Andriamanelo. Instead Rangita bears Andrianamponga who in turn fathers Andriamanelo. Andrianamponga is a cyclical figure, included at the beginning and the end of some royal genealogies of the *vazimba* epoch and so his appearance is structurally parallel to Andriandroka in Antehiroka. In TA II the women are sisters, and Rafohy gives birth to Andriamanelo. TA I; Rainandriamampandry; Savaron, 'Contribution à l'histoire d'Imerina', *Bulletin de l'Académie malgache*, 11 (1928), p. 69; and Lefebre, 'Les Mandiavatos', *Notes, Reconnaissances, Explorations*, IV/2 (1898), p. 895, name Ramanalimanjaka as Rafohy's husband. Nothing more is known of him save Grandidier's unfounded statement in *Ethnographie*, pp. 82–3, that the husbands of Rafohy and Rangita were leaders of a Javanese invasion.

44 TA, p. 16.

45 The following versions are used for this discussion: TA, p. 18; TA, pp. 139 et seq.; *Firaketana*, no. 26 (1939), pp. 332–4, no. 33 (1939), p. 506, no. 35 (1939), p. 552, no. 40 (1940), pp. 79–80, no. 43 (1940), p. 159; TA, pp. 543–4 [A. I]; TA, pp. 544–6 [A. II]; pp. 546–8 [A. III]; TA, pp. 306–10 [A. IV]; TA, pp. 237–8 [A. V]; A. VIa; A. VIb; Rainandriamampandry, fol. 4r [A. VIc]; ibid., fols. 76r–v [A. VIIa]; ibid., fols. 95r–96v [A. VIIb]; ibid., fols. 74v–75r [A. VIIc]; Vig MS., Boky VIII [A. VIII].

46 Alamanga literally means blue forest. Maurice Bloch (Personal Communication) observes that blue (*manga*) is often used to denote male power.

47 See Berg, 'Historical Traditions', pp. 193–221.

48 For Swahili, see L. Dahle, 'The Swahili Element in the New Malagasy-English Dictionary', *Antananarivo Annual*, vol. 9 (1885), p. 110. M. Rasamuël, 'Ny Vazimba', p. 60, notes that 'those called Vazimba are simply ancient ancestors and nothing more'. For *vadzimu* and its relation to the *mhondoro* cult, see Brian Fagan, *Southern Africa during the Iron Age* (New York, 1965), p. 122. For the Common Bantu, see M. Guthrie, *Comparative Bantu*, vol. 2 (Farnborough, Hants., 1971), p. 125, C. S. no. 619.

10. 'The Disease of Writing': Ganda and Nyoro Kinglists in a Newly Literate World[1]

DAVID HENIGE

> If men learn [writing] . . . it will plant forgetfulness in their souls . . . What you have discovered is a recipe not for memory but for reminder.[2]

Not very long ago I argued that the kinglist of Buganda, in contrast to that of Bunyoro, gave every appearance of being reliable and historically accurate. I based this assessment primarily on structural considerations—the plausibly complex succession patterns of the Ganda royal genealogy contrasted with the patently artificial components of the Nyoro list. There was also the argument of consistency to be considered. It was not easy to find many variations among the available lists of Ganda rulers, whereas for Bunyoro differences not only existed but also fell into a suspiciously purposive progression of repetitive kinglists of increasing length. Agreement among the Ganda kinglists, by the rule of confirming independent sources, seemed to speak in favor of their credibility.

Work done in the past few years on the cosmological content of Ganda traditions as well as a recently published discussion of the antithesis of listing and orality have helped to persuade me that I was wrong to have accepted so easily the accuracy of the Ganda kinglists as the centerpieces of their royal traditions. When I began to look more closely at the historical context of their earliest appearance in written forms, even their oral basis seemed suspect. I realized that I had misjudged the timing and intensity of the introduction of literacy into Ganda ruling circles. In fact, a strong argument can be made that much of the size, structure, and sequence of the Ganda kinglist was a product of early Arabic literacy in Buganda, already present at the time at which the kinglist was first collected and published. As a result, in the present paper I propose to draw out the similarities in the Ganda and Nyoro kinglists rather than to contrast them as I had done previously. This reconsideration leads me to the conclusion that the Ganda lists may be no more

240

accurate than those of the Nyoro and therefore less historical than I
had originally thought. It also allows me the opportunity to reflect
on a few important new themes in the study of oral materials today.

Recent clarifications of just what the handy and hallowed term
'oral tradition' should really encompass have hardly influenced the
conclusions drawn elsewhere from allegedly oral data about the
Ganda and Nyoro pasts. Prior to these refinements, the characteristic which has been allowed to determine the 'oralness' of a body of
information seems generally to have been the mode in which it came
to the notice of literate historians. That is to say, if contemporary
historian *X* collected spoken information about a particular past
event, it was thereby deemed to be 'oral' tradition. But this conclusion depended on the simplistic assumption that modern-day verbal
transmission was *prima facie* evidence that the information had also
been transmitted uninterruptedly by oral means across many generations from the time of the event(s) described. Hence it was seen
as 'oral' in its modality and as 'tradition' in its presumed origin in the
more remote past. Similar assumptions were also applied to data
from investigators writing in the past whenever they related that
what they subsequently published had originally been presented
orally. Their reports, though written, thus were accepted as once
having been 'oral tradition'. Such an approach fails to take sufficient
account of possible anomalies in prior transmissions, which may for
instance have involved literacy, so that the chain of transmission
may have included written media among its links. It also entirely
begs the crucial question of ultimate provenance and thus the
central issue of the relationship of a datum to a past event. The
inability or unwillingness of historians to reconstruct fully the chain
of transmission forces them back on an essentially ahistorical and
synchronic attitude toward their data that fails to tie the present
convincingly to the past.

Sometimes historians have not observed carefully the distinction
that properly obtains between the concepts denoted as 'tradition'
and 'testimony'. There are admittedly problems of connotation
here, since in common usage 'tradition' has come to comprehend
what ought to be termed 'testimony'. Nevertheless, legitimate and
important differences must be observed. By any recognized standard, that which is 'traditional' is corporate or collective as a viewpoint, whereas testimony represents individual actions or attitudes
which may diverge from the collective mentality. To carry this
distinction a step further, it should be remembered that the term
'tradition' implies the passage of time and is therefore a point of

view transmitted and inherited from the past. Conversely, testimony properly speaking usually means no more than a new, firsthand, or eyewitness account, either of an event or of some prior description of an event. In short, a single informant or even a small group of informants cannot be considered to have proffered 'oral tradition' unless it can be demonstrated that he, she, or they really stand as proxies for larger, relatively stable and enduring elements of their society.

The failure of students of oral tradition in the interlacustrine region to observe this distinction has led many of them to miss the significance of the spread of literacy for the creation of the Ganda and Nyoro kinglists that became common in the vernacular literature. They assumed in both instances that what they heard from local historians was typical of what was regarded as characteristic of traditional societies—that the historians were operating in a completely oral environment and that the oral historical materials centered on lists of former rulers. In fact, the oral historians of Buganda and Bunyoro used past rulers only as convenient conceptual referents around which they grouped other sorts of remembered historical data. They were making no lists of their own, in the sense of composing sequences of definite order and length. But their use of the names provided grist for the mills of academically trained historians, both native and foreign, who organized these names into kinglists that they could present to doubters as hallmarks of the credibility of Ganda and Nyoro oral traditions. Kinglists of this sort were specific, detailed, and expected kinds of material similar to that already familiar in non-oral societies. Once listed, the names also seemed to provide reliably sequenced events or periods revealing process, change, and causation—the staples of the professional diet of European historians who took over the field after World War II. Western historians of the interlacustrine area industriously compiled the names into kinglists, scrutinized them closely, and conferred on the results of their analyses starring roles in their attempts to reconstruct the contours and duration of the area's past. It became axiomatic that mobilizing and using the kinglists was indispensable for pursuing successful historical research in the area. To judge from the literature, enthusiasm for the kinglists even stimulated an occasional willingness to accept them even when their use implied suspending critical judgment about their reliability.

The main reason for reconsidering the historical meaning of the Ganda and Nyoro kinglists is that literate historians' faith in them falters on recent recognition of the fact that lists *qua* lists are not a natural analytical category. Most individuals in our own society do after all compile lists regularly, whether in organizing their knowledge mentally or in committing that knowledge to writing, so that lists became a recognized form of knowledge organized and demonstrated. In literate societies even the most inconsequential things are listed. The memorizing of lists of almost anything is a common activity and in many schools serves as a mode of transferring and testing knowledge. Who, for instance, does not know the child who delights in reciting in proper order the presidents of the United States or the rulers of England? Or the old man or woman who defines those elusive 'good old days' by abstracting and mentally listing their 'good' qualities from the less well defined unpleasant detritus of the memory?

But, we must ask ourselves, does the compiling of lists extend beyond our own culture—or others like it—as a form of organizing useful knowledge? For instance, should we expect to find this activity occurring in oral societies and, if so, should we expect that oral historians would regard the listing of previous rulers in proper historical sequence as a practical and productive form of activity? Goody has recently argued that we should not hold these expectations.[3] He would see the activity of listing—that is, the abstracting of 'like' elements (in the case under examination, kings) from a mental universe of unlike elements (in this case all those things which were not kings)—as a graphic art which is not only common in, but confined almost entirely to, literate societies. The ability to list is, by this argument, a function of being literate. Furthermore, the construction of lists is, in Goody's opinion, a discontinuous and decontextualized form of mental activity that requires a significant reshaping of an oral society's modes of thought.[4] The fact that so many kinglists have been shown to be distorted and incorrect suggests that Goody's doubts about the appearance of listing in oral societies ought to cause us to question the authenticity of the Ganda as well as the Nyoro kinglists as 'tradition'.[5]

Where Has Suddenly Sprung up This New Tradition?[6]

The circumstances in which these kinglists appeared even raise questions as to whether their sources were oral. In the nineteenth century, Buganda and Bunyoro were contiguous kingdoms in what was to become the Uganda Protectorate. Whatever their respective historical developments may have been before they entered the written record late in the nineteenth century, European influences and colonial rule reached them in markedly different ways. In every possible sense the earliest missionaries and British colonial administrators favored Buganda political and social culture vis-à-vis other African polities of the Protectorate. On the other hand, they denigrated Bunyoro, not only in respect to Buganda but also, and probably more gallingly to the Banyoro, in regard to Toro, an upstart breakaway kingdom from Bunyoro whose ruler had learned well how to gain the efficacious favor of Europeans of every variety.[7] These contrasts in European attitudes seem to have paralleled the presentations of the past by the Baganda and the Banyoro in both kind and degree. The modern Ganda interpretation of their kingdom's past developed very early and once developed it remained remarkably consistent, even with the elaborations that were added to it as time passed. A coherent and comprehensive account of the Nyoro past, on the other hand, developed only several decades after that of Buganda, and when it did it presented several aspects which cannot but give rise to misgivings about its historicity. Since I have elsewhere detailed the arguments against accepting the Bunyoro kinglist and the standard reconstruction of the early history of the state, I will confine myself here to recapitulating only the most salient points as they relate also to a discussion of the Ganda list.[8]

Whereas the kinglist of Buganda and its attendant traditions blossomed quickly, the oral tradition of Bunyoro was much slower to bloom, growing both gradually and fitfully. In 1875, the same year that Stanley, as noted below, was able to secure a list of thirty-five Ganda kings (*bakabaka*), Linant de Bellefonds was able to collect the names of only five Nyoro rulers, or *bakama*.[9] Less than three years later, Emin Pasha, despite taking 'the greatest possible pains' among the Nyoro, was no more successful.[10] Nevertheless, this inchoate Nyoro list grew longer as time passed—to twelve names in the 1890s, fourteen and then seventeen names a decade later (both of these versions from the same informant!), and finally seventeen names again in the 1920s.[11] These kinglists grew at the expense of inconsistencies and contradictions among them, as if the oral data on which they were presumably based were not equal to the new demands for greater and greater length being put on them. No two of the lists agreed on the names or order of the various rulers, and informants were able to provide few details about any but the most recent *bakama* named in them.

These hesitations ended abruptly with the publication in 1935 of what appeared to be a fully matured Nyoro kinglist consisting of no fewer than twenty-three names. To the bare bones of the names in the earlier lists were at last added many details which had apparently hitherto escaped notice.[12] The *mukama* then ruling Bunyoro, Tito Winyi II or IV, who, under the pseudonym 'K.W.' was the purported author of the articles in which all this new information appeared, supported the additional details by referring to long since published names and events in the past of the neighboring Ganda state. In fact this latest Nyoro kinglist almost certainly oriented itself to the well-known Ganda list, with which it marched nearly in lockstep, providing apparent corroboration which, for all its spuriousness, many historians later came to regard as evidence of its essential reliability.

John Nyakatura, who might fairly be called the court historian of modern Bunyoro, later bestowed the final *imprimatur* on K.W.'s list when he published his own work, *Abakama ba Bunyoro-Kitara*, in 1947.[13] Nyakatura later claimed major credit for the florescence of K.W.'s kinglist, recalling that in his early manhood he had been seized by 'a passion to know how many kings had ruled over Bunyoro'.[14] His early researches in this regard were based on testimony of Nyoro 'troubadors', as he called them, and on the royal tombsites scattered throughout and beyond the shrunken colonial boundaries of Bunyoro.[15] On the strength of these tombsites particularly, Nyakatura gradually built up his long list of *bakama*, which he first provided to K.W. and later published under his own authorship. Explaining this rather tardy appearance of the 'full' Nyoro kinglist, Nyakatura stated that the Banyoro were 'not in a hurry to write [the list] down'.[16] He did not account for this very inexpedient reluctance, so inconsistent with Bunyoro's otherwise often demonstrated sense of injustice at British favoritism toward Buganda.

In addition to whatever traditional information K.W. and Nyakatura may have used, they also had recourse to two non-oral kinds of source in their efforts to construct a usable Nyoro past. The first of these was, as noted, the royal tombsites, many of which now exist quite widely scattered in the area. The guardians of these tombs had abandoned and reoccupied them numerous times during the previous 75 years as a result of the parlous political conditions in nineteenth-century Bunyoro. The capacity of these tombsites to confirm the reconstruction of the Nyoro oral kinglists thus seems doubtful. At best, they might verify the names and number of the kings, but they could not provide data for reconstructing sequence.

In fact, later investigations at some sites unearthed no evidence at all of royal burials.[17]

The second non-oral source used by K.W. and Nyakatura was equally important to them and certainly more to the point. This was the written tradition of Buganda accessible in the works of Ganda authors.[18] These works conveniently laid out the structure and duration of an exemplar past, with some helpful details about Bunyoro thrown in. Little more remained for them than to measure the Ganda past in terms of the kings in its list, then correlate these names with the fragmentary recollections of rulers available in Bunyoro, and finally fill the resulting blanks (which were in fact rather numerous) in the assumed one-to-one correspondence between the two by repeating Nyoro royal names. As a result, new 'Winyi' *bakama* appeared and rendered Tito Winyi, who had been calling himself Winyi II for many years, Winyi IV. Several earlier *bakama* underwent similar transformations.

A verdict of straightforward manipulation of this kind may seem harsh, even unfair, to what were probably well-intentioned efforts by K.W. and Nyakatura to bring their own past into what they felt was well-deserved alignment with that already recorded and accepted for Buganda. But a look at the development of the Nyoro list over time and a close comparison of the details of its final published version with the information in previously published Ganda traditions leave the modern historian little alternative but to doubt that it could have had its sources in authentic nineteenth-century Nyoro oral tradition, not to mention its even more problematic relationship to the real Nyoro past.

The protracted and fitful development of the kinglist of Bunyoro presents features almost exaggerated in their starkness. They exhibit a propensity to list and to lengthen which increased throughout the colonial period, probably as a result of cumulative exposure to literacy and, in this case, more specifically to the abundance of Ganda historical literature published during these decades. In this sense the example of Bunyoro has diagnostic value insofar as it stands as an analog, albeit of magnified proportions, for the ways in which history may have been done in Buganda fifty years earlier, when the stimulus of growing literacy and a desire to acquire the respect of Europeans were similar but our ability to discern the Ganda responses to them much less.

> Just as in [B]unyoro the large tobacco pipe is a symbol of the Great Lords, so here [Buganda] it is the large family tree![19]

The Ganda kinglist, and with it the fuller tradition of the kingdom, developed into its final form within little more than a generation after the arrival of the first Europeans there in 1862. As early as 1875 *kabaka* Mutesa gave Henry Stanley lists of thirty-two and thirty-five rulers, with a few details describing the activities of several of them.[20] Other lists, similar in length and always with an increasing amount of circumstantial detail, were collected from Mutesa and some of his high officials during the next several years.

This elaboration of Ganda royal tradition culminated in the appearance of the first edition of Apolo Kaggwa's *Ekitabo kya Basekabaka be Buganda* in 1901.[21] Kaggwa was *katikkiro*, or prime minister, of Buganda, so that his work carried the weight of official sanction, and it quickly came to be, in Rowe's words, 'probably the best known book in Luganda' besides the Bible.[22] In consequence, its appearance then (it underwent two further editions in 1912 and 1927) marked the real end of development in Ganda dynastic traditions.[23] Unlike the Nyoro traditions, where inconsistencies were plentiful, the Baganda agreed not only on who had ruled but also on what they had done. Into this harmonious chorus only a single discordant note is known to have intruded. This was a list of *bakabaka* collected from Stanislas Mugwanya, another high Ganda official, in 1891–2. Mugwanya's list differed from other published versions less in length than in the sequence and placement of rulers. Wrigley has discussed the provenance of Mugwanya's list and considered its implications for the history and the historiography of early Buganda, showing how this alternative *schema* can make good historical sense of the same elements of Ganda tradition presented in other ways by Mutesa and Kaggwa.[24] He concludes that the existence of a different but equally believable kinglist renders plausibility alone an inadequate ground for accepting the Mutesa-Kaggwa version as authentic.

Except insofar as Mugwanya's list demonstrates that alternatives not based on the canonical version of the Ganda kinglist can make sense of the same history, it is not germane to our purposes here, which are to explain how a long and plausible Ganda kinglist could have been available to Stanley as early as 1875. If nothing else, the appearance of the Ganda list long before that of any other kinglist for the area means that Ganda oral historians could not have derived it directly from external written models in the same way that Nyoro historians built theirs half a century later from Ganda historical writings.[25] Furthermore, its internal reasonableness and the apparently adventitious consistency among several versions

(Mugwanya's expected) seemed to favor accepting it as an authentic expression of Ganda oral tradition.[26] However, based on comments made by early observers, on Wrigley's demonstration of reasonable alternative explanations, and on the arguments adduced by Goody regarding listing, I will argue here that the Ganda kinglist first collected by Stanley was an accurate representation neither of the oral resources of mid nineteenth-century Ganda historiography nor of the number of *bakabaka*. The evidence supporting this view relates to the convergence in time and place of factors similar to those present later in Bunyoro that facilitated the accumulation and presentation of a literate-style Ganda kinglist. Within a few decades between 1850 and 1900, the introduction of literacy in Arabic and then in English, the advent of intense missionary activity, and the imposition of colonial rule to the advantage of the Baganda each contributed its measure to this.

The Europeans who began to visit Buganda in the 1860s were naturally interested in learning more about the past of this impressively organized state, which moreover was strategically located in terms of European geopolitical intentions in Africa and which offered tantalizing commercial and missionary possibilities besides. They asked for details about its history, receiving them first through the intermediary of their Swahili guides. The information initially gathered by Speke and Grant in 1862 included only a very short list of rulers, eight in all, but only thirteen years later Mutesa, as we have seen, was able to provide Stanley with lists four times as long.[27] For our purposes the crucial question is whether the longer lists of 1875 had been in existence before Stanley came along in that year—whether they had in fact been available (though not recorded) at the time of Speke's visit at Mutesa's court. We cannot know the answer to this question, of course, but it has commonly been assumed that such lists, or at least the raw materials from which to compile them, had been present. There is, though, no direct evidence that the Baganda had accurately maintained a long kinglist beyond the range of European knowledge until Stanley came along and was able to collect and publish it.

Before turning to ways in which Ganda oral historians might have gone about developing a list, it is necessary to set the stage by discussing Stanley's tendency to exaggerate much of what he reported about Buganda. His interest in whatever Mutesa and others offered him in the way of historical data predisposed him to accept whatever was given him, particularly if it would, in his words, testify to 'the respectable antiquity' of the kingdom.[28] Fired by the

desire to open new mission fields in central Africa, Stanley profes-
sed to see in Mutesa an 'Augustus by whose means the light of
the Gospel will be brought to benighted' Africa.[29] His enthusiasm
to sell Mutesa to the European public led him to accept or infer
much (but variously) magnified estimates of the extent of Mutesa's
authority, the size of his armies, and the population of his kingdom.[30]

Meanwhile Mutesa proved receptive to Stanley's blandishments.
At the time Mutesa appears to have feared the expansive tendencies
of the Egyptian government, whose forces had moved up the Nile
and had already begun to encroach on neighboring Bunyoro. The
fortuitous arrival of Stanley provided him with an alternative
foreign policy at the very moment he needed it most. Mutesa
skillfully used Stanley's credulity by manifesting an apparently
eager desire for Christian missionaries, even though from all
accounts he had by then all but converted to Islam.[31] This convergence of enthusiasms—real or feigned—meant that Stanley was
willing to believe what Mutesa told him on matters that enhanced
the importance of Buganda. It is clear from contemporary descriptions of Mutesa's character that he was shrewd enough to recognize
Stanley's usefulness to him and to profit from it.

Having established the historical circumstances that could have
promoted this joint fabrication of a lengthy list of Ganda kings, we
can now discuss sources from which Mutesa and other Ganda
traditionalists might have sought answers to what must have seemed
to them strange questions coming from Stanley and other similarly
minded Europeans. The two most obvious sources of information
about past Buganda rulers were the royal tombs *cum* jawbone
shrines and the recollections of members of those clans which
claimed affiliation with members of the royal line named in the
kinglists. Known Ganda shrines, unlike the royal Nyoro tombs,
have all been located within a conveniently restricted geographical
compass not far from the royal capital, at least since they first came
to the notice of the outside world.[32] Their accessibility would have
permitted Mutesa the opportunity to use them and their guardians if
he needed them to compose a list of the sort asked for by his visitors.
We do not know whether Mutesa did this, but several points cast
doubt on the usefulness to him or anyone else of the Ganda
tombs/shrines as mnemonics for accurate reconstruction of the
Buganda past.

First, according to Kaggwa and several other authors, Mutesa had
caused the bodies and jawbones of his eight immediate predecessors

to be exhumed and reburied, not always in their previous resting places.[33] Neither these writers nor any modern historian has ever explained Mutesa's motives in doing this, nor why he chose only his immediate predecessors if, as the usual correlation of the longer kinglist with the tombsites implies, there actually existed a much larger 'pool' of burial sites and dead ancestors. It is possible (though perhaps not very likely) that earlier *bakabaka* had commonly followed such procedures but had abandoned them with the advent of Islam and Christianity. Or perhaps Mutesa himself instituted the practice as in some way a response to the newly arrived Islam.[34] In any case, it can readily be seen how a *kabaka*'s manipulation of the tombs of his predecessors would introduce imponderables regarding the recollective value of the modern tombsites —imponderables which might well disconcert even those historians most strongly committed to the reliability of these sources as evidence supporting the evolved official kinglist.

To complicate matters of site identification even further, there are in Buganda today, and presumably were in the past, many shrines which, although indistinguishable in size, accoutrements, and attending personnel from those attributed to reigning *bakabaka*, actually commemorate non-ruling princes and other members of the royal family.[35] These are now remembered as belonging to royal collaterals who lived during the last few generations before the time of Mutesa. If Mutesa, in gathering data, had recourse to such shrines of princes of earlier generations, it is possible that the self-serving claims of guardians of such shrines allowed him to extend his list of kings by inextricably mixing *bakabaka* and non-reigning royals.

The number of Ganda kings identified by the earliest Europeans to visit Buganda turns out to match the eight graves that Mutesa had opened. Speke included the names of seven predecessors of Mutesa in his *Journal* but said nothing about their burial sites.[36] His companion Grant offered no list of named rulers in *A Walk Across Africa*, his major account of the expedition, but in his journal and elsewhere he noted that there had been only eight rulers before Mutesa and that their names (which unhappily he did not include) were known 'from the fact that their tombs are protected and preserved by the crown to the present day'.[37] Now (excepting Kimera, the probably eponymous and ahistorical founder of the line), this is precisely the number of *bakabaka* that Mutesa is credited with having exhumed and reinterred. This unquestionably intriguing coincidence does little to support the hypothesis that the

Baganda of the 1850s and 1860s knew anything like the number of kings identified by later sources.

There are two ways to reconcile Grant's reference to only eight rulers and tombs with Kaggwa's testimony of a much larger number of rulers and the allegedly corroborating existence now of some thirty shrines identified as containing the remains of dead *bakabaka*. On the one hand we can argue that Grant (and by inference Speke) was mistaken and, having become aware of Mutesa's exhumations, had concluded wrongly that the small number of tombsites actually involved all previous *bakabaka*.[38] This assumption, or one like it, would be necessary if we are to retain the hypothesis that the number of tombs known before 1860 matched the evolved kinglist of 1875. Conversely we might argue that in 1862 the Baganda could identify only the shrines of these eight rulers with certainty but that by 1875 the curiosity of the Arabs, Stanley, Linant de Bellefonds, and Chaillé-Long—or perhaps the unsuccessful inquiries of Speke and Grant (Speke, after all, spent more time at Mutesa's court than Stanley)—had forced Mutesa to rummage around and find other sites which might or might not have previously had clearly defined royal associations. These additional tombs would have acquired overtones of royalty during the next quarter of a century. After all, what tomb guardians would eschew the chance to claim a relationship with a previous ruler? If this hypothesis is tenable (it can never be proved true), it means that the value of the Ganda tombs as independent physical evidence authenticating the oral kinglist is nil, except possibly for the half dozen or so rulers immediately preceding Mutesa.

Turning to the clan traditionalists, Mutesa's other likely source for information about his predecessors, we are again faced with opportunities for unhistorical lengthening of the list of kings that arose in the process of assembling disjointed information into an integrated synthesis. Most clans that may have had (or thought they had) royal connections probably maintained some memory of their affiliation. Such recollections would, like any traditions adhering to individual tombsites, be isolated segments rather than parts of a unified whole—bodies of discrete data not related to a wider historical context, unconnected links not yet fashioned into a chain by Kaggwa and other Ganda historians. Nor, for that matter, is it likely that inquiries that Mutesa and others might have carried out among the clans in the 1860s and 1870s were very systematic or impartial, at least not as trained historians prefer to define those terms. It is hardly unthinkable that over time the more powerful and influential

251

David Henige

clans in Buganda, even those without royal ancestors, were able to expand to their advantage the configuration of the Ganda kinglist as it came eventually to be established.[39] Mutesa's inquiries would only have intensified and reinforced such inherent inclusive tendencies. Should we not expect the clan traditionalists to have been as inventive in response to their perceptions of Mutesa's intent as Mutesa himself apparently was in responding to and absorbing new knowledge and new views from his Swahili and European visitors?

In fact the very important question of interchange and absorption of new knowledge enters prominently into the search for an explanation of the appearance of the evolved Ganda kinglist. We have already seen how this list, in contrast to that of Bunyoro, had reached a fully matured form when it first appeared in print. There are therefore no written records of the impact of literate influences on the contents of the list, because these influences took the form of a stimulus for consolidating unorganized oral data rather than borrowing already structured data from printed sources. However, by the time Stanley arrived in 1875, the ruling circles in Buganda had already been exposed quite heavily to Arabic literacy by Swahili traders, teachers, and scribes. Every European observer during the 1870s and 1880s commented on the surprising extent to which Mutesa and his leading officials had absorbed Islamic learning and lore.[40] Mutesa himself was adept and conscientious in reading the Qur'an, and he dabbled in other forms of Arabic literature as well. The Ramadan feast was observed and Arab sartorial styles were adopted widely. Written and oral communication was carried out in Arabic, and several thousand youths were trained in Arabic and Islam in preparation for government service. The influence of Muslim culture in Buganda was at its height just when Stanley was there but waned as Mutesa saw the practical advantages of wooing European missionaries (and, he hoped, in winning European munitions).

In short, the Buganda court was no longer an oral society in 1875. This fact means that literacy in Buganda was having its greatest impact at precisely the moment that remembrances of the past were undergoing their final mutations and consolidation as they were passed along to the Europeans. We have little direct evidence of the role that Islam and Arabic learning might have had in Mutesa's reconstruction of the list of *bakabaka*, but there are hints in the historical record that it was significant. Emin Pasha spoke of a 'journal' that Mutesa was alleged to possess containing the names of his predecessors and which was 'in Arabic naturally', but Emin discounted its details (and perhaps its existence) since he had found

252

no one else who remembered such details 'beyond four generations'.[41]

Another indication that Islamic learning influenced Mutesa's reconstruction of the Ganda past was his insistence on equating the Ganda anthropomorphic ancestor Kintu with Noah's son Ham, the progenitor of the Negro races in the Muslim *schema* of primeval genealogy. Mutesa's identification of the two first appeared in Stanley's work and was confirmed in the correspondence of the earliest Christian missionaries.[42] It is likely that Mutesa became acquainted with Ham through his reading of Arabic literature (he is not mentioned in the Qur'an), since Ham figured more prominently there than in contemporaneous European thought.[43] But, whatever ideas Mutesa gleaned from his introduction to Arabic learning, the widespread use of Arabic script would have facilitated the rapid development of listing and the formulation of an orthodox sequence of Ganda kings in good time for Mutesa (or his officials) to offer an evolved kinglist to Stanley in 1875.

We need not accept the most damning implications of these arguments. At best the data at Mutesa's disposal might have provided elements from which a historically accurate kinglist might be constituted, even if no means of doing this had previously been present. The ways in which Mutesa and others organized the various components could thus have been based on the authentic, though partial, visions of the past then current. Or they might have been subtly modified to serve political functions like antedating Buganda's territorial expansion at the expense of Bunyoro, as happened not far away in Rwanda.[44] But they could also have been completely adventitious.

Historians and anthropologists have long accepted the standard kinglist of Buganda as reliable because it appeared in a consistent and circumstantially detailed form very early in the available documentary record. And they have accepted the K.W./Nyakatura list of Nyoro rulers similarly because it was in turn consistent with the Ganda data. Under the circumstances, it may be best to see consistency as a hallmark of doubt rather than of credibility, since agreement can be explained readily by the similarly literizing environments in which both lists emerged. For the coherence on which historians have relied as evidence of authenticity, it was necessary only that the compilers of the Ganda list ascertain that one available version did not contradict others. Access to Arabic literacy before 1875 and the large amount of vernacular literature produced during the early colonial period made this task easy for neotraditional historians in Buganda. And of course when it came time for Nyoro officials to make a case for their own historical primacy, these same Ganda kinglists, by then handily encapsulated in Kaggwa's *Ekitabo,* provided temptingly convenient referents that they used to render their efforts plausible, consistent and, as it proved, thereby persuasive.

Conclusion

> In filling up the Blanks of old Histories we need not be so scrupulous. For it is not to be feared that time should run backward and by restoring the things themselves to knowledge, make our conjectures appear ridiculous.[45]

Miller's introduction to this volume makes a distinction between what he calls a 'present past' and 'absent past'. Simply put, the absent past is whatever period beyond the first or second hand experience of traditional historians has left few traces evident to people in the present. It is a time often associated with 'origins', when whatever happened has become subject to speculation and to the imagination of the historians who describe it. As a result it is characterized by increased structure and by mythical overtones. The present past is less structured and more circumstantial because direct reminders, if not quite evidence, from it remain to remind historians of what happened then. I would give an ironic but substantive twist to these concepts by adding a third, which might be called the 'absent present'. That is, where modern academic historians attempt to locate uncontaminated orally preserved information about the past in societies that have recently become partially literate, they assume a working present that has in fact already vanished. For Buganda and Bunyoro, the period when undiluted oral data were available had ended by 1925 at the very latest. Neotraditional historians had by then sketched out the basic outlines of Ganda and Nyoro pasts with literate techniques. They later definitively articulated these histories in the form of written kinglists for the benefit of interested Europeans.

In trying to cope at second hand with published data that have emanated from this absent present, the methods of analysis are naturally not the same as those pursued in studying data collected in the field. As a locus of activity for historical research, the armchair has often been denigrated by historians—particularly African historians collecting oral historical data in the field who have justified their activities as resurrecting the past through the discovery of

254

'new' evidence.[46] Clearly the amount of light thrown on the African past during the last twenty years by practitioners of what might be called mouth-to-ear resuscitation goes a long way toward justifying this point of view, although sometimes it is forgotten that light brings with it shadows. The field interview can be an indispensable tool for historical research, but its value should not lead to the conclusion that it is sufficient in all circumstances. For the history of Buganda and Bunyoro it has not been sufficient for nearly fifty years, since almost no authentically new information remained to be found. In these cases a more circuitous approach is required, which may in fact be launched from the comfort of the armchair.

Arguments or conclusions derived from armchair analysis must depend on a wide range of sources but must at the same time remain tentative. The historian of Africa must perforce agree with Auden that 'knowledge may have its purposes but guessing is always more fun than knowing', even if he or she would prefer not to. The speculative posture each historian takes in respect to the evidence will depend on a number of variables, some of which are frankly and inescapably idiosyncratic. Just as some, when faced with a sixteen-ounce container with eight ounces of liquid in it, will think of it as half full and others as half empty, so too there will be different responses to Grant's comments on the royal tombs and Kaggwa's inconclusive stories of exhumations. Put more specifically, some will be surprised that neither the Baganda nor the Banyoro remembered the names, relationships, and sequence of all their past rulers in the form of a classically literate list; others would be just as surprised by arguments that they could have or did. But, setting temperament aside as much as possible, the appropriate task of any investigator is to unearth whatever evidence has survived, sift it to discover and define alternatives, and then weigh and finally select that alternative or series of alternatives that is most compatible with the aggregate data.

To do this in the present instance, it is necessary to consider carefully both the capacity and the propensity of any oral society to take pains to remember various parts of the past in a coherent and accurate synthesis. It is sometimes forgotten that to its practitioners one of the more attractive features of the oral mode is that it allows inconvenient parts of the past to be forgotten by those more interested in the exigencies of the continuing present than in the full exposition of the past. In societies that depend on flexibility and ambiguity in their social and political activities (and this really means all societies, of course) orality can free the present from imprisonment by the past because it permits the remembrance of aspects of that past—like the sequence and activities of former rulers—to accord with ever-changing self-images.

Naturally this flexibility does not appeal to historians, who depend on the immutability of their sources to gain access to this past. They may defend the applicability of the assumption of immutability to Buganda by objecting that it is not possible that anyone could have invented a whole congeries of dead *bakabaka*, since the brief time between Speke's and Grant's visits and that of Stanley would have left far too little time to suppress variants and satisfy ruffled feelings. On two grounds this argument fails. In the first place only a handful of individuals provided Europeans with data about the Ganda past, so that they had little need for extensive backing and filling beyond a small clique. Secondly, the strategy adopted, the addition of new names, would have coopted support rather than alienating it. The lengthening of the roster of kings would have been all the easier if no more was required than to reorganize and amplify with the aid of the newly introduced Arabic literacy existing but vague recollections of past personages associated with tomb sites.

Beyond discussion of the suspect provenance and dubious reliability of the evolved Ganda and Nyoro kinglists, there are indications that even the expanded forms do not reflect the full duration of the area's past. Ironically, the imputed depth of the lengthened Ganda and Nyoro dynastic lists does not do justice to the real antiquity of polities in the area, which is much greater than that of the latterday dynasties. Recent archeological work in the area suggests that organized polities existed many centuries before the dates assigned by conventional reign-length dating techniques to the establishment of the recently existing states there.[47] This view is in line with recent research in Africa, Oceania, and elsewhere which strengthens arguments that telescoping, or the shortening of the apparent period between the time of origins and recent eras, is common in centralized as well as noncentralized societies where it has long been known to be ubiquitous.

To the historian in one of his or her natural guises as chronophile, telescoping is naturally far more alarming than lengthening, since it is much less susceptible to detection through internal analysis and impossible to measure even if it should be discovered. The view that beginnings and ends of ruling lines tend to be remembered while an interval of indeterminate duration is forgotten has often been advanced by anthropologists, but it has usually been rejected by historians on the grounds that it is irreducibly unhistorical. Some historians apparently continue to believe that any tradition should be accepted unless or until it can be proven false. This is an unexceptionable working argument, provided that every effort is made to test its applicability in any given situation. Otherwise it is only to say that any tradition must be accepted uncritically. Those less infatuated with precise dating are aware that characteristics of oral tradition like telescoping tell us far more interesting things about how history works in a nonliterate society than a profusion of dates ever could.

Fieldwork, however industrious or sophisticated, is no substitute for asking basic questions about the status of oral data in a modern environment from the repose of the armchair. The informants who are presently available to field researchers in many cases are decades removed from information that circulated in oral societies before literacy and colonial rule began to affect their politics and traditions. One way in which we partially compensate for this handicap is to penetrate the facade of standardized written traditions by a wide canvass and careful scrutiny of the earlier sources from the period during which the modern canonical versions took shape. Doing so may in this case help to eliminate some of the more obviously quixotic visions of the interlacustrine past, views which serve only to stifle fruitful inquiry in favor of blithe illusion.

Notes

1 'Against the disease of writing one must take special precautions, as it is a dangerous and contagious disease.' Pierre Abelard to Héloise. I wish to thank very much Benjamin Ray, John Rowe, and Christopher Wrigley for their comments and criticisms of earlier drafts of this paper and for their suggestions of other avenues of inquiry.
2 Plato, *Phaedrus*, 275a–b. In this tableau Plato used the story of Thamus, the king of Egypt's debunking of the sage Thoth's invention of writing to publicize his own view of the superiority of the spoken word.
3 Jack Goody, 'What's in a List?' in his *The Domestication of the Savage Mind* (Cambridge, 1977), pp. 74–111.
4 Ibid., pp. 81–4.
5 Goody, ibid., pp. 90–2, speaks briefly of genealogies and kinglists in a literate or literizing context.
6 J. P. Crazzolara, 'The Lwoo People', *Uganda Journal*, vol. 5 (1937), p. 19, referring to the publication of K.W.'s articles discussed below.
7 For the history of Toro and its ruler Daudi Kasagama in the late nineteenth and early twentieth centuries see Kenneth Ingham, *The Kingdom of Toro in Uganda* (London, 1975), pp. 89–118, and E. I. Steinhart,

'Royal Clientage and the Beginnings of Colonial Administration in Toro, 1891–1900', *International Journal of African Historical Studies*, vol. 6 (1973), pp. 265–85.

8 For the full argument see David Henige, *The Chronology of Oral Tradition* (Oxford, 1974), pp. 105–14.

9 L.M.A. Linant de Bellefonds, 'Itinéraire et voyage de service fait entre le post militaire de Fatiko et la capitale de M'tesa, roi d'Uganda, fév-juin 1875', *Bulletin de la Société Khédiviale de Géographie de l'Egypt*, vol. 1 (1876–7), p. 12.

10 Eduard Schnitzer [Emin Pasha], in Franz Stuhlmann (ed.), *Die Tagebücher von Dr. Emin Pascha* (6 vols., Hamburg, 1916–21), vol. 1, p. 381.

11 See David Henige, 'K.W.'s Nyoro Kinglist: Oral Tradition or the Result of Applied Research?' (Paper presented at the 15th Annual Meeting of the African Studies Association, Philadelphia, 1972), for details and references to the published literature.

12 K.W. [Tito Winyi], 'The Kings of Bunyoro-Kitara', *Uganda Journal*, vol. 3 (1935), pp. 155–60; vol. 4 (1936), pp. 75–83; vol. 5 (1937), pp. 53–69.

13 The recent appearance of an English translation of *Abakama* (G.N. Uzoigwe (ed.), *Anatomy of an African Kingdom* [Garden City, N.Y., 1973]) provided the opportunity, but unfortunately not the occasion, for an extended analysis of Nyakatura's background and work. The editor chose to ignore important questions concerning Nyakatura's training, motivation, and sources in favor of the peculiar argument that the historical accuracy of *Abakama* should not be 'an overriding consideration' in using it (*Anatomy*, p. xxvi). Several issues neglected by Uziogwe are taken up in Carole Buchanan, 'Of Kings and Traditions: the Case of Bunyoro-Kitara', *International Journal of African Historical Studies*, vol. 7 (1974), pp. 516–27.

14 Nyakatura to Fr. Antoine Caumartin, [October] 1972. I would like to thank Fr. Caumartin for sharing Nyakatura's letter with me and for providing a translation of it as well as for his own observations based on forty years' residence in Bunyoro as a White Father.

15 Nyakatura to Caumartin, [October] 1972.

16 Ibid to ibid., 10 November 1972.

17 For this argument see David Henige, 'Royal Tombs and Preternatural Ancestors: a Devil's Advocacy', *Paideuma*, vol. 23 (1977), pp. 205–19; Kenneth Ingham, 'The *Amagasani* of the Abakama of Bunyoro', *Uganda Journal*, vol. 17 (1953), pp. 138–45.

18 Although I cite only Kaggwa here, because he was the most influential source in the development of both the Ganda and Nyoro kinglists, numerous other Baganda were writing traditional history in the first decades of this century. For these see John Rowe, 'Myth, Memoir, and Moral Admonition: Luganda Historical Writing', *Uganda Journal*, vol. 33 (1969), pp. 17–40, 217–19; Michael Twaddle, 'On Ganda Historiography', *History in Africa*, vol. 1 (1974), pp. 85–100.

19 Schnitzer, *Tagebücher*, vol. 1, p. 381.

20 H. M. Stanley, *Through the Dark Continent* (2 vols., New York, 1875), vol. 1, p. 344, specifically credited Mutesa with providing him with the

names of his predecessors, and ascribed certain other details in the account he published to other Ganda officials, but see below, note 27.

21 For the influence of Kaggwa's work see M. S. M. Kiwanuka, 'Sir Apolo Kaggwa and the Precolonial History of Buganda', *Uganda Journal*, vol. 30 (1966), pp. 137–52; Rowe, 'Myth.' More generally, Rowe, 'Progress and a Sense of Identity: African Historiography in East Africa', *Kenya Historical Review*, vol. 5 (1977), pp. 23–34.

22 Rowe, 'Myth', p. 21.

23 For the various Ganda kinglists published by 1901, see C. C. Wrigley, 'The Kinglists of Buganda', *History in Africa*, vol. 1 (1974), pp. 129–38.

24 Ibid. Wrigley shows that accepting Mugwanya's sequence of rulers would date Buganda expansion at the presumed expense of Bunyoro to a time when Bunyoro was weak rather than strong, and would group the more mythic elements of the traditions at the beginning where we would normally expect them to be. In addition, parts of Mugwanya's list agree with the sequence of the first published Ganda kinglist, that of Speke discussed below. For other views of the standard Ganda list, see R. R. Atkinson, 'The Traditions of the Early Kings of Buganda: Myth, History, and Structural Analysis', *History in Africa*, vol. 2 (1975), pp. 17–57; Michael Twaddle, 'Towards an Early History of the East African Interior', *History in Africa*, vol. 2 (1974), p. 171.

25 It is true of course that Speke published a 'list' of Karagwe rulers in his *Journal of the Discovery of the Source of the Nile* (London, 1863), p. 250, but this was really no more than two names multiplied by an arbitrary number.

26 See for example Martin Southwold, 'The History of a History: Royal Succession in Buganda', in I. M. Lewis (ed.), *History and Social Anthropology* (London, 1968), p. 132.

27 Although Stanley credited Mutesa with the information he published regarding earlier *bakabaka*, ten years later the CMS missionary A. M. Mackay claimed that it was the *mujasi* (commander-in-chief) Kapalaga who had provided Stanley with 'the lot of fabulous tales of previous kings of Buganda'. Mackay to CMS, May 1885, in *Church Missionary Intelligencer* (October 1885), p. 713. Kapalaga later became chief of the Muslim party during the civil strife in Buganda in the late 1880s.

28 Stanley, *Through the Dark Continent*, vol. 1, p. 380.

29 Stanley to *New York Herald*, 12 April 1875, in Norman R. Bennett (ed.), *Stanley's Dispatches to the New York Herald, 1871–1872, 1874–1877* (Boston, 1970), p. 220. In his dispatch to *The Daily Telegraph* 'Augustus' became, more appropriately, 'Ethelbert'.

30 Stanley, *Dispatches*, pp. 222, 225; idem, *Through the Dark Continent*, vol. 1, p. 401. Stanley's (or Mutesa's) hyperbole was immediately criticized by James Grant, 'On Mr. H. M. Stanley's Exploration of the Upper Nile', *Proceedings of the Royal Geographical Society*, vol. 20 (1875–6), p. 46. Shortly thereafter Mutesa repeated his claims to rule over Busoga and Karagwe in a letter to General Gordon. M. F. Shukry, *Equatoria under Egyptian Rule* (Cairo, 1953), pp. 331–3, 362.

31 M. S. M. Kiwanuka, *A History of Buganda* (London, 1971), pp. 160–6, 168–9; Roland Oliver, *The Missionary Factor in East Africa* (London, 1952), pp. 39–41; Arye Oded, *Islam in Uganda* (New York, 1974).

32 For arguments that the Ganda tombsites and shrines represented historical reminders see R. Oliver, 'The Royal Tombs of Buganda', *Uganda Journal*, vol. 23 (1959), pp. 124–33. For other aspects of these shrines see Benjamin Ray, 'Royal Shrines and Ceremonies in Buganda', *Uganda Journal*, vol. 36 (1972), pp. 35–48; idem., 'Sacred Space and Royal Shrines in Buganda', *History of Religions*, vol. 16 (1976–7), pp. 363–73; idem., 'Death, Kingship, and Royal ancestors in Buganda', in Frank E. Reynolds and Earle H. Waugh (eds.), *Religious Encounters with Death: Insights from the History and Anthropology of Religions* (University Park, Pa., 1977), pp. 56–69.

33 Apolo Kaggwa, in May M. Edel (ed.), *The Customs of the Baganda* (New York, 1934), pp. 34–51.

34 Christianity seems not to have played any part in Mutesa's activities in this regard; Kaggwa dated them to a period prior to its introduction. See Kaggwa in *Customs*, pp. 34–51.

35 Kiwanuka, *History of Buganda*, pp. 2–3; Ray, 'Royal Shrines', p. 38. I owe this point to Benjamin Ray.

36 Speke, *Journal*, p. 252.

37 James A. Grant, 'Summary of Observations on the Geography, Climate, and Natural History of the Lake Region of East Africa', *Journal of the Royal Geographical Society*, vol. 42 (1872), p. 272. in his journal (sub 29 June) Grant noted that the names of these eight kings were mentioned (without naming them himself) and added that 'this accuracy is kept thus carefully on record' from the jawbone shrines. Journals of James A. Grant, f. 207, ms 17915, National Library of Scotland. Speke collected all his historical data into an excursus, but it is possible that he secured his information on earlier Ganda rulers at the same time as Grant. Even earlier (13 June) though, Grant must have been given similar information, since he reckoned that the 'ancestors' of Mutesa and Kamurasi had settled the country about two hundred years earlier. Ibid., f. 203. This time estimate suggests that the prevailing orthodoxy then held the number of previous rulers to be eight.

38 As noted, Kaggwa dated the exhumations to a time after Speke's and Grant's visit, so that this alternative seems unlikely if we accept his dating.

39 Only ten of some fifty Ganda clans are recorded as having provided mothers of reigning *bakabaka*. See Martin Southwold, 'Succession to the Throne in Buganda', in Jack Goody (ed.), *Succession to High Office* (Cambridge, 1966), pp. 82–126. My thanks to Benjamin Ray for suggesting this line of argument.

40 See Oded, *Islam in Uganda, passim*, esp. pp. 60–139, for the most complete account of the Islamization of Uganda during this period.

41 Schnitzer, *Tagebücher*, vol. 1, p. 381.

42 Stanley, *Through the Dark Continent*, vol. 1, p. 345n; C. T. Wilson to H. Wright, 19 April 1878, Church Missionary Society Archives, London, C6 025.

43 One of Roscoe's informants, formerly Mutesa's palace steward, stated that Mutesa picked up the Kintu/Ham identity after he had 'read' Islam. For more on Ham and the Baganda, see Jean Pierre Chrétien, 'Les deux visages de Cham: points de vue français au XIXème siècle sur les races africaines d'après l'exemple de Afrique orientale', in *L'idée de race dans la*

pensée politique française contemporaine, eds., Pierre Guiral and Emile Temine (Paris, 1977), pp. 194–9. John Roscoe and Apolo Kaggwa, 'Enquiry into Native Land in the Uganda Protectorate', Rhodes House Library, MSS Afr. s. 17. For Ham in Islamic thought see G. Vajda, 'Ham', *Encyclopaedia of Islam*, 2nd ed., vol. 3, pp. 104–5. On the other hand, Ham Mukasa recalled that during Stanley's visit Mutesa was much impressed by the way in which the book of Genesis 'reconciles countries and the origins of things', so that there was Biblical reinforcement. Mukasa, 'Some Notes on the Reign of Mutesa', *Uganda Journal*, vol. 2 (1935), p. 68.

44 For Rwandan expansion, which actually took place in the nineteenth century in most cases but was dated much earlier by Rwandan historians, see Jan Vansina, *L'évolution du royaume rwanda des origines à 1900* (Brussels, 1962), pp. 83–91. Mutesa himself seemed to feel the need for the 'unoccupied land' argument since he told Stanley that Kintu 'found the country uninhabited, for not a single soul then dwelt in the area between the lakes Victoria and Albert and Muta Nzigé'. More to the point, 'the fertile valleys of Unyoro were unoccupied': Stanley, *Through the Dark Continent*, vol. 1, p. 345.

45 Walter Ralegh, *The History of the World* (London, 1687), pt. I, bk. 2, ch. xxiii, sec. 4. One is reminded of Swift's typically trenchant comment on the shenanigans of African cartographers of his time in filling similar voids.

46 For a recent disapproving view of armchair historians see J. B. Webster, 'Dating, Totems, and Ancestor Spirits: Methods and Sources in African History', *Journal of Social Science* [Malawi], vol. 5 (1978), p. 5.

47 Among others see Peter R. Schmidt, 'A New Look at Interpretations of the Early Iron Age in East Africa', *History in Africa*, vol. 2 (1975), pp. 127–36; Twaddle, 'Towards an Early History', pp. 147–84.

11. Memory and Oral Tradition

JAN VANSINA

The relationship that exists between history, memory, and myth[1] is the main concern of the historian. All his data are the product of memory and all are myth. Direct messages from the past transit at the least through the memory of an eyewitness, at the most through the memories of a long chain of witnesses. Selection and deformation of the message spring from several sources, but perhaps the most important one of them stems from the very processes of memory itself. Hence studies about memory should interest all historians, and especially those who deal with oral traditions in which the repeated passage of a message through several memories compounds their effects. In this article we first summarize some of the findings of psychologists about memory and then discuss the implications of these findings for personal reminiscences and for oral tradition, which stems from such reminiscences.

Memory[2]

Memory is a representation by interiorized action of an event or situation ('remembrance-image'). Such a remembrance is usually expressed in a narrative form, as connected sequence, however inchoate. Representations are imitative actions, and their presence in a connected form involves creative activity.[3] At both the points of creating the image and of narrating it (processes which in most cases occur together) the perceptual data are either selected or rejected, structuring takes place, and 'gaps' are filled by supplying logical sequences of the type 'it must have been'. All of this is evident in any recollection of a traffic accident, for instance. The testimonies become more structured the more they are repeated, some information is omitted and items that were not observed are added. A witness may declare that car A was coming from one street and car B down another. He clearly was not watching both cars *before* the collision but has deduced their motions from the scene of the accident itself. The memorizing of perceptual data is also strongly colored by emotion in such a way that displeasing perceptions are ignored or suppressed; experiments have shown this to be true when opinions contrary to one's own are to be learned.[4] Lastly, repetition of a message, either to learn it by rote or as one retells it, increases structuration through reduction until a stable narrative has been achieved or until the text to be learned by rote has become firmly linked to other structuring mechanisms.[5]

Memory is like a library.[6] Items are received, labeled according to a system of encoding, and stored. Recall occurs by being given a label and with it tracing the item. Items become lost if they were not labeled, if their label was destroyed later, or if the item was misfiled. The library code is the crucial element in the whole operation. Similarly, the mnemonic code dictates the whole operation of the mind. Three major dimensions of this code are known today. Two of them are congruent with the language code, which underlines the relevance and importance of language and speech in memory processes. The first dimension is the verbal code containing the totality of information and programs that allow the preparation of a verbal expression.[7] The second and truly dominant dimension—the master code—is the semantic memory. Like a library code, it is organized hierarchically by topic and integrated into a single system according to an overall view of the world and the logical relationships perceived in it. This is the same as the 'cognitive categories' or the 'mental map' in anthropological parlance. This code is acquired during infancy and culturally determined.[8] The third dimension is visual. Concrete items easily translated into action/images are much better retained than abstract items because such concrete items undergo a double coding in terms of verbal expression and also visual coding.[9]

Retrieval occurs by an appeal to one of two kinds of searching strategies. One can search by following lines linking data that entered the memory together, scanning the body of information that was memorized during a certain period until the item wanted is recognized, rather like the person who plays back a tape recording until he hits the spot he wants to retrieve. This technique, which is primarily based on the verbal code, is much faster than the second one but less economical since if it does not turn up the desired item, the other code must then be used.[10] The technique has been identified independently by students of oral literature.[11] These have also identified the second technique and called it cueing. Here a cue to the semantic label is given and the cue allows a specific item to be directly recognized. The technique is slower, as would be expected, but much more precise than scanning. The cue can bear on the logical position of the item in the semantic code or on some of the attributes of the item to be recalled, such as its qualities, color, phonetic pronunciation, etc. Such attributes form secondary filing systems that crosscut the main code.[12]

Remembrances once stored are never lost. But we all forget! What then happens to prevent us from remembering? Inhibition as a block to recall has been known since the days of Freud.[13] Many cases of temporary amnesia also prove the point that recall is inhibited when it is too painful. But most memories are forgotten because something went wrong with the coding or decoding processes. Specific events or situations of a repetitive nature are not easily recalled because their labels are practically identical except for a sequential index that differentiates between them. Any time I go to buy bread is like the last time, except for the day. Experiment shows that in such situations only the first and the last experiences are remembered, so that the ability to recall a given instance typically assumes the shape of a U-curve.[14] Coding can have been improper but it is never omitted. If it was never done, the item was never memorized to begin with. As for improper encoding if a 'cat' had been classed under 'mineral' rather than 'animal' and the later 'cat' cue refers to 'a domestic animal', the memory of the original 'cat' can never be found. Even if the code is correct, the stored information may be summoned with a cue which itself is based on an implicit code that interferes with or is incompatible with the memory code. If I remember 'cat' as a 'domestic animal with whiskers' and am asked not for that concrete code but for 'the domestic animal of the household whose feminine form is used as a collective noun for the species' all this abstract grammar interferes with the direct semantic code in use. Either I will not remember 'cat' at all because of the confusion, or I will find the image only after some reasoning.

The semantic code is the key to the whole operation of memory. It is a worldview or a mental map acquired during childhood. Hence it is an acquired system, and because it is taught it is largely part of a shared collective code. Because their mental maps are different, the memories of people in different cultures vary. Memories of small children vary from those of older children and from those of adults, and it can even be argued that in most cultures memories of men and women will vary because their education and occupations were different. There is no such thing as a general 'human memory'. If, then, the relationship between the memory of a community and its socio-cultural framework is well understood,[15] much less can be said

264

about idiosyncratic differences except that they exist. Further research on the interaction between the individual and his or her culture would be highly relevant for students of oral tradition.

Personal Reminiscences

The psychologist's known data about memory are obviously most relevant to oral historians who deal with living witnesses who theoretically could remember everything and whose biases can be studied. Their recollections thus constitute a single oral document with properties that can be defined and taken into account. These witnesses are rather passive in providing information (even when they volunteer it to the interviewer, which is much less frequent than is usually thought), and therefore they can be guided and stimulated to provide evidence in spite of themselves. The historian who deals with a written document also deals with a single memory—provided that the document itself is not a written record of a prior oral tradition and that the original text is at hand. But the written document is the product of an active informant who may have edited far more than the oral informant. As for oral traditions, they all begin as personal reminiscences,[16] all the more reason to explore some of the practical consequences of what we know about memory first in relation to the informant of oral history. All personal memory is in fact a small portion of a much larger life history. The life history is the motherlode out of which flow the data for all other genres of history. And yet 'life history' as a genre itself is ill-understood at best. In principle memory never fades. It should be possible to rediscover all the remembrances of a person, and his or her life history would then become a very long document indeed. To a certain extent this can be done, as psychiatrists know, and the results can be extremely lengthy. But even those life histories which make up book-length autobiographies in fact include only a portion of the recoverable recollections.[17] Given time to recall, people will remember more and more about a given period or event (witness the phenomenon of a language, once studied but since forgotten, 'which comes back to a person'). Clearly, what passes for life history in most oral history programs is no such thing!

Many so-called 'life histories' are in fact a caricature of a full life history. The interviewers clearly limited themselves to certain questions or answers while eliminating others. Often the informant presents as life history what is but an outline of a career history, with or without a collection of anecdotes. Such documents should not be labeled 'life history'. Their label should reflect more accurately the narrow range of reminiscences that was elicited.

The informant who spontaneously begins a search for a genuine life history is exceedingly rare and an oddity in most cultures. Yet life histories can be recovered. Once an informant has grasped that this is the goal of the inquiry and is visited frequently enough, a full life history may result. Even then one obtains an edited version of the person's memories. On the one hand a good many reminiscences are put aside as being too private, too painful to recall, or too bothersome to explain and justify. On the other hand there is fabulation. As a person begins to assemble his memories he begins to see new meaning in his life and stresses data accordingly. He may at first recall bits in no coherent pattern. He mulls over these, creates a new pattern, and goes on to fill in the gaps he now perceives. This is done at least in part to stop further worrisome searching of memory and sometimes to put a stop to the interviewer's probing. In large part it is done because no one lives comfortably with the knowledge that he or she cannot recall a continuous past if one wants to. There is a *horror vacui* here. Fabulations almost always become more 'logical' than the original pattern was and fit better with the current self-image of the informant, especially if he or she is already an older person. It is then up to the interviewer to find such fabulations and to prove that they were so, by showing, for example, that the logic is too neat, or that the informant's self-imputed motivations and opinions which are badly remembered anyway tally too neatly with subsequent events.

Given the ambiguities of life histories, the time it takes to collect them,[18] the rapport that has to be established between informant and inquirer, and the resulting psychological complications that may arise, it usually is wise not to collect a whole life history. But portions of such histories will be desirable. To probe for specific reminiscences in order to complement data from other sources (including other informants), or to find answers to questions for which only scarce data are otherwise available, is an extremely fruitful way of tapping people's memories. For instance, in Africa such data are invaluable for most of the colonial period when other documentation does not exist or is uniformly biased in the same directions. The following points bear on the use of oral interviews of this limited sort, and especially on the question of dating them.

Practitioners know very well that informants often have vivid but self-contained memories from their early childhood of a quite specific nature, in which they 'see' a brief scene rather than narrate an extended event. Such memories are short because the attention span of a child is short compared to that of an adult. They are self-contained because the young child's memory 'program' is as yet only inchoate. Usually such reminiscences contain other diagnostic features, such as the imagined large size of adults (the size is in proportion to that of the child). Such memories can safely be dated to early childhood, usually from 18 months onwards to perhaps ten years of age, with a progressive increase in the action portion of the 'event' recalled and a gradual loss of self-containment with increasing age. For instance when a person remembers a scene but also can tell you—from memory—that he was then going to this school and that the road between the school and home was so and so, he has a cluster of memories. The reminiscences are no longer isolated or self-contained, and so the reminiscence must be dated to late childhood, perhaps around ten years of age. When such self-contained memories form a coherent story, there is a very strong likelihood of fabulation. Often a person mixes up genuine reminiscences with what parents or older siblings later told him about the situation when he first told them about his remembrance. Such fabulation does not introduce serious errors and should not worry a researcher over much, as there probably is no serious distortion of the facts, but it may thwart the attempt to infer dates from others. Self-rationalizing fabulations are quite a different matter, since they distort, but they are rather easily detected.

Practice also teaches that informants always seem to remember more incidents from their youth than from a later age. This probably is due to the greater memorability of first experiences.[19] Repetition of later similar events produces negative interference as we have seen. Usually only the first and last of such experiences are remembered. Thus a person recalls that he was sent out as a child to buy bread and sometimes even remembers how much he paid, especially if change was involved. But no one recalls every purchase of bread ever made in his life.

First experiences of a domestic nature occur at an earlier age than those of a public nature, and first public experiences which involve little knowledge of social relations are earlier than those which presuppose such an understanding. In the absence of knowledge, the later mnemonic code structured around such knowledge cannot function properly. Thus a child's memory of a funeral differs markedly from that of an adult, both because the child remembers the scene but does not 'remember' the relationships between the persons present, and because most children do not as yet realize what death means. Childhood memories start with simple scenes and become more complex as one grows older. When informants recall domestic practices or situations 'from their youth', not only will domestic memories be dated earlier but it is even possible to sequence them in time according to the complexity of knowledge that the ability to remember presupposes.

In practice more coherent remembrances seem to occur from the age of six or seven onwards, while nondomestic memories depend upon the age at which a child is allowed to roam outside the household, an age which in most cultures clearly differs for boys and girls and which varies also from culture to culture. My own fieldwork experience in different African cultures[20] would put a full understanding of kinship relations and the behavior appropriate to them at about ten years of age. A full understanding of relations between kinship *groups*, or a grasp of their economic, political and ritual relationships, occurs only at a much later age, about fifteen years or so. Clearly the above is but a general indication. In some cultures people are taught their genealogies as children, but in others they are not or they learn them only at a later age. In Burundi aristocrats may explain genealogies and marriage alliances to ten-year-old children who learn them by rote without understanding implications, while farmers' children are not taught such niceties. So attention to local practice should modify the rule of thumb: ten years for domestic matters, fifteen for public. The main point here is to argue that seemingly vague references to 'in my youth . . .' can be often pinpointed to a rather precise date in a person's life history and a date assigned to them once the informant's present age is known.

A few variables affecting the likelihood of remembrance must be kept in mind in all genres of oral history,[21] not just life history. These include the degree of repetitiveness of the experience, concreteness of the data, whether opinions or motivations are involved, whether the memory was learned by rote, and the intensity of the emotions associated with the events remembered. We have already pointed to the negative interference of repetitive experience. This and the effect of the fact that concrete items are much better remembered than abstract items explain the well-known fact that people remember so few numbers, even though one always seems to call for concrete numbers! Numbers are abstract. When such an abstract item is combined with repetitive experience, as is the case for prices, the series is simply not recalled. Anyone who claims to remember a series of numbers either made it up or had some very special reason to learn the numbers in question, and the reason must be elucidated by the researcher. So oral history and by extension oral tradition will *a priori* not be fruitful sources for direct quantitative history.[22]

Because abstract items are difficult to remember one must be distrustful also of statements about former norms or general rules. Thus 'bride-wealth amounted to four mats' is a highly suspect memory. Either the informant really recalls one actual case and generalizes from it, or he uses the current norm 'rectified' for the past. If he really does recall the former standard, one will want to know what special event made the informant remember such a norm so precisely. Since informants have a strong tendency to generalize and often speak in terms of 'norms' (to be contrasted, of course, with today's norms!), this caveat applies often.

As for opinions and imputed motivations, these too are abstract. We have seen that people tend to distort opinions opposed to their own, if they do not forget them altogether. Moreover, here too the effect of the repetitive situation interferes. Nevertheless most people in a variety of cultures claim to remember opinions, both their own and those of others. All such claims are suspect. How often do people not genuinely claim as their own opinions which they took in fact from others? Moreover, one's memory cannot record every change of opinion one had held because opinions usually change gradually and often unconsciously. Further, most remembered opinions are distorted by associated strong emotions. Finally, a person's belief about the continuity or discontinuity of his or her opinions in the past is a core part of every personality.[23] No one is schizophrenic enough to sort out the different strata of past opinions and their consequences. Remembrance of opinions must be distrusted unless there are strong grounds to the contrary. Such grounds include concrete action resulting from standing on an opinion, as when a person is jailed for his beliefs, such factors as a particularly strong emotion followed by action as a result of public expression of it, or even a particularly pithy expression of the opinion itself. All the above warnings apply equally to remembrances of motivations, which are as difficult to observe as opinions are, as easily attributed, as often unconscious, and usually more complex than opinions. So the usefulness of oral history, and in its wake oral tradition, for a direct intellectual history is as weak as it is for quantitative history.

Items learned on purpose give the appearance of being better remembered, in part because recall is fast and complete. In some cases, such as learning by rote, the impression is justified, though slippage occurs even here. Learning on purpose involves repetition of the message until it 'sticks'. This type of repetition in fact restructures the message until the labels attached to it are all recalled in the correct sequence. Items which are not learned by rote are invariably simplified and streamlined. Elements in the continuous stream of impressions are provided with points of stress following one another in a logical way to make a narrative. All of these effects are not perceived in texts learned by rote, but they are there. They may lead in fact to the replacement of some words by others, provided the substitutes fit all the tags of the original and tie in even better to clues provided by the preceding and following words. So an easy memory, well expressed, could arouse suspicion on these grounds.[24]

Emotions strongly color perception and hence memory of it. Emotions govern the selection of which items may be remembered. Exciting situations are better remembered than others, perhaps because the senses were more alert, just as fatigue and stress tend to dull observations and hence their remembrance. On the whole, situations involving pleasurable emotions are best remembered, while situations involving unpleasant emotions are forgotten. Many painful memories are blocked. Often this occurs in seemingly innocuous ways. One really remembers 'the good old days'. For instance, draftees in peace time tend to recall the pleasurable 'memorable' events of their stay in the army, not the vexations or the boredom which at the time made them long so fervently for their release. True, there are cases where misfortune was so strong or persistent as to 'scar' a personality and break through inhibitions. The unhappy event then becomes a very vivid part of a person's mental heritage. The contrary case, when the event is not recalled, is much more frequent. Oral historians should keep this in mind, so that they can attempt by specific probing questions to counteract the general tendency to gloss over unpleasantness.

From Personal Remembrance to Oral Tradition

Personal remembrance is not fit for public consumption. Most remembrances are simply not destined to be shared with the public because they are intimate. Reminiscences in an oral history interview situation are already somewhat edited with an eye to their potential impact on others. The informant may indeed want to remember all he can for himself, but his remembrance is a message.

It is directed to the interviewer and most informants are also well aware of the wider public and slant their data accordingly. The resulting texts are a combination of the initiatives of both interviewer and informant. A writer edits his reminiscences in much the same way except that he alone has the initiative, and hence a stronger motivation, and that he definitely writes for a public. He omits more, rearranges his data more, restructures them more to make points or for effects. There is thus a significant difference between a writer and an informant.[25] But we know from practice that there seems to be an even bigger difference between an oral personal reminiscence and most oral traditions.

How does a set of personal reminiscences become an oral tradition? In the case of family oral tradition the process is not so different from the case of the writer. Reminiscences are edited, the general goal being to preserve family identity and cohesion and explain one's individuality to the family. Besides this, reminiscences are given to teach from experience, to assert the visible or invisible prominence of the family, and perhaps for a variety of other reasons as well. Personal reminiscences told to friends nearly always constitute comments on a current situation or express the desire to explain oneself.

Oral traditions of a formal nature—poems, songs, or lists—are different. They involve a new creation from personal reminiscences. Elements in the memory of the witness are discarded, others rearranged, a new structure imposed. In the case of lists the editing is the most extreme, but the criteria for selection are unusually clear. In the composition of poems, epics, or songs, structuring in order to recreate dominates in an activity analogous to that of memorizing itself, which is also creative. Thus we could call these data memories at one remove. The prominence of symbolic elements in these texts has often been remarked upon. Reliance on symbols is not surprising, once it is realized that symbolic thought is very much the same thing as recalling memories. The mind plays with the mnemonic code to evoke rather than remember and uses its potential for association to explore new connections.[26]

Individual innovation marks the transmission of such already formalized traditions or fictional materials as tales, as these data are performed rather than recited, and personal creativity is expected. But innovation is less conspicuous in formal historiographical traditions, i.e. those stories which have developed from personal reminiscences, are claimed to be true, and are handed down as truth from one generation to the descending ones. Here the agents of transmission try to be as accurate as possible. But the very creation of such stories again involves editing and restructuring according to the dominant interests of the community. This sort of editing is an extension of the tendencies inherent in the mnemonic code itself. The code is collective, and so influences initial perceptions, but data stored by it are further deformed to fit collective concerns. Such formal traditions should, unlike any others, have eliminated most idiosyncrasies both in their composition and in their transmission.

There are no empirical data about the transformation of idiosyncratic personal reminiscences into a collective official tradition. But the evidence about the interaction of fictional tales (themselves often traditions) and historical traditions shows how some official traditions are born.[27] In other cases one suspects a number of personal memories to have been conflated in order to reach a common version. Selection here primarily involves generalization, the development of more imagined logical links between events remembered, and the weeding out of discrepant recollections. A further possibility is simply the imposition of one version—usually, one imagines, that of a leader—but perhaps also the one that is performed best. This one version then becomes the collective account by eclipsing the others.

Oral tradition is a memory of memories in the most literal way, since the message is learned from what another person recalled and told. Given its dependence on recitation, it is reassuring to know that all memorization has a verbal dimension to it. In fact many mnemotechnical devices, such as rhyme, verse, assonance, etc., make use of the phonemic characteristics of a language to ensure a more faithful rendering. Even in prose which is not learned by rote these vocal characteristics remain important. As a consequence traditions are the most easily and faithfully remembered and reproduced in the language in which they were told. This is all the more true when one recalls that the mnemonic code, the main dimension of memory, is congruent with the semantic code of the language in which the traditions are told. Hence it is easier to tell the tradition in its original language than to give a translation of it. Whenever possible traditions should be collected in the original language. In cases where the tradition is known only in translated form, e.g. as occurs with Aztec traditions in Mexico, the translated text should be closely analyzed to see where words, expressions, and images differ from their usual meanings in the foreign language used. One expects a shift toward the semantic code of the foreign language in such translations, and since this is what occurs even in written translations of writings, how much more it must affect speech.

Memory is collective to a large extent, and the contents of oral tradition are even more collective, but no one quite knows to what extent. As the semantic code is congruent with the linguistic code, one can reason from the linguistic analogy that individual idiosyncrasy will have no more—but no less—effect than idiolects have upon dialects and the transformation of languages. And as languages often change only very slowly,[28] we can presume that idiosyncratic effects on oral traditions—especially for historiographical traditions—are in fact very restricted. The semantics of language may vary somewhat faster than the overall change, but again there is no reason to believe that change in this sphere is extremely fast in the absence of rapid social change or confrontations between different cultures. Therefore the mnemonic code of all the witnesses in a chain of testimony is almost identical barring sudden sociocultural upheavals. Unless traditions are more than a few centuries old, deformations due to a changing collective mnemonic code need not be feared. Idiosyncrasy plays a minor role, especially for historiographical traditions, and collective views of the world are slow to change. This means that if we can identify the mental maps which underlie a body of traditions today, we have also identified the major source of deformation during transmission as well.

How is this code to be elucidated? As most of the patterns of cognition making up a mental map are unconscious, direct inquiry yields data which result from introspection by the informant. There is some value to these evaluations, but they need to be controlled because idiosyncrasies and imaginative interpretations are common to introspection.[29] Several other approaches also can elucidate the outline of the code. The corpus of the oral tradition itself carries the elements needed to discover its own bias, because children learn the mnemonic code from their elders and mainly through the oral corpus. Thus the historian can examine the whole corpus of tradition, whether it refers to fiction or to history. He lists the themes broached, especially those in the historiographical accounts. This gives him a rough guide as to what was thought to be significant and how selection has proceeded. In this analysis he concentrates on traditions of origin and on religious texts, because a good part of the worldview is explicitly expressed by them. Such texts also yield further clues—preoccupations, central symbols—that will help to account for many of the common features of the whole corpus. Such

273

an approach soon identifies a number of key concepts and terms for which the semantic fields can be studied directly from the contexts in which they occur. These semantic fields carry the researcher to the heart of the culture, as Delivré has shown in his work.[30] A further approach concentrates on fiction for children, or for both children and adults. This involves tales, proverbs, riddles, games, etc. What do these data teach to children? Here exegesis by adults is very valuable, as they give the same exegesis that they give to children and thus reveal directly how the mental maps are formed.[31] The whole ethnography of education is relevant here. No single approach among those mentioned needs to be privileged. A catholic attitude enables the researcher to crosscheck and thus to validate results. In this way he overcomes the main obstacle in this type of research, where validity cannot be established by referring directly to an informant, but where the subjective input of the researcher's imagination tends to be high.[32]

Because the mnemonic code is largely collective, it differs, as dialects differ, from society to society. It follows that when testimonies which emanate from members of the same community are compared this collective bias remains undetected. Hence the need to search systematically for the mnemonic code. Hence also the exceptional value of comparing accounts about the same events but stemming from different communities or even from different societies. Often such attempts fail to turn up accounts bearing on the same events. A famous case is that of Benin. The written documents do not allow a check on the oral traditions, and the historian who attempted to cross-verify them was not able to find any reference in his documents that refers unambiguously to the events narrated in the traditions collected by others.[33] Documents do not mention the names of the Benin kings, so that even a chronological control of the traditions remains so far out of reach. Clearly writers and traditionalists were not on the same mental wavelength. Their principles of selection diverged widely. Their views of the world and of reality and therefore their respective memory codes were so different that two histories of Benin result. As a case proving the importance in history of mental maps, both written and oral, Benin is outstanding. As an example of what will happen when one compares sources from different cultures, its discouraging results may be the exception rather than the rule. In any case, it should not dissuade us from searching complementary sources from different societies for evidence in the mnemonic codes of each.

Conclusion

Since memory is a recreation based on impressions from the past, it is in a way amazing that the relation of a memory to what actually happened can be so close[34] and that different witnesses can in fact give statements which agree with each other and with other data. The reliability of memory is little more remarkable for oral tradition than it is for oral history or even for the written source. At the same time, its limitations show us better the truth of the old adage: *testis unus, testis nullus*. The Romans who developed this criterion of relying only on multiply confirmed facts thought only about willful deformation of an account presented in a court of law. The realization that all memory is creative action makes the rule all the wiser, especially as it becomes more difficult to find with certainty which kinds of subconscious, unintended deformation may have occurred. By the same token the value of independent confirming statements is enhanced, although the notion of *independence* becomes hazier than it formerly was. For instance, we have a large number of statements about the invasions of the Northmen in ninth and tenth century Western Europe, independent in the sense that they come from witnesses who did not know one another. But these were all written by clerics, usually monks. Not only did these people share a single status as choice targets for the Vikings, but the whole outlook on life of these witnesses was essentially identical. The sources are not truly independent, at least not in the sense that a Viking report and a monastery report would be in relation to each other. It follows that for large segments of history the degree of reliability of such sources as these is somewhat less than was formerly believed. But no practicing historian would eliminate such information either on the grounds of 'contamination' or by the *testis unus* rule. He knows from everyday life, as does the judge, how often confirming statements in fact reflect a reality of the past, the amazing phenomenon with which this paragraph started.

The same standards should apply to testimony from oral traditions. If the lines of transmission are independent, then independence has the same value as for written sources or oral history. If not, or if this cannot be shown positively,[35] the sources can still be used in a probationary status as grounds for a hypothesis. Crosscultural confirmation constitutes the most certain type of evidence.

The study of memory teaches historical practitioners of oral tradition what kinds of bias occur in a culture and when to become suspicious. Suspicion should be rife when series of numbers are reported, when a single instance of a series of recurrent events is claimed to be precisely remembered, when the narrative is too elegant or too logical, the picture too rosy, or norms or motivations too clearly recalled. Suspicion once aroused invites not rejection but closer scrutiny.

The study of memory teaches us that all historical sources are suffused by subjectivity right from the start. As the source is created, even anticipated in the act of perceiving, the subjectivity is already there. If some of the past masters of the historical method had fully grasped this fact it would have driven them to despair. And yet precisely this biased quality of the sources is what enables the historian in the end to reach a greater degree of objectivity. As Marrou said, every work of history is the product of a ratio of subjectivities, that of the witnesses and that of the historian.[36] But this implies that the subjectivity of the historian is bounded, not only by the data he has, but also by the subjective interpretations of the witnesses. Others who reconstruct the past as, for instance, archeologists, are not so constrained and can freely impose their own frameworks on the data. Thus, unusual objects can be ritual objects for one generation of archeologists, an expression of class differences for another one, and the remains of a technical gadget for yet another.[37] Such interpretations, not limited by the views of the creators of their sources, often reveal more about the prejudice of the author than anything else. Paradoxically, then, historians cannot err as much, because there is more subjectivity in their data. They are constrained by the voices of the past themselves.

This subjectivity of the witnesses moreover is also part and parcel of that very past and once taken into account gives the historian's reconstruction of it a little more authenticity. It helps us to understand the past much better, So here is the paradox: the more subjective the source, the better it reflects a reality of the past! Such a statement needs qualification. The past reality of the interpretation may not be the same past as that of the events. Nevertheless, by this token oral traditions are sources of exceptional value since they convey not only the interpretation of the witnesses to an event but those of the minds who have transmitted it, however slight the alterations may be. More historical reflection has gone into the creation of an oral tradition than into the composition of other sources. To a large extent it acquires these extra levels through the process of memorization. To a very large extent the oral tradition is a collective thought because the mnemonic code it reveals is a collective enterprise.

Notes

1 Moses I. Finley, 'Myth, Memory, and History', *History and Theory*, vol. 4 (1965), pp. 281–302.
2 As I write this article, I do not have access to a good library. Hence the footnoting is somewhat limited. A basic survey of psychological findings about memory is Alain Lieury, *La mémoire: résultats et théories* (Brussels, 1975). It has full references to the authors of experiments and theories, so that the reader can find there the sources for conclusions presented here.
3 Ibid., p. 177. This terminology refers to the theories of Piaget, as in pp. 175–6.
4 Ibid., pp. 185–6 for an experiment about opinions; p. 176 for 'logical reconstruction'.
5 Ibid., p. 130.
6 Ibid., pp. 21–7, 153–6.
7 Ibid., pp. 133–41.
8 Ibid., pp. 141–9.
9 Ibid., pp. 149–53.
10 Ibid., pp. 154–6.
11 Harold Scheub, *The Xhosa Ntsomi* (Oxford, 1975), pp. 12–16.
12 Lieury, *La mémoire*, pp. 154–72.
13 Ibid., pp. 189–92, quotes two cases from Sigmund Freud, *The Psychopathology of Everyday Life* (New York, 1914).
14 Lieury, *La mémoire*, pp. 42–7, 63–7, 93–7.
15 Ibid., pp. 35–6, 193–8 where he cites the theories of Pierre Janet, *Principles of Psychotherapy* (New York, 1924), and Maurice Halbwachs, *Les cadres sociaux de la mémoire* (Paris, 1925). The latter, a follower of Durkheim, is said to underestimate the role of the individual.
16 Even a writer first formulates his reminiscence as a narrative orally, as experiments with the 'echo-box' effect show. Cf. Lieury, *La mémoire*, pp. 90–1, 97–105.
17 A good introduction to the anthropological genre of life history is L. L. Langness, *The Life History in Anthropological Science* (New York, 1965).
18 I estimate that a life history of a person forty years old would take six months to a year to be constituted and that one researcher could probably not pursue more than two such endeavours at the same time. Given the practice of psychoanalysts, my impression from empirical research does not seem excessive.
19 First experience refers to the first time a person realizes that something novel happens to him, not necessarily the first time the event happened. The distinction is important when dealing with remembrances from early childhood.
20 Direct experimentation with this was undertaken in 1954 with Kuba children. They played house, with the older children correcting the mistakes of the younger ones. The experiment's goal was to find more rapidly appropriate kinship behavior towards all types of relatives. I thank Prof. L.

de Heusch who, at that time, gave me this very useful tip. Later observations among the Rwanda, Rundi, and Tio also generally support the generalizations made.

21 These genres are: public accounts as narrative, public accounts as songs or poems, private personal accounts, induced information—whether induced 'naturally' or not, teaching by example, life history. This typology is probably not definitive.

22 This does not mean that oral data cannot be quantified. Such techniques as prosopography show the contrary.

23 This is as true when total reversal of opinions occurs as in other cases. In such cases of 'conversion' a person seems to have a tendency to recast his previous opinions either at the antipodes of his present views or, more commonly, mostly at the antipodes but with doubts.

24 It was believed that learning by rote was learning associations which were strengthened by repetition. But association does not explain the phenomenon. Cf. Lieury, *La mémoire*, p. 168; also pp. 126–30, basing himself on the famous discovery by Miller of the magic number seven (pp. 24–5).

25 The case of the diarist is an especially ambiguous one. He keeps a private diary for his eyes only; yet it is also clear that most diarists hope that one day their diaries will be found.

26 Cf. Dan Sperber, *Rethinking Symbolism*, trans. Alice L. Morton (Cambridge, 1975).

27 Cf. Jan Vansina, *La Légende du passé: Traditions orales du Burundi* (Tervuren, Belgium, 1972).

28 The rate of change in speech is not constant as was once believed by the glottochronologists. Nevertheless empirical evidence again suggests a rather slow rate under most circumstances. For instance, seventeenth-century Kongo texts are easily grasped by Kongo today and differences in language are minor.

29 A good African instance of idiosyncrasy is the case of Muchona 'the hornet', who strongly influenced the intrepretations of Ndembu symbolism and religion proposed by V. Turner. See 'Muchona the Hornet', in J. Casagrande (ed.), *In the Company of Man* (New York, 1959).

30 Alain Delivré, *L'histoire des rois d'Imerina: interprétation d'une tradition orale* (Paris, 1974). His chapters on 'the ethnography of kingship' are central to the understanding of traditions. Moreover, he also shows that ethnography and history were carried together by the same traditions.

31 Thus riddles are used during Kuba initiation to teach directly some basic attitudes and opinions about life to the young initiates.

32 This lack of possible checks is the major drawback of most structuralist analysis. Structural analysis should use the approaches outlined in this paragraph as well.

33 A. F. C. Ryder, *Benin and the Europeans, 1485–1897* (New York, 1969); Jacob U. Egharevba, *A Short History of Benin* (Ibadan, 1968); R. E. Bradbury, *Benin Studies* (London, 1973), pp. 17–43. In general, Daniel F. McCall, *Africa in Time Perspective* (Boston, 1964), conclusion.

34 But not so amazing on second thought. Memory is essential for the survival of the human species, and evolutionary theory suggests that it has to be accurate enough for this purpose.

35 Contamination between oral sources, especially in the same society, is extremely frequent.

36 Henri-Irènée Marrou, *De la connaissance historique*, 2nd ed. (Paris, 1955).

37 Even the olive presses in ancient Tripolitania were taken to be 'monuments of some prehistoric cult' by classical archeologists before the true nature of these machines dawned upon modern investigators. Cf. D. E. L. Haynes, *The Antiquities of Tripolitania* (Tripoli, 1965), pp. 142–3.

Index

Index

Index

ritual installers of chiefs—(*cont.*)
  122–3, 145–50, 164–5, 165–6,
  166–7, 172–3
ritualists, 134, 143–4
royal burialists, 133–4, 136–7
Rwanda, 133, 141, 143, 144, 147

Sala Mpasu, 87
Sanga, 121
selection, 35–9, 49, 50, 51
semantic code(s), in the memory, 263–4
sequence, 15, 17, 228–9
Shambaa, 158
Shi, 9, 16, 23, 28, 33, 38–9, 126–55
Shimat dynasty, 89, 91, 93, 101–2,
  102–3
Sine, 160, 163–5
Speke, John, 67, 248, 250, 251, 259 fn
  25
Stanley, Henry Morton, 66, 244, 247,
  248–9
structuralism, 82–3, 108, 278 fn 32
structure, 126–7, 132–3, 133–5,
  138–9, 150–1, 160
structuring, 12–15, 21–2, 35–9, 44–9,
  50, 51, 262–3, 270–4
symbols, 271

Tantara ny Andriana eto Madagascar,
  221, 223
telescoping, 17–18, 256–7
testimony, 241–2
Tio, 195–7
Tito Winyi II (IV), *see* K.W.
tombs, 224, 245–6, 249–51; *see also*
  graves
toponyms, 211
Toro, 169, 244
tribes, 34
Turner, Victor, 48

Vansina, Jan, 82–3, 108, 157–8, 206,
  217–18 fn 7
variation, 9, 10, 19–20, 28–9, 50, 130,
  132–3, 160
vazimba, 19, 28, 41–2, 161, 221, 222–7,
  228, 230, 231, 232, 233

Wamara, 64, 73–4, 76
Wambuzi, 202
White, C. M. N., 121
Womunafu, 201–19
Wrigley, C. C., 61, 63–4, 72, 157, 247
writing, *see* literacy